I0123685

Coat of Arms

Bossard

Bossards, Bozards, and Buzzards

The Descendants of

Phillip Bossard

Who Landed in Philadelphia
September 30, 1740 and Settled
in Hamilton Township, Pennsylvania

A Genealogy
Compiled and Written by

Mary Smith Jackson

HERITAGE BOOKS
2011

HERITAGE BOOKS
AN IMPRINT OF HERITAGE BOOKS, INC.

Books, CDs, and more—Worldwide

For our listing of thousands of titles see our website
at
www.HeritageBooks.com

Published 2011 by
HERITAGE BOOKS, INC.
Publishing Division
100 Railroad Ave. #104
Westminster, Maryland 21157

International Standard Book Numbers
Paperbound: 978-0-7884-5346-5
Clothbound: 978-0-7884-8860-3

Bossard Homestead in Bossardsville, Pennsylvania
(Now called the Gum Farm)

Christ Church in Hamilton Square
Land donated by Phillip Bossard

FORWARD

This book was written primarily for the interest and whatever pleasure may be derived from it by the descendants of Phillip Bossard. Hopefully, they will enjoy reading it as much as I have enjoyed doing the research for it. This research involved years of searching in historical societies, court houses, reading through rolls and rolls of microfilm and tramping through old cemeteries. It is a result of writing hundreds of letters requesting information on family records. Most all of the people I contacted were very helpful and interested in knowing more about their ancestry.

Most of the early records for the family in the Monroe County, Pennsylvania area were taken from the church records of the Hamilton Township Christ Church. Baptisms in this church dates back to 1763 and includes most of the Bossard family from that time on who remained in that area. Other records were obtained from cemeteries, wills, vital records, bible records, family records, newspapers and various other sources. When all these were exhausted, names, dates and places may have been taken from census records. In some cases, the dates taken from census records are approximate dates, and are usually indicated by using 'ca' before the date.

As in any genealogy there is margin for error, either a typing error, a record that has been copied wrong or more than one record on a person that disgree as to dates, etc. I have tried to be as accurate as possible, using the best available information. Also, it does not include every descendant of Phillip in the United States, covering the 250 years since his arrival. This would be an impossible task for anyone, especially an amateur genealogist like myself, and would probably fill several volumes of this size.

A numbering system is used in the book to easily follow your ancestry back to Phillip. Roman numerals are used in listing the children in each family. If there is a number preceding that child's name, there will be additional information in the following chapter. After each name for the head of a family, the ancestry for that person is in parenthesis. By following that ancestry in the preceding chapters, it will lead you back to Phillip.

TABLE OF CONTENTS

ACKNOWLEDGMENTS

I would like to thank everyone who has contributed information on their families and has helped so much in bringing this writing up to the present day.

A special thanks to Mrs. Elizabeth Walters of the Monroe County Historical Society, now retired, who helped me so much with the early records of the family and for the wonderful records she made available at the Historical Society in Stroudsburg.

Also, to Dale Burger who has added so much to those records with his cemetery indexing and marriage reports and for much of the information he contributed, especially on the Altemose branch of the family.

A special thanks to my son, Edward Jackson, for his expertise with the computer. Without his help, this project would never have been completed.

Last, but by no means least of all, a special thanks to my late husband, Eugene Jackson, who could never quite understand my 'Genes', but was always there to help. He was my companion, my chauffeur on so many research trips and even tramped through old forgotten cemeteries with me. I know that he would be happy to know that this work is finished.

LIST OF ILLUSTRATIONS

Tombstone for Phillip Bossard
and wife Eva Catherine

Placque Placed at the homesite of Phillip Bossard
By the Monroe County Historical Society

CHAPTER 1

FIRST GENERATION

1 **BOSSARD Johannes Phillip**: was born in 1706, possibly in Alsace-Lorraine. At the age of 34 he sailed for America on the ship "Samuel and Elizabeth", William Chilton, Commander. The ship sailed from Rotterdam, last from Deal, England, arriving in Philadelphia on September 30, 1740.

It is unknown whether or not Phillip was married when he came to this country, since I have not found the names of wives or children under the age of 16 in the passenger lists for that time period. However, from events that took place later, I assume that he brought with him his wife, Eva Catherine, and at least two or three children.

Soon after his arrival, Phillip made his way to Cherry Valley and settled there between the Wind-Gap and the settlements on the Delaware River. It was here that Phillip and John Moor purchased the plantation of over 250 acres from Joseph Farmer, who was the executor for the estate of Edward Farmer. He paid one hundred and fifty pounds, lawful money of the state of Pennsylvania and the deed is recorded in Easton, Northampton County dated October 11, 1752. Later, by an endorsement, John Moor released all of his part to Phillip.

The location of the plantation was in the town of Lower Smithfield, but in 1762 part of Lower Smithfield became Hamilton Township. In 1842 the town of Bossardsville was projected by Melchior Bossard, a descendant of Phillip. To anyone passing through the town of Bossardsville it would seem to be only a crossroad, but to this family it is a very important place on the map. Near this crossroad stands a large stone house, built in the German fashion to last, and is the home of our ancestors who helped to build this country. The first home that Phillip built was probably a log house located about 100 yards North of the stone house now standing there. This house was probably built by his son or his grandson in the early 1800's.

The first few years in their new home were peaceful and prosperous. No doubt it was a busy time, clearing the land to be worked, planting, harvesting and caring for his family. With the primitive tools for farming they had at that time, it must have been extremely hard work and long hours to work a farm of that size.

As more settlers moved into the area the Indians became more and more resentful. They were determined to drive the white settlers south of the Blue Mountains. On the 11th day of December, 1755, over 200 Indians attacked the settlements in what is now known as Lehigh, Northampton and Monroe counties. All the buildings were burned north of East Stroudsburg and the people were killed or taken prisoner. Cherry Valley was next and in the middle of January 1756 an attack was made on the settlers there.

There was a man working for Phillip named Mulhausen and on the day of the attack, he was shot by one of the five Indians. One of Phillip's sons tried to come to his rescue but was also killed by the Indians. Phillip wounded one of the attackers and might have been killed himself if some of his neighbors had not come to his assistance and scared the attackers away. This was the first of Phillip's sons to be killed by the Indians.

After this happened, a chain of forts were built along the ridge from the Susquehanna to the Delaware to protect the settlers. There was Fort Norris near Kresgeville, Fort De-Pui at Shawnee and Fort Hynshaw at Bushkill. The Bossard home was located about half way between Fort Norris and Fort Hamilton and it was the very center of activity during this time. Officers and troops would stop off at their home on their way from one fort to another. Among them was General James Young, who spent the night of June 23rd at the Bossard home, while making an inspection of the Provincial forts in 1756. Neighbors would congregate there to discuss the difficult times and to make decisions on their best course of action. His home became a place of refuge for his neighbors during Indian attacks. At one time, there were nine families staying there, as there was safety in numbers.

A second major attack was made about the 20th of April on Cherry Valley and the surrounding area. It was decided that this was such a serious matter, they would send a representative to Easton and ask for protection. They chose Michael Roup and the depositon he gave is so interesting that I would like to include it here:

> The 24th day of April, one thousand seven hundred and fifty seven, appeared before me, William Parsons, Esquire, one of his Majesty's Justices of the Peace for the county of Northampton, one Michael Roup, of Lower Smithfield, in the said county, age 52 years, a person to me well known and worthy of credit, and being duly sworn on the Holy Evangelists of almighty God, did depose and declare, that his neighbor, Phillip Bozart, being at Fort Norris last Saturday week, heard a letter read there, which was dispatched by Major Parsons to acquaint the garrison that he had received information that some enemy Indians intended shortly to come and attack the inhabitants at and about Minisink and to desire them to be on their guard; which was soon made known to all the neighboring inhabitants. And this deponent further saith that on Friday morning last, John LeFever, passing by a house of Phillip Bozart and this deponent informed them that the Indians had murdered Casper Gundryman last Wednesday evening; whereupon this deponent went immediately to the house of Phillip Bozart to consult which was best to be done. Their house, being about a half mile apart, that they concluded it best for the neighbors to collect themselves together, as many as they could in some one house. And this deponent further saith, that he immediately returned home and loaded his wagon as fast as he could with his most valuable affects which he carried to Bozart's house. That as soon as he unloaded his wagon, he drove to his son-in-law, Peter Soan's house, about two miles, and loaded as much of his effects as the time would admit and took them also to Bozart's house, where nine families were retired; That a great number of inhabitants were also retired to the houses of Conrad Bittenbender and John McDowell; That Bozart's house is 7 miles from Fort Hamilton and 12 miles from Fort Norris. And this deponent further saith that yesterday morning about 9 o'clock the said Peter Soan and Christian Klein, with his daughter, about 13 years of age, went from Bozart's house to the house of the said Klein and thence to Soan's house to look after their cattle and to bring some more effects. And this deponent further saith, that about a half hour after the above three persons were gone from Bozart's house, a certain George Hartleib, who also fled with his family to the Bozart house and had been to his own house about a mile from Soan's to look after his creatures and to bring away what he could, returned to Bozart's and reported that he had heard three guns fired very quick, one after the other, and toward Soan's place which made them conclude the above three persons were killed by the Indians. And this deponent further saith, that their little company were afraid to venture to go and see what had happened that day as they had many women and children to take care of. who had they left might have fallen prey to the

> enemy. And this deponent further saith, that this morning, nine men of the neighborhood armed themselves as best as they could and went toward Peter Soan's house in order to discover what had happened to the above three persons. That when they came within about three hundred yards of the house, they found the bodies of the said Soan and Klein lying about twenty feet from each other, killed and scalpt, but did not find Klein's daughter. Soan was killed by a bullet which entered the upper part of his back and came out his breast. Klein was killed with their tomahawks. The nine men immediately returned to Bozart's house and reported the above. That this deponent was not one of the nine, but that he had remained at Bozart's with the women and children. That the rest of the people desired this deponent to come to Easton and acquaint the Justice with what had happened. That the nine men did not think it was safe to stay and bury the dead. And further this deponent saith not
>
> The mark (X) of
> Michael W. Roup

Col. Rec., Vol. VII p. 49

This deposition gives us an insight into what life must have been like for our ancestors during that time.

A short time after this, two more of Phillip's sons were killed by Indians during another attack. I know of no records giving the names of these three sons, but they are probably buried in the small family plot behind Phillip's house along with his hired man Mulhausen. According to a descendant of Phillip, Mulhausen had purchased a small plot of land from Phillip for his burial, and that he asserted that this burial place was to be kept in good shape for all time. This plot was only used before the church cemetery was started about 1775.

As previously stated, it is difficult to determine whether or not Phillip was married before he came to this country in 1740. We know that his son, Melchior, was born in 1745 and that he would have been 10 or 11 years old during the Indian attacks of 1755 and 1756. It would seem very likely that the sons who were fighting Indians during this time would have to be older than Melchior. Since Melchior was born just five years after Phillip came to this country, it is reasonable to believe that Phillip was married and had at least two or three children when he arrived here.

When the French and Indian war was over, peace once again returned to the valley and there was time to think of church and school, the many duties of caring for his family and his plantation. He was active in community affairs and at times, he acted as viewer of new roads. It was during this time that Phillip donated land for the new church and school.

In 1775, the first log church was built and at the same time a new school. The Christ Church in Hamilton Township has records of baptisms as early as 1763 and include nearly all of the Bossard family for many years. Phillip and his family were very active in the church and we find them acting as sponsors for many of the children born of their children and friends. Altho it was Phillip who donated the land for this church, it was his son Melchior who actually gave the deed for the land, which is in Easton, Northampton County, dated June 23rd 1792 and was recorded on January 12th, 1795.

The log church was used until 1829, when the new Hamilton Square Church was built. It is a beautiful stone church and the interior is exceptionally beautiful. The pulpit is high and on each side are winding stairs leading up to it. The work was all done by hand, including the delicate spindles in the balustrade and the altar rail. There have been almost no changes made since the church was built and the church is still being used today.

There is a cemetery in the back of the church and it is here that Phillip and his wife Eva Catherine are buried. At least two of his known children are also buried here. His tombstone states that he died in 1797, in the 90th year of his life and also that his wife, Eva Catherine, died in her 77th year, altho no dates were given for her. The tombstone, written in German, was replaced by the descendants of the sixth and seventh generation and is an exact replica of the original.

The tax list of 1785 shows that his son Melchior paid taxes of one pound, eight shillings, three pence on 300 acres of land, 3 horses and 5 cows. By this time, he had evidently taken over the farm for his Father, altho he did not receive a deed until 1790. This deed is recorded in Deed Book B2, page 102 in the town of Easton, County of Northampton. It reads in part as follows:

This indenture made the twenty seventh day of July in the year of our Lord one thousand and ninety between Phillip Bozsert of Hamilton Township in the state of Pennsylvania, Yeoman of the one part and Melchior Bozsert (son of the said Phillip) of Hamilton Township aforesaid, Yeoman of the other part, witnessth that the said Phillip Bozsert as well for and in consideration of the natural love and affection which he hath and doth bear towards his son and of the sum of four hundred pounds lawful money of the State of Pennsylvania, to him heretofore paid and five shillings now at the execution hereof paid by his son Melchior Bozsert, etc.

This the same tract or piece of land which the executors of Edward Farmer, deceased, by indenture bearing date of October 1752 granted and sold unto a certain John Moor and the said Phillip Bozsert; and the said John Moor, by an endorsement on said indenture, released all his part thereof unto the said Phillip Bozsert, etc.

The memorial stone, placed at the homesite of Phillip by the Monroe County Historical Society, is a tribute to this man, a true pioneer, Indian fighter and one of the builders of our country. He was loved and respected by his neighbors, friends and an ancestor we can be proud of.

HOMESITE OF PHILLIP BOSSARD
BORN 1706--DIED 1797
PIONEER SETTLER OF CHERRY VALLEY
DONOR OF LAND FOR HAMILTON SQUARE
CHURCH
HERE WAS A PLACE OF REFUGE FROM INDIAN
RAIDS DURING THE FRENCH AND INDIAN
WARS OF 1754-1760

Known surviving children of Phillip and Eva Catherine:

2 **BOSSARD Heinrich:** (*Phillip*) was born ca 1740, believed to be a son of Phillip and Eva Catherine, altho there has been no record found to prove his relationship to Phillip, other than Phillip and Eva Catherine were sponsors for at least one of his children born in Hamilton Township and christened in the Hamilton Square Church. Therefore, the children of Heinrich and his wife Anna Catherine will be included here.

3 **BOSSARD Melchior:** (*Phillip*) born December 18 1745

4 **BOSSARD Christina:** (*Phillip*) born ca 1746

The number of children born to Phillip and Eva Catherine is unknown. There is evidence that they were living in Williams Township in Northampton Co., before settling in Hamilton Township, with Eva Catherine attending communion at church in 1752. There was also a George Peter Bossard, who was a sponsor for a child born in 1752 in Williams Township and this is probably the same Peter Bossard listed in the 1761 tax lists for Hamilton Township. No other records have been found for him.

There was mentioned a record of a Samuel Bossard, son of Phillip, for confirmation, no dates or place, and no other records found of a Samuel. He might also be a son, and may have been one of the sons that was killed by the Indians in 1756.

This would account for at least seven children in the family, including the three known surviving children, George Peter, and the three sons that were killed by Indians. There may have been others that are unaccounted for and some records may show up at a later date.

Tombstone of Melchior Bossard
(Died Febuary 9, 1830)

CHAPTER 2

SECOND GENERATION

2 **BOSSARD Heinrich:** (*Phillip*) was born ca 1740. This is probably the son of Phillip and Eva Catherine, living in Hamilton Township until about 1790. They were sponsors of at least one of Henry's children. Phillip's son, Melchior, was also sponsor for at least one of his children. He married Anna Catherina ca 1763 in Hamilton Township. The descendants of Heinrich spell the name 'BUZARD' or 'BUZZARD'.

Children of Heinrich and Anna Catherina:

i- **BUZARD Anna Elizabeth:** born December 12 1763
5 ii- **BUZARD Phillip Jacob:** born September 26, 1764
iii- **BUZARD J. Valentine:** born April 5, 1769
6 iv- **BUZARD J. George:** born March 11, 1771
7 v- **BUZARD J. Melchior:** born April 11, 1772
8 vi- **BUZARD Heinrich:** born July 16, 1773
vii- **BUZARD Anna Catherine:** born June 3, 1776
viii- **BUZARD Sarah:** born August 5, 1786
ix- **BUZARD Johan:** born September 27, 1790

Heinrich is on the tax assessment list for the year 1772 through 1788. His name no longer appears after 1788, when he removed to Unity Township, now called Pleasant Unity in Westmoreland County, Pennsylvania. There he purchased a large plantation of 5,568 acres from the Penn family for the sum of 155 pounds. This deed was recorded in Westmoreland County on May 20, 1790. The name in all the records of Westmoreland County was spelled 'Buzard', and the descendants of Heinrich used this spelling, which will be used hereafter for those descendants.

Heinrich died in 1791, just a year after he purchased his plantation in Unity Township. It is not known when his wife died. There is a report of a Buzzard, who was killed by a tree falling on him in that area (often called Buzzardtown). This may have been Heinrich, since it was only one year after buying the large plantation and he was only 51 years old when he died, it seems likely that his death may have been accidental.

3 **BOSSARD Melchior:** (*Phillip*) was born December 18, 1745 in Hamilton Township, son of Phillip and Eva Catherine. He married ca 1768, Margaretha Catherine Keller, daughter of Christofel and Margaretha Keller, born ca 1746 and died July 16, 1796. Melchior then married Veronica (Heller) Conrad, widow of Peter Conrad. She was born June 28, 1747, and died Oct. 31. 1809. Melchior died

on February 9, 1830. He and his wife Margaretha Catherina are buried in the Hamilton Square Churchyard next to his Father and Mother.

Melchior was just a boy of ten or twelve years during the French and Indian War, so he probably did not take an active part in the fighting. However, during the Revolutionary War, his name appears five times on the muster rolls and served as a 30, 60, or 90 day militiaman. At one time he served under his brother-in-law, Captain Christopher Keller. The records of the muster rolls for Melchior are as follows:

1778-May 14-6th Bn. 5th Co. 7th class Melchior Buzard
1780-5th bn.-8th co. 7th class-Melher Busard
1781-5th Bn.-5th Co.-7th class-Walker Basard
1782-5th Bn.-8th Co.-7th class-Melker Buzzard
1784-Capt. Keller's Co.-Col. Kern's Battalion-Melchior Bossart

Note the varied spelling of his name.
He is listed in the D. A. R. Patriot Index, published in 1966, page 73 as:
Melchior Bossart (Buzard, Buzzard) b. Dec. 18, 1745, died Feb. 8, 1830. Married Margaretha Catherine Keller, private, Pennsylvania.

His wife, Margaretha Catherine, was born in Germany and came to this country with her parents and her brother Christopher, arriving in Philadelphia in 1751. Her Father, Christophel No. 1, died at sea on the way over to this country, and her Mother, Margaretha, married George Hartlieb, before coming to Cherry Valley.

Melchior and Christopher Keller became very close friends as well as brothers-in-law. for each had married the sister of the other. They served in the same company, during the Revolutionary War, and in 1795, when Christopher made his will, he chose Melchior to be the guardian of his minor children. They acted as sponsors for each other's children and each named a child after the other.

In 1813, Melchior sold land to his son Peter, part of the land left to him by his Father. There are two seperate deeds. both dated January 20, 1813. One deed contains 53 acres and the other deed contains 194 acres. Peter remained on the farm until his death.

He also sold land to his son Christopher in 1813, who sold the land by 1820, when he removed to New York State.

Children of Melchior and Margaretha born in Hamilton Township are:

9 **i- BOSSARD Christina**: born September 15, 1769
10 **ii- BOSSARD Eva Catherine**: born March 27, 1771
iii- BOSSARD Johan George: born August 8, 1772 and died young

11 iv- **BOSSARD Phillip**: (twin) born December 28, 1773
12 v- **BOSSARD Christopher**: (twin) born December 28, 1773
13 vi- **BOSSARD Elizabeth**: born January 14, 1776
14 vii- **BOSSARD Melchior**: born February 19, 1778
15 viii- **BOSSARD George**: born December 22, 1779
16 ix- **BOSSARD Andreas**: born March 3, 1782
17 x- **BOSSARD Peter**: born May 13, 1784
xi- **BOSSARD Margaret**: born April 22, 1786
Child by Melchior's second marriage:
18 xii- **BOSSARD Melchior**: born Febuary 28, 1800

4 **BOSSARD Christina**: (*Phillip*) was probably born about 1746, daughter of Phillip and Eva Catherine. She married Christopher Keller, son of Christophel and Margaretha Keller, born October 12, 1743 in Germany. He died June 10, 1795 in Hamilton Township and Christina died age 64. They are both buried in the Hamilton Square churchyard.

The children of Christopher Keller and Margaretha Catherina Bossard, born in Hamilton township are:

19 i- **KELLER Margaretha Catherine**: born May 6, 1770
20 ii- **KELLER Christina**: March 17, 1772
21 iii- **KELLER Johan George**: born March 5, 1774
iv- **KELLER Johan Phillip**: born May 3, 1776 and died young
22 v- **KELLER Andreas**: born August 8, 1778
23 vi- **KELLER Maria**: born April 15, 1782
24 vii- **KELLER Susanna**: born August 2, 1784
25 viii- **KELLER Christoffel**: born July 20, 1788

CHAPTER 3

THIRD GENERATION

5 **BUZARD Phillip Jacob**: (*Heinrich, Phillip*) was born September 26, 1764 in Hamilton Township, son of Heinrich and Anna Catherine. He married Margaretha (unknown maiden name). They removed to Westmoreland County ca 1790. Spelling used was 'Buzard'.

Children born in Hamilton Township:
i- **BUZARD Maria**: born ca 1783
ii- **BUZARD Jonathan**: born July 31,1788. He moved to Ohio from Westmoreland Co., before 1850.
Children born in Westmoreland Co.:
iii- **BUZARD Heinrich**: born January 12, 1795
iv- **BUZARD Johannes**: cr. July 30, 1797

6 **BUZARD Johanne George**: (*Heinrich, Phillip*) was born March 11, 1771 in Hamilton Township, son of Heinrich and Anna Catherine. He married Margaretta (unknown maiden name) and removed to Westmoreland County.

Children born in Mt. Pleasant, Westmoreland County:
i- **BUZARD Anna Maria**: cr. July 18, 1793
ii- **BUZARD George Vetter**: cr. December 13, 1795
iii- **BUZARD Melchior**: cr. March 30, 1798
iv- **BUZARD Magdelena**: born January 19, 1806
v- **BUZARD Catharina**: born June 9, 1808
vi- **BUZARD Susanna**: born September 19, 1809

7 **BUZARD Johann Melchior**: (*Heinrich, Phillip*) was born April 11, 1772 in Hamilton Township, son of Heinrich and Eva Catherine. He married Maria Susanna Snyder, born July 10, 1775, daughter of Valentine and Maria Elizabeth Snyder. He removed to Westmoreland County and died ca. 1850-52 in Madison Township, Pennsylvania.

Children born in Westmoreland County:
i- **BUZARD John Henrich**: born May 3, 1794
ii- **BUZARD Maria Elizabeth**: born November 12, 1795
iii- **BUZARD Jacob**: born December 26, 1797
iv- **BUZARD Johann (John)**: born July 11, 1799
v- **BUZARD Anna**: born March 11, 1806
vi- **BUZARD George W.**: born ca 1807

vii- BUZARD James: born April 24, 1812
Possibly others: Samuel-Thomas-Sara

8 **BUZARD Heinrich**: (*Heinrich, Phillip*) was born July 16, 1773 in Hamilton Township, son of Heinrich and Eva Catherine, He married Catrina (unknown maiden name).

Known children born in Westmoreland Co:
i- BUZARD John: cr. Febuary 7, 1796
ii- BUZARD Elisabeth: cr. December 9, 1797

9 **BOSSARD Christina**: (*Melchior, Phillip*) was born September 15, 1769 in Hamilton Township, daughter of Melchior Bossard and Margaretha Catherine Keller. She married Simon Heller, born March 13, 1767, son of Simon Heller and Louisa Deitz. Simon died July 26, 1833 and Christina died November 15, 1822. They are buried in the Hamilton Square Churchyard.

Children born in Hamilton Township:
i- HELLER Johan Melchior: born January 10, 1788
ii- HELLER Simon Jr.: born June 6, 1789
iii- HELLER Elizabetha: born November 24, 1789 died in infancy of small pox
iv- HELLER Kathrina: born September 10, 1794
v- HELLER Sara: born April 20, 1797 and died September 11, 1805
vi- HELLER Fronica: born December 15, 1799

10 **BOSSARD Eva Catherine**: (*Melchior, Phillip*) was born March 27, 1771 in Hamilton Township, daughter of Melchior Bossard and Margaretha Catherine Keller, and died April 3, 1837. She married Felix Weiss, born January 22, 1764, and died September 5, 1854. Both are buried in the Hamilton Square Churchyard.

Known children born in Hamilton Township:
26 **i- WEISS Felix II**: born in 1790
27 **ii- WEISS George**: born April 19, 1798

11 **BOSSARD Phillip**: (*Melchior, Phillip*) was born December 28, 1773 in Hamilton Township, twin son of Melchior Bossard and Margaretha Catherine Keller. He married Maria Heller, ca 1800 and moved to Lansing, Tompkins Co. New York. He died May 6, 1810 in Lansing, and is buried in the cemetery at the Dutch and German Reformed Church in North Lansing, New York. Maria Married (2) John Haas.

When Phillip arrived in New York, he purchased 138 Acres from Christopher Johnson. In 1812, after his death, the land was sold and the deed was signed by John Haas and his wife Polly (nickname often used for Mary or Maria).

Children of Phillip and Maria born in Lansing:
28 i- **BOSSARD John**: born September 3, 1802
29 ii- **BOSSARD Joseph**: born November 6, 1804
iii- **BOSSARD Susannah**: born May 5, 1808
iv- **BOSSARD Melchior**: born April 10, 1810

12 **BOSSARD Christopher**: (*Melchior, Phillip*) was born December 28, 1773, twin son of Melchior Bossard and Margaretha Catherine Keller. He married Sarah, by whom he had eight children, all born in Hamilton Township.

He bought land from his Father in 1813 and in 1814 which he sold by 1820, when he removed to Lansing, Tompkins Co., New York. On September 8, 1831, he sold the land in Lansing to Ephriam Heller, deed recorded in Ithaca, New York, and removed to the town of Humphrey in Cattaraugus Co. When the land was sold in Lansing, the deed was signed by Christopher and Elizabeth. Sarah may have died before 1831 and he married Elizabeth, or her name may have been Sarah Elizabeth if she used her middle name. No records were found to verify this.

Christopher is listed in the 1850 census in Humphrey, New York, age 77, living with his son John. There is no wife listed, so his wife Elizabeth must have died before 1850. No death record or cemetery stones have been found for Christopher or his wife, but he was no longer in the census records for 1860. Therefore, he must have died between 1850-60. In the census records, the spelling is 'Bozard' and his descendants continue to spell it this way.

Children of Christopher and Sarah born in Hamilton Township:
i- **BOZARD Hanna**: born December 31, 1796
ii- **BOZARD Milchert**: bp. March 7, 1799 and died young
30 iii- **BOZARD Johan Melchior**: born March 8, 1801
31 iv- **BOZARD Peter**: born April 4, 1803
32 v- **BOZARD Richart**: born July 27, 1805
33 vi- **BOZARD Phillip**: born March 8, 1811
34 vii- **BOZARD Charles**: born May 23, 1814
viii- **BOZARD George**: born October 18, 1816

13 **BOSSARD Elizabeth**: (*Melchior, Phillip*) was born January 14, 1776 in Hamilton Township, daughter of Melchior Bossard and Margaretha Keller and died October 18, 1828 in Pahaquarry Township, New Jersey. She married Benjamin De Puy, born May 28, 1771 in Wyoming Valley. He died November 2, 1831 in Pahaquarry Township, New Jersey

Children born in Hamilton Township:
i- **DE PUY Susannah**: born August 27, 1792

ii- **DE PUY Margaret**: born April 15, 1794
iii- **DE PUY Elijah**: born January 29, 1796
iv- **DE PUY Elizabeth**: born March 10, 1798

Children born in Walpack New Jersey, Dutch Reform records of baptisms:

v- **DE PUY Melchior**: born February 24, 1800
vi- **DE PUY Hannah**: born June 18, 1802
vii- **DE PUY Nicholas**: born July 29, 1804
viii- **DE PUY Anny**: born August 29, 1806
ix- **DE PUY Eva Catherine**: born September 24,1808
x- **DE PUY Moses**: born March 13, 1811
xi- **DE PUY Ency**: born June 10, 1813
xii- **DE PUY Benjamin**: born December 18, 1815 and died 1837 buried in Smithfield, Presbytarian cemetery. Unmarried.
xiii- **DE PUY James Van Campen**: born December 22, 1818

14 BOSSARD Melchior Jr.: (*Melchior, Phillip*) was born February 19, 1778 in Hamilton Township, son of Melchior Bossard and Margaretha Catherine Keller, died 1813 in Upper Mt. Bethel, Pennsylvania. This may be the Melchior who married Mary Shaw, daughter of John and Hannah Shaw. Mary died February 23 1800 and is buried in the Cherry Valley Methodist church cemetery. He then married Anna Shaw. After Melchior died in 1813, Anna married an Evans and removed to Lansing, Tompkins Co., New York. Or, this Melchior may have died young, since a second son was named Melchior to Melchior and his second wife, Veronica Conrad.
This has not been verified.

Children:

i- **BOSSARD Melchior**:
ii- **BOSSARD Hannah**: born April 13, 1806 in Hamilton Township
iii- **BOSSARD Mary Ann**: born ca 1810 in Mt. Bethel Pa. She married Lorenzo Giles. No other records.
iv- **BOSSARD Sarah Ann**: born ca 1813. She died in Lansing, Tompkins Co., New York in 1833.

15 BOSSARD George: (*Melchior, Phillip*) was born December 22, 1779 in Hamilton Township, son of Melchior Bossard and Margaretha Keller. He married Elizabeth Rhohn, daughter of John and Elizabeth Rhohn, born July 11, 1787 in Bethlehem, Pennsylvania. She died in Dix, Schuyler County, New York, May 13, 1851 and George died in 1854. They are buried in a small cemetery outside of Montour Falls, south of the McCarthy farm.

By 1808, the family had removed to Lansing in Tompkins County, New York, where he purchased 36 acres of land from David Beardsley, being a part of lot number 57, according to deed of June 5, 1817 recorded in Tompkins County. He later sold this land and removed to the Town of Dix in Chemung County, now in Schuyler County, New York.

Children:
35 i- **BOSSARD Margaretha**: born Nov 5, 1804 in Hamilton Township.
ii- **BOSSARD Mary**: born 1808 , unmarried, died November 2, 1895 in Beaver Dams, New York.
Children born in Lansing, New York:
36 iii- **BOSSARD Sarah**: born March 29, 1818
37 iv- **BOSSARD Simon**: born September 14, 1820
38 v- **BOSSARD Veronica**: bpt. June 19, 1823
vi- **BOSSARD Elizabeth Jennie**: born April 14, 1825 and she died in 1845. She is buried with her parents in Montour.
39 vii- **BOSSARD Anson**: born April 3, 1827

16 **BOSSARD Andrew**: (*Melchior, Phillip*) was born March 3, 1782 in Hamilton Township, son of Melchior Bossard and Margaretha Catherine Keller. He married Nancy Hammond on February 22, 1804. She was born April 4, 1784 in Litchfield, Connecticutt. In 1809 they were living in Chemung Co., New York and then removed to Osceola, Pennsylvania in 1813. Andrew died August 20, 1858 and Nancy died November 24, 1839. They are buried in Fairview cemetery in Osceola. Their name is spelled with one 's', BOSARD.

Children born in Chemung Co., New York:
i- **BOSARD James Huntington**: born 1808 and died 1834
40 ii- **BOSARD Alvers**: born September 23, 1810
Children born in Osceola, Pennsylvania:
iii- **BOSARD Emma**: born December 22, 1813 and died 1831
41 iv- **BOSARD Maria**: born ca 1814
42 v- **BOSARD Arthur F.**: born December 28, 1816
43 vi- **BOSARD Andrew Keller**: born December 27, 1819
44 vii- **BOSARD Melchior De Poi**: born ca 1821-2
viii- **BOSARD Nancy**: born 1824 and died 1836
ix- **BOSARD Peter**: born in Osceola, no other records

17 **BOSSARD Peter**: (*Melchior, Phillip*) was born May 13 1784 in Hamilton Township, son of Melchior Bossard and Margaretha Catherine Keller. He married Anna Margaret Kern, born August 22, 1787. He died December 19, 1835 and she died March 29, 1866. They are buried in Rock's cemetery.

Peter purchased most of the land from his Father by deed dated January 20, 1813 and recorded in Easton, Northampton County Pennsylvania, where he lived for the rest of his life.

Children born in Hamilton Township:
45 i- **BOSSARD Hanna**: born January 14, 1805
46 ii- **BOSSARD John**: born September 16, 1807

47 iii- **BOSSARD Anna Catherine**: born December 21, 1810
48 iv- **BOSSARD Johan Melchoir**: born August 5, 1813
49 v- **BOSSARD Samuel**: born April 22, 1816
50 vi- **BOSSARD Johan Jacob**: born December 16, 1818
51 vii- **BOSSARD Peter K.**: born July 7, 1821
52 viii- **BOSSARD Eliza Ann**: March 12, 1824
ix- **BOSSARD Jesia Caspes**: born December 9, 1825
53 x- **BOSSARD Joseph**: born 1828

18 BOSSARD Melchior: (*Melchior, Phillip*) was born January 24, 1800 in Hamilton Township, son of Melchior Bossard and Veronica Heller Conrad. He married Elizabeth (unknown maiden name), born September 25, 1801. She died April 19, 1878 and Melchior died March 26, 1879. They are buried in the Middle Smithfield Presbytarian Church cemetery.

Known children:
i- **BOSSARD Samuel**: born December 17, 1826 and died February 7, 1861.
ii- **BOSSARD Elizabeth**: born 1828 and died April 19, 1878.

19 KELLER Margaretha Catherine: (*Christina, Phillip*) was born May 6, 1770, daughter of Christopher Keller and Christina Bossard. She married December 11, 1787 in Easton, Pennsylvania, Michael Butz born May 1, 1767, son of Michael Butz and Elizabeth Weaver. He died February 28, 1826. No record for the death of Margaretha Catherina has been found.

Children:
i- **BUTZ Elizabeth**: born July 28, 1788 in Easton
ii- **BUTZ Maria**: born July 10, 1789 in Easton
iii- **BUTZ John George**: born January 11, 1792
iv- **BUTZ Jacob**: born September 10, 1793
v- **BUTZ Henry**: removed to Warren County New Jersey
vi- **BUTZ Catherine**: born November 21, 1796
vii- **BUTZ Susanna**: born April 6, 1798. The Mother was not at the christening for Susanna. It is possible that she died at this time.

20 KELLER Christina: (*Christina, Phillip*) was born March 17, 1772 in Hamilton Township, daughter of Christopher Keller and Christina Bossard. She married in 1791, Conrad Deiter (Teeter), son of Henry and Elizabeth Teeter. They removed to Lansing, New York by 1800.

NOTE: In the book "Kellers of Pennsylvania and New York", by David Keller, he states that Christina was disinherited by her Father. However, the deed clearly states that 'said bequests to my three daughters, Catherine, Mary and

Susanna, hereinbefore named, do in my opinion by no means overrun the advantage and allowance which my son-in-law Conrad Deiter, obtained of me in the purchase of his land'. Apparently, Conrad Deiter had recieved some land from Christopher and he felt that this was his daughter's inheritance.

As for Christopher not attending his grandaughter's christening perhaps he was ill, or for some other reason, was not able to attend. I can see no reason to believe that there was any conflict between Christina and her Father.

Perhaps the Cristina Deiter, who attended communion in 1814, was another Christina. Records of the Evangelical United Congregation In Lansing, New York, shows that this family was here as early as July of 1800, when their son Jacob was born and were still here, at least until 1807.

Children born in Hamilton Township:
i- **TEETER Susanna**: born March 15, 1794
ii- **TEETER Andrew**: born November 13, 1795
Children born in Lansing:
iii- **TEETER Jacob**: born July 31, 1800
iv- **TEETER Rachel**: born July 11, 1802
v- **TEETER Isaac**: born October 1, 1804
vi- **TEETER Anna**: born November 5, 1807

21 **KELLER Johan George**: (*Christina, Phillip*) was born March 15, 1774 in Hamilton Township, son of Christopher Keller and Christina Bossard. He married October 20, 1794, Rachel Dills born October 13, 1776, daughter of John and Rachel Dills. He died October 16, 1833 and Rachel died August 7, 1838. They are buried in the Mt. Zion cemetery, Hamilton Township.

Children:
i- **KELLER Johanne**: born February 18, 1795
ii- **KELLER Christopher D.**: born July 12, 1797
iii- **KELLER Joseph**: born February 7, 1800
Two daughters died in infancy.

22 **KELLER Andrew**: (*Christina, Phillip*) was born August 8, 1788 in Hamilton Township, son of Christopher Keller and Christina Bossard. He married Elizabeth Bauer. They removed to Lansing, New York for a short time and then moved to Cuba, Allegany County.

Children born in Lansing except Katie.
i- **KELLER Katie**:
ii- **KELLER Sarah**: born August 17, 1802
iii- **KELLER Tillman**: January 27, 1805
iv- **KELLER Elizabeth**: born May 17, 1812
v- **KELLER Mariette**: born Febuary 1, 1815

vi- **KELLER Albert**: born November 1, 1822
vii- **KELLER Susan**: died young with diptheria
viii- **KELLER Flora**: died young with diptheria
ix- **KELLER Alfred**: died young with diptheria
Children probably born in Allegany Co.:
ix- **KELLER George**:
x- **KELLER James**:
xi- **KELLER Betsey**:
xii- **KELLER Calvin B.**:

23 **KELLER Maria**: (*Christina, Phillip*) was born April 15, 1782 in Hamilton Township, daughter of Christopher Keller and Christina Bossard. She married Jacob Deiter, possibly a brother of Conrad Deiter, and they removed to Lansing, New York before 1800, where three of their children were born. They may have moved to Allegany Co. after that. No further records. Name spelled 'Teeter' in New York.

Children born in Lansing, New York:
i- **TEETER Anna**: born February 21, 1800
ii- **TEETER Catherine**: born May 8, 1803
iii- **TEETER Simeon**: born March 27, 1804

24 **KELLER Susanna**: (*Christina, Phillip*) was born August 2, 1784 in Hamilton Township, daughter of Christopher Keller and Christina Bossard. She married James Shafer and removed to Lansing and then to Cuba, Allegany Co., New York.

Children born in Hamilton Township, Pennsylvania:
i- **SHAFER Jacob**: born December 28, 1802
ii- **SHAFER Sara**: born March 8, 1813
Children probably born in New York State:
iii- **SHAFER Rachel**:
iv- **SHAFER Christopher**: born September 6, 1820
v- **SHAFER Louise**:
vi- **SHAFER Maria**: born April 27, 1827
vii- **SHAFER Joseph**:
viii- **SHAFER George**:

25 **KELLER Christopher**: (*Christina, Phillip*) was born July 20, 1788 in Hamilton Township, son of Christopher Keller and Christina Bossard, and died 1880 in Cuba, New York. He married Anna Hauser ca 1810, born February 16, 1793, and died 1880, daughter of Heinrich and Margaretha Hauser. The family removed to Cuba, New York State about 1823.

Children born Hamilton Township:
i- **KELLER Anna**: born November 14, 1810

ii- **KELLER Katarina**: born August 29, 1812
iii- **KELLER George**: born October 21,1814
iv- **KELLER Margaretha**: born October 22, 1816
v- **KELLER Christina**: born November 21,1818
vi- **KELLER Amos**: February 18, 1821
vii- **KELLER Elizabeth Ann**: born February 11, 1823
Children born in New York State:
viii- **KELLER Enos**: born 1824
ix- **KELLER Sarah Ann**: born 1827
x- **KELLER Andrew**: born 1829
xi- **KELLER William Henry**: born 1830
xii- **KELLER Elizabeth Marie**: born 1833

NOTE:

Since there has already been a genealogy of the Keller family, in Pennsylvania and New York, the descendants of this family will not be continued in this writing. Refer to 'The Kellers of Hamilton Township' by David Henry Keller.

Several books have been published on the 'Heller' familes of Pennsylvania. Therefore, I am not including any further descendants of Simon Heller and his wife Christina Bossard.

Very little information has been available on the De Puy family of Pennsylvania and New Jersey. I will include the information that I have found in the next chapter.

For more information on some of the descendants of Henry Buzzard see the book "The Buzzards of Pennsylvania", by Edward Buzard Reighard and another book on the Buzzards in Pennsylvania, by Josiah Buzzard.

CHAPTER 4

Fourth Generation

26 **WEISS Felix II**: (*Eva Catherine, Melchior, Phillip*) was born September 29, 1790 in Hamilton Township. Pennsylvania, son of Felix Weiss and Eva Catherine Bossard. He married Susannah Brong born October 15, 1790, daughter of Sebastian and Barbara Brong. He died April 26, 1863 and Susannah died September 25, 1866. They are both buried in the Salem Church cemetery in Chestnuthill, Pennsylvania.

Children born in Hamilton Township:
i- **WEISS Sebastian**: born December 31, 1815
54 ii- **WEISS Daniel F.**: born April 15, 1818
55 iii- **WEISS George B.**: born December 10, 1820
56 iv- **WEISS Susannah**: born June 27, 1824
57 v- **WEISS Felix III**: born May 5, 1827
58 vi- **WEISS Sally Ann**: born January 5, 1830
59 vii- **WEISS Elizabeth**: born April 8, 1833

27 **WEISS George**: (*Eva Catherine, Melchior, Phillip*) was born April 19, 1798, son of Felix Weiss and Eva Catherine Bossard. He married Susannah Snyder born December 28, 1804, daughter of John and Louisa Snyder. George died April 20, 1830 and Susannah died January 21, 1887. They are buried in Mt. Zion cemetery in Hamilton Township. After Felix died, Susannah married Henry Fenner and had five children.

Children born in Hamilton Township:
60 i- **WEISS Amelia**: born January 23, 1824
ii- **WEISS Simon**: born May 6, 1827 and died April 5, 1828
61 iii- **WEISS Catherine Anna**: born April 14, 1829

28 **BOSSARD John**: (*Phillip, Melchior, Phillip*) was born September 3, 1802 in Lansing New York, son of Phillip Bossard and Maria Heller. He was still in Lansing in 1826, when he signed a quitclaim on his father's property. No other records have been found for him in New York State, but he could possibly be the Father of a Roswell Bossard born in 1829 in Lansing, New York, who married Rachel Millage.

29 **BUZZARD Joseph**: (*Phillip, Melchior, Phillip*) was born November 6, 1804, son of Phillip Bossard and Maria Heller. He married December 3, 1826, Mary Ann

(Polly) Osman, daughter of John and Mary Osman, born October 2, 1811 in Lansing, New York. About 1831 they moved to Cattaraugus Co., New York and shortly after that they moved to Oakland Co., Michigan. They bought 160 acres for $1.25 and $1.50 an acre. At that time it was a wilderness, but Joseph and some of Mary Ann's family cleared the land and built a log home. Here they raised their family of 14 children. The descendants of Joseph spell the name 'BUZZARD'.

Children born in New York State:
62 i- **BUZZARD Almira**: born April 12, 1827
63 ii- **BUZZARD Adeline**: born August 11, 1829
64 iii- **BUZZARD Israel**: born July 1831
65 iv- **BUZZARD John**: born January 1833
Children born in Michigan:
66 v- **BUZZARD Eli**: born in 1836
67 vi- **BUZZARD Jacob L.**: born May 9, 1838
vii- **BUZZARD Elizabeth**: born in 1840
68 viii- **BUZZARD Edwin Joseph**: born January 5, 1842
69 ix- **BUZZARD George M.**: born November 1844
70 x- **BUZZARD Isabelle**: born in 1847
xi- **BUZZARD Archie**: born February 7, 1848
xii- **BUZZARD Louise**:
xiii- **BUZZARD Charles**:
71 xiv- **BUZZARD William**: born November 1856

30 BOZARD Johan Melchior: (*Christopher, Melchior, Phillip*) was born March 8, 1801 in Hamilton Township, son of Christopher and Sarah Bossard. He married Sally (unknown maiden name). He sold land in Cattaraugus Co. in 1853. No further records have been found for him or his children.

Children born in Cattaraugus Co.:
i- **BOZARD Alfred**: born in 1831
ii- **BOZARD Ann**: born in 1836

31 BOSSARD Peter: (*Christopher, Melchior, Phillip*) was born April 4, 1803 in Hamilton Township, son of Christopher and Sarah Bossard. He married Margaret Bossard, born November 5, 1804 in Hamilton Township. She was the daughter of George Bossard and Elizabeth Rhohn. When his Father moved to Cattaraugus Co., Peter and Margaret remained with her family in the Town of Dix in Schuyler Co., New York, and is the only one of Christopher's family who used the spelling of 'BOSSARD', altho the name was spelled 'Bozzard' on a land record of 1870. It is not known when Peter died, but he was living in 1870, when he sold his farm, containing 25 acres to his son, Jarvis. Margaret died November 7, 1891 in Horseheads, New York and is buried in the cemetery in Watkins Glen, New York.

Children born in Dix, Schuyler Co., New York:

72 i- **BOSSARD Edson**: born June 16, 1835
73 ii- **BOSSARD George**: born May 11, 1838
iii- **BOSSARD Mandis**: died an infant August 31, 1839
74 iv- **BOSSARD Marcus**: born Febuary 21, 1842
75 v- **BOSSARD Jarvis L.**: born April 1843

32 **BOZARD Richard**: (*Christopher, Melchior, Phillip*) was born July 27, 1805 in Hamilton Township, son of Christopher and Sarah Bossard. He married January 10, 1829, Elinor Learn, born October 17, 1809. She died November 6, 1866 and Richard married (2) on January 8, 1868, Harriet Cherryman, born January 17, 1822. She died August 16, 1870 and Richard died September 16, 1870. They are buried in the Pierce cemetery in Ischua, New York.

Children born in Humphrey, Cattaraugus Co., New York:
76 i- **BOZARD Henry M.**: born June 21, 1830
77 ii- **BOZARD Andrew J.**: born December 29, 1833
78 iii- **BOZARD Cyrus Peter**: born April 8, 1835
79 iv- **BOZARD Barnard S.**: born March 5, 1838
80 v- **BOZARD Ashbel Lacy**: born Febuary 24, 1841
81 vi- **BOZARD Rebecca**: born June 17, 1844
82 vii- **BOZARD Joseph M.**: born September 10, 1847
83 viii- **BOZARD Laura H.**: born November 20, 1852
84 ix- **BOZARD Judson O.**: born March 5, 1855

33 **BOZARD Phillip**: (*Christopher, Melchior, Phillip*) was born March 8, 1811 in Hamilton Township, Pennsylvania, son of Christopher and Sarah Bossard. He was in Leicester, Livingston Co. New York in 1840 and moved to Oakland Co., Michigan soon after that. He married Susannah (unknown maiden Name), born ca 1813. The spelling of his name became 'Buzzard' in Michigan. No further records.

One known child:
i- **BUZZARD Catherine**: born ca 1848

34 **BOZARD Charles**: (*Christopher, Melchior, Phillip*) was born May 23, 1814 in Hamilton Township, son of Christopher and Sarah Bossard. He married (1) Patty Bush and (2) Martha. He sold land in Cattaraugus Co. in 1853 and removed to Oakland Co. Michigan. Unknown date of death.

Children born in New York State:
85 i- **BOZARD Sylvanus**: born June 1837
86 ii- **BOZARD Sylvester Lorenzo**: born March 1844
87 iii- **BOZARD William E.**: born October 1852

35 **BOSSARD Margaret**: (*George, Melchior, Phillip*) was born November 5, 1804 in Hamilton Township, daughter of George Bossard and Elizabeth Rhohn. She married Peter Bossard, son of Christopher and Sarah Bossard.
See number 31, Peter Bossard.

36 **BOSSARD Sarah**: (*George, Melchior, Phillip*) was born March 30, 1818 in Lansing, New York, daughter of George Bossard and Elizabeth Rhohn. She married David Backer ca 1840 and she died April 16, 1892. David Backer was born ca 1817 and died before April 4, 1874, when his wife and children sold 46 acres, (half of the farmland he owned) in the Town of Dix, New York.

Children born in Dix:

88 **i- BACKER Amanda**: born 1842
89 **ii- BACKER Jane**: born December 3, 1843
90 **iii- BACKER Juliet**: born ca 1845
iv- BACKER Frances: born 1847 and died December 10, 1925 in Montour Falls, New York. She is buried in the Montour cemetery, unmarried.
91 **v- BACKER Harriet M.**: born 1848
92 **vi- BACKER George L.**: born ca 1850
vii- BACKER David A.: born ca 1852, unmarried
93 **viii- BACKER Emmett**: born 1853

37 **BOSSARD Simon**: (*George, Melchior, Phillip*) was born September 14, 1820 in Lansing, New York, son of George Bossard and Elizabeth Rhohn. He married (1) September 14, 1842, Hannah Norris. She died June 22, 1863 and he married (2) September 25, 1867, Mrs. Julia S. Smith, born September 21, 1827. She died September 26, 1868 and Simon died December 9, 1868. He was, at one time, a postmaster in Sullivanville, Chemung Co., New York. They are buried in the Newton cemetery in Sullivanville, New York.

Children of Simon and Hannah:

i- BOSSARD Abbot: born June 11, 1843 and died on November 4, 1867, buried with his parents.
94 **ii- BOSSARD George A.**: born in 1846
95 **iii- BOSSARD Iona**: born Febuary 1858

Child of Simon and Julia:

96 **iv- BOSSARD Judd**: born June 3, 1868

38 **BOSSARD Veronica**: (*George, Melchior, Phillip*) was baptized March 31, 1823 in Lansing New York, daughter of George Bossard and Elizabeth Rhohn. Altho she was baptized Veronica, she always used the name Fanny. She married March 24, 1847, John Cross born 1821, son of Joshua Cross and Kezia Turk. She died March 31, 1897 and John died June 11, 1895. They are both buried in the New Reading cemetery in Reading, Schuyler Co., New York.

Children born in Reading, New York:

97 i- **CROSS Elizabeth**: born May 28, 1848
98 ii- **CROSS Virginia**: born 1852
99 iii- **CROSS Miles**: born 1853
100 iv- **CROSS Maria**: born 1855
101 v- **CROSS Mary**: born 1861
102 vi- **CROSS Maude**: born 1867

39 **BOSSARD Anson**: (*George, Melchior, Phillip*) was born April 3, 1829 in Lansing, New York, son of George Bossard and Elizabeth Rhohn. He married July 17, 1853, Cornelia Annette Eddy born Febuary 14, 1835 in Townsend, New York, daughter of Thomas Eddy and Elizabeth Shreeves. They made their home in the Town of Dix on a farm where the Watkins Glen race track is now located. The house is still there close to the entrance of the race track. He later sold that farm and moved to Enfield in Tompkins Co., where he lived until he died November 1, 1919. His wife died December 14, 1914 and they are buried in North Lansing.

Children born in Dix:

103 i- **BOSSARD Clara Eddy**: born July 12, 1854
104 ii- **BOSSARD Charles E.**: born August 17, 1857
105 iii- **BOSSARD William Delevan**: born July 19, 1862
iv- **BOSSARD Charlotte Maude**: born June 20, 1864 and died January 30, 1870
106 v- **BOSSARD Fred Anson**: born April 24, 1871

40 **BOSARD Alvers**: (*Andrew, Melchior, Phillip*) was born September 23, 1810 in Osceola Pennsylvania, son of Andrew Bossard and Nancy Hammond. He married September 1849, Elizabeth Peck Bosworth born April 10, 1819. Alvers remained on the farm that was once his Father's. He died August 1, 1883 in Bath, New York. Elizabeth died August 8, 1900 in Osceola. They are both buried in Fairview cemetery in Osceola.

One child:

107 i- **BOSARD Susan A.**: born July 22, 1850

41 **BOSARD Maria**: (*Andrew, Melchior, Phillip*) was born 1814 in Osceola, Pennsylvania, daughter of Andrew Bossard and Nancy Hammond. She married in 1843, Dr. Henry C. Bosworth born ca 1811. Maria died in 1870 and Henry died November 14, 1898 in Osceola.

Children:

108 i- **BOSWORTH Edward E.**: born in 1846
109 ii- **BOSWORTH Urbana A.**: born May 1848
110 iii- **BOSWORTH Charles H.**: born 1851

42 **BOSARD Arthur F.**: (*Andrew, Melchior, Phillip*) was born ca 1817 in Osceola, son of Andrew Bossard and Nancy Hammond. He married Elizabeth (unknown maiden name) from Orangeville, Ohio. They lived in Deerfield, Pennsylvania. Alvers died in 1890 and Elizabeth died November 28, 1898.

Children:
111 i- **BOSARD Adelaide**: born 1847
112 ii- **BOSARD Kirtland A.**: born January 1849
iii- **BOSARD Cora**: born ca 1854
iv- **BOSARD Frank**: born ca 1856

43 **BOSARD Andrew Keller**: (*Andrew, Melchior, Phillip*) was born December 27, 1819 in Osceola, Pennsylvania, son of Andrew Bossard and Nancy Hammond. He married Hetty Cilly born 1819, daughter of John Cilly and Marcia Goodwin. Hetty died November 22, 1865 and on June 16, 1867 he married Anne Flanders Sherman, born April 5, 1837. Andrew K. died March 12, 1877 in Osceola and Anne died July 14, 1882. She is buried in the cemetery on Butler Hill, near Knoxville. He is buried in Osceola.

Children of Andrew K. and Hetty:
113 i- **BOSARD James Huntington**: born April 1845
114 ii- **BOSARD George Leroy**: born June 1847
115 iii- **BOSARD Jerome Leon**: born May 29, 1849
116 iv- **BOSARD Florence H.**: born May 11, 1851
117 v- **BOSARD Sara Louise**: born July 1853
118 vi- **BOSARD William Burns**: born July 1854
119 vii- **BOSARD Maria**: born 1859
Children of Andrew K. and Anne:
120 viii- **BOSARD Emma**: born February 1870
121 ix- **BOSARD Stella M.**: born 1869
122 x- **BOSARD Elizabeth Ann**: born February 1875

44 **BOSARD Melchior De Poi**: (*Andrew, Melchior, Phillip*) was born in 1822, Town of Osceola, son of Andrew Bossard and Nancy Hammond. He married February 29, 1848, Eleanor Campbell born April 27, 1828. Melchior served in Co. L., 2nd Pennsylvania Cavalry, during the Civil War. He died September 4, 1864 of Emeritis, while serving near City Point, Virginia and is buried there. Eleanor remained a widow until her death, February 16, 1914.

Children born in Osceola:
123 i- **BOSARD John Mahlon**: born November 10, 1848
124 ii- **BOSARD Laura Jane**: born August 1851
125 iii- **BOSARD Anna Maria**: born April 4, 1860

45 **BOSSARD Hanna**: (*Peter, Melchior, Phillip*) was born January 14, 1805 in

Hamilton Township, Pennsylvania, daughter of Peter Bossard and Anna Margaret Kern. She married Phillip Huffsmith born May 10, 1801, son of Adam Huffsmith and Julianna Ritter. Hanna died December 8, 1866 and Phillip died November 1, 1864. They are buried in the cemetery at Brodheadsville.

Children born in Hamilton Township:

i- **HUFFSMITH Lisa Ann**: born October 19, 1824 and died January 1, 1829. She is buried in the Salem Church cemetery.

126 ii- **HUFFSMITH Lavina**: born August 19, 1826

iii- **HUFFSMITH Catherine Anna**: born June 28, 1828 and died April 11, 1833. She is buried in Salem Church cemetery.

iv- **HUFFSMITH Elizabeth**: born September 2, 1830 and died May 5, 1833. She is buried in Salem Church cemetery.

127 v- **HUFFSMITH Lynford**: born August 20, 1832

vi- **HUFFSMITH Hannah Maria**: born December 9, 1834 and died May 16, 1836. She is buried Salem Church cemetery.

vii- **HUFFSMITH Margaret**: born June 1, 1835 and died May 9, 1840. She is buried in Salem Church cemetery.

viii- **HUFFSMITH Phillip Jr.**: born February 19, 1837 and died September, 1837. He is buried in the Salem Church cemetery.

128 ix- **HUFFSMITH Samuel**: born July 1, 1838

129 x- **HUFFSMITH Sarah Jane**: born August 29, 1840

130 xi- **HUFFSMITH Margaret Ann**: born January 16, 1843

131 xii- **HUFFSMITH George Washington**: born September 21, 1845

46 BOSSARD **John**: (*Peter, Melchior, Phillip*) was born September 16, 1807 in Hamilton Township, son of Peter Bossard and Anna Margaret Kern. He married Sarah Erdman, daughter of John and Sara Erdman, born November 2, 1805 in Hamilton Township. No record found for their date of death in Monroe Co., Pennsylvania.

Children born in Hamilton Township:

i- **BOSSARD Susannah**: born December 9, 1834

ii- **BOSSARD Catharina**: born January 7, 1838 and died March 27, 1838, buried in Rock's cemetery.

132 iii- **BOSSARD Sarah**: born ca 1831

iv- **BOSSARD Andrew**: born December 24, 1839 and died January 4, 1858, buried in Rock's cemetery.

133 v- **BOSSARD Isaiah**: born Febuary 7, 1844

47 BOSSARD **Anna Catherine**: (*Peter, Melchior, Phillip*) was born December 21, 1810 in Hamilton Township, daughter of Peter Bossard and Anna Margaret Kern. She married Jacob Ruth, born September 17, 1804 in Hamilton Township. Anna died December 18, 1898 and Jacob died October 1, 1879. They are buried in the cemetery at Brodheadsville.

Children born in Hamilton Township:

134 i- **RUTH Lynford**: born August 8, 1830

ii- **RUTH Hannah**: born June 18, 1832 and died Febuary 2, 1835, buried in Rock's cemetery.

iii- **RUTH Margaret**: born March 17, 1835 and died May 19, 1840, buried in Rock's cemetery.

135 iv- **RUTH Joseph**: born August 18, 1837

136 v- **RUTH Jacob**: born April 25, 1840

137 vi- **RUTH Samuel**: born January 14, 1843

138 vii- **RUTH James**: born December 10, 1846

viii- **RUTH Sarah Catherine**: born October 6, 1849

139 ix- **Ruth Martha Jane**: born August 20, 1853

48 **BOSSARD J. Melchior**: (*Peter, Melchior, Phillip*) was born August 5, 1813 in Hamilton Township, Pennsylvania, son of Peter Bossard and Anna Margaret Kern. He married January 12, 1833, Hanna Arnold born October 2, 1818, daughter of George and Elizabeth Arnold. Melchior died October 27, 1871 and Hanna died March 14, 1884. They are buried in the Bossard Heller cemetery in Hamilton Township.

Children born in Hamilton Township:

140 i- **BOSSARD Charles**: born July 26, 1834

141 ii- **BOSSARD Margaret**: born October 24, 1835

142 iii- **BOSSARD Joseph H.**: born October 4, 1837

143 iv- **BOSSARD Susannah**: born October 3, 1839

144 v- **BOSSARD Peter**: born April 30, 1841

145 vi- **BOSSARD Florinda**: born March 1843

146 vii- **BOSSARD Mary Jane**: born April 1845

147 viii- **BOSSARD James**: born February 1848

148 ix- **BOSSARD Anna E.**: born August 27, 1851

149 x- **BOSSARD John M.**: born July 7, 1854

150 xi- **BOSSARD Franklin**: born June 12, 1857

xii- **BOSSARD Andrew**: (twin) born September 2, 1850

xiii- **BOSSARD George**: (twin) born September 2, 1850

The twins both died in November 1850 and they are buried in the Bossard-Heller cemetery.

49 **BOSSARD Samuel**: (*Peter, Melchior, Phillip*) was born April 22, 1816 in Hamilton Township, son of Peter Bossard and Anna Margaret Kern. There is no record of a marriage for him in the Monroe Co. records, but there was a Matilda that was born on October 5, 1832 to a Samuel and Sarah Bossard. If they were the parents, his wife may have died young. Matilda was living with John and Sarah Bossard in the 1850 census. She married October 15, 1857, Jerome Shaw. No other records were found. Samuel died June 4, 1892 and he is in buried Rock's cemetery, Jackson Township.

50 **BOSSARD J. Jacob:** (*Peter, Melchior, Phillip*) was born December 16, 1818 in Hamilton Township, son of Peter Bossard and Anna Margaret Kern. He married October 20, 1839, Christina Rees, born October 20, 1839, daughter of Samuel Rees and Magdelena Rinker. Jacob and Christina moved to Ida Grove, Iowa sometime before 1900. He died May 22, 1909 and his wife died August 18, 1902. They are both buried in the Ida Grove cemetery.

Children born in Hamilton Township:
151 i- **BOSSARD Samuel:** born April 29, 1841
152 ii- **BOSSARD Edwin:** born February 22, 1845
153 iii- **BOSSARD Sarah Catherine:** born June 16, 1847
Children probably born in Jackson Township:
154 iv- **BOSSARD Rachel J.:** born 1851
v- **BOSSARD Idella:** born March 1, 1852 and died October 27, 1852, buried in Rock's cemetery.
155 vi- **BOSSARD Mary Alice:** born ca 1854
vii- **BOSSARD Emmaline:** born April 15, 1855, and died July 22, 1855, buried in Rock's cemetery.
viii- **BOSSARD Susie:** born ca 1859. No other records
156 ix- **BOSSARD Ida J.:** born August 17, 1857
x- **BOSSARD Lizzie:** born March 24, 1859 and died November 4, 1862, buried in Rock's cemetery.
xi- **BOSSARD Alvin:** born September 12, 1860 and died September 26, 1860, buried in Rock's cemetery.
157 xii- **BOSSARD Layton:** born March 19, 1865

51 **BOSSARD Peter K.:** (*Peter, Melchior, Phillip*) was born July 7, 1821 in Hamilton Township, Pennsylvania, son of Peter Bossard and Anna Margaret Kern. He married November 15, 1850, Anna Elizabeth Levering born July 8, 1827. Peter K. died October 3, 1897 and Anna Elizabeth died May 11, 1910. They are both buried in Mt. Zion cemetery in Hamilton Township.

Children born in Hamilton Township:
158 i- **BOSSARD Emma:** born June 8, 1853
159 ii- **BOSSARD William H.:** born November 20, 1855
iii- **BOSSARD Joseph A.:** born 1862
160 iv- **BOSSARD Eugene Abraham:** born December 10, 1860
161 v- **BOSSARD Mary Ann:** born July 4, 1863
vi- **BOSSARD Elnora:** born November 30, 1864 and died April 14, 1865

52 **BOSSARD Eliza Ann:** (*Peter, Melchior, Phillip*) was born March 12, 1824 in Hamilton Township, daughter of Peter Bossard and Anna Margaret Kern. She married November 9, 1845, Jacob Eyer born March 19, 1816, son of Heinrich and Elizabeth Eyer. Eliza Ann died March 23, 1867 and is buried in Mt. Zion cemetery. Jacob died January 22, 1898 and most of their family removed to Northampton Co., Pennsylvania.

Children:

162 i- **EYER Isaiah**: born April 4, 1847

ii- **EYER Edwin**: born January 27, 1849 and died March 30, 1861

163 iii- **EYER Peter**: born January 27, 1850

iv- **EYER Mary Alice**: born May 4, 1852 and died March 14, 1861, buried in Mt. Zion cemetery.

164 v- **EYER Emma Catherine**: born December 23, 1853

vi- **EYER Franklin Bossard**: born April 8, 1856 and died March 18, 1861, buried in Mt. Zion cemetery.

vii- **EYER Amanda**: born December 11, 1857 and died March 16, 1861, buried in Mt. Zion cemetery.

viii- **EYER Margarette**: born November 12, 1860 and died March 12, 1927, buried in Mt. Zion cemetery.

ix- **EYER Ellnora**: born June 13, 1862

x- **EYER Charles Henry**: born December 2, 1864

xi- **EYER Joseph**: born March 2, 1867

53 **BOSSARD Joseph**: (*Peter, Melchior, Phillip*) was born 1828 in Hamilton Township, son of Peter Bossard and Anna Margaret Kern. He married July 11, 1850, Sophia Cornelia Fetterman, born May 24, 1830, daughter of Abraham and Rachel Fetterman. Sophia died March 8, 1852 and is buried in Mt. Zion cemetery. Joseph married (2) Mary Ann Kemmerer, born 1827. He died September 27, 1913 and Mary Ann died January 30, 1915. They are buried in the Stroudsburg cemetery.

Child of Joseph and Sophia:

165 i- **BOSSARD Alice**: born in 1852

Child of Joseph and Mary Ann:

ii- **BOSSARD Norton A.**: born in December 2, 1863 and died in 1869. He is buried in Stroudsburg cemetery.

Andrew and Eliza Bozard

Andrew Bozard with his brothers and sisters

CHAPTER 5

FIFTH GENERATION

54 **WEISS Daniel F.**: (*Felix Weiss Jr., Eva Catherine, Melchior, Phillip*) was born April 15, 1818 in Hamilton Township, son of Felix Weiss and Susannah Brong. He married Susan ca 1840, (unknown maiden name). He died November 13, 1847 and is buried in the Salem Church cemetery in Gilbert, Pennsylvania.

Children born in Chestnuthill:
166 i- **WEISS Mary Ann**: born December 27, 1840
ii- **WEISS Francis H.**: born ca 1843
iii- **WEISS Davalt**: born ca 1844
167 iv- **WEISS Martha Jane**: born ca 1846

55 **WEISS George B.**: (*Felix Weiss Jr., Eva Catherine, Melchior, Phillip*) was born December 10, 1820, son of Felix Weiss Jr. and Susannah Brong. He married Elizabetha Altemose born April 23, 1827, daughter of Jacob Altemose and Elizabeth Greenamoyer. In 1863, at the time of his Father's death, they were in Luzerne Co., Pennsylvania. No records after that date.

Children born in Gilbert, Pennsylvania:
i- **WEISS Amelia**: born October 9, 1842
ii- **WEISS Regina**: born October 20, 1844
iii- **WEISS Sarah**: born February 18, 1846
iv- **WEISS Daniel**: born June 25, 1848
v- **WEISS William Henry**: born February 28, 1850
vi- **WEISS Thomas Jefferson**: born December 5, 1852
vii- **WEISS Mary J.**: born ca 1855
viii- **WEISS Alice**: born ca 1858

56 **WEISS Susannah**: (*Felix Weiss Jr., Eva Catherine, Melchior, Phillip*) was born June 27, 1824 in Hamilton Township, daughter of Felix Weiss and Susannah Brong. She married Linford Altemose, born December 3, 1825 in Chestnuthill, son of Jacob Altemose and Lydia Greenamoyer. She died February 14, 1888 and Linford died August 15, 1895. They are buried in Old Brodheadsville cemetery.

Children:
168 i- **ALTEMOSE Julia Arvilla**: born March 5, 1854
ii- **ALTEMOSE Mary Jane**: born February 3, 1856, and died July 29, 1857, buried Brick church cemetery.
iii- **ALTEMOSE Emma**: born July 31, 1857

iv- **ALTEMOSE Jacob**: born October 10, 1859 and died January 11, 1861. Buried in Brodheadsville.
169 v- **ALTEMOSE Diana**: born September 28, 1863
170 vi- **ALTEMOSE Stewart A.**: born December 30, 1865

57 **WEISS Felix III**: (*Felix Weiss Jr., Eva Catherine, Melchior, Phillip*) was born May 5, 1827 in Hamilton Township, son of Felix Weiss and Susannah Brong. He married Eliza Ann (unknown maiden name), born March 1837. He died before 1900 and Eliza died March 8, 1903.

Children born in Chestnuthill:
171 i- **WEISS Charles F.**: born July 1859
ii- **WEISS Adeline**: born ca 1862
iii- **WEISS Lucinda**: born ca 1867
iv- **WEISS Levering**: born ca 1869
172 v- **WEISS Stewart**: born ca 1872
vi- **WEISS Benjamin**: born ca 1875
vii- **WEISS Ellen L.**: born December 1879

58 **WEISS Sally Ann**: (*Felix Weiss Jr., Eva Catherine, Melchior, Phillip*) was born January 25, 1830 in Hamilton Township, daughter of Felix Weiss and Susannah Brong. She married ca 1852, Henry Hoodmaker born 1829. No records found after their fourth child was born.

Children:
i- **HOODMAKER Nathan**: born ca 1853
ii- **HOODMAKER Ellen**: born ca 1854
iii- **HOODMAKER Edwin**: born ca 1857
iv- **HOODMAKER Franklin**: born Nov 1859

59 **WEISS Elizabeth**: (*Felix Weiss Jr., Eva Catherine, Melchior, Phillip*) was born April 8, 1833, daughter of Felix Weiss and Susannah Brong. She married Samuel Reese Gearhart born October 22, 1836. Elizabeth died February 18, 1926 and S. Reese died March 21, 1914. They are buried in the Buena Vista cemetery in Chestnuthill Township, Pennsylvania.

Children:
173 i- **GEARHART Cicero**: born April 18, 1858
174 ii- **GEARHART Anna Elizabeth**: born March 1860
175 iii- **GEARHART Theodore**: born October 25, 1862
iv- **GEARHART Alice**: born October 17, 1863 and died February 2, 1886, buried in Buena Vista Cemetery.
176 v- **GEARHART Ulyssis**: born 1865
177 vi- **GEARHART John H.**: born June 4, 1868
178 vii- **GEARHART Thomas**: born September 21, 1870

179 viii- **GEARHART Lucy E.**: born March 24, 1875
ix- **GEARHART Phillip**: born June 6, 1876 and died February 25, 1877, buried Buena Vista cemetery.

60 **WEISS Amelia**: (*George Weiss, Eva Catherine, Melchior, Phillip*) was born July 23, 1824 in Hamilton Township, Pennsylvania, daughter of George Weiss and Susannah Snyder. She married Emmanuel Shoemaker born December 19, 1820, son of Johanne Shoemaker and Hannah Trach. Amelia died October 26, 1864 and Emmanuel married (2) Mrs. Mary Hulsheiser. He died March 28, 1895 and they are buried in Mt. Zion cemetery in Hamilton Township.

Children born in Hamilton Township:
180 i- **SHOEMAKER Abner**: born June 8, 1845
181 ii- **SHOEMAKER Louisa**: born October 15, 1846
182 iii- **SHOEMAKER Susan Ellen**: born August 26, 1849
iv- **SHOEMAKER Edwin S.**: born April 1850 and died May 6, 1850.
183 v- **SHOEMAKER Lynford Milton**: born June 8, 1851
184 vi- **SHOEMAKER William Marvin**: bp. August 21, 1852
185 vii- **SHOEMAKER Mary Alice**: born October 9, 1855
186 viii- **SHOEMAKER Catherine Ardella**: born May 16, 1861
ix- **SHOEMAKER Amelia**: born September 24, 1864 and died July 17, 1878.

61 **WEISS Catherine Anna**: (*George Weiss, Eva Catherine, Melchior, Phillip*) was born April 14, 1829, daughter of George Weiss and Susannah Snyder. She married Lynford Marsh born December 19, 1822, son of Isaak Marsh and Margaretha Williams. He died February 3, 1889. No record of her death date.

Children:
i- **MARSH Milton**: born May 31, 1849 and died August 1, 1894 in Belvidere, New Jersey, buried in Stroudsburg cemetery.
ii- **MARSH Howard Wilson**: born October 10, 1850

62 **BUZZARD Almira**: (*Joseph, Phillip, Melchior, Phillip*) was born April 12, 1827 in Lansing, New York, daughter of Joseph Bossard and Mary Ann Osman. She married July 1848, Henry French in Michigan. No further records.

63 **BUZZARD Adeline**: (*Joseph, Phillip, Melchior, Phillip*) was born August 11, 1829 in Lansing, New York, daughter of Joseph Buzzard and Mary Ann Osman. She married Almor Stanley in Oakland Co., Michigan. No further records.

64 **BUZZARD Israel**: (*Joseph, Phillip, Melchior, Phillip*) was born July 1831 in Lansing, New York, son of Joseph Buzzard and Mary Ann Osman. He married

Rozella Perry and resided in Tyrone Township, Michigan. She died before 1900 and Israel died between 1900 and 1910. No further records.

Children born in Michigan:

187 i- **BUZZARD Joseph**: born May 1862
ii- **BUZZARD Mary Ann**: born ca 1864
iii- **BUZZARD Adelia**: born ca 1866
iv- **BUZZARD John W.**: born ca 1871
v- **BUZZARD Nelson**: born ca 1874

65 **BUZZARD John**: (*Joseph, Phillip, Melchior, Phillip*) was born January 1833, probably in Cattaraugus Co. New York, son of Joseph Buzzard and Mary Ann Osman. He went to Michigan with with his parents and became a Captain on the Great Lakes. Wife's name unknown.

Children:

188 i- **BUZZARD Edward J.**:
189 ii- **BUZZARD Walter H.**: born ca 1861
190 iii- **BUZZARD Coray**: born ca 1864

66 **BUZZARD Eli**: (*Joseph, Phillip, Melchior, Phillip*) was born ca 1836 in Oakland Co. Michigan, son of Joseph Buzzard and Mary Ann Osman. He married Effie Pettie in 1857. He died in 1862.

One child:

i- **BUZZARD Louisa**: born 1858

67 **BUZZARD Jacob L.**: (*Joseph, Phillip, Melchior, Phillip*) was born May 9, 1838 in Oakland Co. Michigan, son of Joseph Buzzard and Mary Ann Osman. He married May 1, 1861, Polly Myers, born 1831 in Detroit, Michigan. In February 1861, he purchased 160 acres in Williams Township, Oakland Co., Michigan.

Children born in Williams Township:

191 i- **BUZZARD Armus H.**: born December 1863
192 ii- **BUZZARD Alice F.**: born ca 1867
193 iii- **BUZZARD Polly A.**: born ca 1874
194 iv- **BUZZARD Frank J.**: born August 1877
195 v- **BUZZARD Laura**: born June 1880

68 **BUZZARD Edwin Joseph**: (*Joseph, Phillip, Melchior, Phillip*) was born January 5, 1842 in Clarkston, Michigan, son of Joseph Buzzard and Mary Ann Osman. He married December 26, 1866, Eleanor D. Moore born May 1846, in Bay City, Michigan. Edwin enlisted in Owego, New York on December 26, 1863 and served in the 116th Regiment of the New York Volunteers. His description

was: Gray eyes, brown hair and 5 feet 6 1/2 inches. After serving three years, he returned to Williams Township in Michigan and settled on a small piece of land in Section 15. He retired from farming after 45 years and moved to Bay City.

Children:

196 i- **BUZZARD Lucy Bell**: born August 20, 1868
197 ii- **BUZZARD Ralph Eugene**: born March 7, 1870
198 iii- **BUZZARD Roy Vernon**: born February 12, 1875
199 iv- **BUZZARD Mary Eleanor**: born April 20, 1879
200 v- **BUZZARD Alice Louise**: born March 18, 1885
201 vi- **BUZZARD William Joseph**: born August 17, 1887

69 **BUZZARD George M.**: (*Joseph, Phillip, Melchior, Phillip*) was born November 1844, in Clarkston, Michigan, son of Joseph Buzzard and Mary Ann Osman. He married Mary E. (unknown maiden name) and resided in Fenton, Genesee Co. Michigan.

Known children:

i- **BUZZARD Olive**: born October 1872
ii- **BUZZARD Mathias**: born November 1876
iii- **BUZZARD Hazel**: born June 1886

70 **BUZZARD Isabelle**: (*Joseph, Phillip, Melchior, Phillip*) was born ca 1847 in Clarkston, Michigan, daughter of Joseph Buzzard and Mary Ann Osman. She married Daniel Addis born ca 1840, son of Peter and Mary Addis. No further records.

71 **BUZZARD William**: (*Joseph, Phillip, Melchior, Phillip*) was born November 1856 in Clarkston, Michigan, son of Joseph Buzzard and Mary Ann Osman. He married Nellie (unknown maiden name), born March 1864.

Children:

i- **BUZZARD Cleveland**: born December 1884
ii- **BUZZARD Lucille**: born September 1887
iii- **BUZZARD Iva**: (twin) born May 1891
iv- **BUZZARD Vera**: (twin) born May 1891
v- **BUZZARD Harold**: born August 1892

72 **BOSSARD Edson**: (*Peter, Christopher, Melchior, Phillip*) was born June 16, 1835 in The Town of Dix, New York, son of Peter Bossard and Margaret Bossard. He married Margaret Miller, born 1832. During the Civil War, Edson served as a private in Company B, 161 New York Infantry. He died January 23, 1863. Margaret died in 1861. They are buried in the Miller cemetery, Hurd's Corners, New York.

One child:

i- **BOSSARD Ida May**: born October 13, 1861 and died April 18, 1877, buried in Miller cemetery.

73 **BOSSARD George**: (*Peter, Christopher, Melchior, Phillip*) was born May 11, 1838 in Dix, New York, son of Peter Bossard and Margaret Bossard. He married Emma Holly born February 23, 1852 in Dundee, New York, daughter of Lewis Holly and Susannah Case. During the Civil War, he served as a private in Co. D., 1st New York Veteran Cavalry. He died July 9, 1919 in Dundee, New York. Emma died May 19, 1922. They are buried in the Dundee cemetery.

Children born in Dix:

202 i- **BOSSARD Lewis G.**: born June 29, 1879
203 ii- **BOSSARD Ethelyn Marie**: born October 7, 1883
204 iii- **BOSSARD Mabel**: born September 2, 1871 in Reading, New York

74 **BOSSARD Marcus**: (*Peter, Christopher, Melchior, Phillip*) was born February 21, 1842 in Dix, New York, son of Peter Bossard and Margaret Bossard. He married Mary Amelia Van Nortrick, born May 26, 1846, daughter of Floyd C. and Hattie L. Van Nortrick. During the Civil War he served as a private in Co. M., 4th New York Heavy Artillery and, also, the 8th New York Heavy Artillery. He died in 1894 and Mary Amelia died October 20, 1896. They are buried in Deckertown, Steuben Co., New York.

Children:

i- **BOSSARD Charles**: died young, not in his Mother's will of 1896.
205 ii- **BOSSARD Leon M.**: born ca 1876
iii- **BOSSARD Viola**: born 1881 and died 1903
iv- **BOSSARD Mattie**: born 1885 and died 1896
v- **BOSSARD Phillip**: born July 1889

75 **BOSSARD Jarvis L.**: (*Peter, Christopher, Melchior, Phillip*) was born April 1843 in Dix, New York, son of Peter Bossard and Margaret Bossard. He married July 3, 1873, Hattie O. Richardson, born May 1851. Jervis died February 2, 1910, in Binghamton, New York. Hattie died April 19, 1918 in Horseheads, New York and is buried in Watkins. No issue.

76 **BOZARD Henry M.**: (*Richard, Christopher, Melchior, Phillip*) was born June 21, 1830 probably in Lansing, New York, son of Richard Bozard and Elinor Learn. He married September 14, 1858, Mary Barker born ca 1835. He died in Livonia, New York, December 6, 1900 and Mary died May 1, 1906 in Rochester, New York.

Children born in Olean, New York:

206 i- **BOZARD Dela**: born ca 1859

207 ii- **BOZARD Earl W.**: born January 1862
208 iii- **BOZARD Mary**: born ca 1869
209 iv- **BOZARD Richard**: born June 22, 1878

77 **BOZARD Andrew J.**: (*Richard, Christopher, Melchior, Phillip*) was born December 29, 1833 in Humphrey, Cattaraugus Co. New York, son of Richard Bozard and Elinor Learn. He married June 5, 1861, Sarah Eliza Winters Pierce born January 1836, daughter of Alphonso Winters. He died July 16, 1908 and Sarah died October 14, 1912. Sarah had two children by her first marriage, Kelly and George. They are buried in Humphrey.

One child:
i- **BOZARD Alphonzo**: born 1862 and died 1864

78 **BOZARD Cyrus Peter**: (*Richard, Christopher, Melchior, Phillip*) was born April 8, 1835 in Humphrey, New York, son of Richard Bozard and Elinor Learn. He married July 10, 1861, Julia Pierce born August 26, 1840, daughter of Lyartus Pierce and Catherine Fosmer. He died March 16, 1905 in Humphrey and Julia died October 14, 1931 In Olean, New York.

Children born in Humphrey:
210 i- **BOZARD Truman Cyrus**: born September 30, 1862
211 ii- **BOZARD Edward Harrison**: born October 29, 1864
212 iii- **BOZARD Blanche C.**: born April 7, 1871

79 **BOZARD Barnard S.**: (*Richard, Christopher, Melchior, Phillip*) was born March 5, 1838, in Humphrey, New York, son of Richard Bozard and Elinor Learn. He married Susan Carr and moved to Chicago, Illinois. He died July 1908. Unknown children.

80 **BOZARD Ashbel Lacy**: (*Richard, Christopher, Melchior Phillip*) was born February 24, 1841 in Humphrey, New York, son of Richard Bozard and Elinor Learn. He married January 12, 1869, Catherine G. Conlan, born August 26, 1852. During the Civil War, he served as a private and a corporal in Co. A., 133rd New York Infantry. He died March 27, 1926 and Catherine died June 24, 1942 in Allegany. They are buried in Allegany cemetery.

Children born in Humphrey:
213 i- **BOZARD Alphonzo A.**: born September 24, 1869
214 ii- **BOZARD Iva L.**: born 1874
215 iii- **BOZARD Harrison B.**: born November 1878
216 iv- **BOZARD Ralph Raymond**: born September 24, 1885
217 v- **BOZARD Kittie**: born June 2, 1890

81 BOZARD Rebecca: (*Richard, Christopher, Melchior, Phillip*) was born ca 1843 in Humphrey, New York, daughter of Richard Bozard and Elinor Learn. She married Harrison Newell, born ca 1837. Rebecca died December 6, 1932 in Allegany, New York. No records found for Harrison. No issue.

82 BOZARD Joseph M.: (*Richard, Christopher, Melchior, Phillip*) was born September 10, 1847 in Humphrey, New York, son of Richard Bozard and Elinor Learn. He married April 1, 1872, Calista Snyder born August 1845 and moved to Michigan. He was living in Durand, Michigan in 1908. No further records found.

One child listed in 1900 census:
i- **BOZARD Glen**: born October 1886

83 BOZARD Laura H.: (*Richard, Christopher, Melchior, Phillip*) was born November 20, 1851 in Humphrey, New York, daughter of Richard Bozard and Elinor Learn. She married Eliab Barber, who served in the Civil War, Co. H. New York 37th Infantry. Laura died April 2, 1927, in Allegany, New York and Eliab died November 6, 1910 in Olean, New York. They are buried in the Allegany cemetery.

Children:
i- **BARBER Elmer E.**: born ca 1868
ii- **BARBER Charles**: born ca 1871
iii- **BARBER Andrew**: born ca 1874
iv- **BARBER Maggie**: born ca 1876

84 BOZARD Judson O.: (*Richard, Christopher, Melchior, Phillip*) was born March 4, 1855 in Humphrey, New York, son of Richard Bozard and Elinor Learn. He married (1) Rose Conlon and married (2) May M. Barber, born May 1862. He died March 10, 1946 in Allegany, New York and May M. died January 28, 1927.

Children by first wife:
218 i- **BOZARD Arthur**: born ca 1879
219 ii- **BOZARD Glen Weir**: born ca 1885
220 iii- **BOZARD Marcia Rose**: born November 1886
Children by second wife:
221 iv- **BOZARD Howard Raymond**: born January 24, 1899
v- **BOZARD Harry**: born 1900 and he died in 1942
vi- **BOZARD Ella Mae**: born September 1903. She is living in 1989 in the nursing home at Salamanca, New York. Unmarried.

85 BOZARD Sylvanus: (*Charles, Christopher, Melchior, Phillip*) was born June 1837 in Cattaraugus Co., New York, son of Charles Bozard and Patty Bush. He married Sarah (unknown maiden name) and they were living in Groveland Co.,

Michigan in 1900. No further records.

Known Children:
222 i- **BOZARD Arthur C.**: born April 1869
ii- **BOZARD Herbert M.**: born ca 1872
iii- **BOZARD Durbin S.**: born June 1874

86 **BOZARD Sylvester Lorenzo**: (*Charles, Christopher, Melchior, Phillip*) was born March 1844 in Cattaraugus Co., New York, son of Charles Bozard and Patty Bush. He married Etta J. (unknown maiden name) born September 1855. They were living in Holly, Michigan in 1900. No further records.

Known child:
i- **BOZARD Mabel Louise**: born 1879

87 **BOZARD William E.**: (*Charles, Christopher, Melchior, Phillip*) was born October 1852 in Cattaraugus Co., New York, son of Charles Bozard and Patty Bush. He married Mary S. (unknown maiden name) born November 1858. They were living in Kalamazoo, Michigan in 1910. No further records.

Known children:
i- **BOZARD George W.**: born January 1879
ii- **BOZARD Bertha M.**: born April 1885
iii- **BOZARD Willard W.**: born May 1888
iv- **BOZARD Donald D.**: born March 1898

88 **BACKER Amanda**: (*Sarah, George, Melchior, Phillip*) was born 1842 in Dix, New York, daughter of David Backer and Sarah Bossard. She married Edward Quin, born November 18, 1823, son of Dominick Quin and Maria Smith.. She died October 30, 1920 and Edward died March 18, 1910. They are buried in the Glenview cemetery at Urbana, Steuben Co., New York.

Children:
223 i- **QUIN Sarah M.**: born July 3, 1876
224 ii- **QUIN George E.**: born 1878
iii- **QUIN William**:

89 **BACKER Jane**: (*Sarah, George, Melchior, Phillip*) was born December 3, 1843 in Dix, New York, daughter of David Backer and Sarah Bossard. She married Frank Hedden, born July 24, 1838, son of Henry Hedden and Mary Howe. She died September 3, 1883 and Frank married (2), Mary Smith. Frank Hedden died August 26, 1908 in Montour Falls.

Children born in Dix, New York:

225 **i- HEDDEN Henry Ambrose**: born October 29, 1869
226 **ii- HEDDEN Charles D.**: born 1871
227 **iii- HEDDEN Albert Elmer**: born 1878

90 **BACKER Juliet**: (*Sarah, George, Melchior, Phillip*) was born ca 1845 in Dix, New York, daughter of David Backer and Sarah Bossard. She married George Sturdevant, born ca 1843. George died before 1900 and Juliet was living with her mother. No further records found.

One child born in Beaver Dams, New York:
i- STURDEVANT George: born September 1868

91 **BACKER Harriet M.**: (*Sarah, George, Melchior, Phillip*) was born 1848 in Dix, New York, daughter of David Backer and Sarah Bossard. She married John D. Fero born 1847, son of Peter and Evaline Fero. He was in the Civil War. Harriet died May 14, 1898 in Hornby, New York and John Married (2) Susan L., born 1848 and died March 16, 1929. John died February 28, 1915 in Willard, New York. They are buried in the cemetery at Montour Falls.

Children:
228 **i- FERO Emmett**: born December 26,1872
229 **ii- FERO Evaline**: born January 1874
230 **iii- FERO Sarah**: born December 1882
231 **iv- FERO Lewis Ray**: born ca 1883
v- FERO May: born May 1887
232 **vi- FERO Margaret May**: born May 29, 1888
233 **vii- FERO Maude** : born August 1890
viii- FERO Dean G.: born January 16, 1891
234 **ix- FERO Victor**: born March 22, 1893

92 **BACKER George L.**: (*Sarah, George, Melchior, Phillip*) was born ca 1850 in Dix, New York, son of David Backer and Sarah Bossard. He married Eva Tompson, born ca 1850. No further records found.

Known child:
i- BACKER Bertha F.: born July 1879

93 **BACKER Emmett**: (*Sarah, George, Melchior, Phillip*) was born March 8, 1853 in Dix, New York, son of David Backer and Sarah Bossard. He married Sarah Tompkins. He died November 4, 1926 in Corning, New York and is buried in Fairview cemetery, Painted Post, New York.

One known child born in Hornby, New York:
235 **i- BACKER Elmond D.**: born 1878

94 BOSSARD George A.: (*Simon, George, Melchior, Phillip*) was born 1846 in Sullivanville, New York, son of Simon Bossard and Hannah Norris. No record found of his wife. He went to Rockford, Washington about 1900 and purchased a large farm, which he rented and lived in the small house on the property. He taught school in Rockford and traveled throughout Western Canada, writing articles about the places he visited for the Rockford Times. Some of these articles were printed in the Elmira paper. He died 1936 in Rockford.

One child:

i- BOSSARD Arthur: no information found for him except that he remained in New York State.

95 BOSSARD Iona: (*Simon, George, Melchior, Phillip*) was born February 1858 in Sullivanville, New York, daughter of Simon Bossard and Hannah Norris. She married Augustus Van Wort, born October 1851. She died January 10, 1932 and he died September 20, 1914, both in Tompkins Cove, New York.

One child:

i- VAN WORT Annette: born April 1879

96 BOSSARD Judd: (*Simon, George, Melchior, Phillip*) was born June 3, 1868 in Sullivanville, New York, son of Simon Bossard and Julia Smith. He was an infant when his parents died and he went to live with his uncle, Anson Bossard. He married Jennie Richards, born 1872. He died June 27, 1909 and Jennie died in 1972. They are buried in West Milford, New Jersey.

Children:

236 i- **BOSSARD Clarence**: born December 31, 1892
237 ii- **BOSSARD Roy**: born ca 1895
238 iii- **BOSSARD Helen**: born 1900
239 iv- **BOSSARD Edna**: born 1906
240 v- **BOSSARD William**:

97 CROSS Elizabeth: (*Veronica, George, Melchior, Phillip*) was born May 28, 1848 in Lansing, New York, daughter of John Cross and Veronica Bossard. She married Eugene K. Smith born July 12, 1845 in Augusta, New York. She died September 19, 1897 and Eugene died April 16, 1925 in Reading, New York. They are buried in the New Reading cemetery.

One child born in Reading, New York:

241 i- **SMITH Fred R.**: born September 12, 1871

98 CROSS Virginia: (*Veronica, George, Melchior, Phillip*) was born in 1852 in Reading, New York, daughter of John Cross and Veronica Bossard. She married

December 31, 1870, John Erway and moved to Kansas before 1895. No other records found.

Known children:
i- ERWAY Levi:
ii- ERWAY John:
iii- ERWAY Frank:

99 CROSS Miles: (*Veronica, George, Melchior, Phillip*) was born 1853 in Reading, New York, son of John Cross and Veronica Bossard. He married Emma Fox. He died November 30, 1929 and Emma died in 1922, in Erie, Pennsylvania. No issue.

100 CROSS Mary: (*Veronica, George, Melchior, Phillip*) was born 1861 in Reading, New York, daughter of John Cross and Veronica Bossard. She married April 2, 1888, Will Palmer Baker born 1856, son of Edwin Baker and Adelia Shauger. Mary died November 30, 1929 and Will died June 14, 1923 in Reading, New York. No issue.

101 CROSS Maria: (*Veronica, George, Melchior, Phillip*) was born 1855 in Reading, New York, daughter of John Cross and Veronica Bossard. She married Frank A. Smith born 1854, son of Philetus and Edith Smith. She died June 3, 1935 and he died February 13, 1902. They are buried in the New Reading cemetery.

Children born in Reading:
i- SMITH Ethel: unknown date of birth. unmarried
ii- SMITH Leon C.: born May 17, 1891. He served in World War I and died November 13, 1918. He is buried in the New Reading cemetery.

102 CROSS Maude: (*Veronica, George, Melchior, Phillip*) was born 1867 in Reading, New York, daughter of John Cross and Veronica Bossard. She married September 3, 1885, William Phinney born 1863, son of Obediah Phinney. They were divorced in 1897. Maude died February 13, 1902 and is buried in the New Reading cemetery. He married (2) Elizabeth Billinghurst. and he died December 30, 1930.

One child:
242 i- PHINNEY Grace: born January 23, 1889

103 BOSSARD Clara Eddy: (*Anson, George, Melchior, Phillip*) was born July 12, 1854 in Dix, New York, daughter of Anson Bossard and Cornelia Annette Eddy. She married January 15, 1879, Myron Personius born 1854. She died February 23,

1936 and he died August 28, 1925 in Ithaca, New York. They are buried in the North Lansing cemetery.

Children:

i- **PERSONIUS Orran**: born October 2, 1881 and died December 16, 1891 in Ithaca, New York.
243 ii- **PERSONIUS Grace A.**: born December 28, 1885
244 iii- **PERSONIUS Adrian**: born March 27, 1896

104 **BOSSARD Charles E.**: (*Anson, George, Melchior, Phillip*) was born August 27, 1857 in Dix, New York, son of Anson Bossard and Cornelia Annette Eddy. He married January 15, 1879, Charlotte Elizabeth Smith born October 23, 1856, in Ithaca, New York, daughter of Alfred Smith and Mary Jane Ketchum. They were married in Ithaca New York and resided in Enfield. He died May 2, 1916 in Enfield and she died April 22, 1924 in Ithaca. They are buried in Hayt's cemetery.

Children:

245 i- **BOSSARD Arthur Alfred**: born April 23, 1882
246 ii- **BOSSARD Lottie Annette**: born June 30, 1887
247 iii- **BOSSARD Florence Catherine**: born July 24, 1889
248 iv- **BOSSARD Jessie Elizabeth**: born June 4, 1894
v- **BOSSARD Fred**: died an infant

105 **BOSSARD William Delevan**: (*Anson, George, Melchior Phillip*) was born July 19, 1862 in Dix, New York, son of Anson Bossard and Cornelia Annette Eddy. He married December 10, 1882, Sarah Ann Allen born July 23, 1864, daughter of Elnathan Allen and Mary Holley. They resided in the town of Odessa for about five years and then moved to the Town of Howard in Steuben Co. New York. In 1895, he purchased 111 acres from the heirs of Charles H. Hartshorn and later bought land from heirs of George Appi. He was well known as one of the most prosperous farmers in the area. He died February 13, 1946 in Hornell, New York and Sarah died November 13, 1942 in Howard, New York. They are buried in Rural cemetery in Hornell, New York.

Children:

249 i- **BOSSARD Claude**: born May 6, 1885 in Odessa
250 ii- **BOSSARD Mary**: born June 16, 1886 in Dix

Children born in Howard, New York:

251 iii- **BOSSARD Fred**: born May 24, 1888
252 iv- **BOSSARD Roy**: born September 2, 1896
253 v- **BOSSARD Charlotte Maude**: born January 9, 1901
254 vi- **BOSSARD Lawrence Orlo**: born December 14, 1903
255 vii- **BOSSARD Inez Velma**: born April 4, 1906

106 **BOSSARD Fred Anson**: (*Anson, George, Melchior, Phillip*) was born April 24,

1871 in Dix, New York, son of Anson Bossard and Cornelia Annette Eddy. He married March 9, 1891, Lorena Alvira Pike born October 13, 1873, daughter of Charles Pike and Eliza Owens. He died August 22, 1952 in Syracuse, New York and Lorena died September 4, 1934 in W. Groton, New York. They are buried in W. Groton.

Children:

256 i- **BOSSARD Lorena Althea**: born June 4, 1894 in Watkins, New York
257 ii- **BOSSARD Anson Chester**: born February 22, 1896 Townsend, New York
258 iii- **BOSSARD Charlie Asil**: born August 21, 1898 in Newfield, New York
259 iv- **BOSSARD Marjorie Eliza**: born February 8, 1901 in Lake Ridge, New York
260 v- **BOSSARD Irma Stella**: born September 30, 1903 in Goodyears Corners, New York
261 vi- **BOSSARD Kermit Clarence**: born January 4, 1906 Groton, New York
vii- **BOSSARD Melba Naomi**: born April 12, 1909 in W. Groton, New York and died May 7, 1925 In Cortland, New York
262 viii- **BOSSARD Winona Armorel**: born April 6, 1914 in W. Groton, New York

107 BOSARD Susan A.: (*Alvers, Andrew, Melchior, Phillip*) was born July 22, 1850 in Osceola, Pennsylvania, daughter of Alvers Bosard and Elizabeth Peck Bosworth. She married November 9, 1870, Myron Bonham born May 12, 1845. She died February 4, 1912 and Myron died October 20, 1919. They are buried in the Fairview cemetery in Osceola.

Children born in Osceola:

i- **BONHAM Jessie**: born 1871
263 ii- **BONHAM Wallace Lee**: born September 5, 1874
264 iii- **BONHAM Edward H.**: born June 13, 1887

108 BOSWORTH Edward E.: (*Maria, Andrew, Melchior, Phillip*) was born 1846 in Osceola, Pennsylvania, son of Dr. Henry G. Bosworth and Maria Bosard. He married January 7, 1888, Adelaide Bosard born 1847, daughter of Arthur F. and Elizabeth Bosard. He died 1917 and Adelaide died 1926 and they are buried in Osceola. No known children. See number 111.

109 BOSWORTH Urbana A.: (*Maria, Andrew, Melchior, Phillip*) was born May 1848 in Osceola, Pennsylvania, son of Dr. Henry G. Bosworth and Maria Bosard. He married November 15, 1871, Ann Hoyt born February 1851. He died 1926 and Ann died in 1917.

Children:

265 i- **BOSWORTH Henry L.**: born October 1875
266 ii- **BOSWORTH May S.**: born May 1878

110 **BOSWORTH Charles H.**: (*Maria, Andrew, Melchior, Phillip*) was born 1851 in Osceola, Pennsylvania, son of Dr. Henry G. Bosworth and Maria Bosard. He married (1), Ida V. Seeley born 1851, daughter of Morgan Seeley and Harriet Beebe. She died April 11, 1896 and he married (2), October 28, 1897, Stella G. Taylor. He died in 1928.

Children:
267 i- **BOSWORTH Ford E.**: born January 1878
ii- **BOSWORTH Reed S.**:

111 **BOSARD Adelaide**: (*Arthur, Andrew, Melchior, Phillip*) was born 1847, in Osceola, Pennsylvania, daughter of Arthur and Elizabeth Bosard. See number 108, Edward E. Bosworth.

112 **BOSARD Kirtland A.**: (*Arthur, Andrew, Melchior, Phillip*) was born June 1849 in Tioga Co., Pennsylvania, son of Arthur F. and Elizabeth Bosard. He married Hattie (unknown maiden name) born January 1854. He died 1920 and Hattie died 1946 in Osceola.

Children:
i- **BOSARD May**: (twin) born July 24, 1879
268 ii- **BOSARD Ray F.**: (twin) born July 24, 1879
269 iii- **BOSARD Adelaide**: born February 7, 1894.

113 **BOSARD James Huntington**: (*Andrew K., Andrew, Melchior, Phillip*) was born April 1845 in Osceola, Pennsylvania, son of Andrew K. Bosard and Hetty Cilly. He married June 27, 1872, Rebecca Faulkner born September 1851 and removed to Grand Forks, North Dakota. He was a prominent lawyer in Grand Forks. No death records found.

Children born in Tioga Co., Pennsylvania:
i- **BOSARD Florence H.**: born July 1873
270 ii- **BOSARD Robert H.**: born April 1875
iii- **BOSARD Helen D.**: born 1877
Children born in Grand Forks:
iv- **BOSARD Gerald F.**: born September 1881
v- **BOSARD Sarah K.**: born December 1882
vi- **BOSARD Daphne H.**: born August 1884

114 **BOSARD George Leroy**: (*Andrew K., Andrew, Melchior, Phillip*) was born

January 1848 in Osceola, Pennsylvania, son of Andrew K. Bosard and Hetty Cilly. He married Mary Beagle. No other records found.

115 BOSARD Jerome Leon: (*Andrew K., Andrew, Melchior, Phillip*) was born May 29, 1849 in Osceola, Pennsylvania, son of Andrew K. Bosard and Hetty Cilly. He married May 9, 1871, Alice M. Smith born August 1851, daughter of Henry Smith and Phebe M. Cook. He died in 1906 and Alice died in 1921. They are buried in Osceola.

Children:

271 i- **BOSARD Myra S.**: born June 1873

ii- **BOSARD Andrew K.**: born July 1878 and died 1945, unmarried. He is buried in Osceola.

iii- **BOSARD Edith M.**: born August 1881

116 BOSARD Florence H.: (*Andrew K., Andrew, Melchior, Phillip*) was born May 11, 1851 in Osceola, Pennsylvania, daughter of Andrew K. Bosard and Hetty Cilly. She married, May 23, 1872, Willis R. Bierly. She died March 20, 1873 in Williamsport, Pennsylvania and Willis married her sister, Sarah Louise Bosard.

One child:

i- **BIERLY Florence Hortense**: born March 16, 1873 and died August 11, 1873. Buried Fairview cemetery in Osceola.

117 BOSARD Sara Louise: (*Andrew K., Andrew, Melchior, Phillip*) was born July 1853 in Osceola, Pennsylvania, daughter of Andrew K. Bosard and Hetty Cilly. She married September 24, 1874, Willis R. Bierly. They removed to Grand Forks, North Dakota, where he was in newspaper publishing. No records of their death dates found.

Children born in Tioga Co.:

i- **BIERLY Arthur L.**: born December 1877

ii- **BIERLY Grace L.**: born November 1879

Children born in Grand Forks:

iii- **BIERLY Robert B.**: born April 1883

iv- **BIERLY Ernest P.**: born March 1886

v- **BIERLY Jessee B.**: born June 1888

vi- **BIERLY Carl R.**: born September 1890

vii- **BIERLY Phillip S.**: born March 1895

118 BOSARD William Burns: (*Andrew K., Andrew, Melchior, Phillip*) was born 1854, in Osceola, Pennsylvania, son of Andrew K. Bosard and Hetty Cilly. He married in 1878, Carrie Fical born September 1854, and removed to Grand Forks, North Dakota. No further records.

Children:

272 i- **BOSARD Louise**: born August 7, 1880
273 ii- **BOSARD James Huntington**: born August 1882
274 iii- **BOSARD Ralph Mortimer**: born 1886
iv- **BOSARD Gertrude**: died aged 5 of Scarlet fever

119 **BOSARD Maria:** (*Andrew K., Andrew, Melchior, Phillip*) was born 1859 in Osceola, Pennsylvania, daughter of Andrew K. Bosard and Hetty Cilly. She married Judge Herbert B. Mitchell, son of Judge John I. Mitchell, and moved to Rock Island, Illinois. No further records.

120 **BOSARD Emma**: (*Andrew K., Andrew, Melchior, Phillip*) was born October 9, 1867 in Osceola, Pennsylvania, daughter of Andrew K. Bosard and Anne Sherman. She married Joseph B. Redfield born August 1868, son of Joseph B. and Martha Redfield. They lived in Farmington, Pennsylvania. Emma died April 1, 1915 and Joseph married (2) Amy K. (unknown maiden name), born 1883 and died 1971. Joseph died in 1942 and they are buried in the Keeneyville cemetery, Keeneyville, Pennsylvania.

Children:

275 i- **REDFIELD Helen**: born March 1891
276 ii- **REDFIELD Albert Lee**: born September 1894
277 iii- **REDFIELD Mark B.**: born March 3, 1898

121 **BOSARD Stella M.**: (*Andrew K., Andrew, Melchior, Phillip*) was born 1869 in Osceola, Pennsylvania, daughter of Andrew K. Bosard and Anne Sherman. She married Fred Ellison who was Mayor of Corning in the 1930's. No further records.

Known children:

i- **ELLISON Henry B.**:
ii- **ELLISON Harold**:

122 **BOSARD Elizabeth Ann**: (*Andrew K., Andrew, Melchior, Phillip*) known as 'Lizzie', was born February 1875 in Osceola, Pennsylvania, daughter of Andrew K., Bosard and Anne Sherman. She married Jesse O. Treat, born April 5, 1867, son of Rufus Treat and Mary J. Snyder. He died in 1926 and Lizzie died in 1927. They are buried in the cemetery on Butler Hill, near Knoxville, Pennsylvania.

Children born in Chatham, Pennsylvania:

278 i- **TREAT Mabel Almina**: born June 4, 1894
279 ii- **TREAT Jessie Ethel**: born May 9, 1897
280 iii- **TREAT Ernestine Maude**: born May 13, 1899
iv- **TREAT Glenn B.**:
281 v- **TREAT Ernest Bosard**: born July 30, 1909

123 **BOSARD John Mahlon**: (*Melchior, Andrew, Melchior, Phillip*) was born November 10, 1848 in Osceola, Pennsylvania, son of Melchior De Poi Bosard and Eleanor Campbell. He married April 24, 1872, Jennie Crane born 1852 in Addison, New York. He died September 9, 1889 at Dunkirk, New York and is probably buried in Lawrenceville, Pennsylvania. Jennie was living in Elmira, New York in 1900.

Children:
i- **BOSARD Mary E.**: born July 1873
ii- **BOSARD Eleanor C.**: (twin) born July 1879
iii- **BOSARD Florence H.**: (twin) born July 1879

124 **BOSARD Laura Jane**: (*Melchior, Andrew, Melchior, Phillip*) was born 1857 in Osceola, Pennsylvania, daughter of Melchior De Poi Bosard and Eleanor Campbell. She married Charles Lowry. No further records.

One known child:
i- **LOWRY Elva R.**: born 1878 and died 1905

125 **BOSARD Anna Maria**: (*Melchior, Andrew, Melchior, Phillip*) was born April 4, 1860 in Osceola, Pennsylvania, daughter of Melchior De Poi Bosard and Eleanor Campbell. She married April 4, 1883, Andrew Owlet born January 3, 1850, son of Thomas Owlet and Mary Treat. She died in 1934 and Andrew died September 19, 1924. They are buried in the Nelson cemetery at Nelson, Pennsylvania.

Children:
282 i- **OWLET Fordyce Deroy**: born February 17, 1884
283 ii- **OWLET Fay Dollie**: born August 19, 1886
284 iii- **OWLET Jessie Luella**: born January 26, 1888
285 iv- **OWLET John Bosard**: born November 26, 1890
286 v- **OWLET Charles E.**: born September 9, 1892
287 vi- **OWLET Carlton Andrew**: born July 26, 1894
288 vii- **OWLET Mark F.**: born June 24, 1897
289 viii- **OWLET Burton Wesley**: born July 15, 1899
290 ix- **OWLET Thomas Mack**: born December 13, 1902

126 **HUFFSMITH Lavina**: (*Hanna, Peter, Melchior, Phillip*) was born August 19, 1826 in Hamilton Township, Pennsylvania, daughter of Phillip Huffsmith and Hanna Bossard. She married Henry Laufer, born July 30 1825. She died December 4, 1875, in Stroudsburg, Pennsylvania, and Henry married (2), September 28, 1879, Mrs. Harriet Miltenberger born 1820. Harriet died March 28, 1892 in Petersville and he died December 30, 1905. They are buried in Stroudsburg.

Children:
i- **LAUFER Anna Elizabeth**: born February 18, 1850 and died Septem-

ber 5, 1852
ii- LAUFER Franklin: born ca 1853 and died before 1905
291 **iii- LAUFER Stewart**: born September 2, 1855
iv- LAUFER Emma Lydia: born ca 1858
292 **v- LAUFER Alice**: born November 12, 1864
293 **vi- LAUFER Ellen**: born September 1869

127 HUFFSMITH Lynford: (*Hanna, Peter, Melchior, Phillip*) was born August 20, 1832 in Hamilton Township, Pennsylvania, son of Phillip Huffsmith and Hanna Bossard. He married August 17, 1854, Catherine Erdman born February 7, 1828. She died May 20, 1895 and Lynford married (2) Anna Maria Gruber. Lynford died February 28, 1905 and is buried in Mt. Zion cemetery in Hamilton Township.

One child:
i- HUFFSMITH Stewart: born July 9, 1855 and died October 31, 1855. He is buried in Mt. Zion cemetery

128 HUFFSMITH Samuel: (*Hanna, Peter, Melchior, Phillip*) was born July 1, 1838 in Hamilton Township, Pennsylvania, son of Phillip Huffsmith and Hanna Bossard. He married August 17, 1867, Angeline Frantz born ca 1848, daughter of Levi and Ann Frantz. No further records.

129 HUFFSMITH Sarah Jane: (*Hanna, Peter, Melchior, Phillip*) was born August 29, 1840 in Hamilton Township, Pennsylvania, daughter of Phillip Huffsmith and Hanna Bossard. She married Amandis Rinker born October 7, 1834, son of Solomon Rinker and Rebecca Kunkle. She died January 4, 1903 in Stroudsburg, and is buried in the Stroudsburg cemetery. No death record found for Amandis.

Children:
294 **i- RINKER Hanna L.**: born ca 1860
295 **ii- RINKER Peter L.**: born October 8, 1862
296 **iii- RINKER Stewart**: born October 1865
297 **iv- RINKER Charles S.**: born August 2, 1866
298 **v- RINKER Mary F.**: born November 22, 1868
299 **vi- RINKER Edwin**: born May 1874
vii- RINKER Cora Martha: born November 4, 1878
Possibly two others. No records found.

130 HUFFSMITH Margaret Ann: (*Hanna, Peter, Melchior, Phillip*) was born January 16, 1843 in Hamilton Township, Pennsylvania, daughter of Phillip Huffsmith and Hanna Bossard. She married October 9, 1868, Jacob Root. Believed to have moved to Northampton Co., Pennsylvania. No further records.

131 **HUFFSMITH George Washington**: (*Hanna, Peter, Melchior, Phillip*) was chr. September 21, 1845 in Hamilton Township, Pennsylvania, son of Phillip Huffsmith and Hanna Bossard. He married Emma (unknown maiden name), born 1848. He died 1917 and Emma died in 1911 and they are buried in the Stroudsburg cemetery.

Children:
300 i- **HUFFSMITH William**: born 1876
ii- **HUFFSMITH Harry Clinton**: born July 8, 1877. He was unmarried and died December 25, 1910.
iii- **HUFFSMITH Maggie May**: born April 6, 1880
301 iv- **HUFFSMITH Carrie**: born March 6, 1881

132 **BOSSARD Sarah**: (*John, Peter, Melchior, Phillip*) was born ca 1831 in Hamilton Township, Pennsylvania, daughter of John Bossard and Sarah Erdman. She married November 20, 1849, Jacob Klinker born February 1826 and they removed to Bethlehem, Northampton Co., Pennsylvania. Jacob was a pensioner of the Civil War. Sarah died before 1900. Jacob was living with son William in 1900. No further records.

Known children:
i- **KLINKER Mary E.**: born September 19, 1855
ii- **KLINKER John Joseph**: born December 18, 1859
302 iii- **KLINKER Frank Isaiah**: born August 31, 1862
303 iv- **KLINKER William W.**: born June 1870

133 **BOSSARD Isaiah**: (*John, Peter, Melchior, Phillip*) was born February 7, 1844 in Hamilton Township, Pennsylvania, son of John Bossard and Sarah Erdman. He married January 27, 1866, Clara Ann E. Seifert, born January 1845. They removed to Braintree, Wyoming Co., Pennsylvania before 1900. No further records.

Known children born in Hamilton Township
i- **BOSSARD David Grant**: born October 18, 1866
ii- **BOSSARD Florence May**: born May 17, 1868

134 **RUTH Lynford**: (*Anna Catherine, Peter, Melchior, Phillip*) was born August 8, 1830 in Hamilton Township, Pennsylvania, son of Jacob Ruth and Anna Catherine Bossard. He married August 27, 1854, Christine Heller born February 22, 1832, daughter of Simon and Elizabeth Rebecca Heller. He died March 4, 1907 in Stroudsburg and Christine died in 1913. They are buried in the Stroudsburg cemetery.

Children:
304 i- **RUTH Matilda**: born ca 1856
305 ii- **RUTH Adeline**: born ca 1857

iii- **RUTH Mary Ardella**: born September 1, 1857
iv- **RUTH Ella M.**: born October 1859
306 v- **RUTH Catherine E.**: born September 21, 1861
vi- **RUTH Simon J.**: born ca 1864 and died before 1900
vii- **RUTH Arthur L.**: born ca 1866
307 viii- **RUTH Robert E.**: born December 31, 1870
ix- **RUTH George Ferguson**: born April 26, 1873 and died September 14, 1878
x- **RUTH Roger**: born December 1879 and died young

135 **RUTH Joseph**: (*Anna Catherine, Peter, Melchior, Phillip*) was born August 18, 1837 in Hamilton Township, Pennsylvania, son of Jacob Ruth and Anna Catherine Bossard. He married June 30, 1860, Sarah Frances Decker, born August 1, 1841. He died February 9, 1917 and Sarah died September 12, 1916. They are buried in the Delaware Water Gap cemetery.

Children:
308 i- **RUTH Ervin**: born December 1861
ii- **RUTH Howard D.**: born ca 1862. Never married
iii- **RUTH Elmer**: born March 27, 1865 and died January 11, 1867
309 iv- **RUTH Harry**: born ca 1865
310 vi- **RUTH Sanderson**: born ca 1868
311 v- **RUTH Clarence**: born August 1870
312 vii- **RUTH Bertha**: born ca 1870

136 **RUTH Jacob**: (*Anna Catherine, Peter, Melchior, Phillip*) was born April 25, 1840 in Hamilton Township, Pennsylvania, son of Jacob Ruth and Anna Catherine Bossard. He married 1862, Anna Maria Williams, born October 14, 1836. He died March 5, 1920 in Stroudsburg and Anna died November 5, 1903. They are buried in the Stroudsburg cemetery.

Children:
313 i- **RUTH Martha A.**: born August 8, 1863
ii- **RUTH Catherine E.**: born June 11, 1865 and died March 26, 1866
314 iii- **RUTH Ellen Frances**: born ca 1866
315 iv- **RUTH Mary A.**: born ca 1867
v- **RUTH Willie**: born August 1869
316 vi- **RUTH Edward M.**: born January 9, 1872
317 vii- **RUTH John**: born March 22, 1877
318 viii- **RUTH Ada**: born March 1880

137 **RUTH Samuel**: (*Anna Catherine, Peter, Melchior, Phillip*) was born January 14, 1843 in Hamilton Township, Pennsylvania, son of Jacob Ruth and Anna Catherine Bossard. He married Margaret (unknown maiden name) and believed to have resided in Williamsport, Pennsylvania. No further records.

138 **RUTH James**: (*Anna Catherine, Peter, Melchior, Phillip*) was born December 10, 1846 in Hamilton Township, Pennsylvania, son of Jacob Ruth and Anna Catherine Bossard. He married ca 1870, Ellen M. Arnold, born November 24, 1852. He died April 24, 1921 and Ellen died December 23, 1925. They are buried in Mt. Zion cemetery in Hamilton Township.

Children:

319 i- **RUTH Clara M.**: born March 11, 1877

ii- **RUTH Minnie C.**: born February 28, 1878 and died October 23, 1909, buried in Mt. Zion cemetery.

320 iii- **RUTH Edith Adella**: born June 3, 1888

iv- **RUTH Walter**: born ca 1896, died May 22, 1937

v- **RUTH Bertha**: died as an infant and is buried in Bossard Heller cemetery. Also two other infants are buried there.

139 **RUTH Martha Jane**: (*Anna Catherine, Peter, Melchior, Phillip*) was born August 20, 1853 in Hamilton Township, Pennsylvania, daughter of Jacob Ruth and Anna Catherine Bossard. She married ca 1870, Israel Haney born November 30, 1850, son of William and Margaret Haney. He died April 5, 1933 and Martha Jane died October 17, 1934. They are buried in the Mt. Zion cemetery in Hamilton Township.

Children:

321 i- **HANEY William J.**: born December 24, 1870

322 ii- **HANEY Catherine E.**: born ca 1872

323 iii- **HANEY Maggie M.**: born July 3, 1875

324 iv- **HANEY Ellen S.**: born ca 1878

v- **HANEY Romanus**: born April 3, 1881 and died April 5, 1881, buried in Mt. Zion cemetery.

325 vi- **HANEY Elwood Clayton**: born December 29, 1883

326 vii- **HANEY Floyd M.**: born 1886

140 **BOSSARD Charles**: (*Melchior, Peter, Melchior, Phillip*) was born July 26, 1834 in Hamilton Township, Pennsylvania, son of Melchior Bossard and Hannah Arnold. He married ca 1860, Elizabeth Shoemaker, born May 1836. He died January 3, 1902 and Elizabeth died March 10, 1917. They are buried in Mt. Zion cemetery in Hamilton Township.

Children:

327 i- **BOSSARD Lillie Louise**: born December 21, 1862

ii- **BOSSARD Ellenora**: born November 29, 1864 and died April 14, 1865

328 iii- **BOSSARD Fannie**: born October 9, 1866

iv--**BOSSARD Mary Eda**: born December 22, 1873 and died August 12, 1875

329 v- **BOSSARD Laura**: born March 31, 1869

141 BOSSARD Margaret: (*Melchior, Peter, Melchior, Phillip*) was born October 24, 1835 in Hamilton Township, Pennsylvania, daughter of Melchior Bossard and Hanna Arnold. She married November 7, 1863, Jacob Harmon born November 28, 1836 in Hamilton Township, son of Joseph and Eunice Harmon. He died June 21, 1907 and Margaret died April 25, 1888. They are buried in Rock's cemetery in Jackson Township.

Children:

i- **HARMON Clara:** born 1864 and died December 2, 1949, unmarried.

330 ii- **HARMON Minnie:** born 1870

142 BOSSARD Joseph H.: (*Melchior, Peter, Melchior, Phillip*) was born October 4, 1837 in Hamilton Township, Pennsylvania, son of Melchior Bossard and Hannah Arnold. He married Maria (unknown maiden name) born May 1842. He died July 6, 1906 and Maria died in 1922. They are buried in the Bossard Heller cemetery in Hamilton Township.

Children:

i- **BOSSARD Henry:** born August 7, 1858 and died September 24, 1878.

ii- **BOSSARD Norton Allen:** born October 20, 1863 and died 1869, buried in Stroudsburg cemetery.

143 BOSSARD Susannah: (*Melchior, Peter, Melchior, Phillip*) was born October 23, 1839 in Hamilton Township, Pennsylvania, daughter of Melchior Bossard and Hanna Arnold. She married September 6, 1866, Samuel Hood born May 23, 1842. He died May 20, 1927 and Susannah died November 8, 1915. They are buried in the Stroudsburg cemetery.

One child:

331 i- **HOOD William C.:** born July 9, 1874

144 BOSSARD Peter: (*Melchior, Peter, Melchior, Phillip*) was born April 30, 1841 in Hamilton Township, Pennsylvania, son of Melchior Bossard and Hanna Arnold. He married Louisa (unknown maiden name) born February 1846. She died February 2, 1929. Peter served in Co. C. Pa. Militia during the Civil War. They are buried in Stroudsburg cemetery. No date of death found for Peter. No issue.

145 BOSSARD Florinda: (*Melchior, Peter, Melchior, Phillip*) was born March 1843 in Hamilton Township, Pennsylvania, daughter of Melchior Bossard and Hanna Arnold. She married Barnet Mansfield born May 8, 1839, son of Jacob Mansfield. She died May 4, 1920 and Barnet died December 4, 1923. They are buried in the Stroudsburg cemetery.

Children:

i- **MANSFIELD Allie Trivilla**: born February 15, 1864 and died young.
ii- **MANSFIELD Willie M.**: born December 21, 1865 and died young.
iii- **MANSFIELD Howard**: born August 1868 and died 1919
332 iv- **MANSFIELD Charles**: born June 1874
333 v- **MANSFIELD Mamie**: born 1881
334 vi- **MANSFIELD Paul**: born January 1883

146 BOSSARD Mary Jane: (*Melchior, Peter, Melchior, Phillip*) was born April 1845 in Hamilton Township, Pennsylvania, daughter of Melchior Bossard and Hanna Arnold. She married July 8, 1866, Stephen J. Giersch born November 20, 1834. son of John Giersch and Sophia Ehret. He died December 24, 1901 and Mary Jane died January 7, 1933. They are buried in the Stroudsburg cemetery.

One child born in Stroudsburg:
335 i- **GIERSCH Harry C.**: born September 1877

147 BOSSARD James: (*Melchior, Peter, Melchior, Phillip*) was born February 1848, son of Melchior Bossard and Hanna Arnold. He married 1872, Sarah H. Sceurman born October 1845. He died in 1915 and Sarah died in 1924. They are buried in Mt. Zion cemetery in Hamilton Township.

Children:
336 i- **BOSSARD Melchior W.**: born in 1873
337 ii- **BOSSARD Mary Catherine**: born April 4, 1874
iii- **BOSSARD Florence C.**: born November 1875 and died September 4, 1913, buried in Stroudsburg.
iv- **BOSSARD Joseph F.**: born August 29, 1883 and died June 6, 1898, buried in Stroudsburg.

148 BOSSARD Anna E.: (*Melchior, Peter, Melchior, Phillip*) was born August 27, 1851 in Hamilton Township, Pennsylvania, daughter of Melchior Bossard and Hanna Arnold. She married 1871, Jerome Henry Haney born June 1, 1845, son of William and Rebecca Haney. Anna died December 13, 1912 in Hamilton Township and he died October 7, 1930. Jerome was first married to Mary Elizabeth Sceurman, born May 5, 1843. She died August 4, 1869. They had two children, Catherine, born in 1865, who married December 25, 1884, William Eyer. John L. Haney, born May 31, 1867, who married Alice Laufer. See number 292 for Alice Laufer.

Children of Jerome and Anna E.:
338 i- **HANEY Nettie**: born June 1872
339 ii- **HANEY Minnie**: born 1875
340 iii- **HANEY Tilton**: born October 29, 1876
341 iv- **HANEY Harry**: born June 1882
342 v- **HANEY Charles B.**: born May 22, 1888

343 **vi- HANEY Mabel Ruth**: born January 10, 1892

149 **BOSSARD John M.**: (*Melchior, Peter, Melchior, Phillip*) was born July 7, 1854, son of Melchior Bossard and Hanna Arnold. He married (1) December 31, 1887 Lizzie Turn born October 15, 1859, daughter of John Turn and Ency De Puy. She died June 24, 1893 and he married (2) Anna M. Turn. He died December 8, 1913 in Stroudsburg and Anna died in 1939. John was a Judge in Monroe Co. They are buried in the Middle Smithfield cemetery. No issue.

150 **BOSSARD Franklin**: (*Melchior, Peter, Melchior, Phillip*) was born June 12. 1857, son of Melchior Bossard and Hanna Arnold. He married March 21, 1891, Caroline Altemose born March 1859, daughter of Peter and Sarah Altemose. He died May 23, 1926 and Caroline died August 21, 1932. They are buried in the Stroudsburg cemetery.

Children born in Stroudsburg:

344 **i- BOSSARD Frank Sterling**: born April 27, 1892

ii- BOSSARD Foster: born September 1898 and died March 31, 1956, unmarried. He is buried in the Stroudsburg cemetery.

151 **BOSSARD Samuel**: (*Jacob, Peter, Melchior, Phillip*) was born April 29, 1841 in Hamilton Township, Pennsylvania, son of Jacob Bossard and Christina Rees. He married February 11, 1865, Margaret Jane Edinger born September 11, 1840, daughter of Abraham and Sally Ann Edinger. She died March 9, 1909 and Samuel died March 16, 1909, in Chester, Pennsylvania. They are buried in Stroudsburg cemetery.

Children:

345 **i- BOSSARD Martha**: born March 27, 1866

ii- BOSSARD Susan: born November 8, 1867 and died April 29, 1943, unmarried.

346 **iii- BOSSARD Catherine**: born June 21, 1869

347 **iv- BOSSARD Frederick Phillip**: born June 4, 1870

348 **v- BOSSARD Robert Lee Phillip**: born August 27, 1874

152 **BOSSARD Edwin**: (*Jacob, Peter, Melchior, Phillip*) was born February 22, 1845 in Hamilton Township, Pennsylvania, son of Jacob Bossard and Christina Rees. He married December 11, 1864, Emma Walter born March 26, 1846, daughter of John S. Walter and Lavina Huston. Edwin served in Co. H., 214 Regiment, Pa. Infantry, during the Civil War. He enrolled March 21, 1865. His description was: Hazel eyes, brown hair, ruddy complexion, 5ft. 6ins. He received a pension of $8.00 a month. They moved to Moosic, Lackawanna Co., Pennsylvania where he died October 20, 1899. Emma died May 1, 1895, in Moosic.

Children:

349 i- **BOSSARD Curvin**: born May 12, 1865

ii- **BOSSARD Arlo**: born February 12, 1867 and died February 28, 1867, buried in Rock's cemetery.

iii- **BOSSARD Annette**: born November 5, 1868 and died February 22, 1869. Also in Rock's cemetery.

350 iv- **BOSSARD John**: born June 23, 1870

v- **BOSSARD Jennie**: born March 1, 1872, Probably died before 1899. Not in Father's obituary.

vi- **BOSSARD Lizzie**: born ca 1874

vii- **BOSSARD Harry**: born August 4, 1875 and died July 29, 1876. Also in Rock's cemetery.

351 viii-**BOSSARD Anna Levina**: born May 12, 1884

153 **BOSSARD Sarah Catherine**: (*Jacob, Peter, Melchior, Phillip*) was born June 16, 1847 in Hamilton Township, Pennsylvania, daughter of Jacob Bossard and Christina Rees. She married March 4, 1868, Jerome J. Woodling born April 24, 1843, son of Andrew and Elizabeth Woodling. She died October 27, 1870 and is buried in Rock's cemetery, Jackson Township. Jerome remarried and he died May 24, 1905 in Hamilton Township.

Children:

i- **WOODLING Lulu**: born December 28, 1868

352 ii- **WOODLING Katie**: born October 23, 1870

154 **BOSSARD Rachel J.**: (*Jacob, Peter, Melchior, Phillip*) was born 1851, daughter of Jacob Bossard and Christina Rees. She married Nathan Lesh born May 1845, son of John and Mary Lesh. He died May 8, 1921 and Rachel died April 1937. They are buried in Stroudsburg cemetery.

Children:

353 i- **LESH M. G. Dayton**: born September 21,1872

ii- **LESH Nettie**: born 1879 and died December 19, 1880. Buried in Mt. Zion cemetery.

155 **BOSSARD Mary Alice**: (*Jacob, Peter, Melchior, Phillip*) was born ca 1854, daughter of Jacob Bossard and Christina Rees. She married December 10, 1870, John B. Houser. They were living in Wilkesbarre, Pennsylvania in 1909. No further records.

Known children born in Hamilton Township:

i- **HOUSER Arlington Brady**: born April 26, 1872

ii- **HOUSER Norton Layton**: born March 14, 1874

iii- **HOUSER Lola Grace**: born October 30, 1875

156 BOSSARD Ida J.: (*Jacob, Peter, Melchior, Phillip*) was born August 17, 1857, daughter of Jacob Bossard and Christina Rees. She married (1) Dr. Cicero H. Drake born 1839. He died January 4, 1889 and she married (2) Edward Maritz. She moved to Ida Grove, Iowa with her parents and died there in 1946. They are buried in Ida Grove.

Children of first marriage:
i- **DRAKE Bessie Vivian:** born March 14, 1887 and died July 19, 1892
ii- **DRAKE Mabel:** born October 11, 1896
Children of second marriage:
354 iii- **MARITZ Marjorie:**
iv- **MARITZ Newell:**

157 BOSSARD Layton: (*Jacob, Peter, Melchior, Phillip*) was born March 19, 1865, son of Jacob Bossard and Christina Rees. He also went to Ida Grove, Iowa, with his parents. There he married Mary, (unknown maiden name) and moved to Pappilleon, Nebraska. No further records

Children born in Ida Grove:
i- **BOSSARD Harry:** born August 1890
ii- **BOSSARD Roy L:** born May 1893
iii- **BOSSARD Ida:** born February 1895
iv- **BOSSARD Alice:** born July 1898

158 BOSSARD Emma: (*Peter K., Peter, Melchior, Phillip*) was born June 8, 1853 in Hamilton Township, daughter of Peter K. Bossard and Anna Elizabeth Levering. She married July 26, 1880, James Fable born 1852. Emma died February 16, 1925. No record found for James.

Children:
i- **FABLE Eugene Abraham:** born October 21, 1880 and died March 17, 1881
ii- **FABLE Burton Bossard:** born December 28, 1881
355 iii- **FABLE Emma:** born February 1883

159 BOSSARD William H.: (*Peter K., Peter, Melchior, Phillip*) was born November 1857, son of Peter K. Bossard and Anna Elizabeth Levering. He married February 25, 1880, Alice Kemmerer born August 1858, daughter of Samuel and Sophia Kemmerer. They removed to Easton, Pennsylvania. No further records.

Children:
i- **BOSSARD Freddie J.:** born October 10, 1880 and died May 2, 1881. He is buried in the Methodist Episcopal Church cemetery in Cherry Valley.
ii- **BOSSARD Harry:** born February 1882

iii- BOSSARD Frederick Newton: born October 2, 1883
iv-BOSSARD Floyd: born January 1888

160 BOSSARD Eugene Abraham: (*Peter K., Peter, Melchior, Phillip*) was born December 10, 1860 in Hamilton Township, Pennsylvania, son of Peter K. Bossard and Anna Elizabeth Levering. He married September 29, 1885, Almira Woodling born May 1862. She died April 5, 1936 and Eugene died September 15, 1952. They are buried in the Stroudsburg cemetery.

Children:
356 **i- BOSSARD Edith Mae:** born March 27, 1887
357 **ii- BOSSARD Harold Frederick:** born May 23, 1896
358 **iii- BOSSARD Miles Franklin:** born October 12, 1898

161 BOSSARD Mary Ann: (*Peter K., Peter, Melchior, Phillip*) known as "Mamie", was born July 4, 1863 in Hamilton Township, daughter of Peter K. Bossard and Anna Elizabeth Levering. She married January 22, 1887, Edward Oyer born June 1868. They resided in Northampton Co., Pennsyvania.

One child known:
i- OYER Frederick: born August 5, 1896

162 EYER Isaiah: (*Eliza Ann, Peter, Melchior, Phillip*) was born April 4, 1847 in Hamilton Township, son of Jacob Eyer and Eliza Ann Bossard. He was living in Plainfield, Northampton Co., where he married Lucinda (unknown maiden name), born 1866. No further records.

Children born in Northampton Co.:
i- EYER Eliza A.: born February 1887
ii- EYER Nellie C.: born August 1888
iii- EYER Steward: born September 1890
iv- EYER Agnes: born May 1897

163 EYER Peter: (*Eliza Ann, Peter, Melchior, Phillip*) was born ca 1850 in Hamilton Township, son of Jacob Eyer and Eliza Ann Bossard. He married October 12, 1873, Sarah Butz. Probably removed to Northampton Co. and he died in 1914. No further records.

Children:
i- EYER Frank: born ca 1874
ii- EYER Howard: born December 21, 1877

164 EYER Emma Catherine: (*Eliza Ann, Peter, Melchior, Phillip*) was born December 23, 1853 in Hamilton Township, Pennsylvania, daughter of Jacob Eyer and Eliza Ann Bossard. She married Adam Werkhiser born October 18, 1848. She died January 24, 1901 in Pen Argyl, Pennsylvania. Adam was still living at that time. No further records.

Children:

i- WERKHISER Estella: born ca 1879

One other daughter, no record of name or birth

165 BOSSARD Alice: (*Joseph, Peter, Melchior, Phillip*) was born 1852, daughter of Joseph Bossard and Sophia Cornelia Fetterman. She married November 17, 1874, John Palmer Carmer born November 22, 1850, son of Augustus and Mary Ann Carmer. He died April 30, 1929 and Alice died April 26, 1934. They are buried in the Stroudsburg cemetery.

Children: (twins)

359 **i- CARMER Grace L.:** born March 15, 1881

360 **ii- CARMER Laura M.:** born March 15, 1881

William and Sarah Bossard

Back row: Fred Front left: Claude Center: Matie

Curvin and Minnie Bossard

Back Row left to right: Murriel, Ina May, Gladys, Vera, Cecil
Front Row left to right: Calvin, Minnie, Curvin, Carmen
Center front: Marcelle

CHAPTER 6

SIXTH GENERATION

166 **WEISS Mary Ann**: (*Daniel Weiss, Felix Weiss, Eva Catherine, Melchior, Phillip*) was born December 27, 1840 in Chestnuthill, Pennsylvania, daughter of Daniel F. and Susan Weiss. She married George W. Altemose, born January 17, 1834, son of Adam and Catherina Altemose. He died April 14, 1908 and she died December 8, 1923. They are buried in the Buena Vista cemetery at Brodheadsville, Pennsylvania.

Children:

i- **ALTEMOSE Amanda**: born ca 1859
ii- **ALTEMOSE Edwin F.**: born December 3, 1861 and died May 13, 1928, buried Buena Vista cemetery.
iii- **ALTEMOSE Susan**: born May 11, 1863
361 iv- **ALTEMOSE Emma Catherine**: born November 6, 1864
v- **ALTEMOSE Mary A.**: born 1868 and died 1873
vi- **ALTEMOSE Mary Jane**: born September 16, 1969
362 vii- **ALTEMOSE Electa**: born June 1871
viii- **ALTEMOSE Julia Edith**: born October 30, 1873, and died June 14, 1888, buried in Brodheadsville cemetery.
ix- **ALTEMOSE Rachel W.**: born 1874 and died 1878
x- **ALTEMOSE George T.**: born 1877 and died 1878, buried in Brodheadsville cemetery.
363 xi- **ALTEMOSE Grace**: born September 1879

167 **WEISS Martha Jane**: (*Daniel Weiss, Felix Weiss, Eva Catherine, Melchior, Phillip*) was born April 26, 1846 in Hamilton Township, Pennsylvania, daughter of Daniel F. and Susan Weiss. She married March 25, 1865, Edwin Levering, born April 12, 1842, son of Abraham and Mary Levering. She died June 29, 1870 and Edwin married (2) Susannah B., born September 1860. Martha is buried in Mt. Zion cemetery.

One child:

i- **LEVERING Harry**: born ca 1867

168 **ALTEMOSE Julia Arvilla**: (*Susannah Weiss, Felix Weiss, Eva Catherine, Melchior, Phillip*) was born March 5, 1854 in Gilbert, Pennsylvania, daughter of Linford Altemose and Susannah Weiss. She married August 1874, Thomas Felker born August 4, 1854, son of John Felker and Sallie Ann Miller. He died 1927 and Julia died 1932.

Children:

364 i- **FELKER Ellen E.**: born 1874
365 ii- **FELKER Stewart Ervin**: born March 10, 1877
366 iii- **FELKER Hattie Jane**: born September 18, 1879
367 iv- **FELKER Jennie Diana**: born July 30, 1882
368 v- **FELKER Cora Alice**: born May 13, 1886

169 ALTEMOSE Diana: (*Susannah Weiss, Felix Weiss, Eva Catherine, Melchior, Phillip*) was born September 28, 1863 in Gilbert, Pennsylvania, daughter of Lynford Altemose and Susannah Weiss. She married in 1883, Daniel C. Miller born July 23, 1857, son of Samuel Miller and Sarah A. Kester. He died December 9, 1909 and Diana died February 23, 1944. They are buried in the Buena Vista cemetery.

Children:

i- **MILLER Edgar H.**: born December 31, 1883 and died January 15, 1893. He is buried in the old Brodheadsville cemetery.
369 ii- **MILLER Florence Emma**: born August 15, 1886
370 iii- **MILLER Bertha B.**: born October 1888

170 ALTEMOSE Stewart A.: (*Susannah Weiss, Felix Weiss, Eva Catherine, Melchior, Phillip*) was born December 30, 1865 in Gilbert, Pennsylvania, son of Lynford Altemose and Susannah Weiss. He married August 11, 1898 in Tannersville, Bertha M. Singer born September 16, 1881, daughter of James Singer. He died December 20, 1952 in Wilson Boro and Bertha died February 28, 1963. They are buried in Forks cemetery in Stockertown, Pennsylvania.

Children:

371 i- **ALTEMOSE Vernon G.**: born January 23, 1899
ii- **ALTEMOSE Helen Diana**: born July 9, 1900
372 iii- **ALTEMOSE Emma Lydia**: born July 30, 1902
373 iv- **ALTEMOSE Ralph Arlington**: born September 17, 1904
374 v- **ALTEMOSE Jacob Victor**: born January 26, 1907
375 vi- **ALTEMOSE Beatrice Naomi**: born November 24, 1908
376 vii- **ALTEMOSE Albert Alvin**: born November 17, 1910
377 viii- **ALTEMOSE Woodrow Wilson**: born March 4, 1913
378 ix- **ALTEMOSE Alberta Arvilla**: born July 4, 1918

171 WEISS Charles F.: (*Felix Weiss, Felix Weiss, Eva Catherine, Melchior, Phillip*) was born July 1859 in Chestnuthill Pennsylvania, son of Felix and Eliza Ann Weiss. He married Electa A. Snyder born June 1873, daughter of Reuben and Mary Ann Snyder. He died November 22, 1934.

Children:

i- **WEISS Raymond**: born March 1891
ii- **WEISS Eva May**: born 1894 and died January 18, 1898, buried in

Brodheadsville cemetery.
379 iii- **WEISS Ruth H.**: born May 1896
iv- **WEISS Logan F.**: born July 17, 1898
380 v- **WEISS Iva M.**: born ca 1902
vi- **WEISS Grover S.**: born September 7, 1903
vii- **WEISS Amy A.**: born April 5, 1905
viii- **WEISS John F.**: born ca 1907
381 ix- **WEISS Viola A.**: born 1909

172 **WEISS Stewart**: (*Felix Weiss, Felix Weiss, Eva Catherine, Melchior, Phillip*) was born ca 1872 in Chestnuthill, Pennsylvania, son of Felix and Eliza Ann Weiss. He married Ella (unknown maiden name).

One known child:
i- **WEISS Samuel Eugene**: born December 28, 1905

173 **GEARHART Cicero**: (*Elizabeth Weiss, Felix Weiss, Eva Catherine, Melchior, Phillip*) was born April 18, 1858 in Hamilton Township, Pennsylvania, son of Samuel Rees Gearhart and Elizabeth Weiss. He married August 31, 1887, Blanche Greenswald born February 1870, daughter of Amandis Greenswald and Lorraine Beiber. He died November 20, 1920 in Stroudsburg and she died August 18, 1960. They are buried in the Stroudsburg cemetery.

Children:
382 i- **GEARHART Olive**: born June 12, 1888
383 ii- **GEARHART A. Greenswald**: born November 1890
384 iii- **GEARHART Helen L.**: born December 1891
385 iv- **GEARHART Samuel R.**: born January 22, 1896
386 v- **GEARHART Roberta E.**: born October 10, 1899
vi- **GEARHART Ruth**: born November 16, 1903

174 **GEARHART Anna Elizabeth**: (*Elizabeth Weiss, Felix Weiss, Eva Catherine, Melchior, Phillip*) was born March 1860, daughter of Samuel Rees Gearhart and Elizabeth Weiss. She married December 16, 1876, Samuel Felker born October 26, 1856. He died in 1911 and Anna died October 2, 1929.

Children:
i- **FELKER Emma J.**: born July 25, 1877
ii- **FELKER Minnie**: born June 1879
387 iii- **FELKER John R.**: born December 1880
iv- **FELKER Mabel**: born June 1890

175 **GEARHART Theodore**: (*Elizabeth Weiss, Felix Weiss, Eva Catherine, Melchior, Phillip*) was born October 25, 1862, son of Samuel Rees Gearhart and Elizabeth

Weiss. He married November 15, 1885, Amanda Snyder born November 10, 1870, daughter of Jonas and Susan Snyder. He died February 14, 1923 in Gilbert, and Amanda died February 25, 1940 in Allentown, Pennsylvania. They are buried in the Salem Church cemetery in Gilbert.

Children:

388 i- **GEARHART Lida May**: born July 9,1886
389 ii- **GEARHART Dorothy N.**: born June 16, 1888
iii- **GEARHART Arlington H.**: born April 5, 1890 and died August 27, 1890.
390 iv- **GEARHART Susannah E.**: born June 24, 1891
391 v- **GEARHART Charles R.**: born March 7, 1893
vi- **GEARHART Eva A.**: born May 10, 1894 and died September 26, 1894
392 vii- **GEARHART Edna M.**: born July 31, 1895 in Effort
393 viii- **GEARHART William J.**: born February 20, 1900
394 ix- **GEARHART Nevin A.**: born December 20, 1904
395 x- **GEARHART Lyster M.**: born August 1, 1906
396 xi- **GEARHART Martin F.**: (twin) born September 21, 1909
397 xii- **GEARHART Maurice**: (twin) born September 21, 1909
398 xiii- **GEARHART D. Kenneth**: born October 1, 1911
399 xiv- **GEARHART Franklin**: born November 20, 1913

176 GEARHART Ulyssis: (*Elizabeth Weiss, Felix Weiss, Eva Catherine, Melchior, Phillip*) was born 1865, son of Samuel Rees Gearhart and Elizabeth Weiss. He married July 14, 1886, Abba Jane Burger born 1866 in Effort, Pennsylvania, daughter of Reuben and Mary Burger.

Children:

400 i- **GEARHART Alice**:
401 ii- **GEARHART Mary**:

177 GEARHART John H.: (*Elizabeth Weiss, Felix Weiss, Eva Catherine, Melchior, Phillip*) was born June 4, 1868, son of Samuel Rees Gearhart and Elizabeth Weiss. He married June 28, 1890, Alice Andrew born September 23, 1871, daughter of Levi and Mary Andrew. He died January 15, 1927 and Alice died April 19, 1950. They are buried in the Buena Vista cemetery.

Children:

402 i- **GEARHART Albert**: born May 1891
403 ii- **GEARHART Mabel M.**: born December 1892
404 iii- **GEARHART Stewart Raymond**: born September 3, 1894
405 iv- **GEARHART Grace L.**: born May 7, 1896
406 v- **GEARHART Lois**: born May 14, 1897
407 vi- **GEARHART Minnie E.**: born June 1898
vii- **GEARHART Stella**: born May 25, 1900

408 viii- **GEARHART Florence A.**: born 1901
409 ix- **GEARHART Bertha E.**: born 1902
x- **GEARHART Howard E.**: born November 24, 1903
410 xi- **GEARHART Clifford A.**: born May 26, 1905
411 xii- **GEARHART Elva O.**: born 1908
xiii- **GEARHART Lee**:

178 **GEARHART Thomas**: (*Elizabeth Weiss, Felix Weiss, Eva Catherine, Melchior, Phillip*) was born September 21, 1870, son of Samuel Rees Gearhart and Elizabeth Weiss. He married March 24, 1900, Emma S. Ruff born December 29, 1878, daughter of Michael and Julia A. Ruff. He died December 15, 1954 and Emma died October 29, 1937. They are buried in the Buena Vista cemetery.

Children:
412 i- **GEARHART Blanche Alberta**: born February 18, 1901
413 ii- **GEARHART Ammon R.**: born October 18, 1905
414 iii- **GEARHART Grant G.**: born 1908
iv- **GEARHART Berneda**:
v- **GEARHART Edith**:
vi- **GEARHART Pauline**:
415 vii- **GEARHART Ernest**: born 1911
viii- **GEARHART Arline**: born May 14, 1921

179 **GEARHART Lucy E.**: (*Elizabeth Weiss, Felix Weiss, Eva Catherine, Melchior, Phillip*) was born March 24, 1874, daughter of Samuel Rees Gearhart and Elizabeth Weiss. She married June 1, 1895, Edwin M. Bruch born October 8, 1875, son of George Bruch and Lucinda Kresge. She died April 19, 1962 and he died February 21, 1964.

Children:
416 i- **BRUCH David**: born October 3, 1894
417 ii- **BRUCH Leila**: born January 6, 1897
iii- **BRUCH Luther A.**: born January 2, 1899 and died December 1, 1911.

180 **SHOEMAKER Abner**: (*Emelie Weiss, George Weiss, Eva Catherine, Melchior, Phillip*) was born June 8, 1845 in Hamilton Township, Pennsylvania, son of Emmanuel Shoemaker and Emelie Weiss. He married December 12, 1867, Margaret A. Werkhiser born December 5, 1847, daughter of Henry Werkhiser and Catherine Hauser. He died June 10, 1942 and Margaret died April 1, 1884. They are buried in the Mt. Zion cemetery, Hamilton Township.

Children born in Hamilton Township:
i- **SHOEMAKER baby Etta**: buried Mt. Zion cemetery, no dates
ii- **SHOEMAKER William C.**: born ca 1869
418 iii- **SHOEMAKER Laura F.**: born October 16, 1870

419 iv- **SHOEMAKER Carrie A.**: born September 21, 1872

181 **SHOEMAKER Louisa**: (*Emelie Weiss, George Weiss, Eva Catherine, Melchior, Phillip*) was born October 15, 1846 In Hamilton Township, Pennsylvania, daughter of Emmanuel Shoemaker and Emelie Weiss. She married March 24, 1866, Francis E. Snyder born ca 1831, son of John Snyder. She died November 7, 1875 and Frances died July 25, 1888. She is buried in Mt. Zion cemetery.

Children:
i- **SNYDER Curvin**:
ii- **SNYDER Emmanuel**: born December 10, 1869
iii- **SNYDER Stewart**:
iv- **SNYDER Burton**:

182 **SHOEMAKER Susan Ellen**: (*Emelie Weiss, George Weiss, Eva Catherine, Melchior, Phillip*) was born August 26, 1849 in Hamilton Township, Pennsylvania, daughter of Emmanuel Shoemaker and Emelie Weiss. She married November 18, 1866, Samuel Rinker born December 1, 1843, son of Solomon Rinker and Rebecca Kunkel. She died January 10. 1903 and Samuel died July 25, 1927 in Stroudsburg. They are buried in the Stroudsburg cemetery.

Children:
420 i- **RINKER Florence A.**: born ca 1867
421 ii- **RINKER Emily T.**: born February 1869
422 iii- **RINKER Carrie E.**: born ca 1872
iv- **RINKER Sally May**: born ca 1874
v- **RINKER Edith A.**: born ca 1875
423 vi- **RINKER Mary E.**: born ca 1877
424 vii- **RINKER Clayton G.**: born November 4, 1878
viii- **RINKER William N.**: born ca 1879
425 ix- **RINKER Sherman Morris**: born September 1880
426 x- **RINKER Ada P.**: born April 1885
427 xi- **RINKER Eda B.**: born April 1886
428 xii- **RINKER Floyd A.**: born October 1888
429 xiii- **RINKER Alice E.**:
430 xiv- **RINKER Bertha R.**:

183 · **SHOEMAKER Lynford Milton**: (*Emelie Weiss, George Weiss, Eva Catherine, Melchior, Phillip*) was born June 8, 1851 in Hamilton Township, Pennsylvania, son of Emmanuel Shoemaker and Emelie Weiss. He married Helen Miller, born June 1860. She died in 1921 and he married (2) Mary (unknown maiden name). He died April 1, 1948 and they are buried in the Stroudsburg cemetery.

Children:
431 i- **SHOEMAKER Verna**: born October 11, 1895

ii- **SHOEMAKER Harold**: born February 8, 1898

184 **SHOEMAKER William Marvin**: (*Emelie Weiss, George Weiss, Eva Catherine, Melchior, Phillip*) was baptized August 21, 1852 in Hamilton Township, Pennsylvania, son of Emmanuel Shoemaker and Emelie Weiss. He married May 2, 1883, Rachel Hobbs born July 1856. No other records found.

Known children:
i- **SHOEMAKER Minnie M.**: born August 1886
ii- **SHOEMAKER Emmanuel H.**: born September 1894

185 **SHOEMAKER Mary Alice**: (*Emelie Weiss, George Weiss, Eva Catherine, Melchior, Phillip*) was born October 9, 1855 in Hamilton Township, Pennsylvania, daughter of Emmanuel Shoemaker and Emelie Weiss. She married June 12, 1875, Franklin Fetherman born September 1855, son of Jonathan and Sarah Fetherman. No further records found.

Known children:
i- **FETHERMAN Erhard**: born Januray 1877
ii- **FETHERMAN Alice**: born July 31, 1882
432 iii- **FETHERMAN Edith May**: born April 7, 1885
433 iv- **FETHERMAN Mamie**: born June 1888

186 **SHOEMAKER Catherine Ardella**: (*Emelie Weiss, George Weiss, Eva Catherine, Melchior, Phillip*) was born May 16, 1861 in Hamilton Township, Pennsylvania, daughter of Emmanuel Shoemaker and Emelie Weiss. She married June 12, 1875, Jerome Bonser born July 25, 1862, son of Reuben Bonser and Sabina Frantz. She died November 13, 1936 and Jerome died July 25, 1923. They are buried in the Salem Church cemetery.

Known children:
434 i- **BONSER Stanley W.**: born March 4, 1888
435 ii- **BONSER Muriel T.**: born 1897

187 **BUZZARD Joseph**: (*Israel, Joseph, Phillip, Melchior, Phillip*) was born 1862 in Clarkston, Michigan, son of Israel Buzzard and Rozella Perry. He married Olive, (Unknown maiden name) born October 1869. In 1910, they were living in Livingston Co. Michigan. No further records.

Known children:
i- **BUZZARD Howard**: born ca 1890
ii- **BUZZARD Murdock**: born ca 1891
iii- **BUZZARD Josephine**: born ca 1893
iv- **BUZZARD Dewitt**: born ca 1895

v- **BUZZARD Wheaton**: born ca 1897
vi- **BUZZARD Homer**: born ca 1902
vii- **BUZZARD Richard**: born ca 1905
viii- **BUZZARD Ivan**: born ca 1907

188 BUZZARD Edward J.: (*John, Joseph, Phillip, Melchior, Phillip*) was born ca 1860 in Port Huron, Michigan, son of John Buzzard. He was a Captain on the Great Lakes. Wife's name not known.

189 BUZZARD Walter H.: (*John, Joseph, Phillip, Melchior, Phillip*) was born ca 1861 in Port Huron, Michigan, son of John Buzzard. He married Mary (unknown maiden name), born ca 1860. They lived in Port Huron, Michigan. He was also a Captain on the Great Lakes. No children listed in the 1910 census.

190 BUZZARD Coray: (*John, Joseph, Phillip, Melchior, Phillip*) was born ca 1864 in Michigan, son of John Buzzard. He was a Marine Engineer on the Great Lakes. He married Hulda Richards, born ca 1860 in Germany.

One child:
i- **BUZZARD Henry Eugene**: born 1885

191 BUZZARD Armus H.: (*Jacob L., Joseph, Phillip, Melchior, Phillip*) was born December 1863 in Williams Township, Bay Co. Michigan, son of Jacob L. Buzzard and Polly Myers. He married Margaret Richardson, born September 1868. No further records.

Known children born in Bay Co., Michigan:
i- **BUZZARD Claude H.**: born July 1891
ii- **BUZZARD Marguerite**: born July 1895

192 BUZZARD Alice F.: (*Jacob L., Joseph, Phillip, Melchior, Phillip*) was born ca 1867 in Oakland Co. Michigan, daughter of Jacob L. Buzzard and Polly Myers. She married George Fleming.

Known child:
i- **FLEMING Myrtle**:

193 BUZZARD Polly A.: (*Jacob L., Joseph, Phillip, Melchior, Phillip*) was born ca 1874 in Williams Township, Bay Co., Michigan, daughter of Jacob L. Buzzard and Polly Myers. She married Elmer Hershey born August 1870 in Ohio.

Known children:

i- **HERSHEY Edna**: born Setember 1893
ii- **HERSHEY Hazen**: born January 1896

194 BUZZARD Frank J.: (*Jacob L., Joseph, Phillip, Melchior, Phillip*) was born August 1877 in Williams Township, Bay Co., Michigan, son of Jacob L. Buzzard and Polly Myers. He married 1900, Mina (unknown maiden name) born June 1880.

195 BUZZARD Laura: (*Jacob L., Joseph, Phillip, Melchior, Phillip*) was born June 1880 in Williams Township, Bay Co. Michigan, daughter of Jacob L. Buzzard and Polly Myers. She married Fred W. Hill.

196 BUZZARD Lucy Bell: (*Edwin, Joseph, Phillip, Melchior, Phillip*) was born August 20, 1868 in Williams Township, Bay Co., Michigan, daughter of Edwin J. Buzzard and Eleanor D. Moore. She married April 18, 1888, Richard Clarey born June 1865, son of Michael Clarey and Bridgett Murphy. He died November 16, 1937 and Lucy died April 30, 1944. They are buried in Oakridge cemetery in Bay City, Michigan.

Children:
436 i- **CLAREY Edwin**: born September 1890
437 ii- **CLAREY Richard Dorcey**: born January 1892
438 iii- **CLAREY Ethel**: born July 29, 1894
439 iv- **CLAREY Ivan**: born November 1898
v- **CLAREY Harry**: born 1901 and died 1922
440 vi- **CLAREY Alfred**: born March 9, 1904
441 vii- **CLAREY June**: born June 1907

197 BUZZARD Ralph Eugene: (*Edwin J., Joseph, Phillip, Melchior, Phillip*) was born May 7, 1870 in Williams Township, Bay Co., Michigan, son of Edwin J. Buzzard and Eleanor D. Moore. He married December 20, 1894, Henrietta Middleton born 1875. He died March 18, 1955 in Bay City and is buried in Oakridge cemetery.

Children:
442 i- **BUZZARD Howard**: born 1898
443 ii- **BUZZARD Lloyd**: born 1905

198 BUZZARD Roy Vernon: (*Edwin J., Joseph, Phillip, Melchior, Phillip*) was born February 12, 1875 in Williams Township, Bay Co. Michigan, son of Edwin J. Buzzard and Eleanor D. Moore. He married September 7, 1898, Nellie Helen Horn born September 6, 1878. Roy died September 29, 1953 and Nellie died March 24, 1949. They are buried in Oakridge cemetery Bay City, Michigan.

Children:

444 i- **BUZZARD Roland Lavern**: born June 27, 1899
445 ii- **BUZZARD Ramond Vernon**: born April 29, 1901
446 iii- **BUZZARD Alvin Milford**: born September 13, 1903
447 iv- **BUZZARD Eleanor Geneva**: born November 25, 1905
448 v- **BUZZARD George William**: born January 13, 1909
449 vi- **BUZZARD Alice Leona**: born January 10, 1912
450 vii- **BUZZARD Vera Marie**: born March 13, 1913
451 viii- **BUZZARD Roy Edward**: born April 13, 1923

199 BUZZARD Mary Eleanor: (*Edwin J., Joseph, Phillip, Melchior, Phillip*) was born April 20 1879 in Williams Township, Bay Co., Michigan, daughter of Edwin J. Buzzard and Eleanor D. Moore. She married August 6, 1896, Mercer Richardson.

200 BUZZARD Alice Louise: (*Edwin J., Joseph, Phillip, Melchior, Phillip*) was born March 18, 1885 in Williams Township, Bay Co., Michigan, daughter of Edwin J. Buzzard and Eleanor D. Moore. She married October 18, 1911, John Weed. They are buried in Simms cemetery, Augres, Michigan.

Children:

i- **WEED Viola**: born January 13, 1913
ii- **WEED Irving**:
iii- **WEED Edwin**:

201 BUZZARD William Joseph: (*Edwin J., Joseph, Phillip, Melchior, Phillip*) was born August 17, 1887 in Williams Township, Bay Co., Michigan, son of Edwin J. Buzzard and Eleanor D. Moore. He married (1) Eva White, daughter of Roy White and Emma Sibley. He married (2) Wilhemina Mrohs. Wilhemina had four children by her first marriage to Nathaniel Petee. They were Elton, Garnet E., Arthur and Francis.

Children by first marriage

452 i- **BUZZARD Edwin Howe**: born 1912
453 ii- **BUZZARD Russell Donald**: February 10, 1913

Children by second marriage:

454 iii- **BUZZARD Noreen**: born February 8, 1925
455 iv- **BUZZARD Robert William**: born February 8, 1926
456 v- **BUZZARD Doris**: born September 21, 1928
457 vi- **BUZZARD Dorothy**: born December 21, 1929
458 vii- **BUZZARD Clayton E.**: born April 30, 1935

202 BOSSARD Lewis G.: (*George, Peter, Christopher, Melchior, Phillip*) was born June 29, 1879 in Dix, New York, son of George Bossard and Emma Adele Holly.

He married Martha Belle Urghart Roberts born 1881. He died November 30, 1945 and Martha died in December 12. 1962. They are buried in the Dundee cemetery in Dundee, New York.

One child born in Erwin, New York.
459 i- **BOSSARD George Clay**: born October 15, 1913

203 **BOSSARD Ethelyn Marie**: (*George, Peter, Christopher, Melchior, Phillip*) was born October, 7, 1883 in Reading, New York, daughter of George Bossard and Emma Adele Holly. She married November 14, 1912, Oliver William Snook born December 26, 1884 in Australia, son of Alanson Snook. He died November 25, 1960 in Elmira, New York, and Ethelyn died December 27, 1973 in Elmira. They are buried in Dundee, New York.

One child born in Dundee, New York:
460 i- **SNOOK Raymond**: born April 5, 1914

204 **BOSSARD Mabel**: (*George, Peter, Christopher, Melchior, Phillip*) was born September 2, 1875 in Dundee, New York, daughter of George Bossard and Emma Adele Holly. She married ca 1900, Luther Stanton born October 14, 1878. He first married Elsie Haven, by whom he had one child, Ida. Mabel died January 5, 1911 in Barrington, New York, and Luther died May 13, 1954. They are buried in the Dundee cemetery.

Children:
461 i- **STANTON Gladys**: born August 28, 1901
462 ii- **STANTON Zelma**: born June 23, 1903
463 iii- **STANTON William**: born April 14, 1906

205 **BOSSARD Leon M.**: (*Marcus, Peter, Christopher, Melchior, Phillip*) was born 1876 in Dix, New York, son of Marcus Bossard and Mary Amelia Van Nortrick. He married September 15, 1903, Emily Jenkins born 1877 in England, daughter of Henry W. and Mary A. Jenkins. He died December 8, 1915 in Willard, New York and Emily died July 14, 1919 in Rochester, New York.

Children born in Corning, New York:
i- **BOSSARD Arthur F.**: born April 5, 1905 and died young
464 ii- **BOSSARD Albert George**: born October 12, 1906

206 **BOZARD Dela**: (*Henry, Richard, Christopher, Melchior, Phillip*) was born ca 1859 in Olean, New York, daughter of Henry M. Bozard and Mary Barker. She married Lovella Fuller and they were living in N. Bloomfield, New York in 1908. No further records.

207 BOZARD Earl W.: (*Henry, Richard, Christopher, Melchior, Phillip*) was born January 1862 in Olean, New York, son of Henry W. Bozard and Mary Barker. He married March 22, 1886 in Canandaigua, Nellie W. Clark born August 1862 in Almond, New York. In 1900, they lived in Hornell, New York and then removed to Auburn, New York. Nellie died September 28, 1916 in Auburn. No record found for Earl.

One child:

i- **BOZARD May**: born December 1887. At the time of her Mother's death in Auburn, she was working at the Auburn College. No further records.

208 BOZARD Mary: (*Henry, Richard, Christopher, Melchior, Phillip*) was born 1869 in Olean, New York daughter of Henry M. Bozard and Mary Barker. She married June 26, 1893, George C. Buchia. They were living in Pittsford, New York in 1908. No further records.

209 BOZARD Richard: (*Henry, Richard, Christopher, Melchior, Phillip*) was born June 22, 1878 in Olean, New York, son of Henry M Bozard and Mary Barker. He married February 23, 1903, Nettie Kaeli born 1879, daughter of Andrew and Alice Kaeli. She died October 19, 1909 in Rochester, New York. No issue. No further record for Richard.

210 BOZARD Truman Cyrus: (*Cyrus, Richard, Cristopher, Melchior, Phillip*) was born September 30, 1862 in Humphrey, New York, son of Cyrus Bozard and Julia Pierce. He married July 4, 1882, Eva Lucille Butler born June 27, 1864, daughter of William Butler and Marietta Hopkins. He died October 10, 1920 in Salamanca, New York and Eva died December 1, 1950. They are buried in Wildwood cemetery.

Children born in Humphrey, New York:

465 i- **BOZARD Ross Edward**: born January 7, 1883
466 ii- **BOZARD Grace Blanche**: born April 7, 1883
467 iii- **BOZARD Ruby Emily**: born July 11, 1887
468 iv- **BOZARD Floyd Cyrus**: born May 10, 1890
469 v- **BOZARD Flossie Marietta**: born March 24, 1895
470 vi- **BOZARD Bernice Mae**: born August 2, 1901
471 vii- **BOZARD Beatrice Julia**: born July 11, 1903
472 viii- **BOZARD Clifford James**: born April 11, 1906

211 BOZARD Edward Harrison: (*Cyrus, Richard, Christopher, Melchior, Phillip*) was born October 29, 1864 in Humphrey, New York, son of Cyrus P. Bozard and Julia Pierce. He married March 6, 1907, Mary M. Ganung born June 4, 1885, daughter of Charles Ganung and Susan Sweet. He died April 25, 1953 and Mary died March 31 1969 in Allegany, New York.

Children born in Humphrey:

i- **BOZARD Helen Amelia**: born January 12, 1908 and died in 1973, unmarried.

473 ii- **BOZARD Rena**: born August 22, 1909

iii- **BOZARD Julia Marion**: born December 26, 1910 and died September 17, 1923 in Humphrey.

474 iv- **BOZARD Bertha Eldene**: born November 20, 1916

212 BOZARD Blanche C.: (*Cyrus, Richard, Chrsitopher, Melchior, Phillip*) was born April 7, 1871 in Humphrey, New York, daughter of Cyrus P. Bozard and Julia Pierce. She married September 27, 1900, William C. Mosman born March 29, 1866 in Humphrey, New York, son of Mathias Mosman and Mary Elizabeth Ganung. She died April 25, 1953 and William died in 1923 in Allegany, New York.

Children born in Allegany, New York:

475 i- **MOSMAN Lynford**: born June 25, 1904

476 ii- **MOSMAN William Devere**: born March 25, 1908

213 BOZARD Alphonzo A.: (*Ashbel, Richard, Christopher, Melchior, Phillip*) was born September 24, 1868 in Humphrey, New York, son of Ashbel Bozard and Kate Conlon. He married June 25, 1899, Luella J. Wilbur born May 1869. He died March 3, 1951 and Luella died May 6, 1946. They are buried in Allegany.

One child:

i- **BOZARD Earl Hanford**: born December 1, 1900

214 BOZARD Iva L : (*Ashbel, Richard, Christopher, Melchior, Phillip*) was born ca 1874, daughter of Ashbel and Catherine G. Conlon. She married (1) December 23, 1890, John Matteson. He died April 30, 1897 in Wright's Corners, New York and she married (2) Sydney G. Hale in 1897. No further records.

One child by second marriage:

477 i- **HALE Lora D.**: born April 15, 1900

215 BOZARD Harrison B.: (*Ashbel, Richard, Christopher, Melchior, Phillip*) was born November 1878 in Humphrey, New York, son of Ashbel Bozard and Catherine B. Conlon. He married Mabel V. Vance born ca 1883 in Lincoln, Nebraska. He died February 18, 1922 in Allegany, New York. No record found for Mabel. No issue.

216 BOZARD Ralph Raymond: (*Ashbel, Richard, Christopher, Melchior, Phillip*) was born September 24, 1885 in Humphrey, New York, son of Ashbel Bozard and Catherine B. Conlon. He married October 6, 1914 in Allegany, Ann Conhiser, born 1888. He died February 28, 1922 and Ann died November 26, 1944. They are buried in Allegany. No issue.

217 **BOZARD Kittie**: (*Ashbel, Richard, Christopher, Melchior, Phillip*) was born June 2, 1890 in Humphrey, New York, daughter of Ashbel Bozard and Kate Conlon. She married January 21, 1913 in Olean, Alfred Rehler born March 22, 1888, son of Andrew and Marguerite Rehler. She died May 7, 1983 and Alfred is still living in Allegany as of 1990.

Children:

i- REHLER Kenneth Alfred: born November 22, 1913 and died the same day.

ii- REHLER Donald Leslie: born January 2, 1915 and died in 1915

478 **iii- REHLER Margaret Rose**: born October 16, 1916

218 **BOZARD Arthur**: (*Judson, Richard, Christopher, Melchior, Phillip*) was born ca 1879 in Humphrey, New York, son of Judson Bozard and Rose Conlon. He married in Olean, February 16, 1898. Wife's name unknown.

219 **BOZARD Glen Weir**: (*Judson, Richard, Christopher, Melchior, Phillip*) was born ca 1884 in Humphrey, New York, son of Judson Bozard and Rose Conlon. He married December 30, 1903, Blanche C. Button, daughter of Andrew Button and Hannah Duncan. He died December 31, 1945 in Allegany, New York. No record found for Blanche.

One child:

479 **i- BOZARD Thurman Andrew**: born May 28, 1907

220 **BOZARD Marcia Rose**: (*Judson, Richard, Christopher, Melchior, Phillip*) was born November 1886 in Humphrey, New York, daughter of Judson Bozard and Rose Conlon. She married December 31, 1902, Glen Grover Ford born 1884, son of Frank F. Ford and Judith (Julia) Foot. No further records.

221 **BOZARD Howard Raymond**: (*Judson, Richard, Christopher, Melchior, Phillip*) was born January 24, 1899 in Humphrey, New York, son of Judson Bozard and May M. Barber. He married September 8, 1926, Myrtle Elizabeth Morgan born 1895, daughter of Nelson and Blanche Morgan. He died March 2, 1986 in Allegany, New York. His wife died January 7, 1984. They are buried in Allegany, New York.

One child:

i- BOZARD Donald:

222 **BOZARD Arthur C.:** (*Sylvanus, Charles, Christopher, Melchior, Phillip*) was born April 1869 in Oakland Co. Michigan, son of Sylvanus and Sarah S. Bozard. He married Rose L. (unknown maiden name) born February 1871 in Michigan.

Known children born in Oakland Co. Michigan.
i- BOZARD Winifred F.: born June 1894
ii- BOZARD Ernest C.: born June 1897

223 **QUIN Sarah M.:** (*Amanda Backer, Sarah, George, Melchior, Phillip*) was born July 3, 1876, daughter of Edward Quin and Amanda Backer. She married April 12, 1900, Floyd Gibson, born 1875, son of Judson Gibson and Sarah Drew. Sarah died October 3, 1948 and Floyd died 1955. They are buried in the Glenwood cemetery in Pulteney, New York.

Known children:
480 **i- GIBSON Edward J.:** born December 22, 1909
481 **ii- GIBSON Virginia L.:** born March 9, 1913

224 **QUIN George E.:** (*Amanda Backer, Sarah, George, Melchior, Phillip*) was born 1878 in Pulteney, New York, son of Edward Quin and Amanda Backer. He married October 17, 1906, Lizzie Wixom, daughter of Fred J. Wixom and Ida H. Austin. He died in 1961 and is buried in the Glenview cemetery in Pulteney, New York.

Known child:
i- QUIN Edward J.: born 1910
One other child, an infant, died December 31, 1911

225 **HEDDEN Henry Ambrose:** (*Jane Backer, Sarah, George, Melchior, Phillip*) was born October 29, 1869 in Dix, New York, son of Frank Hedden and Jane Backer. He married June 24, 1914, Josephine Edmister born February 14, 1887, daughter of John Edmister and Ashsah Jackson. He died February 9, 1927 in Hornell, New York and Josephine died June 16, 1978.

Children born in Hornell, New York:
482 **i- HEDDEN William Franklin:** born August 11, 1915
483 **ii- HEDDEN Raymond Albert:** born June 22, 1917
484 **iii- HEDDEN Mary Jane:** born May 18, 1920
iv- HEDDEN Ruth: born October 2, 1921, unmarried
485 **v- HEDDEN Esther:** born April 9, 1927

226 HEDDEN Charles D.: (*Jane Backer, Sarah, George, Melchior, Phillip*) was born 1871 in Dix, New York, son of Frank Hedden and Jane Backer. He married March 21, 1900, Mary B. Williams born 1876. He died 1950 and she died 1956. They are buried in the Beaver Dams cemetery. No issue.

227 HEDDEN Albert Elmer: (*Jane Backer, Sarah, George, Melchior, Phillip*) was born 1878 in Dix, New York, son of Frank Hedden and Jane Backer. He married Georgia Crout, born 1891. He died 1951 and Georgia died March 8, 1950. They are buried in Beaver Dams. No issue.

228 FERO Emmett: (*Harriet Backer, Sarah, George, Melchior, Phillip*) was born December 26, 1872 in Trumansburg, New York son of John D. Fero and Harriet Backer. He married August 9, 1899, Claudia Pangbourne born 1874. He died November 12, 1933 and Claudia died April 16, 1955 in Watkins Glen, New York. No issue.

229 FERO Evaline: (*Harriet Backer, Sarah, George, Melchior, Phillip*) was born January 1874 in Dix, New York daughter of John D. Fero and Harriet Backer. She married September 23, 1897, Thomas Albert Decker, born April 1870. She died May 3, 1949 in Beaver Dams. No death record found for Thomas.

Children:

486 i- **DECKER Lawrence**: born August 1898
487 ii- **DECKER Florence**: born November 24, 1900
488 iii- **DECKER Clifford**: born 1902
489 iv- **DECKER Harriet**: born 1907
490 v- **DECKER Harold E.**: born 1910
491 vi- **DECKER Martha**: born ca 1912
492 vii- **DECKER Erma**: born ca 1914

230 FERO Sarah: (*Harriet Backer, Sarah, George, Melchior, Phillip*) was born December 1882 in Dix, New York, daughter of John D. Fero and Harriet Backer. She married Norman Johnson. No further records.

One known child:
i- **JOHNSON Norman**:

231 FERO Lewis Ray: (*Harriet Backer, Sarah, George, Melchior, Phillip*) was born ca 1883 in Dix, New York, son of John D. Fero and Harriet Backer. He married (1) June 12, 1912, Bertha Kniffen born December 19, 1891. She died July 28, 1957 and he married (2) Helena Pulhamus. She died January 3, 1978 in Watkins Glen, New York. No death records found for Lewis Ray. No issue.

232 **FERO Margaret May:** (*Harriet Backer, Sarah, George, Melchior, Phillip*) was born May 29, 1888 in Dix, New York, daughter of John D. Fero and Harriet Backer. She married Dr. John Pritchard, born December 31, 1879. He practiced medicine in Buffalo, New York and then moved to Ogdensburg, New York. A new wing at the Ogdensburg hospital was named in his honor. Margaret died September 1974 and John died May 9, 1952 in Ogdensburg.

One child born in Ogdensburg:
493 i- **PRITCHARD Elizabeth:** born September 19, 1916

233 **FERO Maude:** (*Harriet Backer, Sarah, George, Melchior, Phillip*) was born ca 1891, daughter of John D. Fero and Harriet Backer. She married William Suchcuhardt and they were living in New York City in 1933. No issue. No further records found.

234 **FERO Victor:** (*Harriet Backer, Sarah, George, Melchior, Phillip*) was born March 26, 1893 in Hornby, New York, son of John D. Fero and Harriet Backer. He married December 6, 1922, Nina La Maureaux in Rochester, New York. He died in January 1954 at Rochester.

One child:
494 i- **FERO Dean:** born July 1, 1930

235 **BACKER Elmond D.:** (*Emmett Backer, Sarah, George, Melchior, Phillip*) was born 1878 in Hornby, New York, son of Emmett Backer and Sarah Tompkins. He married Viola (unknown maiden name). He died in 1954 and is buried in the Fairview cemetery in Erwin, New York. No further records.

236 **BOSSARD Clarence:** (*Judd, Simon, George, Melchior, Phillip*) was born December 31, 1892 in West Milford, New Jersey, son of Judd Bossard and Jennie Richards. He married May 21, 1916, Anna Lehman born October 11, 1896 in Brooklyn, New York, daughter of August Lehman and Minnie Frank. He died in January 27, 1967 in West Milford, New Jersey and Anna died October 11, 1986. They are buried in West Milford.

Children born in West Milford New Jersey:
i- **BOSSARD Walter:** born March 12, 1917
ii- **BOSSARD Clayton:** born September 14, 1918
495 iii- **BOSSARD Raymond:** born January 16, 1921
iv- **BOSSARD Anna Gertrude:** born June 1, 1923
v- **BOSSARD Harry Peters:** born February 6, 1926

237 **BOSSARD Roy:** (*Judd, Simon, George, Melchior, Phillip*) was born ca 1895

in West Milford, New Jersey, son of Judd Bossard and Jennie Richards. He married Gloria (unknown maiden name). No issue. No further records.

238 **BOSSARD Helen**: (*Judd, Simon, George, Melchior, Phillip*) was born 1900 in West Milford, New Jersey, daughter of Judd Bossard and Jennie Richards. She married (1) Mr. Parker and (2) Russell Roome. They have two children.

239 **BOSSARD Edna**: (*Judd, Simon, George, Melchior, Phillip*) was born 1906 in West Milford, New Jersey, daughter of Judd Bossard and Jennie Richards. She married John Decker. She died 1973 in West Milford. No further records.

One child:
i- DECKER John:

240 **BOSSARD William**: (*Judd, Simon, George, Melchior, Phillip*) was born in West Milford, New Jersey, son of Judd Bossard and Jennie Richards. Wife's name unknown. They have three children. No further records.

241 **SMITH Fred R.**: (*Elizabeth Cross, Veronica, George, Melchior, Phillip*) was born September 12, 1871 in Reading, New York, son of Eugene K. Smith and Elizabeth Cross. He married November 18, 1895, Lizzie B. Barrett born October 1874, daughter of Anson Barrett and Susan Mc Intyre. He died February 13, 1901 and is buried in the New Reading cemetery.

One child:
i- SMITH Harry E.: born ca 1900. He was in Fulton, New York in 1925.

242 **PHINNEY Grace**: (*Maude Cross, Veronica, George, Melchior, Phillip*) was born January 23, 1889 in Reading, New York, daughter of William Phinney and Maude Cross. She married Frank Burton and they moved to Utah or Montana. No further records.

One known child:
i- BURTON Jane Elizabeth: born December 12, 1915

243 **PERSONIUS Grace A.**: (*Clara, Anson, George, Melchior, Phillip*) was born December 28, 1885 in Spencer, New York, daughter of Myron Personius and Clara Eddy Bossard. She married (1) October 4, 1905, Miles Lane born March 2, 1879. He died June 14, 1948 in Ithaca, New York and she married (2) Clarence Ashton Wood on August 2, 1952. She married (3), October 8, 1961, Joseph Britten Koons. She died October 22, 1982 in Oriskany Falls, New York. No issue.

244 **PERSONIUS Adrian:** (*Clara, Anson, George, Melchior, Phillip*) was born March 27, 1896 in Lansing, New York, son of Myron Personius and Clara Eddy Bossard. He married March 4, 1920, Olive Sill. Olive died June 29, 1985 in Painted Post, New York.

One child born in Lansing, New York
496 i- **PERSONIUS Doris:** born May 9, 1923

245 **BOSSARD Arthur Alfred:** (*Charles, Anson, George, Melchior, Phillip*) was born April 23, 1882 in Schuyler Co. New York, son of Charles Bossard and Elizabeth Smith. He married December 17, 1902, Mabel Wilson born November 5, 1883, daughter of Fremont Wilson and Della Babcock. He died in Enfield, New York, September 27, 1952 and Mabel died December 28, 1964. They are buried in Hayts Corners, New York.

Children born in Enfield, New York:
497 i- **BOSSARD Margaret Thelma:** born December 7, 1907
498 ii- **BOSSARD Lucelia Elizabeth:** born April 14, 1910
iii- **BOSSARD Foster Wilson:** born September 26, 1911. He is living in Ithaca, New York, unmarried.
499 iv- **BOSSARD Winifred Martha:** born November 12, 1913
500 v- **BOSSARD Myron Arthur:** born August 31,1918
501 vi- **BOSSARD Robert William:** born August 14, 1920
vii- **BOSSARD Stanley:** infant, died October 24, 1921
502 viii- **BOSSARD Betty Jane:** born April 16, 1926 in Ithaca

246 **BOSSARD Lottie Annette:** (*Charles, Anson, George, Melchior, Phillip*) was born June 30, 1887 in Townsend, New York, daughter of Charles Bossard and Elizabeth Smith. She married November 11, 1909, Burt Kibbe born March 10, 1883 in North Bingham, Pennsylvania, son of George W. Kibbe and Dorothy Fuller. She died January 3, 1971 and Burt died February 15, 1958. They are buried in Ulyssis, Pennsylvania.

Children born in Genessee, Pennsylvania:
503 i- **KIBBE Vivian Florence:** born March 30, 1911
504 ii- **KIBBE Ramon:** born May 6, 1913

247 **BOSSARD Florence Catherine:** (*Charles, Anson, George, Melchior, Phillip*) was born July 14, 1889 in Enfield, New York, daughter of Charles Bossard and Elizabeth Smith. She married April 24, 1918, Roy Duncan Mc Millan born September 19, 1893, son of John Mc Millan and Emma Ball. She died September 5, 1978 and Roy died September 22, 1981 in Paris, Texas.

Children born in Ithaca, New York:
i- **MC MILLAN John Duncan:** born March 9, 1922 and died March 10,

1922, buried in Hayts corners.
505 **ii- MC MILLAN Charles Duncan**: born May 20, 1923

248 **BOSSARD Jessie Elizabeth**: (*Charles, Anson, George, Melchior, Phillip*) was born June 4, 1894 in Enfield, New York, daughter of Charles Bossard and Elizabeth Smith. She married (1) April 4, 1917, Harold Bowman Genung born September 2, 1893 in Ithaca, New York, son of John Aubrey and Isabelle Genung. She married (2) May 17, 1944, Riley Henry Heath. She died January 1985 in Binghamton, New York and was cremated.

Children by first marriage:
506 **i- GENUNG Harold Bowman Jr.**: born August 18, 1919
507 **ii- GENUNG John Bossard**: born January 13, 1922

249 **BOSSARD Claude**: (*William, Anson, George, Melchior, Phillip*) was born May 6, 1885 in Odessa, New York, son of William Bossard and Sarah Allen. He married December 15, 1910 in Fremont, New York, Cora Voltz born December 14, 1892, daughter of George Voltz and Elizabeth Emmer. He died May 22, 1960 and Cora died 1974. They are buried in Rural cemetery in Hornell, New York.

Children born in Howard, New York:
508 **i- BOSSARD Clarence Albert**: born August 18, 1913
509 **ii- BOSSARD Harold Willis**: born February 11, 1916
510 **iii- BOSSARD Doris Alta**: born October 15, 1922

250 **BOSSARD Mary**: (*William, Anson, George, Melchior, Phillip*) known as 'Matie', was born June 16, 1886 in Dix, New York, daughter of William Bossard and Sarah Allen. She married (1) December 19, 1906 in Howard, New York, Walter Horton. They were divorced and she married (2) Reuben Hurlburt. She died May 3, 1966 in Hornell, New York and is buried in the Rural cemetery of Hornell. Reuben died November 18, 1964.

Children of first marriage, born in Hornell, New York:
i- HORTON Thelma Arline: born November 16, 1910 and is living in Hornell, unmarried.
511 **ii- HORTON Orlo Lauren**: born March 14, 1917

251 **BOSSARD Fred**: (*William, Anson, George, Melchior Phillip*) was born May 24, 1888 in Howard, New York, son of William Bossard and Sarah Allen. He married (1) Anna (Roe) Coots, born 1888. She was adopted by James Coots and Hattie Page. She died August 18, 1933 in Hornell, New York and Fred married (2) October 9, 1938 in Wellsboro, Pennsylvania, Sophia Lenchiki. Fred died January 28, 1943. Fred and Anna are buried in Rural cemetery in Hornell.

Children:
512 **i- BOSSARD Harriet**: born April 11, 1910
513 **ii- BOSSARD William Anson**: born February 6, 1913
514 **iii- BOSSARD Merlin**: born March 15, 1915
515 **iv- BOSSARD Marion**: born February 11, 1920
516 **v- BOSSARD Kenneth**: born March 10, 1922
Children by 2nd marriage:
vi- BOSSARD Fred: born May 14, 1940
vii- BOSSARD Robert: born September 4, 1941

252 **BOSSARD Roy**: (*William, Anson, George, Melchior, Phillip*) was born September 2, 1896 in Howard, New York, son of William Bossard and Sarah Allen. He married June 22, 1915 in Hornell, New York, Florence Mabel Jaynes born June 8, 1896 in Hornell, New York, daughter of Charles Jaynes and Ervie Alger. Roy was in an automobile accident near Dansville, New York and died in the Dansville Hospital, August 1, 1938. Florence died December 23, 1978 and they are buried in Rural cemetery in Hornell, New York.

Children:
517 **i- BOSSARD Aletha Ruth**: born May 6, 1916 in Howard
Children born in Hornell, New York:
518 **ii- BOSSARD Mildred Inez**: born April 25, 1922
519 **iii- BOSSARD Merle Roy**: born October 8, 1926
520 **iv- BOSSARD Glenn Allen**: born June 27, 1931

253 **BOSSARD Charlotte Maude**: (*William, Anson, George, Melchior, Phillip*) known as 'Lottie', was born January 9, 1901 in Howard, New York, daughter of William Bossard and Sarah Allen. She married (1) November 18, 1919 in Howard, Frank Hobart Smith born May 4, 1897 in Hornellsville, New York, son of Hobart Clinton Smith and Hannah Belle Leonard. He died September 15, 1951 and Lottie married (2) October 12, 1964, Michael Cannella. He died June 21, 1965 and is buried on Long Island. She died March 19, 1985 in Hornell. Frank and Lottie are buried in the Rural cemetery in Hornell.

Children:
521 **i- SMITH Ernest Glen**: born September 13, 1920
522 **ii- SMITH Mary Louise**: born May 30, 1928

254 **BOSSARD Lawrence Orlo**: (*William, Anson, George, Melchior, Phillip*) was born December 14, 1903 in Howard, New York, son of William Bossard and Sarah Allen. He married August 18, 1924 in Fremont, New York, Marion Josephine Schaumberg born July 23, 1901 in Hornellsville, New York, daughter of John Casper Schaumberg and Jeanette Wells. He died March 27, 1961 in Howard, New York and is buried in Rural cemetery in Hornell. Marion is living in Hornell with her son, Gerald.

Children born in Hornell, New York:

523 i- **BOSSARD Gerald Louis**: born June 19, 1926
524 ii- **BOSSARD Dorothy Jean**: born January 2, 1930
iii- **BOSSARD Elizabeth Ann**: born August 9, 1935
525 iv- **BOSSARD Jacqueline Lou**: born April 26, 1941

255 **BOSSARD Inez Velma**: (*William, Anson, George, Melchior, Phillip*) was born April 4, 1906 in Howard, New York, daughter of William Bossard and Sarah Allen. She married October 30, 1924 in Howard, New York, Lloyd Cameron Palmer born November 27, 1902 in Fremont, New York, son of Chester Arthur Palmer and Minnie Myers. She died June 18, 1969 in Rochester, New York and Lloyd died February 11, 1978. They are buried in the Howard cemetery.

Children born in Hornell, New York:

526 i- **PALMER Lorena June**: born July 10, 1928
527 ii- **PALMER Luella Ann**: born January 17, 1931
528 iii- **PALMER Allen Duane**: born May 27, 1932
529 iv- **PALMER Betty Joanne**: born September 2, 1933
530 v- **PALMER Barbara Jean**: born January 14, 1935
vi- **PALMER Alvin Carl**: born November 30, 1940. He was killed in a corn picker accident on March 25, 1957 on the Bennett farm in Howard, New York and is buried in the Howard cemetery.

256 **BOSSARD Lorena Althea**: (*Fred, Anson, George, Melchior, Phillip*) known as 'Aletha' was born June 4, 1894 in Watkins, New York, daughter of Fred Bossard and Lorena Pike. She married June 30, 1925 in Groton, New York, Howard Eugene De Camp born November 11, 1894 in Brighton, New York, son of Dana De Camp and Sarah Cushman. Howard was a veteran of World War I and served as an industrial dentist at Corning Glass Works, retiring in 1958. He died October 27, 1960 and Aletha died March 6, 1978 in Corning, New York. No issue.

257 **BOSSARD Anson Chester**: (*Fred, Anson, George, Melchior, Phillip*) was born February 22, 1896 in Townsend, New York, son of Fred Bossard and Lorena Pike. He married (1) October 25, 1923, Margaretta Peguese Priestly born November 5, 1895 in Philadelphia, daughter of Emil Peguese and Martha Daley. She died December 15, 1940 and Anson married (2) Mildred Theresa Myers, born October 17, 1911, daughter of George Myers and Florence Decker. She is living in Philadelphia. Anson died August 12, 1970 and is buried at Groton, New York.

Children of first marriage:

531 i- **BOSSARD Charles Priestly**: born December 29,1915 son of Herman Priestly and Margaretta Peguese and adopted by Anson Bossard.
532 ii- **BOSSARD Anson Chester Jr.**: born August 12, 1927 at Cortland, New York

533 iii- **BOSSARD Margaretta Lorena**: born August 28, 1936 at Syracuse, New York
Children by second marriage born in Philadelphia:
534 iv- **BOSSARD Mary Joan Mildred**: born October 9, 1946
535 v- **BOSSARD Peter Robert John**: born June 12, 1949
536 vi- **BOSSARD Paul Delmer John**: born May 18, 1950
537 vii- **BOSSARD Diane Denise Rose**: born June 5, 1952

258 BOSSARD Charlie Asil: (*Fred, Anson, George, Melchior, Phillip*) was born August 21, 1898 at Newfield, New York, son of Fred Bossard and Lorena Pike. He married March 18, 1921 at East Lansing, New York, Florence Leola Buck born February 9, 1902, daughter of Alson Buck and Hattie Luce. He died May 25, 1956 at Groton, New York. Florence is still living in Groton.

Children born at E. Lansing, New York:
538 i- **BOSSARD Lawrence Alson**: born December 5, 1923
Children born at W. Groton, New York:
539 ii- **BOSSARD Clifton Asil**: born June 5, 1926
540 iii- **BOSSARD Beverly Ann**: born August 11, 1935
541 iv- **BOSSARD Charlie Alton**: born July 3, 1938
542 v- **BOSSARD Beth Elaine**: born November 9, 1941

259 BOSSARD Marjorie Eliza: (*Fred, Anson, George, Melchior, Phillip*) was born February 8, 1901 at Lake Ridge, New York, daughter of Fred Bossard and Lorena Pike. She married October 27, 1927 at Groton, New York, Charles Wesley Bogardus born April 24, 1899 in Weedsport, New York, son of Marcus Bogardus and Mary Hoffman. Charles died July 17, 1968 at Syracuse, New York and Marjorie died in 1986 at Syracuse.

Children born at Weedsport, New York:
543 i- **BOGARDUS Neale Fred**: born May 6, 1932
ii- **BOGARDUS Gerald Charles**: born April 22, 1935. He was killed in an industrial plane crash near St. Augustine, Florida, October 2, 1962.

260 BOSSARD Irma Stella: (*Fred, Anson, George, Melchior, Phillip*) known as 'Stella' was born September 30, 1904 at Goodyears Corners, New York, daughter of Fred Bossard and Lorena Pike. She married May 18, 1927 at Groton, New York, Glen Hoffman Bogardus born January 27, 1902 at Weedsport, New York, son of Marcus Bogardus and Mary Hoffman.

One child born in Buffalo:
544 i- **BOGARDUS Clinton Glen**: born July 15, 1930

261 **BOSSARD Kermit Clarence**: (*Fred, Anson, George, Melchior, Phillip*) was born January 5, 1906 at Groton, New York, son of Fred Bossard and Lorena Pike. He married May 16, 1943 at Cohoes, New York, Theresa Hebert born July 18, 1914 at Rouse's Point, New York, daughter of Domina Hebert and Regina Bourgeois. He died November 23, 1973 at Troy, New York. Theresa is still living in Troy.

One child born at Troy, New York:
545 i- **BOSSARD Kermit Jr.**: born April 5, 1951

262 **BOSSARD Winona Armorel**: (*Fred, Anson, George, Melchior, Phillip*) was born April 6, 1914 at Groton, New York, daughter of Fred Bossard and Lorena Pike. She married September 18, 1937 at Groton, New York, Edward Towner. He died November 19, 1944 in Belgium, during World War II. Winona died April 21, 1983 in Phildelphia.

One child born in Phildelphia:
546 i- **TOWNER Douglas Edward**: born February 1, 1941

263 **BONHAM Wallace Lee**: (*Susan Alvers, Andrew, Melchior, Phillip*) was born September 5, 1874 in Osceola, Pennsylvania, son of Myron Bonham and Susan A. Bosard. He died January 11, 1933. No further records.

264 **BONHAM Edward H.**: (*Susan, Alvers, Andrew, Melchior, Phillip*) was born June 13, 1887 in Osceola, Pennsylvania, son of Myron Bonham and Susan A. Bosard. He married Vera Brown, born May 17, 1888 at Osceola. She died October 8, 1918 and Edward died September 12, 1921. No records found of any children.

265 **BOSWORTH Henry L.**: (*Urbana Bosworth, Maria, Andrew, Melchior, Phillip*) was born October 1875 in Osceola, son of Urbana Bosworth and Anna Hoyt. See Myra Bosard #271 for further records.

266 **BOSWORTH May S.**: (*Urbana Bosworth, Alvers, Andrew, Melchior, Phillip*) was born May 1878 Osceola, Pennsylvania, daughter of Urbana Bosworth and Ann Hoyt. She married July 10, 1901, Dr. David Arthur Patterson born 1868 in Osceola. He died in 1927 and May died in 1961. They are buried in the Fairview Cemetery in Osceola. No records found of any children.

267 **BOSWORTH Ford E.**: (*Charles Bosworth, Maria, Andrew, Melchior, Phillip*) was born January 1878, son of Charles Bosworth and Ida V. Seely. He married Leah (unknown maiden name) born November 1878. He was in Wyalusing,

Bradford Co., Pennsylvania in 1900. No further records.

One known child:
i- BOSWORTH John: born April 1900

268 BOSARD Ray F.: (*Kirtland, Arthur, Andrew, Melchior, Phillip*) a twin, born June 24, 1879 in Chatham, Tioga Co., Pennsylvania, son of Kirtland and Harriet Bosard. He married Fannie (unknown maiden name), born 1873. She died in 1958 and he died in 1935. No records found for any children.

269 BOSARD Adelaide: (*Kirtland, Arthur, Andrew, Melchior, Phillip*) was born February 7, 1894 in Osceola, Pennsylvania daughter of Kirtland and Harriet Bosard. She married Walter G. Cole, born 1899. She died in 1916 in Middlebury, Pennsylvania and Walter died in 1947. They are buried in the Hammond cemetery in Middlebury. No further records.

270 BOSARD Robert H.: (*James, Andrew, K., Andrew, Melchior, Phillip*) was born April 1875 in Wellsboro, son of James Huntington Bosard and Rebecca Faulkner. He married June 1889 in Grand Forks, N. Dakota Jessie A. Miller, born March 1880. He attended North Dakota Agricultural College and the State University and entered the Columbian Law School of Washington, D. C. as as senior, graduating in 1897. He went into partnership with his Father in his law firm in Grand Forks. No further records.

271 BOSARD Myra S.: (*Jerome, Andrew K., Andrew, Melchior, Phillip*) was born June 1873 in Osceola, Pennsylvania, daughter of Jerome Bosard and Alice M. Bosworth. She married December 22, 1897, Henry L. Bosworth born 1875, son of Urbana Bosworth and Ann Hoyt. She died 1947 and Henry died 1957 in Osceola. They are buried in Fairview cemetery. No records of children. See number 265, Henry Bosworth.

272 BOSARD Louise: (*William B., Andrew K., Andrew, Melchior, Phillip*) was born July 7, 1880 in Osceola, Pennsylvania, daughter of William B. Bosard and Carrie Fical. She married October 31, 1912, Wilbur Leroy Longfellow born ca 1880. She died September 1956 in Port Angeles, Washington and Wilbur died November 1957, same place.

Children:
547 **i- LONGFELLOW Allen Leroy**: born October 21, 1913
548 **ii- LONGFELLOW Lila Louise**: born May 6, 1915

273 BOSARD James Huntington: (*William B., Andrew K., Andrew, Melchior,*

Phillip) was born August 1882 in Grand Forks, North Dakota, son of William B. Bosard and Carrie Fical. He married Sade Wells. He died September 1976 in Roseburg, Oregon. No further records.

274 **BOSARD Ralph Mortimer**: (*William B., Andrew K., Andrew, Melchior, Phillip*) was born February 1887 in Grand Forks, North Dakota, son of William B. Bosard and Carrie Fical. He married Irene Van Hoot, born April 15, 1906. He died August 29, 1965 in Emerado, North Dakota. Irene was still living in Emerado in 1989.

Children:
i- **BOSARD James Rogers**:
ii- **BOSARD Roy L.**:
iii- **BOSARD Rita**:
iv- **BOSARD William B.**:

275 **REDFIELD Helen**: (*Emma, Andrew K., Andrew, Melchior, Phillip*) was born March 1891 in Osceola, Pennsylvania, daughter of Joseph Redfield and Emma Bosard. She married John O. Pattison. No further records.

Children:
549 i- **PATTISON Helen C.**: born 1912
ii- **PATTISON John R.**: born 1915 and died 1916
550 iii- **PATTISON Jane R.**: born 1921

276 **REDFIELD Albert Lee**: (*Emma, Andrew K., Andrew, Melchior, Phillip*) was born September 1894 in Osceola, Pennsylvania, son of Joseph Redfield and Emma Bosard. He married (1) Florence Webb, born 1888. She died 1959 and he married (2) Jamesia Longwell. He died in 1973 and is buried in the Keeneyville cemetery in Keeneyville, Pennsylvania.

One child:
i- **REDFIELD Joseph B.**: born 1927 and died at birth

277 **REDFIELD Mark B.**: (*Emma, Andrew K., Andrew, Melchior, Phillip*) was born March 3, 1898 in Osceola, Pennsylvania, son of Joseph Redfield and Emma Bosard. He married Dorothy Bauer. Mark died in 1989 and is buried in the Keeneyville cemetery in Keeneyville, Pennsylvania.

Children:
551 i- **REDFIELD Joseph B.**: born 1939 and died 1971. He is also buried in the Keeneyville cemetery.
552 ii- **REDFIELD Mark Jr.**: born 1942
553 iii- **REDFIELD Anthony Lee**: born 1949

278 **TREAT Mabel Almina**: (*Elizabeth, Andrew K., Andrew, Melchior, Phillip*) was born June 4, 1894 in Chatham, Pennsylvania, daughter of Jesse Treat and Elizabeth Ann Bosard. She married March 18, 1916, Waldo Seldon Butler. She died December 24, 1922 in Deerfield, Pennsylvania and is buried in the Butler Hill cemetery near Knoxville. Waldo is still living.

Children:
554 i- **BUTLER Franklin Jesse**: born September 27, 1917
555 ii- **BUTLER Erma Maude**: born April 8, 1920
iii- **BUTLER infant**: died at birth December 1922

279 **TREAT Jessie Ethel**: (*Elizabeth, Andrew K., Andrew, Melchior, Phillip*) was born May 9, 1897 in Chatham, Pennsylvania, daughter of Jesse Treat and Elizabeth Ann Bosard. She married June 20, 1917, Louis Jacob Zundel born August 6, 1891. She died December 19, 1971 and Louis died July 22, 1974.

Children:
556 i- **ZUNDEL Ruth Evelyn**: born May 31, 1918
557 ii- **ZUNDEL Thelma Louise**: born May 23, 1925
558 iii- **ZUNDEL Betty Joette**: born December 23, 1927

280 **TREAT Ernestine Maude**: (*Elizabeth, Andrew K., Andrew, Melchior, Phillip*) was born May 21, 1899 in Chatham, Pennsylvania, daughter of Jesse Treat and Elizabeth Ann Bosard. She married (1) in 1930, Arthur Cooney and (2) William Karschner. No issue.

281 **TREAT Ernest Bosard**: (*Elizabeth, Andrew K., Andrew, Melchior, Phillip*) was born July 30, 1909 in Chatham Township, Pennsylvania, son of Jesse Treat and Elizabeth Ann Bosard. He married December 19, 1932, Helen Rizer born July 18, 1908. He died April 20, 1968 in Cumberland, Maryland.

One child born Cumberland, Maryland:
559 i- **TREAT Sondra Ann**: born June 3, 1938

282 **OWLET Fordyce Deroy**: (*Anna Maria, Melchior, Andrew, Melchior, Phillip*) was born February 17, 1884 in Chatham, Pennsylvania, son of Andrew Owlet and Anna Maria Bosard. He married March 31, 1916, Emily M. Perry born 1879, daughter of W. H. and Ada Perry. She died November 26, 1919 and Fordyce died December 11, 1961. They are buried in the Riverside cemetery in Knoxville, Pennsylvania. No issue.

283 **OWLET Fay Dollie**: (*Anna M., Melchior, Andrew, Melchior, Phillip*) was born August 19, 1886 in Chatham Township, Pennsylvania, daughter of Andrew Owlet

and Anna Maria Bosard. She married July 4, 1902, John E. Whitney born 1870. He died 1937 and she died April 8, 1961. They are buried in the Nelson cemetery.

Children:
i- WHITNEY Dallas:
ii- WHITNEY Douglas:
560 **iii- WHITNEY Marie:**

284 OWLET Jessie Luella: (*Anna Maria, Melchior, Andrew, Melchior, Phillip*) was born January 26, 1888, daughter of Andrew Owlet and Anna Maria Bosard. She married February 17, 1914, James B. Leonard Jr. born 1887, son of James and Kate Leonard. He died in 1960 and Jessie died September 6, 1969 in Wellsboro, Pennsylvania. They are buried in the Nelson cemetery. No issue.

285 OWLET John Bosard: (*Anna Maria, Melchior, Andrew, Melchior, Phillip*) was born November 26, 1890 in Chatham Township, Pennsylvania, son of Andrew Owlet and Anna Maria Bosard. He married November 4, 1914, Eva Mateson born June 22, 1888, daughter of J. S. Mateson and Florence Short. He died February 14, 1960 and Eva died August 15, 1977. They are buried in the Nelson cemetery.

Children:
561 **i- OWLET John Bosard Jr.:**
562 **ii- OWLET Florence:**

286 OWLET Charles E.: (*Anna Maria, Melchior, Andrew, Melchior, Phillip*) was born September 9, 1892 in Chatham Township, Pennsylvania, son of Andrew Owlet and Anna Maria Bosard. He married May 7, 1919, Leah Butler born July 27, 1897, daughter of Harvey Butler and Martha Gee. He died February 3, 1944 and Leah died January 17, 1974. They are buried in the Riverside cemetery in Knoxville.

Children:
i- OWLET Martha: born February 10, 1921
563 **ii- OWLET Charles B.:** born July 20, 1924
564 **iii- OWLET Gweneth:** born March 26, 1928
565 **iv- OWLET Andrew V.:** born June 22, 1930

287 OWLET Carlton Andrew: (*Anna Maria, Melchior, Andrew, Melchior, Phillip*) was born July 26, 1894 in Nelson, Pennsylvania, son of Andrew Owlet and Anna Maria Bosard. He married March 25, 1917, Fay Leonard. He died June 20, 1963 and is buried in the Nelson cemetery. No death record found for Fay.

Children:
566 **i- OWLET Harold:** born March 8, 1923
567 **ii- OWLET Wilma:** born February 16, 1918

288 **OWLET Mark F.**: (*Anna Maria, Melchior, Andrew, Melchior, Phillip*) was born June 24, 1897 in Gold, Potter Co., Pennsylvania. son of Andrew Owlet and Anna Maria Bosard. He married April 16, 1922, Martha O. Buck born 1903, daughter of Walter Buck and Jennie May Bliss. He died November 5, 1979 in Wellsboro, and is buried in the Nelson cemetery.

Children:
568 i- **OWLET Elva**: born September 9, 1923
569 ii- **OWLET Helen Marie**: born February 28, 1926.
570 iii- **OWLET Franklin Deroy**: born November 4, 1928
571 iv- **OWLET Marion Louella**: born November 8, 1931

289 **OWLET Burton Wesley**: (*Anna Maria, Melchior, Andrew, Melchior, Phillip*) was born July 15, 1899 in Gold, Potter Co., Pennsylvania, son of Andrew Owlet and Anna Maria Bosard. He married Alice Bowman, born July 14, 1893, daughter of Joseph Bowman and Amelia Owlet. He died September 22, 1968 at the Robert Packer Hospital of Sayre, Pennsylvania and is buried in the Liberty Corners cemetery in Bradford Co., Pennsylvania. No death record found for Alice Owlet.

Children adopted by Burton and Alice:
572 i- **OWLET Kenneth**: born March 13, 1939
ii- **OWLET Mary**: born April 20, 1940

290 **OWLET Thomas Mack**: (*Anna Maria, Melchior, Andrew, Melchior, Phillip*) was born December 13, 1902, son of Andrew Owlet and Anna Maria Bosard. First marriage unknown. His second marriage was to Mary Bower and he married (3) Nora Miller in 1969. No record of children or death dates found.

291 **LAUFER Stewart**: (*Lavina Huffsmith, Hanna, Peter, Melchior, Phillip*) was born September 2, 1855 in Hamilton Township, Pennsylvania, son of Henry Laufer and Levina Huffsmith. He married January 22, 1880, Miriam Stucker born April 28, 1863. He died June 14, 1915 and Miriam died December 27, 1947. They are buried in the Buena Vista cemetery in Chestnuthill, Pennsylvania.

292 **LAUFER Alice**: (*Levina Huffsmith, Hanna, Peter, Melchior, Phillip*) was born November 12, 1864 in Hamilton Township, Pennsylvania, daughter of Hanry Laufer and Levina Huffsmith. She married October 9, 1886 in Stroudsburg, John Leonard Haney born May 31, 1967, son of J. Henry Haney and Mary Elizabeth Sceurman. She died 1933 and John married (2) Laura Ebersole. He died August 26, 1954. They are buried in the Stroudsburg cemetery. No issue.

293 **LAUFER Ellen**: (*Levina Huffsmith, Hanna, Peter, Melchior, Phillip*) was born September 1869 in Hamilton Township, Pennsylvania, daughter of Henry Laufer

and Lavina Huffsmith. She married Horace Wolf and removed to Connecticutt. No further records.

294 **RINKER Anna L.**: (*Sarah Huffsmith, Hanna, Peter, Melchior, Phillip*) was born November 1859 in Hamilton Township, Pennsylvania, daughter of Amandis Rinker and Sarah Jane Huffsmith. She married November 21, 1891, Franklin Eckert born December 1852, son of James and Susan Eckert. He died in 1948 and Anna died 1953 in Middletown, New York. They are buried in the Stroudsburg cemetery.

One child:

573 **i- ECKERT Leroy**: born April 9, 1896

295 **RINKER Peter L.**: (*Sarah Huffsmith, Hanna, Peter, Melchior, Phillip*) was born October 8, 1862 in Hamilton Township, Pennsylvania, son of Amandis Rinker and Sarah Jane Huffsmith. He married, April 2, 1886, Ella A. Kerrick born ca 1866. No records of death dates found.

Children born in Stroudsburg, Pennsylvania:

i- RINKER Howard: born October 1886

574 **ii- RINKER Russell**: born January 30, 1893

296 **RINKER Stewart**: (*Sarah Huffsmith, Hanna, Peter, Melchior, Phillip*) was born October 1865 in Hamilton Township, Pennsylvania, son of Amandis Rinker and Sarah Jane Huffsmith. He married September 22, 1888, Mrs. Fannie Walton. He died July 8, 1931 and Fannie died in 1931. They are buried in the Stroudsburg cemetery. No known children.

297 **RINKER Charles S.**: (*Sarah Huffsmith, Hanna, Peter, Melchior, Phillip*) was born August 2, 1866 in Hamilton Township, Pennsylvania, son of Amandis Rinker and Sarah Jane Huffsmith. He died May 20, 1899 in Stroudsburg, leaving a wife and one son. No names found. He is buried in the Stroudsburg cemetery.

298 **RINKER Mary F.**: (*Sarah Huffsmith, Hanna, Peter, Melchior, Phillip*) was born November 22, 1868 in Hamilton Township, Pennsylvania, daughter of Amandis Rinker and Sarah Jane Huffsmith. She married December 24, 1888, Lewis E. Rhodes born November 16, 1866, son of Jacob and Lucinda Rhodes. He died October 14, 1924 and Mary died December 29, 1968. They are buried in the Stroudsburg cemetery.

One known child:

575 **i- RHODES Grover C.**: born 1890

299 RINKER Edwin: (*Sarah Huffsmith, Hanna, Peter, Melchior, Phillip*) was born May 1874 in Hamilton Township, Pennsylvania, son of Amandis Rinker and Sarah Jane Huffsmith. He married in 1894, Ida Francis Smith born February 1878. He died March 1932. No death record found for Ida.

Children born in Stroudsburg:

i- **RINKER Elmer**: born July 9, 1894 and died August 2, 1894
ii- **RINKER Earl Arlington**: born August 1, 1896 and died July 17, 1953. Unknown if married.
iii- **RINKER Cora**: born November 1897
576 iv- **RINKER Horace William**: born January 21, 1899
577 v- **RINKER Clarence Franklin**: born January 18, 1902

300 HUFFSMITH William: (*George Huffsmith, Hanna, Peter, Melchior, Phillip*) was born 1876 in Hamilton Township, Pennsylvania, son of George and Emma Huffsmith. He married in 1906, Alta Lee born in Shawnee, Pennsylvania, daughter of George Lee and Harriet Derricke. She died, in Hornell, New York and is buried in the Shawnee cemetery in Monroe Co., Pennsylvania.

Children born in Stroudsburg:

578 i- **HUFFSMITH Clara**: born August 6, 1907
579 ii- **HUFFSMITH Harold**: born January 6, 1915
iii- **HUFFMSITH William Lloyd**: (twin) born May 18, 1911
iv- **HUFFSMITH Judson**: (twin) born May 18, 1911 and died September 19, 1940. He is buried in the Shawnee cemetery.
580 v- **HUFFSMITH George**: born February 28, 1919

301 HUFFSMITH Carrie: (*George Huffsmith, Hanna, Peter, Melchior, Phillip*) was born March 6, 1881 in Hamilton Township, Pennsylvania, daughter of George and Emma Huffsmith. She married October 9, 1903, Harry Williamson born 1878, son of James Williamson. She died 1920 and Harry died 1943.

Child:

i- **WILLIAMSON Harry R.**: born 1913

302 KLINKER Frank Isaiah: (*Sarah, John, Peter, Melchior, Phillip*) was born August 1862 in Hamilton Township, Pennsylvania, son of Jacob Klinker and Sarah Bossard. He married Laura V. Dash born December 1865, daughter of Henry H. and Annie E. Dash. No further records.

303 KLINKER William W.: (*Sarah, John, Peter, Melchior, Phillip*) was born June 1870 in Bethlehem, Pennsylvania, son of Jacob Klinker and Sarah Bossard. He married Viola L.(unknown maiden name), born February 1874. No further records.

304 **RUTH Matilda:** (*Lynford Ruth, Anna Catherine, Peter, Melchior, Phillip*) was born ca 1856, daughter of Lynford Ruth and Christina Heller. She married Edward Nixon born ca 1860. He died May 4, 1942 in Stroudsburg, Pennsylvania. No record found for Matilda.

305 **RUTH Adeline:** (*Lynford Ruth, Anna Catherine, Peter, Melchior, Phillip*) was born ca 1857, daughter of Lynford Ruth and Christina Heller. She married ______ Beck and lived in Phillipsburg, New Jersey in 1909. No further records.

306 **RUTH Catherine A.:** (*Lynford Ruth, Anna Catherine, Peter, Melchior, Phillip*) was born September 1, 1861, daughter of Lynford Ruth and Christina Heller. She married February 14, 1880, William L. Bates.

307 **RUTH Robert E.:** (*Lynford Ruth, Anna Catherine, Peter, Melchior, Phillip*) was born December 31, 1870 in Hamilton Township, Pennsylvania, twin son of Lynford Ruth and Christina Heller. He married May (unknown maiden name) born August 1875. He died October 12, 1900 in Stroudsburg. No issue.

308 **RUTH Ervin:** (*Joseph Ruth, Anna Catherine, Peter, Melchior, Phillip*) was born December 1861, son of Joseph Ruth and Sarah Frances Decker. He married in 1884, Mary E. Ward born September 1864. No record of death dates found.

Children:

581 i- **RUTH William:** born July 1884
ii- **RUTH Arlington:** born March 1886
iii- **RUTH Leroy:** born March 6, 1894

309 **RUTH Harry:** (*Joseph Ruth, Anna Catherine, Peter, Melchior, Phillip*) was born ca 1865, son of Joseph Ruth and Sarah Frances Decker. He married October 24, 1885, Mary M. Heller born 1860, daughter of Henry and Rachel Heller. No further records.

310 **RUTH Sanderson:** (*Joseph Ruth, Anna Catherine, Peter, Melchior, Phillip*) was born ca 1868, son of Joseph Ruth and Sarah Frances Decker. He married May 2, 1899, Ida Williams.

Children:

i- **RUTH Hazel Kirk:** born February 13,1900
ii- **RUTH Florence Bertha:** born August 12, 1901
iii- **RUTH Ethel Bell:** born September 23, 1904

311 **RUTH Clarence:** (*Joseph Ruth, Anna Catherine, Peter, Melchior, Phillip*) was born August 1870, son of Joseph Ruth and Sarah Frances Decker. He married November 4, 1893, Ida Coffman born September 1865 in New Jersey. He died 1940 and Ida died 1938.

Children:

i- **RUTH Elsa:** born August 1894
ii- **RUTH Joseph:** born March 10, 1899 and died young
582 iii- **RUTH Virginia:** born ca 1901
iv- **RUTH Richard Paul:** born April 20, 1903
v- **RUTH Mary Elnora:** born January 3, 1905

312 **RUTH Bertha:** (*Joseph Ruth, Anna Catherine, Peter, Melchior, Phillip*) was born ca 1871, daughter of Joseph Ruth and Sarah Frances Decker. She married June 1, 1903, Dewitt Clinton De Puy born December 14, 1852, son of Enos and Mary Ann De Puy. No further records.

313 **RUTH Martha A.:** (*Jacob Ruth, Anna Catherine, Peter, Melchior, Phillip*) was born August 8, 1863, daughter of Jacob and Anna Marie Ruth. She married February 20, 1889, John C. Sullivan born March 6, 1860, son of John A. and Hannah Sullivan. She died November 24, 1935 and John died April 13, 1932. They are buried in the Stroudsburg cemetery.

Children:

i- **SULLIVAN Ruth:** born ca 1890
583 ii- **SULLIVAN Mary:** born May 2, 1892
584 iii- **SULLIVAN Samuel:** born June 8, 1894
585 iv- **SULLIVAN Anna Marion:** born January 14, 1898

314 **RUTH Ellen Frances:** (*Jacob Ruth, Anna Catherine, Peter, Melchior, Phillip*) was born ca 1866, daughter of Jacob and Anna Marie Ruth. She married July 11, 1893, Edward A. Wolfe born 1865, son of Edward and Ernestine Wolfe. He died May 13, 1943 in Stroudsburg, Pennsylvania. No known children.

315 **RUTH Mary A.:** (*Jacob Ruth, Anna Catherine, Peter, Melchior, Phillip*) was born ca 1867, daughter of Jacob and Anna Marie Ruth. She married December 8, 1886, Charles H. Huntzman born 1863, son of William and Miriam Huntzman. No further records.

316 **RUTH Edward M.:** (*Jacob Ruth, Anna Catherine, Peter, Melchior, Phillip*) was born January 9, 1872 in Stroudsburg, Pennsylvania, son of Jacob and Anna Marie Ruth. He married March 19, 1893, Mary E. Mareau born August 23, 1872 in Chester, Pennsylvania. She died October 7, 1918 and Edward married (2) June 16,

1923, Claudine Henry born 1873, daughter of John Newton and Alexia Stone. He died July 2, 1927 and they are buried in Stroudsburg.

One child by first marriage, born in Stroudsburg:
586 i- **RUTH Anna Geneva**: born August 21, 1897

317 RUTH John: (*Jacob Ruth, Anna Catherine, Peter, Melchior, Phillip*) was born March 22, 1877, son of Jacob and Anna Marie Ruth. He married Sarah (unknown maiden name). He died December 15, 1932 and is buried in Cherry Valley cemetery, Pennsylvania.

Children:
587 i- **RUTH Theodore Franklin**: born February 1, 1908
ii- **RUTH Irvin J.**:
588 iii- **RUTH Lorraine**:

318 RUTH Ada: (*Jacob Ruth, Anna Catherine, Peter, Melchior, Phillip*) was born March 1880, daughter of Jacob and Anna Marie Ruth. She married January 5, 1907, Amos J. Hartman.

319 RUTH Clara M.: (*James Ruth, Anna Catherine, Peter, Melchior, Phillip*) was born March 1877 in Hamilton Township, Pennsylvania, daughter of James and Ellen Ruth. She married May 12, 1900, George A. Frable born May 10, 1866, son of Charles Frable and Semaema Hawk. She died 1936 and George died 1939 in Gilbert, Pennsylvania. They are buried in the Gilbert cemetery.

Children:
i- **FRABLE Beulah**: born March 16, 1902

320 RUTH Edith Adella: (*James Ruth, Anna Catherine, Peter, Melchior, Phillip*) was born June 3, 1888 in Hamilton Township, Pennsylvania, daughter of James and Ellen Ruth. She married February 18, 1911, Robert R. Mittman of Northampton Co. No further records.

321 HANEY William J.: (*Martha Ruth, Anna Catherine, Peter, Melchior, Phillip*) was born December 24, 1870 in Hamilton Township, Pennsylvania, son of Israel Haney and Martha Jane Ruth. He married ca 1870, Rebecca (unknown maiden name). He died July 24, 1900 and is buried in Mt. Zion cemetery.

One child:
i- **HANEY William**: born 1899

322 HANEY Catherine E.: (*Martha Ruth, Anna Catherine, Peter, Melchior, Phillip*) was born ca 1872 in Hamilton Township, daughter of Israel Haney and Martha Jane Ruth. She married _____ Walsh.

323 HANEY Maggie M.: (*Martha Ruth, Anna Catherine, Peter, Melchior, Phillip*) was born July 3, 1875 in Hamilton Township, daughter of Israel Haney and Martha Jane Ruth. She married _____ Miller.

One child born in Stroudsburg, Pennsylvania:
i- MILLER Ethel: born September 4, 1894

324 HANEY Ellen S.: (*Martha Ruth, Anna Catherine, Peter, Melchior, Phillip*) was born ca 1878 in Hamilton Township, Pennsylvania, daughter of Israel Haney and Martha Jane Ruth. She married ______ Miller.

325 HANEY Elwood Clayton: (*Martha Ruth, Anna Catherine, Peter, Melchior, Phillip*) was born December 29, 1883 in Hamilton Township, Pennsylvania, son of Israel Haney and Martha Jane Ruth. He married 1905, Dorothy (unknown maiden name) born ca 1888.

Children:
589 **i- HANEY William J.**: born 1906
ii- HANEY Blanche Evelyn: born April 18 1907
iii- HANEY Richard Harvey: born April 13, 1908
iv- HANEY Burton Elwood: born August 21, 1914

326 HANEY Floyd M.: (*Martha Ruth, Anna Catherine, Peter, Melchior, Phillip*) was born 1886 in Hamilton Township, Pennsylvania, son of Israel Haney and Martha Jane Ruth. He married Alice Susan Kemmerer, born 1881. She died in 1957 and is buried in the Stroudsburg cemetery. No death record found for Floyd.

Known children:
i- HANEY Russell E.: born January 13,1906
ii-HANEY Evelyn Marguerite: born September 10, 1911

327 BOSSARD Lillie Louise: (*Charles, Melchior, Peter, Melchior, Phillip*) was born December 21, 1862 in Hamilton Township, Pennsylvania, daughter of Charles Bossard and Elizabeth Shoemaker. She married in 1882, Edwin A. Bartholomew born December 9, 1849, son of Frederick and Sarah Bartholomew. She died August 5, 1949 and Edwin died November 7, 1926. They are buried in Mt. Zion cemetery in Hamilton Township.

Children:

590 **i- BARTHOLOMEW Charles F.**: born August 2, 1884
ii- BARTHOLOMEW Harry M.: born June 24, 1886 and he died October 29, 1957, unmarried.
591 **iii- BARTHOLOMEW William Edwin**: born May 3, 1889
592 **iv- BARTHOLOMEW Lucy A.**: born February 2, 1897

328 **BOSSARD Fannie A.**: (*Charles, Melchior, Peter, Melchior Phillip*) was born October 9, 1866. She married (1) May 18, 1882, Alvin Fleyte born August 1857. He died in 1936 and is buried in Lakeview cemetery. She married (2) C. A. Goble. She is buried in Mt. Zion cemetery in Hamilton Township, no dates.

One child:
i- FLEYTE Mae: born September 1885

329 **BOSSARD Laura A.**: (*Charles, Melchior, Peter, Melchior, Phillip*) was born March 31, 1869 in Hamilton Township, Pennsylvania, daughter of Charles Bossard and Elizabeth Shoemaker. She married February 7, 1889, William A. Streepy born 1864, son of Samuel and Elizabeth Streepy. She died February 3, 1949 and is buried in Mt. Zion cemetery in Hamilton Township. No record of death date found for William. He died before 1949.

Children:
i- STREEPY Miles A.: born July 2, 1892 and died 1933.
593 **ii- STREEPY Helen E.**: born March 26, 1901

330 **HARMON Minnie**: (*Margaret, Melchior, Peter, Melchior, Phillip*) was born 1870 in Hamilton Township, Pennsylvania, daughter of Jacob Harmon and Margaret Bossard. She married Rev. C. W. T. Strasser. She died May 21, 1937 and he died March 4, 1960. No issue.

331 **HOOD William C.**: (*Susannah, John, Peter, Melchior, Phillip*) was born July 9, 1874, son of Samuel Hood and Susannah Bossard. He married Bessie M. Weaver. He died October 18, 1939 in Stroudsburg and Bessie died March 22, 1957. They are buried in the Stroudsburg cemetery.

One child:
i- HOOD Charlotte: born June 10, 1904 and died July 29, 1915 in Stroudsburg.

332 **MANSFIELD Charles**: (*Florinda, Melchior, Peter, Melchior, Phillip*) was born January 20, 1879 in Sroudsburg, Pennsylvania, son of Barnet Mansfield and Florinda Bossard. He married Gwen Johns. He died October 20, 1933 in Stroudsburg and Gwen died August 18, 1942. They are buried in the Stroudsburg

cemetery.

Children:
i- MANSFIELD Willetta: born May 1903
594 **ii- MANSFIELD Mary Catherine**: born July 28, 1905
iii- MANSFIELD Ralph:
595 **iv- MANSFIELD Ethel Elizabeth**: born June 16, 1914

333 **MANSFIELD Mamie**: (*Florinda, Melchior, Peter, Melchior, Phillip*) was born 1881, daughter of Barnet Mansfield and Florinda Bossard. She married George Smiley born 1880. He died in Stroudsburg in 1961. No death record found for Mamie. They are buried in the Stroudsburg cemetery. No issue.

334 **MANSFIELD Paul**: (*Florinda, Melchior, Peter, Melchior, Phillip*) was born January 1883, son of Barnet Mansfield and Florinda Bossard. He married Eletta Cadoo, born 1878. He died 1959 and she died January 27, 1969. They are buried in the Stroudsburg cemetery.

Children born in Stroudsburg, Pennsylvania:
596 **i- MANSFIELD Thomas Cadoo**: born August 31, 1907
ii- MANSFIELD Paul Jr.: born April 21, 1911 and died 1978 in Allentown, Pennsylvania, buried in Stroudsburg cemetery.
iii- MANSFIELD Florinda: born October 17, 1912

335 **GIERSCH Harry C.**: (*Mary Jane, Melchior, Peter, Melchior, Phillip*) was born September 1877 in Stroudsburg, Pennsylvania, son of Stephen Giersch and Mary Jane Bossard. He married May 19, 1903, Anna Ward born ca 1877 in Yorkshire, England. He died 1939 in Stroudsburg. No date of death found for Anna.

One known child:
597 **i- GEIRSCH Donald**: born 1905

336 **BOSSARD Melchior W.**: (*James, Melchior, Peter, Melchior, Phillip*) was born 1873 in Hamilton Township, Pennsylvania, son of James Bossard and Sarah H. Sceurman. He married September 2, 1896, Sarah Elizabeth Meixell born 1875, daughter of Andrew and Julia Meixell. He died February 2, 1952 in Riverdale, New Jersey and and she died in 1962. They are buried in Mt. Zion cemetery.

Known children:
i- BOSSARD James: He was living in Riverdale, New Jersey in 1952. No further records.
ii- BOSSARD Paul: He was living in Andover, New Jersey in 1952. No further records.
iii- BOSSARD Joseph: He was living in San Diego, California in 1952.

No further records.

337 **BOSSARD Mary Catherine:** (*James, Melchior, Peter, Melchior, Phillip*) was born April 4, 1874, daughter of James Bossard and Sarah H. Sceurman. She married August 16, 1894, Jacob Hartman born March 9, 1871, son of Jacob and Eva Jane Hartman. She died August 4, 1915 and he died December 23, 1937. They are buried in the Stroudsburg cemetery.

Children:

598 **i- HARTMAN Bessie Hilda:** born March 1, 1895
ii- HARTMAN Margaret Anna: born April 28, 1903 and died May 7, 1920, unmarried.
599 **iii- HARTMAN Helen Irene:** born September 30, 1907

338 **HANEY Nettie:** (*Anna E., Melchior, Peter, Melchior, Phillip*) was born 1873, daughter of Jerome Henry Haney and Anna E. Bossard. She married 1893, Benjamin Mackes born October 1866 in Stroudsburg, son of John Mackes and Elizabeth Wagner. He died April 15, 1951 and Nettie died April 20, 1951.

One child:

600 **i- MACKES John Henry:** born January 24, 1895

339 **HANEY Minnie:** (*Anna E., Melchior, Peter, Melchior, Phillip*) was born July 1874 in Hamilton Township, Pennsylvania, daughter of Jerome Henry Haney and Anna E. Bossard. She married 1894, Dayton Lesh born September 21, 1872, son of Nathan Lesh and Rachel Bossard. She died April 17, 1960 and he died November 15, 1960. They are buried in Stroudsburg cemetery.

Children:

i- : one child died in infancy
601 **ii- LESH Violet W.:** born September 14, 1896. She was adopted.

340 **HANEY Tilton:** (*Anna E., Melchior, Peter, Melchior, Phillip*) was born October 20, 1876 in Hamilton Township, Pennsylvania, son of Jerome Henry Haney and Anna E. Bossard. He married July 14, 1900, Laura Seigel born November 3, 1877, daughter of Alfred and Amanda Seigel. She died March 28, 1923 and Tilton married (2) Blanche Clements. She died in 1952 and is buried in Mt. Eaton cemetery.

One known child:

i- HANEY Claude: born December 1900 and died February 13, 1901.

341 **HANEY Harry:** (*Anna E., Melchior, Peter, Melchior, Phillip*) was born 1880

in Hamilton Township, Pennsylvania, son of Jerome Henry Haney and Anna E. Bossard. He married September 2, 1903, Bertha Snyder, born January 20, 1882, daughter of Frank and Ada Snyder. He died 1918 and is buried in Mt. Zion cemetery in Hamilton Township. She died July 26, 1973.

Children:
602 i- **HANEY Ada Blanche**: born September 16, 1904
603 ii- **HANEY Ruth Adaline**: born June 19, 1909

342 **HANEY Charles B.**: (*Anna E., Melchior, Peter, Melchior, Phillip*) was born May 22, 1888 in Hamilton Township, Pennsylvania, son of Jerome Henry Haney and Anna E. Bossard. He married December 2, 1911, Jennie L. Rinker born June 13, 1886, daughter of Edward and Mary Rinker. She died January 12, 1953 and Charles died August 8, 1960.

One Child:
604 i- **HANEY Mary Ellen**: born September 9, 1912

343 **HANEY Mabel Ruth**: (*Anna E., Melchior, Peter, Melchior, Phillip*) was born January 10, 1892, daughter of Jerome Henry Haney and Anna E. Bossard. She married April 19, 1919, William Ernest Snyder born September 25, 1888, son of Romanus Snyder and Martha A. Kirkhuff. She died June 7, 1960 and he died February 20, 1971. They are buried in the Kellersville cemetery in Hamilton Township.

Children:
605 i- **SNYDER Dora Madlyn**: born January 28, 1920
606 ii- **SNYDER Anna Elizabeth**: born February 25, 1922
iii- **SNYDER Roe Jerome**: born April 30, 1930 and died January 31, 1931 buried in Kellersville cemetery.

344 **BOSSARD Frank Sterling**: (*Franklin, Melchior, Peter, Melchior, Phillip*) was born April 1882, son of Franklin Bossard and S. Caroline Altemose. He married Ruth Fox, born 1892. He died April 28, 1948 and Ruth died March 13, 1970, both in Stroudsburg. They are buried in the Stroudsburg cemetery.

One child:
i- **BOSSARD William Fox**: born 1927 and died 1934

345 **BOSSARD Martha**: (*Samuel, Jacob, Peter, Melchior, Phillip*) was born March 27, 1866 in Hamilton Township, Pennsylvania, the daughter of Samuel Bossard and Margaret Jane Edinger. She married January 17, 1893, George F. Bartholomew, born 1867 in Jackson Township, son of George and Elizabeth Bartholomew.

Children:

i- **BARTHOLOMEW Margretta**: born November 2, 1893, She is living in Trumbull, Connecticutt, age 96.

ii- **BARTHOLOMEW Harold**: born November 24, 1894, and died October 3, 1895, buried Stroudsburg.

607 iii- **BARTHOLOMEW Sarah**: born September 23 1900

346 **BOSSARD Catherine**: (*Samuel, Jacob, Peter, Melchior, Phillip*) was born June 21, 1869 in Hamilton Township, Pennsylvania, daughter of Samuel Bossard and Margaret Jane Edinger. She married June 25, 1896, Allen P. Musselman born ca 1866, son of William and Catherine Musselman. He died January 1949 in Chester, Pennsylvania.

Children:

608 i- **MUSSELMAN Jean**:

ii- **MUSSELMAN Frederick**:

347 **BOSSARD Frederick Phillip**: (*Samuel, Jacob, Peter, Melchior, Phillip*) was born June 4, 1870 in Hamilton Township, Pennsylvania, son of Samuel Bossard and Margaret Jane Edinger. He married June 16, 1909, Elizabeth M. Morgan born May 31, 1882, daughter of Edward Morgan and Nora Tims. He died December 27, 1949 in Stroudsburg and Elizabeth died July 7, 1946. They are buried in Mt. Hope cemetery in Delaware Co., Pennsylvania.

Children born in Delaware Co.:

609 i- **BOSSARD Katherine**: (twin) born February 6, 1913

610 ii- **BOSSARD Elizabeth**: (twin) born February 6, 1913

348 **BOSSARD Robert Lee Phillip**: (*Samuel, Jacob, Peter, Melchior, Phillip*) was born August 27, 1874 in Hamilton Township, Pennsylvania, son of Samuel Bossard and Margaret Jane Edinger. He married November 20, 1906 in New York City, Margaret Brennan born March 4, 1888 in Tremont, Pennsylvania, daughter of Martin and Mary Ann Brennan He died June 27, 1942 and she died September 17, 1975. They are buried in the Stroudsburg Cemetery.

Children born in Chester, Pennsylvania:

i- **BOSSARD Samuel**: born February 4, 1912, and is living in New York City, unmarried.

611 ii- **BOSSARD Roberta**: born December 20, 1907

349 **BOSSARD Curvin**: (*Edwin, Jacob, Peter, Melchior, Phillip*) was born May 12, 1865 in Jackson Township, Pennsylvania, son of Edwin Bossard and Emma Walters. He went to Ida Grove, Iowa with his Grandparents, Jacob and Christina Bossard. He married January 1893, Minnie Maritz born May 9, 1874 in Pennsylvania,

daughter of John and Elizabeth Maritz. He died May 7, 1943 and Minnie died March 1954, both in Ida Grove, Iowa. They are buried in the Ida Grove Cemetery.

Children born in Ida Grove:

612 i- **BOSSARD Ina Mae**: born October 10, 1893
613 ii- **BOSSARD Carman Lloyd**: (twin) born February 3, 1896
614 iii- **BOSSARD Calvin Floyd**: (twin) born February 3, 1896
615 iv- **BOSSARD Gladys Irene**: born August 30, 1898
616 v- **BOSSARD Vera Emma**: born January 6, 1901
617 vi- **BOSSARD Cecil Alfred**: born August 6, 1903
618 vii- **BOSSARD Murriel Curvin**: born July 3, 1908
619 viii- **BOSSARD Marcelle Minnie**: born March 20, 1911

350 BOSSARD John: (*Edwin, Jacob, Peter, Melchior, Phillip*) was born June 23, 1870 in Hamilton Township, Pennsylvania, son of Edwin Bossard and Emma Walters. He married Ida, (unknown maiden name) and they resided in Moosic, Lackawanna Co., Pennsylvania. No further records.

351 BOSSARD Anna Levina: (*Edwin, Jacob, Peter, Melchior, Phillip*) was born May 12, 1884, daughter of Edwin Bossard and Emma Walters. She married January 19, 1903, Walter H. Robinson born 1882, son of Edward J. Robinson. Last known, was living in Hillsdale, New Jersey, when she applied for her Father's Civil War pension.

One known child born in Stroudsburg:

i- **ROBINSON Howard E.**: born September 5, 1903

352 WOODLING Katie: (*Sarah Catherine, Jacob, Peter, Melchior, Phillip*) was born October 23, 1870 in Jackson Township, Pennsylvania, daughter of Jerome J. Woodling and Sarah Catherine Bossard. Her Mother died when she was an infant and she lived with her Grandparents, Jacob and Christina. She went to Ida Grove, Iowa with them and there she married December 13, 1893, George R. Wilcox born May 31, 1870 in Sherman, New York, son of Lyman Wilcox. He died in Ida Grove (no date) and she remarried. No further records.

Children:

620 i- **WILCOX Dewayne**:
621 ii- **WILCOX Sylvia**:

353 LESH M. G. Dayton: (*Rachel, Jacob, Peter, Melchior, Phillip*) was born September 21, 1872, son of Nathan Lesh and Rachel J. Bossard. He married 1894, Minnie Haney born July 1874, daughter of Jerome Henry Haney and Anna Bossard. (See Minnie Haney number 339).

354 **MARITZ Margery:** (*Ida, Jacob, Peter, Melchior, Phillip*) was born in Ida Grove, Iowa, daughter of Edward Maritz and Ida Bossard. She married Blair Swallum and lived in Macon, Georgia. No further records.

355 **FABLE Emma:** (*Emma, Peter K., Peter, Melchior, Phillip*) was born February 1883 in Hamilton Township, Pennsylvania, daughter of James Fable and Emma S. Bossard. She married February 24, 1912, Lloyd C. Serfass born August 1884, son of Jackson Serfass and Cornelia Shupp. He died 1917 and Emma died 1977. They are buried in the Kellersville cemetery in Hamilton Township. No known issue.

356 **BOSSARD Edith Mae:** (*Eugene, Peter K., Peter, Melchior, Phillip*) was born March 27, 1887 in Hamilton Township, Pennsylvania, daughter of Eugene Abraham Bossard and Almira Woodling. She married November 5, 1909, Clarence Dailey born January 20, 1884, son of Andrew and Diane Dailey. He died 1957 and Edith died February 9, 1961. They are buried in the Stroudsburg cemetery. No issue.

357 **BOSSARD Harold Frederick:** (*Eugene, Peter K., Peter, Melchior, Phillip*) was born May 23, 1896 in Hamilton Township, Pennsylvania, son of Eugene Abraham Bossard and Almira Woodling. He married June 11, 1919, Corinne Williams born February 27, 1893 in Scranton, Pennsylvania, daughter of Albert E. Williams and Caroline Krona. He died February 4, 1944 and Corinne died April 18, 1981. They are buried in the Stroudsburg cemetery. No issue.

358 **BOSSARD Miles Franklin:** (*Eugene, Peter K., Peter, Melchior, Phillip*) was born October 12, 1898 in Hamilton Township, Pennsylvania, son of Eugene Abraham Bossard and Almira Woodling. He married November 16, 1923, Laurette Fabel born May 13, 1898, daughter of Alfred and Martha J. Fabel. He died February 17, 1961 and Laurette died May 27, 1981. They are buried in the Stroudsburg cemetery.

Children:

622 i- **BOSSARD Miles Franklin Jr.:** born April 17, 1926
623 ii- **BOSSARD Bettiejane:** born March 15, 1928

359 **CARMER Grace L.:** (*Alice, Joseph, Peter, Melchior, Phillip*) was born March 15, 1881, twin daughter of John Palmer Carmer and Alice L. Bossard. She married Amzi Dennis born October 18, 1883 in Hamilton Township, Pennsylvania, son of John E. and Catherine Dennis. He died January 24, 1942 and she died December 1, 1941. They are buried in the Stroudsburg cemetery.

Children born in Hamilton Township, Pennsylvania:

624 i- **DENNIS Harold Lawrence:** born July 4, 1905
625 ii- **DENNIS Nina O.:** January 22, 1918

360 CARMER Laura M.: (*Alice, Joseph, Peter, Melchior, Phillip*) was born March 15, 1881, twin daughter of John Palmer Carmer and Alice L. Bossard. She married Henry Hester, born July 17, 1875. She died December 18, 1955 and Henry died January 21, 1961. They are buried in the Stroudsburg cemetery.

Children:

626 i- **HESTER Leroy**: born June 10, 1904
627 ii- **HESTER Lottie**: born 1911
628 iii- **HESTER Allison A.**: July 30, 1914

CHAPTER 7

SEVENTH GENERATION

361 **ALTEMOSE Emma Catherine**: (*Mary Ann Weiss, Daniel Weiss,, Felix Weiss, Eva Catherine, Melchior, Phillip*) was born November 6, 1864, daughter of George W. Altemose and Mary Ann Weiss. She married (1) February 14, 1894, Charles Mill born September 17, 1861 in Gouldsboro, son of Christian and Mary Mill. He died October 1, 1902 and is buried in Brodheadsville cemetery. She married (2) October 1908, Henry Frey born December 26, 1864, in Whitehall Township, son of Israel Frey and Justina Roth. No known issue.

362 **ALTEMOSE Electa**: (*Mary Ann Weiss, Daniel Weiss, Felix Weiss, Eva Catherine, Melchior, Phillip*) was born June 1871 in Brodheadsville, Pennsylvania, daughter of George W. Altemose and Mary Ann Weiss. She married September 26, 1900, William O. Bonser born 1873, son of William and Catherine Bonser. She died November 29, 1951 in Saylorsburg and is buried in Arndts Church cemetery. No issue.

363 **ALTEMOSE Grace**: (*Mary Ann Weiss, Daniel Weiss, Felix Weiss, Eva Catherine, Melchior, Phillip*) was born September 1879, daughter of George W. Altemose and Mary Ann Weiss. She married September 3, 1907, Albert M. Kretzing born 1877 in Newfort, Pennsylvania, son of John and Sarah Kretzing. He died 1960 and Grace died April 26, 1971. They are buried in Buena Vista cemetery in Chestnuthill, Pennsylvania.

Children:

629 i- **KRETZING Mary**: born 1908
630 ii- **KRETZING Kathryn**:
631 iii- **KRETZING Martha**:

364 **FELKER Ellen E.**: (*Julia A. Altemose, Susannah Weiss, Felix Weiss, Eva Catherine, Melchior, Phillip*) was born 1874 in Gilbert, Pennsylvania, daughter of Thomas Felker and Julia Arvilla Altemose. She married J. Ulyssis Everitt, born 1866. He died in 1935 and Ellen died 1954. They are buried in the Appenzel cemetery, Jackson Township.

Children:

632 i- **EVERITT Abbie M.**: born 1896
ii- **EVERITT L. Leroy**:

365 FELKER Stewart Ervin: (*Julia A. Altemose, Susannah Weiss, Felix Weiss, Eva Catherine, Melchior, Phillip*) was born March 10, 1877 in Gilbert, Pennsylvania, son of Thomas Felker and Julia Arvilla Altemose. He married Ida May (unknown maiden name) born 1883. She died 1952 and Stewart died December 15, 1953. They are buried in the Appenzel cemetery, Jackson Township.

One child:
633 **i- FELKER Emma**: born ca 1910

366 FELKER Hattie Jane: (*Julia A. Altemose, Susannah Weiss, Felix Weiss, Eva Catherine, Melchior, Phillip*) was born September 18, 1879 in Gilbert, Pennsylvania, daughter of Thomas Felker and Julia Arvilla Altemose. She married either Reuben Heller or Clark Raish. They were living in Nazareth, Pennsylvania in 1953. No further records.

367 FELKER Jennie Diana: (*Julia A. Altemose, Susannah Weiss, Felix Weiss, Eva Catherine, Melchior, Phillip*) was born July 30, 1882 in Hamilton Township, Pennsylvania, daughter of Thomas Felker and Julia Arvilla Altemose. She married Benjamin Dorshimer, born 1883, son of James Dorshimer and Rosa Snyder. He died 1965 and Jennie died 1954. They are buried in the Appenzel cemetery, Jackson Township. They had three daughters, one who married Arthur Fritz and they lived in Dover, New Jersey. One married Julian Kresge and they lived in Gilbert, Pennsylvania. The other one married Richard Brown and they lived in Portland, Pennsylvania.

One son:
634 **i- DORSHIMER Arthur**: born 1908

368 FELKER Cora Alice: (*Julia A. Altemose, Susannah Weiss, Felix Weiss, Eva Catherine, Melchior, Phillip*) was born May 13, 1886 in Hamilton Township, Pennsylvania, daughter of Thomas Felker and Julia Arvilla Altemose. She married either Reuben Heller or Clark Raish and they lived in Nazareth, Pennsylvnaia. No further records.

369 MILLER Florence Fayette: (*Diana Altemose, Susannah Weiss, Felix Weiss, Eva Catherine, Melchior, Phillip*) was born August 15, 1886 in Jackson Township, Pennsylvania, daughter of Daniel C. Miller and Diana Altemose. She married James Bonser born October 22, 1880. She died March 14, 1913 and James died June 21, 1954. They are buried in Buena Vista cemetery in Chestnuthill.

Children:
635 **i- BONSER Lloyd Kenneth**: born February 10, 1906
636 **ii- BONSER Mitchell Fayette**: born September 2, 1908

370 MILLER Bertha B.: (*Diana Altemose, Susannah Weiss, Felix Weiss, Eva Catherine, Melchior, Phillip*) was born October 1888, in Hamilton Township, Pennsylvania, daughter of Daniel C. Miller and Diana Altemose. She married Edwin F. Kunkle born July 1881, son of Andrew and Catherine Kunkle. He died in 1958 and Bertha died in 1949. They are buried in the Buena Vista cemetery in Chestnuthill. No issue.

371 ALTEMOSE Vernon G.: (*Stewart Altemose, Susannah Weiss, Felix Weiss, Eva Catherine, Melchior, Phillip*) was born January 23, 1899, son of Stewart Altemose and Bertha M. Singer. He married October 21, 1925, Anna Naomi Miller born February 18, 1905. She died August 5, 1936 and he married (2), November 27, 1937, Elda Stout Clauss born July 1, 1906. She died November 20, 1964 and Vernon died June 7, 1984.

Children:

637 i- **ALTEMOSE Edith Catherine**: born December 5, 1925
638 ii- **ALTEMOSE Marion Elizabeth**: born December 14, 1926
639 iii- **ALTEMOSE Elwood Charles**: born May 1, 1928
640 iv- **ALTEMOSE Frances Louise**: born December 24, 1929
641 v- **ALTEMOSE Vernon Grover Jr.**: born August 23, 1932
642 vi- **ALTEMOSE Alice May**: born April 11, 1939

372 ALTEMOSE Emma Lydia: (*Stewart Altemose, Susannah Weiss, Felix Weiss, Eva Catherine, Melchior, Phillip*) was born July 30, 1902, daughter of Stewart Weiss and Bertha M. Singer. She married April 19, 1924, Alfred Franklin Seiple born September 29, 1903. He died November 29, 1971.

Children:

643 i- **SEIPLE Marie Bertha**: born December 23, 1924
644 ii- **SEIPLE William Henry**: born October 15, 1927
645 iii- **SEIPLE Alfred Franklin Jr.**: born July 31, 1930

373 ALTEMOSE Ralph Arlington: (*Stewart Altemose, Susannah Weiss, Felix Weiss, Eva Catherine, Melchior, Phillip*) was born September 17, 1904, son of Stewart Altemose and Bertha M. Singer. He married (1) Minnie Schmidt born November 13, 1905 and he married (2) on June 8, 1935, Thelma Ferguson Shaneberger born February 15, 1903.

One child:

646 i- **ALTEMOSE Paul Arlington**: born September 29, 1926

374 ALTEMOSE Jacob Victor: (*Stewart Altemose, Susannah Weiss, Felix Weiss, Eva Catherine, Melchior, Phillip*) was born January 26, 1907, son of Stewart Altemose and Bertha M. Singer. He married (1) February 10, 1926, Irene May

Buss, born February 10, 1908. She died June 5, 1963 and he married (2) on July 11, 1964, Alma W. Riddle Wildonger born May 13, 1914. Jacob died December 17, 1981.

Children:

647 i- **ALTEMOSE Geraldine M.**: born February 21, 1926
648 ii- **ALTEMOSE Jean Grace**: born June 11, 1927
649 iii- **ALTEMOSE Richard James**: born December 26, 1928
650 iv- **ALTEMOSE Lee Linford**: born March 5, 1931
651 v- **ALTEMOSE Robert Franklin**: born October 21, 1932
652 vi- **ALTEMOSE Wayne Stewart**: born April 16, 1937
653 vii- **ALTEMOSE Labert Dale**: born August 5, 1940

375 ALTEMOSE Beatrice Naomi: (*Stewart Altemose, Susannah Weiss, Felix Weiss, Eva Catherine, Melchior, Phillip*) was born November 24, 1908, daughter of Stewart Altemose and Bertha M. Singer. She married December 3, 1938, Elwood Lee Werkhiser. In 1952 they were living in West Orange, New Jersey. No further records.

376 ALTEMOSE Albert Alvin: (*Stewart Altemose, Susannah Weiss, Felix Weiss, Eva Catherine, Melchior, Phillip*) was born November 17, 1910 in Chestnuthill Township, son of Stewart Altemose and Bertha Singer. He married October 6, 1934, Dorothy Noble born May 10, 1914.

Children:

654 i- **ALTEMOSE Harold Albert**: born February 9, 1936
655 ii- **ALTEMOSE Rollin Amos**: born February 16, 1938
656 iii- **ALTEMOSE Thomas Sherwood**: born June 15, 1943
657 iv- **ALTEMOSE Dorothy Ann**: born October 15, 1946

377 ALTEMOSE Woodrow Wilson: (*Stewart Altemose, Susannah Weiss, Felix Weiss, Eva Catherine, Melchior, Phillip*) was born March 4, 1913, son of Stewart Altemose and Bertha Singer. He married September 16, 1939, Alice E. Kindt born September 7, 1919, daughter of Frederick Kindt and Estella Susan Arnold.

One child:

658 i- **ALTEMOSE Carol Ann**: born October 3, 1940

378 ALTEMOSE Alberta Arvilla: (*Stewart Altemose, Susannah Weiss, Felix Weiss, Eva Catherine, Melchior, Phillip*) was born July 4, 1918, daughter of Stewart Altemose and Bertha Singer. She married September 16, 1939, Eugene A. Shraver born June 27, 1915.

Children:

659 i- **SHRAVER Gary Lynn**: born June 27, 1941
660 ii- **SHRAVER Kirk Lee**: born November 23, 1946
661 iii- **SHRAVER Bart Altemose**: born October 8, 1951

379 **WEISS Ruth H.**: (*Charles Weiss, Felix Weiss, Felix Weiss, Eva Catherine, Melchior, Phillip*) was born May 1896, daughter of Charles and Electa Weiss. She married June 20, 1918, George Counterman born ca 1887, son of William Counterman and Sara E. Hineline.

Children:
662 i- **COUNTERMAN Charles**: born 1918
663 ii- **COUNTERMAN Viola**:
664 iii- **COUNTERMAN Idella**:
665 iv- **COUNTERMAN Dorothy**:

380 **WEISS Iva M.**: (*Charles Weiss, Felix Weiss, Felix Weiss, Eva Catherine, Melchior, Phillip*) was born ca 1902, daughter of Charles and Electa Weiss. She married March 18, 1919 in East Stroudsburg, Pennsylvania, Eugene H. Wolbert born ca 1897, son of Charles Wolbert and Elizabeth Miller. He died 1968 in Buffalo, New York and is buried in Reeders, Pennsylvania.

Children:
i- **WOLBERT Joan**:
ii- **WOLBERT Wardell**:

381 **WEISS Viola A.**: (*Charles Weiss, Felix Weiss, Felix Weiss, Eva Catherine, Melchior, Phillip*) was born 1909, daughter of Charles and Electa Weiss. She married March 26, 1927, Lloyd K. Bonser, born February 6, 1906, son of James Bonser and Florence Miller. He died September 1961 and is buried in the Buena Vista Cemetery in Chestnuthill, Pennsylvania. Viola still living in Stroudsburg in 1989. See Lloyd K. Bonser number 635 for further records.

382 **GEARHART Olive**: (*Cicero Gearhart, Elizabeth Weiss, Felix Weiss, Eva Catherine, Melchior, Phillip*) was born June 12, 1888, in Stroudsburg, Pennsylvania, daughter of Cicero Gearhart and Blanche Greenswald. She married September 19, 1908, Ernest Harrison Taylor born September 5, 1888. He died March 23, 1965 and Olive died March 23, 1975. They are buried in the Stroudsburg cemetery.

Children:
666 i- **TAYLOR Ernest Harrison Jr.**: born October 7, 1909
667 ii- **TAYLOR Elizabeth Louise**: born October 30, 1913
668 iii- **TAYLOR John Fletcher**: born May 12, 1916
669 iv- **TAYLOR William Henry**: born July 1, 1928

383 GEARHART A. Greenswald: (*Cicero Gearhart, Elizabeth Weiss, Felix Weiss, Eva Catherine, Melchior, Phillip*) was born November 29, 1890 in Stroudsburg, Pennsylvania, son of Cicero Gearhart and Blanche Greenswald. He married April 29, 1923, Ruth Barthold born December 21, 1898, daughter of Alan and Agnes Barthold. He died August 11, 1943 and Ruth died December 13, 1979. They are buried in the Stroudsburg cemetery.

Children:

670 i- **GEARHART Joan Agnes**: born September 24, 1927
671 ii- **GEARHART Peter Barthold**: born June 28, 1933

384 GEARHART Helen L.: (*Cicero Gearhart, Elizabeth Weiss, Felix Weiss, Eva Catherine, Melchior, Phillip*) was born December 27, 1891 in Stroudsburg, Pennsylvania, daughter of Cicero Gearhart and Blanche Greenswald. She married April 14, 1914, Dr. James L. Jenson born April 23, 1886. He practiced medicine in Colby, Kansas, and died there before 1978. Helen died January 14, 1978 in Colby.

Children:

i- **JENSON James L. Jr.**: born April 21, 1915
ii- **JENSON Helen Lorraine**: born June 7, 1920
iii- **JENSON Robert L.**: born March 19, 1922
672 iv- **JENSON William Keen**: born November 6, 1923

385 GEARHART Samuel R.: (*Cicero Gearhart, Elizabeth Weiss, Felix Weiss, Eva Catherine, Melchior, Phillip*) was born January 22, 1896 in Stroudsburg, Pennsylvania, son of Cicero Gearhart and Blanche Greenswald. He married (1) Jean Davis and (2) Rebecca Eleanor Mc Call, born August 16, 1905. Samuel served as a Corporal in the infantry during World War I. He died in 1965 and his wife died July 26, 1986. They are buried in the Stroudsburg cemetery.

Children:

i- **GEARHART Samuel Frederick**: born November 20, 1930
673 ii- **GEARHART Robert Morris**: born April 23, 1933

386 GEARHART Roberta E.: (*Cicero Gearhart, Elizabeth Weiss, Felix Weiss, Eva Catherine, Melchior, Phillip*) was born October 10, 1899 in Stroudsburg, Pennsylvania, daughter of Cicero Gearhart and Blanche Greenswald. She married June 21, 1924, H. Evans Morris. They were living in Ft. Myers. Florida. No issue.

387 FELKER John R.: (*Anna E. Gearhart, Elizabeth Weiss, Felix Weiss, Eva Catherine, Melchior, Phillip*) was born December 31. 1880, son of Samuel Felker and Anna Elizabeth Gearhart. He married (1) Flora Shupp, born April 18, 1881, daughter of Josiah Shupp and Sara Jane Kresge. She died April 27, 1908 and is buried in the Gilbert cemetery. He married (2) August 12, 1909, Carrie M. Bond born April 1882, daughter of Lyman and Amelia Bond. He died in 1944 and is buried in Effort cemetery, Effort, Pennsylvania.

Children by first marriage:
674 i- **FELKER Sarah**: born February 19, 1902
ii- **FELKER D. Luther**: born November 15, 1905 and died August 16, 1917, buried in Gilbert cemetery.
675 iii- **FELKER Beatrice**: born July 12,, 1903
676 iv- **FELKER Elsie**: born July 18, 1904
677 v- **FELKER Paul**: born April 20, 1907
Child by second marriage:
678 vi- **FELKER Amelia**: born October 8, 1916

388 GEARHART Lida May: (*Theodore Gearhart, Elizabeth Weiss, Felix Weiss, Eva Catherine, Melchior, Phillip*) was born July 9, 1886 in Gilbert, Pennsylvania, daughter of Theodore Gearhart and Amanda Snyder. She married December 26, 1908, Dr. John E. Gregory born March 5, 1879, son of William Gregory and Elizabeth Shafer. She died October 17, 1963 in Allentown, Pennsylvania and John died November 6, 1965. They are buried in the Salem Church cemetery in Gilbert.

One child:
679 i- **GREGORY Barbara G.**: born March 8, 1913

389 GEARHART Dorothy N.: (*Theodore Gearhart, Elizabeth Weiss, Felix Weiss, Eva Catherine, Melchior, Phillip*) was born July 16, 1888 in Gilbert, Pennsylvania, daughter of Theodore Gearhart and Amanda Snyder. She married Burton R. Leffler born April 30, 1890. He died May 29, 1956 and Dorothy died April 30, 1986. No issue.

390 GEARHART Susannah E.: (*Theodore Gearhart, Elizabeth Weiss, Felix Weiss, Eva Catherine, Melchior, Phillip*) was born June 24, 1891, daughter of Theodore Gearhart and Amanda Snyder. She married Leon Nusbaum. They were living in Allentown, Pennsylvania. No issue.

391 GEARHART Charles R.: (*Theodore Gearhart, Elizabeth Weiss, Felix Weiss, Eva Catherine, Melchior, Phillip*) was born March 7, 1893 in Gilbert, Pennsylvania, son of Theodore Gearhart and Amanda Snyder. He married Mabel Cooper, born September 2, 1902. She died June 14, 1977.

Children:
680 i- **GEARHART Gayle**: born December 18, 1923
681 ii- **GEARHART Gerald**: born February 21, 1926

392 **GEARHART Edna M.**: (*Theodore Gearhart, Elizabeth Weiss, Felix Weiss, Eva Catherine, Melchior, Phillip*) was born April 31, 1895 in Gilbert, Pennsylvania, daughter of Theodore Gearhart and Amanda Snyder. She married Albert W. Courtwright born October 1, 1895 in Pocono, Pennsylvania, son of Henry Courtwright and Emma Shook. He died October 18, 1981. No death record found for Edna.

One child:

682 **i- COURTWRIGHT Leslie**: born January 29, 1916

393 **GEARHART William J.**: (*Theodore Gearhart, Elizabeth Weiss, Felix Weiss, Eva Catherine, Melchior, Phillip*) was born February 20, 1900 in Gilbert, Pennsylvania, son of Theodore Gearhart and Amanda Snyder. He married Mabel A. Buck born September 17, 1894, daughter of Eugene Buck. He died in 1968 and Mabel died January 2, 1981 in Bethlehem, Pennsylvania. They are buried in the Salem Church cemetery in Gilbert, Pennsylvania.

Children:

683 **i- GEARHART William E.**: born January 25, 1924
684 **ii- GEARHART Leroy M.**: (twin) born April 4, 1925
685 **iii- GEARHART Lemar**: (twin) born April 4, 1925
686 **iv- GEARHART Barbara J.**: born October 4, 1930

394 **GEARHART Nevin A.**: (*Theodore Gearhart, Elizabeth Weiss, Felix Weiss, Eva Catherine, Melchior, Phillip*) was born December 20, 1904 in Gilbert, Pennsylvania, son of Theodore Gearhart and Amanda Snyder. He married Amelia Mohr, born June 20, 1911. She died in 1976 and Nevin died January 28, 1981.

Children:

687 **i- GEARHART James**: born July 25, 1943
688 **iii- GEARHART Sarah**: born August 8, 1944
689 **iv- GEARHART Ruth**: born July 14, 1945
690 **ii- GEARHART Charles**: born July 8, 1949

395 **GEARHART Lyster M.**: (*Theodore Gearhart, Elizabeth Weiss, Felix Weiss, Eva Catherine, Melchior, Phillip*) was born August 1, 1906 in Gilbert, Pennsylvania, son of Theodore Gearhart and Amanda Snyder. He married Frances Tuttle, born January 8, 1906. They are presently living in Allentown, Pennsylvania.

Children:

691 **i- GEARHART Austin Tuttle**: born April 12, 1933
692 **ii- GEARHART David**: born July 29, 1944
693 **iii- GEARHART John**: born August 10, 1946

396 GEARHART Martin F.: (*Theodore Gearhart, Elizabeth Weiss, Felix Weiss, Eva Catherine, Melchior, Phillip*) was born September 21, 1908 in Gilbert, Pennsylvania, twin son of Theodore Gearhart and Amanda Snyder. He married Olga Balson, born September 16, 1909. They are presently living in Nazareth, Pennsylvania.

Children:
694 **i- GEARHART Joanne**: born August 11, 1942
695 **ii- GEARHART Nadine**: born February 12, 1945

397 GEARHART Maurice: (*Theodore Gearhart, Elizabeth Weiss, Felix Weiss, Eva Catherine, Melchior, Phillip*) was born September 21, 1908 in Gilbert, Pennsylvania, twin son of Theodore Gearhart and Amanda Snyder. He married Eilene Heydt, born April 11, 1914. Maurice died October 6, 1976 and Eilene is presently living in Allentown, Pennsylvania. No issue.

398 GEARHART D. Kenneth: (*Theodore Gearhart, Elizabeth Weiss, Felix Weiss, Eva Catherine, Melchior, Phillip*) was born October 1, 1911 in Gilbert, Pennsylvania, son of Theodore Gearhart and Amanda Snyder. He married Doris Koehler. He died June 17, 1981 in Poughkeepsie, New York. Doris is still living there. No issue.

399 GEARHART Franklin: (*Theodore Gearhart, Elizabeth Weiss, Felix Weiss, Eva Catherine, Melchior, Phillip*) was born November 20, 1913 in Gilbert, Pennsylvania, son of Theodore Gearhart and Amanda Snyder. He married Mada Brong, born April 14, 1918.

One child:
i- GEARHART Theodore: born September 18, 1938

400 GEARHART Alice: (*Ulyssis Gearhart, Elizabeth Weiss, Felix Weiss, Eva Catherine, Melchior, Phillip*) the daughter of Ulyssis Gearhart and Abba Jane Burger. (no birthdate found). She married Alfred Kleckner. No further records.

401 GEARHART Mary: (*Ulyssis Gearhart, Elizabeth Weiss, Felix Weiss, Eva Catherine, Melchior, Phillip*) the daughter of Ulyssis Gearhart and Abba Jane Burger. (no birthdate found). She married James Weigand. No further records.

402 GEARHART Albert: (*John Gearhart, Elizabeth Weiss, Felix Weiss, Eva Catherine, Melchior, Phillip*) was born May 1891, son of John H. Gearhart and Alice Andrew. He married Emma E. Rockefeller, born 1896. He died May 26, 1965 and Emma died 1978. They are buried in the Buena Vista cemetery in Chestnuthill, Pennsylvania.

One child:
696 **i- GEARHART John W.**:

403 GEARHART Mabel M.: (*John Gearhart, Elizabeth Weiss, Felix Weiss, Eva Catherine, Melchior, Phillip*) was born December 1892, in Monroe Co., Pennsylvania, daughter of John H. Gearhart and Alice Andrew. She married Markley and they were living in Lehighton, Pennsylvania in 1962. No further records.

404 GEARHART Stewart Raymond: (*John Gearhart, Elizabeth Weiss, Felix Weiss, Eva Catherine, Melchior, Phillip*) was born September 2, 1894 in Monroe Co., Pennsylvania, son of John H. Gearhart and Alice Andrew. He married (1) Mazie Arnold born 1893. She died February 28, 1933 and he married (2) Mada Switzgable, born 1900. Stewart died August 1962 and they are buried in the Buena Vista cemetery in Chestnuthill.

Children:
697 **i- GEARHART Claire**:
ii- GEARHART Paul G.:

405 GEARHART Grace L.: (*John Gearhart, Elizabeth Weiss, Felix Weiss, Eva Catherine, Melchior, Phillip*) was born November 1896 in Monroe Co., Pennsylvania, daughter of John H. Gearhart and Alice Andrew. She married (1) ______ Nelson and (2) ______ Jones. No further records.

406 GEARHART Lois: (*John Gearhart, Elizabeth Weiss, Felix Weiss, Eva Catherine, Melchior, Phillip*) was born May 14, 1897 in Monroe Co., Pennsylvania, daughter of John H. Gearhart and Alice Andrew. She married Benjamin Stein. No further records.

407 GEARHART Minnie E.: (*John Gearhart, Elizabeth Weiss, Felix Weiss, Eva Catherine, Melchior, Phillip*) was born June 1898, in Monroe Co., Pennsylvania, daughter of John H. Gearhart and Alice Andrew. She married February 22, 1916, Samuel Kresge born June 1895, son of Wilson Kresge and Emma L. Brong. He died 1955 and Minnie died 1963. They are buried in the Buena Vista cemetery in Chestnuthill.

Children:
698 **i- KRESGE Doris**:
699 **ii- KRESGE June**: born 1924

408 GEARHART Florence A.: (*John Gearhart, Elizabeth Weiss, Felix Weiss, Eva Catherine, Melchior, Phillip*) was born 1901 in Monroe Co., Pennsylvania, daughter of John H. Gearhart and Alice Andrew. She married Fred Field. In 1962, they were living in Scranton, Pennsylvania. No further records.

409 **GEARHART Bertha E.**: (*John Gearhart, Elizabeth Weiss, Felix Weiss, Eva Catherine, Melchior, Phillip*) was born 1902 in Monroe Co., Pennsylvania, daughter of John H. Gearhart and Alice Andrew. She married February 1, 1919, Charles Edwin Gouger born ca 1898, son of John Gouger and Mary A. Ripley. He died August 20, 1950 and she married (2) _____ Graham. They were living in Camden, New Jersey in 1962.

410 **GEARHART Clifford A.**: (*John Gearhart, Elizabeth Weiss, Felix Weiss, Eva Catherine, Melchior, Phillip*) was born May 26, 1905, in Monroe Co., Pennsylvania, son of John H. Gearhart and Alice Andrew. He married May 31, 1927, Eva Rebecca Hinkle born 1898, daughter of John H. Hinkle and Mary A. Warner. She died July 26, 1986, probably in Allentown. No further records.

411 **GEARHART Elva O.**: (*John Gearhart, Elizabeth Weiss, Felix Weiss, Eva Catherine, Melchior, Phillip*) was born ca 1908 in Monroe Co., Pennsylvania, daughter of John H. Gearhart and Alice Andrew. She married Charles Van Billiard. No further records.

412 **GEARHART Blanche Alberta**: (*Thomas Gearhart, Elizabeth Weiss, Felix Weiss, Eva Catherine, Melchior, Phillip*) was born February 18, 1901 in Monroe Co., Pennsylvania, daughter of Thomas Gearhart and Emma S. Ruff. She married _____ March. No further records.

413 **GEARHART Ammon R.**: (*Thomas Gearhart, Elizabeth Weiss, Felix Weiss, Eva Catherine, Melchior, Phillip*) was born October 18, 1905, son of Thomas Gearhart and Emma S. Ruff. He married August 29, 1931, Doris B. Altemose born October 31, 1910. They are presently living in Saylorsburg, Pennsylvania.

414 **GEARHART Grant G.**: (*Thomas Gearhart, Elizabeth Weiss Felix Weiss, Eva Catherine, Melchior, Phillip*) was born ca 1908, son of Thomas Gearhart and Emma S. Ruff. He was married and had no issue.

415 **GEARHART Ernest**: (*Thomas Gearhart, Elizabeth Weiss, Felix Weiss, Eva Catherine, Melchior, Phillip*) was born 1911, son of Thomas Gearhart and Emma S. Ruff. He died March 9, 1975 in Stroudsburg, Pennsylvania and is buried in the Stroudsburg cemetery. No further records.

416 **BRUCH David:** (*Lucy Gearhart, Elizabeth Weiss, Felix Weiss, Eva Catherine, Melchior, Phillip*) was born October 3, 1895 in Stroudsburg, Pennsylvania, son of Edwin M. Bruch and Lucy E. Gearhart. He married Helen Frisbie. David died January 12, 1951. No death date found for Helen.

One child:
i- BRUCH Charles:

417 **BRUCH Leila:** (*Lucy Gearhart, Elizabeth Weiss, Felix Weiss, Eva Catherine, Melchior, Phillip*) was born January 6, 1897 in Stroudsburg, Pennsylvania, daughter of Edwin M. Bruch and Lucy Gearhart. She married after 1951, James Shafer born 1898. He died December 7, 1972 and Liela died February 21, 1989. They are buried in Laurelwood cemetery in South Stroudsburg, Pennsylvania. No issue.

418 **SHOEMAKER Laura F.:** (*Abner Shoemaker, Emelie Weiss, George Weiss, Eva Catherine, Melchior, Phillip*) was born October 16, 1870 in Hamilton Township, Pennsylvania, daughter of Abner Shoemaker and Margaret Werkhiser. She married January 1, 1889, George Anglemyer born April 6, 1865, son of Charles and Hannah Anglemyer. He died December 1, 1891 and Laura died in November 26, 1915. They are buried in Mt. Zion cemetery in Hamilton Township.

One child:
i- ANGLEMYER Edith: born September 1889

419 **SHOEMAKER Carrie A.:** (*Abner Shoemaker, Emelie Weiss, George Weiss, Eva Catherine, Melchior, Phillip*) was born September 1, 1872 in Hamilton Township, Pennsylvania, daughter of Abner Shoemaker and Margaret Werkhiser. She married in 1894, Francis Mengel born October 15, 1873. She died February 20, 1915 and Francis died March 1, 1953. They are buried in the Stroudsburg cemetery.

One child:
i- MENGEL Pearl: born 1894

420 **RINKER Florence A.:** (*Susan Shoemaker, Emelie Weiss George Weiss, Eva Catherine, Melchior, Phillip*) was born ca 1867, daughter of Samuel Rinker and Susan Ellen Shoemaker. She married March 5, 1887, Albert Shafer born June 29, 1862, son of Daniel and Christina Shafer. He died February 12, 1912 and is buried in Mt. Zion cemetery in Hamilton Township. She married (2) ______ Lake and they were living in Stroudsburg in 1952. No further records.

421 **RINKER Emily T.:** (*Susan Shoemaker, Emelie Weiss, George Weiss, Eva Catherine, Melchior, Phillip*) was born February 1869, in Hamilton Township, Pennsylvania, daughter of Samuel Rinker and Susan Ellen Shoemaker. She married

December 19, 1894, Jervis Hartman born May 1859, son of Jacob and Eva Jane Hartman. He died March 3, 1915. No date of death found for Emily.

Known child born in Bartonsville, Pennsylvania
i- HARTMAN Burnetta: born January 12, 1900

422 **RINKER Carrie E.**: (*Susan Shoemaker, Emelie Weiss, George Weiss, Eva Catherine, Melchior, Phillip*) was born 1872, daughter of Samuel Rinker and Susan Ellen Shoemaker. She married December 22, 1893, Daniel E. Newell born 1871, son of Gershom and Emma Newell. Carrie died in 1949 and Daniel died November 29, 1951 in Stroudsburg. They are buried in the Stroudsburg cemetery.

One child:
700 **i- NEWELL Sheldon**:

423 **RINKER Mary E.**: (*Susan Shoemaker, Emelie Weiss, George Weiss, Eva Catherine, Melchior, Phillip*) was born ca 1877, daughter of Samuel Rinker and Susan Ellen Shoemaker. She married ______ Dennis. They were living in Easton, Pennsylvania in 1949. No further records.

424 **RINKER Clayton G.**: (*Susan Shoemaker, Emelie Weiss, George Weiss, Eva Catherine, Melchior, Phillip*) was born November 4, 1878, son of Samuel Rinker and Susan Ellen Shoemaker. He married March 5, 1906, Nettie Frantz born March 11, 1884. He died November 13, 1921 and Nettie died January 12, 1930. They are buried in Stroudsburg cemetery

One known child:
i- RINKER Dayton: born March 22, 1907

425 **RINKER Sherman Morris**: (*Susan Shoemaker, Emelie Weiss, George Weiss, Eva Catherine, Melchior, Phillip*) was born September 1880, son of Samuel Rinker and Susan Ellen Shoemaker. He married December 24, 1903, Ada M. Leap born ca 1885. He died June 5, 1961 in the Cherry Valley area when a tractor overturned on him. His wife died before him.

One child:
701 **i- RINKER Earl R.**: born 1907

426 **RINKER Ada P.**: (*Susan Shoemaker, Emelie Weiss, George Weiss, Eva Catherine, Melchior, Phillip*) was born April 10, 1885, daughter of Samuel Rinker and Susan Ellen Shoemaker. She married ______ Fehr and they were living in Stroudsburg, Pennsylvania in 1949. No further records.

427 **RINKER Eda B.**: (*Susan Shoemaker, Emelie Weiss, George Weiss, Eva Catherine, Melchior, Phillip*) was born April 1886, daughter of Samuel Rinker and Susan Ellen Shoemaker. She married _____ Bonney. They were living in Penargyl, Pennsylvania in 1949. No further records.

428 **RINKER Floyd A.**: (*Susan Shoemaker, Emelie Weiss, George Weiss, Eva Catherine, Melchior, Phillip*) was born October 1888, son of Samuel Rinker and Susan Ellen Shoemaker. He was living in Freeland, Pennsylvania in 1949. No further records.

429 **RINKER Alice E.**: (*Susan Shoemaker, Emelie Weiss, George Weiss, Eva Catherine, Melchior, Phillip*) was born ca 1890, daughter of Samuel Rinker and Susan Ellen Shoemaker. She married _____ Hartzell and was living in Nazareth, Pennsylvania in 1949.

430 **RINKER Bertha R.**: (*Susan Shoemaker, Emelie Weiss, George Weiss, Eva Catherine, Melchior, Phillip*) was born ca 1895, daughter of Samuel Rinker and Susan Ellen Shoemaker. She married _____ Allen and was living in Easton, Pennsylvania in 1949.

431 **SHOEMAKER Verna**: (*Lynford Shoemaker, Emelie Weiss, George Weiss, Eva Catherine, Melchior, Phillip*) was born October 1895 in Stroud Township, Pennsylvania, daughter of Lynford Shoemaker and Helen Miller. She married March 29, 1916, David H. Warrick born May 30, 1889, son of John Warrick and Louisa Hunt. She died 1985 and David died June 29, 1978. They are buried in the Stroudsburg cemetery.

One known child:
702 **i- WARRICK Helen**: born ca 1920

432 **FETHERMAN Edith May**: (*Mary A. Shoemaker, Emelie Weiss, George Weiss, Eva Catherine, Melchior, Phillip*) was born July 31, 1882 in Hamilton Township, Pennsylvania, daughter of Franklin Fetherman and Mary Allis Shoemaker. She married March 12, 1903, Charles F. Werkhiser born July 5, 1876, son of Theodore Werkhiser. She died August 6, 1967 in Paradise, Pennsylvania and Charles died in 1951. They are buried in the Cherry Valley cemetery.

Children born in Cherry Valley, Pennsylvania:
i- WERKHISER Ernest Franklin: born October 3, 1903
ii- WERKHISER Bernita Ardella: born August 27, 1905
iii- WERKHISER Orwell Theodore: born November 26, 1906
iv- WERKHISER Albert Calvin: born September 8, 1908
v- WERKHISER Edgar Dewey: born November 27, 1911

vi- WERKHISER Ruth Elizabeth: born August 19, 1913
vii- WERKHISER Howard Wilson: born February 1, 1916

433 **FETHERMAN Mamie:** (*Mary A. Shoemaker, Emelie Weiss, George Weiss, Eva Catherine, Melchior, Phillip*) was born June 1888 in Hamilton Township, Pennsylvania, daughter of Franklin Fetherman and Mary Allis Shoemaker. She married Lovine Peters. born October 5, 1888 in Hamilton Township, son of Frank and Cecelia Peters. He died November 24, 1958 in Stroudsburg. No death date found for Mamie. No known issue.

434 **BONSER Stanley M.:** (*Catherine Shoemaker, Emelie Weiss, George Weiss, Eva Catherine, Melchior, Phillip*) was born March 4, 1888 in Gilbert, Pennsylvania, son of Jerome Bonser and Catherine Ardella Shoemaker. He married (1) Martha Mc knight and married (2) Mary Maryzuk. Stanley had a band called the 'Lew Stanley and the Nighthawks'. They played in the Poconos and Middle Atlantic State resorts. He served in World War I. He died February 1976 in Gilbert, Pennsylvania and is buried in the Salem Church cemetery in Gilbert. Mary was last known to be living in Florida. No issue.

435 **BONSER Muriel T.:** (*Catherine Shoemaker, Amelia Weiss, George Weiss, Eva Catherine, Melchior, Phillip*) was born 1897 in Gilbert, Pennsylvania, daughter of Jerome Bonser and Catherine Ardella Shoemaker. She married Elwood P. Shafer born 1880, son of Henry Shafer and Amelia Kline. He died April 1962 in Allentown, Pennsylvania and Muriel died 1955. They are buried in the Gilbert cemetery. No issue.

436 **CLAREY Edwin:** (*Lucy, Edwin, Joseph, Phillip, Melchior, Phillip*) was born September 1890 in Williams Township, Bay Co., Michigan daughter of Richard Clarey and Lucy Bell Buzzard. He married Louise Simmons. Edwin died November 17, 1962 in Bay City and is buried in the Oakwood cemetery.

437 **CLAREY Richard Dorcey:** (*Lucy, Edwin, Joseph, Phillip, Melchior, Phillip*) was born January 1892 in Williams Township, Bay Co., Michigan, son of Richard Clarey and Lucy Bell Buzzard. He married (1) Edna Kent and on June 20, 1936, he married (2) Maxine Weston. Richard died May 28, 1955 in Bay City and is buried in the Oakwood cemetery. He had four children by his first marriage and four children by his second marriage.

438 **CLAREY Ethel:** (*Lucy, Edwin, Joseph, Phillip, Melchior, Phillip*) was born July 1894 in Williams Township, Bay Co., Michigan, daughter of Richard Clarey and Lucy Bell Buzzard. She married _____ Rosenbrock. No further records.

439 CLAREY Ivan: (*Lucy, Edwin, Joseph, Phillip, Melchior, Phillip*) was born November 1898 in Williams Township, Bay Co. Michigan, son of Richard Clarey and Lucy Bell Buzzard. He married Rose Simmons. Ivan died in 1963 in Bay City and is buried in the Oakwood cemetery.

440 CLAREY Alfred: (*Lucy, Edwin, Joseph, Phillip, Melchior, Phillip*) was born March 9, 1904 in Williams Township, Bay Co., Michigan, son of Richard Clarey and Lucy Bell Buzzard. He married December 19, 1936, Helen Hearit. He died February 8, 1989 in Fisherville, Michigan and is buried in Pine Grove cemetery.

One child:
i- CLAREY Geraldine: (She married James Schanck).

441 CLAREY June: (*Lucy, Edwin, Joseph, Phillip, Melchior, Phillip*) was born June 1907 in Williams Township, Bay Co. Michigan, daughter of Richard Clarey and Lucy Bell Buzzard. She married Geneseo Bernard. She died March 3, 1984 in Fisherville, Michigan and is buried in Pine Grove cemetery.

442 BUZZARD Howard: (*Ralph, Edwin, Joseph, Phillip, Melchior, Phillip*) was born ca 1898 in Williams Township, Bay Co., Michigan, son of Ralph Eugene Buzzard and Henrietta Middleton. He married January 2, 1918, Hazel Reid born November 13, 1898 in Tuscola Co., Michigan. Howard died in 1971 and Hazel died May 5, 1982. They are buried in Oakwood cemetery.

Children:
i- BUZZARD Ralph:
ii- BUZZARD Alfred:

443 BUZZARD Lloyd: (*Ralph, Edwin, Joseph, Phillip, Melchior, Phillip*) was born ca 1905 in Williams Township, Bay Co., Michigan, son of Ralph Eugene Buzzard and Henrietta Middleton. He married ______ Teal and last known was living in Hawaii.

444 BUZZARD Roland Lavern: (*Roy V., Edwin, Joseph, Phillip, Melchior, Phillip*) was born June 27, 1899 in Williams Township, Bay Co., Michigan, son of Roy Vernon Buzzard and Nellie Helen Horn. He married (1) Lillie Zelma Burns born June 14, 1903. She died February 20, 1925 and he married (2) September 29, 1929, Gertrude Matilda Brown born June 21, 1909. They are presently living in Bay City, Michigan.

Child by first marriage:
703 **i- BUZZARD Beryle Genevieve:** born July 13, 1923
Children by second marriage:

704 ii- **BUZZARD Lloyd Roland**: born June 27, 1930
705 iii- **BUZZARD Lyle Leroy**: born November 15, 1932
706 iv- **BUZZARD Dale Vernon**: born June 23, 1936
707 v- **BUZZARD Gertrude Joy**: born May 10, 1938

445 BUZZARD Ramond Vernon: (*Roy V., Edwin, Joseph, Phillip, Melchior, Phillip*) was born April 29, 1901 in Williams Township, Bay Co., Michigan, son of Roy Vernon Buzzard and Nellie Helen Horn. He married September 29, 1928, Ida May Snyder. Ramond died February 28, 1938 in Bay City and is buried in the Oakridge cemetery.

446 BUZZARD Alvin Milford: (*Roy V., Edwin, Joseph, Phillip, Melchior, Phillip*) was born September 13, 1903 in Williams Township, Bay Co., Michigan, son of Roy Vernon Buzzard and Nellie Helen Horn. He married October 18, 1925, Beulah Fay Miller.

447 BUZZARD Eleanor Geneva: (*Roy V., Edwin, Joseph, Phillip, Melchior, Phillip*) was born November 25, 1905 in Williams Township, Bay Co. Michigan, daughter of Roy Vernon Buzzard and Nellie Helen Horn. She married before 1925, Peter Reff.

448 BUZZARD George William: (*Roy V., Edwin, Joseph, Phillip, Melchior, Phillip*) was born January 13, 1909 in Bay City, Michigan, son of Roy Buzzard and Nellie Helen Horn. He married October 8, 1929, Thelma Irene Skinner.

449 BUZZARD ALICE Leona: (*Roy V., Edwin, Joseph, Phillip, Melchior, Phillip*) was born January 10, 1912 in Bay City, Michigan, daughter of Roy Vernon Buzzard and Nellie Helen Horn. She married November 7, 1928, John Reff.

450 BUZZARD Vera Marie: (*Roy V., Edwin, Joseph, Phillip, Melchior, Phillip*) was born March 13, 1913 in Williams Township, Bay Co., Michigan, daughter of Roy Vernon Buzzard and Nellie Helen Horn. She married April 25, 1934, Emery Joseph Goulet born June 7, 1903.

Children:
708 i- **GOULET Eugene Joseph**: born May 15, 1935
709 ii- **GOULET Jerry**: born April 11, 1937
710 iii- **GOULET Donald Emery**: born February 9, 1949
711 iv- **GOULET Michael**: born August 8, 1951

451 BUZZARD Roy Edward: (*Roy V., Edwin, Joseph, Phillip, Melchior, Phillip*) was born April 13, 1923 in Bay City, Michigan, son of Roy Vernon Buzzard and Nellie Helen Horn. He married October 4, 1947, Norma Tanner born February 15, 1927.

Children:
712 i- **BUZZARD Danelle Kay**: born October 24, 1948
713 ii- **BUZZARD Elaine M.**: born September 2, 1958

452 **BUZZARD Edwin Howe**: (*William, Edwin, Joseph, Phillip, Melchior, Phillip*) was born in 1912 in Bay City, Michigan, son of William J. Buzzard and Eva White. He married August 3, 1934, Alice Lambert, daughter of Herman Lambert and Ann L. Ruterbush. Edwin died April 1, 1961 in Bay City and is buried in Elm Lawn cemetery.

Children:
714 i- **BUZZARD Kenneth Alvin**:
715 ii- **BUZZARD Pauline**:

453 **BUZZARD Russell Donald**: (*William, Edwin, Joseph, Phillip, Melchior, Phillip*) was born February 10. 1913 in Bay City, Michigan, son of William J. Buzzard and Eva White. He married (1) Lillian Griffith and he married (2) June 16, 1934, Loraine Love. He died June 15, 1949 and Loraine died March 31, 1954 in Bay City. They are buried in Elm Lawn cemetery.

One child by first marriage:
716 i- **BUZZARD Maureen**:
Children by second marriage:
717 ii- **BUZZARD Shirley**:
718 iii- **BUZZARD Russell D. Jr.**: born April 15, 1936

454 **BUZZARD Noreen**: (*William, Edwin, Joseph, Phillip, Melchior, Phillip*) was born February 8, 1925 in Bay City, Michigan, daughter of William J. Buzzard and Wilhemina Mrohs. She married (1) August 22, 1945 Matthew Len and (2) in 1948, Albert Wesenick. She married (3) November 23, 1957, Ivan Weston born June 28, 1919, son of John Weston and Carrie Nast.

Child of first marriage born in Bay City:
719 i- **LEN Linda**: born May 27, 1946
Children of second marriage:
720 ii- **WESENICK Darlene**: born December 3, 1949, Bay City
721 iii- **WESENICK Carol**: born March 19, 1951, Port Huron
Children of third marriage born in Bay City:
722 iv- **WESTON Sharon**: born August 1, 1959
v- **WESTON William Ivan**: born 1961 and he was killed in a car accident October 28, 1986. He is buried in Oakridge cemetery

in Bay City.

455 **BUZZARD Robert William:** (*William, Edwin, Joseph, Phillip, Melchior, Phillip*) was born February 8, 1926 in Bay City, Michigan, son of William J. Buzzard and Wilhemina Mrohs. He married July 29, 1950, Marlan Fayetta Barclay born September 1, 1928 in Detroit, Michigan, daughter of Roy W. Barclay and Leona Robertson. They are presently living in Auburn, Michigan.

Children born in Bay City:

723 i- **BUZZARD Janice Lea**: born March 26, 1948 and adopted by Robert and Marlan.
724 ii- **BUZZARD Ellen Marie**: born January 6, 1951
725 iii- **BUZZARD Ruth Evelyn**: born July 22, 1953
iv- **BUZZARD Robert Jr.**: born February 1, 1955

456 **BUZZARD Doris**: (*William, Edwin, Joseph, Phillip, Melchior, Phillip*) was born September 21, 1928 in Bay City, Michigan, daughter of William J. Buzzard and Wilhemina Mrohs. She married February 17, 1950, Laurence Villaire born August 3, 1918 in Jacksonville, Florida. They are presently living in Bay City.

Children:

726 i- **VILLAIRE Daniel L.**: born July 25, 1950
727 ii- **VILLAIRE Barbara E.**: born August 3, 1951

457 **BUZZARD Dorothy**: (*William, Edwin, Joseph, Phillip, Melchior, Phillip*) was born December 21, 1929 in Bay City, Michigan, daughter of William J. Buzzard and Wilhemina Mrohs. She married November 1, 1947, Harry E. Wood born April 21, 1929 in Bay City, son of Guy Wood and Bertha Ross.

Children born in Saginaw, Michigan:

i- **WOOD William Guy**: born March 12, 1950
ii- **WOOD David Edward**: born April 25, 1952
728 iii- **WOOD Marcia Jane**: born September 10, 1954
729 iv- **WOOD Beverly Jean**: born January 10, 1959
730 v- **WOOD Amy Lee**: born December 31, 1960

458 **BUZZARD Clayton E.**: (*William, Edwin, Joseph, Phillip, Melchior, Phillip*) was born April 30, 1935 in Bay City, Michigan, son of William J. Buzzard and Wilhemina Mrohs. He married August 27, 1955, Captola V. Jarsey born January 16, 1936.

One child born in Pincunning, Michigan:

i- **BUZZARD Joseph Jacob**: born March 22, 1971

459 BOSSARD George Clay: (*Lewis, George, Peter, Christopher, Melchior, Phillip*) was born October 15, 1913 in Painted Post, New York son of Lewis G. Bossard and Martha Roberts. He married September 9, 1932, Emma Graham in Cayuga Co. New York.

Children born in Geneva, New York.
731 **i- BOSSARD Sylvia Arline**: born July 11, 1933
732 **ii- BOSSARD Shirley Ann**: born November 18, 1935

460 SNOOK Raymond: (*Ethelyn, George, Peter, Christopher, Melchior, Phillip*) was born April 5, 1914 in Dundee, New York, son of Oliver William Snook and Ethelyn Marie Bossard. He married June 26, 1937 in Pine City, New York, Corabelle Crumb born August 7, 1914 in Deposit, New York, daughter of Fred Crumb and Elizabeth Kittel. They are presently living in Southern Pines, N. Carolina.

Children:
733 **i- SNOOK Carolyn Marie**: born July 20, 1942
734 **ii- SNOOK Patricia Ann**: born February 25, 1945

461 STANTON Gladys: (*Mabel, George, Peter, Christopher, Melchior, Phillip*) was born August 28, 1901 in Dundee, New York, daughter of Luther Stanton and Mabel Bossard. She married February 11, 1920, Charles F. Smith born March 10, 1900.

Children:
735 **i- SMITH June**: born March 24, 1922
736 **ii- SMITH William**: born April 14, 1923
737 **iii- SMITH Harry**: born May 5, 1925
738 **iv- SMITH Frederick**: born January 1, 1934
739 **v- SMITH Charles F. Jr.**: born September 8, 1942

462 STANTON Zelma: (*Mabel, George, Peter, Christopher, Melchior, Phillip*) was born June 23, 1903 in Dundee, New York, daughter of Luther Stanton and Mabel Bossard. She married October 1924, Harry Sharp. She is presently living in Dundee, New York.

One child born in Dundee, New York:
740 **i- SHARP Mary**: born May 10, 1931

463 STANTON William: (*Mabel, George, Peter, Christopher, Melchior, Phillip*) was born April 14, 1906 in Dundee, New York, son of Luther Stanton and Mabel Bossard. He married (1) December 31, 1930, Floreen Morse. He married (2) in 1940, Helen Lynch born June 5, 1903. William died September 19, 1980 and Helen died September 7, 1981.

Children:
741 i- **STANTON Charlotte**: (twin) born October 23, 1932
742 ii- **STANTON Charleen**: (twin) born October 23, 1932

464 **BOSSARD Albert George**: (*Leon, Marcus, Peter, Christopher, Melchior, Phillip*) was born October 14, 1906 in Corning, New York, son of Leon Bossard and Emily Jenkins. He married July 17, 1937 in Rochester, New York, Evelyn M. Hart born 1902, daughter of George A. Hart and Rena Wager.

465 **BOZARD Ross Edward**: (*Truman, Cyrus, Richard, Christopher, Melchior, Phillip*) was born June 7, 1883 in Humphrey, New York, son of Truman Bozard and Eva Butler. He married Bertha Zigler. Ross disappeared from Humphrey in 1938 and was never heard from again. No issue.

466 **BOZARD Grace Blanche**: (*Truman, Cyrus, Richard, Christopher, Melchior, Phillip*) was born April 7, 1885, in Humphrey, New York, daughter of Truman Bozard and Eva Butler. She married August 25, 1912, Walter Storms born July 14, 1889. She died March 30, 1959 in Sugar Grove, Pennsylvania.

Children born in Sugar Grove, Pennsylvania:
743 i- **STORMS Walter T. Jr.**: born September 1, 1913
744 ii- **STORMS Clifford C.**: born June 15, 1916

467 **BOZARD Ruby Emily**: (*Truman, Cyrus, Richard, Christopher, Melchior, Phillip*) was born July 11, 1887 in Humphrey, New York, daughter of Truman Bozard and Eva Butler. She married December 30, 1916, in Buffalo, New York, Charles Frederick Miller. He died December 12, 1951 and Ruby died August 18, 1971 in Buffalo, New York.

Children:
745 i- **MILLER Charles F. Jr.**: born December 16, 1919
746 ii- **MILLER Robert**: born December 3, 1922, unmarried. He was murdered in San Francisco in 1970.
747 iii- **MILLER Stanley**: born February 19, 1924
748 **8 iv- MILLER Richard**: born January 20, 1923

468 **BOZARD Floyd Cyrus**: (*Truman, Cyrus, Richard, Christopher, Melchior, Phillip*) was born May 10, 1890 in Humphrey, New York, son of Truman Bozard and Eva Butler. He married October 6, 1913 in Salamanca, Bessie Harkness born March 26, 1892, daughter of Howard Harkness and Nina Abbott. She died July 22, 1977 and Floyd died June 20, 1979. They are buried in Salamanca.

Children born in Salamanca, New York:

i- **BOZARD Howard Truman**: born February 22, 1915
749 ii- **BOZARD Eva**: born February 7, 1917
750 iii- **BOZARD Mildred**: born January 17, 1919
751 iv- **BOZARD Paul Floyd**: born December 3, 1920
752 v- **BOZARD Donald**: born April 16, 1923
vi- **BOZARD Donna**: born October 4, 1932 and died in September 1933, buried in Salamanca.

469 **BOZARD Flossie Marietta**: (*Truman, Cyrus, Richard, Christopher, Melchior, Phillip*) was born March 24, 1895 in Humphrey, New York, daughter of Truman Bozard and Eva Butler. She married March 24, 1920 in Buffalo, New York, Arthur Zuver born March 24, 1891. He died April 4, 1948 and Flossie died February 8, 1965.

Children born in Pennsylvania:
753 i- **ZUVER James**: born October 22, 1921
754 ii- **ZUVER Eva**: (twin) born January 8, 1923
iii- **ZUVER Jack**: (twin) born January 8, 1923. He was killed in the Korean War, November 28, 1950.
755 iv- **ZUVER Kenneth**: born December 20, 1931

470 **BOZARD Bernice Mae**: (*Truman, Cyrus, Richard, Christopher, Melchior, Phillip*) was born August 2, 1901 in Humphrey, New York, daughter of Truman Bozard and Eva Butler. She married April 30, 1920, Ralph W. Langley born December 3, 1899 in Olean, New York, son of William and Ethel Langley. He died May 10, 1951 in Hornell, New York. Bernice is still living in N. Hornell.

Children born in Salamanca, New York:
756 i- **LANGLEY Beatrice Jean**: born June 14, 1922
757 ii- **LANGLEY Barbara Eva**: born August 19, 1925

471 **BOZARD Beatrice Julia**: (*Truman, Cyrus, Richard, Christopher, Melchior, Phillip*) was born July 11, 1903 in Humphrey, New York, daughter of Truman Bozard and Eva Butler. She married November 5, 1923, Ernest Hokanson born August 17, 1903 in Kinzu Junction, Pennsylvania, son of Emil Hokanson and Sadie Ruff. He died March 18, 1979 and Beatrice is living in a nursing home in East Aurora, New York.

Children:
758 i- **HOKANSON Ernest Jr.**: born July 23, 1926
759 ii- **HOKANSON Dean Russell**: born December 5, 1928
760 iii- **HOKANSON Constance Louise**: born June 22, 1938

472 **BOZARD Clifford James**: (*Truman,Cyrus, Richard, Christopher, Melchior,*

Phillip) was born April 11, 1906 in Humphrey, New York, son of Truman Bozard and Eva Butler. He married Rena Thiel born January 10, 1910 in Barker, New York. They are presently living in Rochester, New York.

Children born in Buffalo, New York:
761 i- **BOZARD Bruce T.**: born February 23, 1942
762 ii- **BOZARD Mary K.**: born November 26, 1947

473 **BOZARD Rena**: (*Edward, Cyrus, Richard, Christopher, Melchior, Phillip*) was born August 22, 1909 in Humphrey, New York, daughter of Edward H. Bozard and Mary M. Ganung. She married September 2, 1930 in Olean, New York, Ralph R. Halladay born August 3, 1910, in Great Valley, New York, son of Raymond and Rose Halladay. She died March 16, 1942 in Allegany, New York. The family moved to Kansas City, Missouri. Ralph died April 6, 1969.

Children born in Great Valley, New York:
763 i- **HALLADAY Harry E.**: born April 6, 1939
764 ii- **HALLADAY Ralph Arthur**: born March 3, 1942

474 **BOZARD Bertha Eldene**: (*Edward, Cyrus, Richard, Christopher, Melchior, Phillip*) was born November 20, 1916 in Humphrey, New York, daughter of Edward H. Bozard and Mary M. Ganung. She married January 1, 1940 in Olean, New York, Raymond Sawdey born November 19, 1910, son of Henry Sawdey and Hattie Turner. They are presently living in Cuba, New York.

Children born in Olean, New York
765 i- **SAWDEY Lawrence James**: born June 11, 1942
766 ii- **SAWDEY Margaret Mary**: born September 16, 1943
767 iii- **SAWDEY Marcia Ann**: born February 10, 1945 in Hornell, New York

475 **MOSMAN Lynford**: (*Blanche, Cyrus, Richard, Christopher, Melchior, Phillip*) was born June 25, 1904 in Allegany, New York, son of William C. Mosman and Blanche Bozard. He married December 2, 1924 in Salamanca, New York, Harriet Laura Fiester born May 27, 1927, daughter of George Ralph Fiester and Laura Delia Tidd. They are presently living in Lancaster, New York and celebrated their 65th wedding anniversary last Thanksgiving Day. Lynford was owner and operator of the Wood's Wallpaper and Paint Store in Lancaster.

Children:
768 i- **MOSMAN William Lynford**: born December 16, 1925 in Olean, New York
769 ii- **MOSMAN Vivian Harriet**: born June 3, 1928 in Olean
770 iii- **MOSMAN Edward George**: born September 17, 1931, in Rochester, New York
771 iv- **MOSMAN Phyllis Elaine**: born December 16, 1938, in Buffalo, New

York

772 v- **MOSMAN Judith Marie**: born August 21, 1944, in Buffalo, New York

476 **MOSMAN William Devere**: (*Blanche, Cyrus, Richard, Christopher, Melchior, Phillip*) was born March 25, 1908 in Allegany, New York, son of William C. Mosman and Blanche Bozard. He married (1) Betty (unknown maiden name) and married (2) Margaret (unknown maiden name) and (3) Mildred Youngberg. He died January 1, 1977 in Cheektowaga, New York. He was the founder of the Buffalo Spray Co., which later became the Mosman Decorators. They had three children. No further records.

477 **HALE Lora D.**: (*Iva, Ashbel, Richard, Christopher, Melchior, Phillip*) was born April 15, 1900, daughter of Sidney G. Hale and Iva Bozard. She married January 6, 1920, Frank E. Woodward born 1895, son of John D. Woodward and Sarah Raymond. No further records.

478 **REHLER Margaret Rose**: (*Kittie, Ashbel, Richard, Christopher, Melchior, Phillip*) was born October 16, 1916 in Allegany, New York, daughter of Alfred Rehler and Kittie Bozard. She is presently living in Allegany, New York with her father, Alfred.

479 **BOZARD Thurman Andrew**: (*Glen, Judson, Richard, Christopher, Melchior, Phillip*) was born April 4, 1907 in Humphrey, New York, son of Glen Bozard and Blanche C. Button. He married Mary Ruth (unknown maiden name). He died May 4, 1957 and Mary Ruth died May 23, 1985. They are buried in Allegany.

One child:
773 i- **BOZARD Bernice**:

480 **GIBSON Edward J.**: (*Sarah Quin, Amanda Backer, Sarah, George, Melchior, Phillip*) was born December 22, 1909 in Pulteney, New York, son of Floyd D. Gibson and Sarah Quin. He married January 1, 1929, Dorothy Cole born May 28, 1912 in Pulteney, daughter of Jeptha Cole and Stella Squires.

Children:
774 i- **GIBSON Eleanor**:
775 ii- **GIBSON Edward J.**:
776 iii- **GIBSON Janice**: born 1937
777 iv- **GIBSON Jerry A.**:

481 **GIBSON Virginia**: (*Sarah Quin, Amanda Backer, Sarah, George, Melchior,*

Phillip) was born March 9, 1913 in Pulteney, New York, daughter of Floyd D. Gibson and Sarah Quin. She married August 28, 1937, Gerald Sick born August 9, 1908, son of Walter B. Sick and Lulu B. Harvey.

482 **HEDDEN William Franklin**: (*Henry Hedden, Jane Backer, Sarah, George, Melchior, Phillip*) was born August 11, 1915, son of Henry Ambrose Hedden and Josephine Edmister. He married October 17, 1940, Marjorie Allen born October 9, 1914, daughter of Harry Allen and Ethel Crites. They are presently living in Hornell, New York.

Children born in Hornell, New York:

i- **HEDDEN Linda Jo Ethel**: born July 8, 1941

778 ii- **HEDDEN William Harry**: born October 11, 1945

483 **HEDDEN Raymond Albert**: (*Henry Hedden, Jane Backer, Sarah, George, Melchior, Phillip*) was born June 22, 1917, son of Henry Ambrose Hedden and Josephine Edmister. He married September 14, 1942, Dorothy Allen born October 1, 1918, daughter of Harry Allen and Ethel Crites. They are presently living in Hornell, New York.

Children born in Hornell, New York:

i- **HEDDEN Raymond Albert Jr.**: born October 14, 1943 and died the same day.

779 ii- **HEDDEN Henry Andrew**: born December 21, 1944

780 iii- **HEDDEN Sue Ann**: born January 12, 1947

iv- **HEDDEN Norman Arthur**: born January 31, 1949 and died June 25, 1949.

781 v- **HEDDEN Marjorie Jean**: born March 1954

484 **HEDDEN Mary Jane**: (*Henry Hedden, Jane Backer, Sarah, George, Melchior, Phillip*) was born May 18, 1920, daughter of Henry Ambrose Hedden and Josephine Edmister. She married September 4, 1943, Robert Frederick Hurne born October 5, 1916. They are presently living in Hornell, New York.

Children:

782 i- **HURNE Marcia Joanne**: born June 15, 1944

ii- **HURNE Ronald Eugene**: born October 7, 1946

783 iii- **HURNE Marlene Ruth**: born December 24, 1949

485 **HEDDEN Esther**: (*Henry Hedden, Jane Backer, Sarah, George, Melchior, Phillip*) was born April 9, 1925 in Hornell, New York, daughter of Henry Ambrose Hedden and Josephine Edmister. She married June 17, 1944, Douglas Leroy Kerr born March 23, 1923. They are presently living in Hornell, New York.

Children:

784 i- **KERR Thomas James**: (twin) born May 4, 1947
785 ii- **KERR Douglas Leroy**: (twin) born May 4, 1947
786 iii- **KERR Nancy Jane**: born May 14, 1949
787 iv- **KERR Roger**: born February 14, 1957

486 DECKER Lawrence: (*Evaline Fero, Harriet Backer, Sarah, George, Melchior, Phillip*) was born August 1898 in Dix, New York, son of Thomas Bert Decker and Evaline Fero. He married Alta G. (unknown maiden name). She died October 29, 1956 in Beaver Dams, New York and he married (2) Mrs. Ethel Gleason. He married (3) Inez Arnold. He died January 9, 1981 in Montour Falls, New York.

Children:

i- **DECKER Hugh**:
ii- **DECKER Eldon G.**:
iii- **DECKER Delmar**:
iv- **DECKER Mildred**:

487 DECKER Florence: (*Evaline Fero, Harriet Backer, Sarah, George, Melchior, Phillip*) was born May 1900 in Dix, New York, daughter of Thomas Bert Decker and Evaline Fero. She married Leon Mapes, born 1884. He died November 27, 1982 and is buried in Beaver Dams, New York. No further records.

488 DECKER Clifford: (*Evaline Fero, Harriet Backer, Sarah, George, Melchior, Phillip*) was born 1902, son of Thomas Bert Decker and Evaline Fero. He died October 15, 1937 in Syracuse, New York. Wife' name unknown.

Children:

i- **DECKER Jack**:
ii- **DECKER Richard**:
iii- **DECKER Norman**:
iv- **DECKER James**:
v- **DECKER Marjorie**:

489 DECKER Harriet: (*Evaline Fero, Harriet Backer, Sarah, George, Melchior, Phillip*) was born ca 1907, daughter of Thomas Bert Decker and Evaline Fero. She married June 4, 1923, Francis Riley. No further records.

490 DECKER Harold E.: (*Evaline Fero, Harriet Backer, Sarah, George, Melchior, Phillip*) was born ca 1910, son of Thomas Bert Decker and Evaline Fero. He married Elizabeth (unknown maiden name). He died July 12, 1959 in Watkins, New York.

Children:
- i- **DECKER Betty:**
- ii- **DECKER Edith:**
- iii- **DECKER Roger:**
- iv- **DECKER Rodney:**

491 **DECKER Martha:** (*Evaline Fero, Harriet Backer, Sarah, George, Melchior, Phillip*) was born, daughter of Thomas Bert Decker and Evaline Fero. She married Jesse Kress. She died July 6, 198_ in Elmira, New York and is buried in Beaver Dams.

Children:
- i- **KRESS Norma J.:**
- ii- **KRESS Clifford:**
- iii- **KRESS Thomas:**
- iv- **KRESS Tina:**
- v- **KRESS Katrina:**
- vi- **KRESS Heidi E.:**
- vii- **KRESS Gunner:**
- viii- **KRESS Daniel:**
- ix- **KRESS John:**

492 **DECKER Erma:** (*Evaline Fero, Harriet Backer, Sarah, George, Melchior, Phillip*) was born, daughter of Thomas Bert Decker and Evaline Fero. She married Joseph Leonardo and lived in Phoenix, Arizona. No further records.

493 **PRITCHARD Elizabeth:** (*Margaret Fero, Harriet Backer, Sarah, George, Melchior, Phillip*) was born September 19, 1916 in Ogdensburg, New York, daughter of Dr. John Pritchard and Margaret Fero. She married (1) name unknown and married (2) Edwin Mitchell, born January 15, 1916 in Brockville, Ontario, Canada. They are presently living in Ogdensburg, New York. She had three children by her first marriage.

494 **FERO Dean:** (*Victor Fero, Harriet Backer, Sarah, George, Melchior, Phillip*) was born July 1, 1930 in Rochester, New York, son of Victor W. Fero and Nina Lamaureau. He married March 17, 1972, Karolina Seidenbusch born October 26, 1940. He is an attorney in Rochester, New York.

Children:
- i- **FERO Shela Karolina:** born December 28, 1972
- ii- **FERO Mathew John:** born October 5, 1975

495 **BOSSARD Raymond:** (*Clarence, Judd, Simon, George, Melchior, Phillip*) was

born January 16, 1921 in West Milford, New Jersey, son of Clarence Bossard and Anna Lehman. He married November 15, 1952, Dolores Furey, daughter of Thomas and Catherine Furey. He died May 25, 1959 in West Milford.

Children born in West Milford, New Jersey:
788 i- **BOSSARD Raymond Jr.**: born October 5, 1953
ii- **BOSSARD Thomas**: born October 10, 1957

496 PERSONIUS Doris: (*Adrian Personius, Clara, Anson, George, Melchior, Phillip*) was born May 9, 1923 in Ithaca, New York, daughter of Adrian Personius and Olive Sill. She married January 26, 1946, Daniel Henry Knowles born March 13, 1923, son of Wilbur Garfield and Katie Sage. They are presently living in Corning, New York.

Children:
789 i- **KNOWLES Denis**: born February 12, 1952
790 ii- **KNOWLES Nancy**: born October 31, 1953

497 BOSSARD Margaret Thelma: (*Arthur, Charles, Anson, George, Melchior, Phillip*) was born December 7, 1902 in Enfield, New York, daughter of Arthur Alfred Bossard and Mabel Wilson. She married October 1, 1933, Homer S. Pringle. Margaret died June 6, 1982. No issue.

498 BOSSARD Lucelia Elizabeth: (*Arthur, Charles, Anson, George, Melchior, Phillip*) was born April 14, 1910 in Enfield, New York, daughter of Arthur Alfred Bossard and Mabel Wilson. She married (1) June 12, 1929, Harvey Gordon Hill born December 24, 1908 in Lindley, New York. They were divorced and she married (2) March 11, 1949, George L. Compton born April 11, 1915 in Ithaca, New York. She is presently living in Newfield, New York.

Children:
791 i- **HILL Jean Lorraine**: born November 8, 1930
792 ii- **COMPTON William George**: (adopted) born July 12, 1952

499 BOSSARD Winifred Martha: (*Arthur, Charles, Anson, George, Melchior, Phillip*) was born November 12, 1913 in Enfield, New York, daughter of Arthur Alfred Bossard and Mabel Wilson. She married (1) July 3, 1937, Norman Arthur Mabee born 1913 in Ithaca, New York. She married (2) December 31, 1948, Kent Compton at Long Beach, California and married (3) February 14, 1959, John Donald Brewster. He died April 18, 1985 and Winifred is presently living in Slaterville Springs, New York. No issue.

500 BOSSARD Myron Arthur: (*Arthur, Charles, Anson, George, Melchior, Phillip*) was born August 31, 1918 in Enfield, New York, son of Arthur Alfred Bossard and Mabel Wilson. He married (1) August 9, 1947 in Ithaca, New York, Clella Stetson. He married (2) Rachel Jane Stuart and (3) Gertrude Tuckerman. They are presently living in Waterloo, New York.

Children:
793 i- **BOSSARD Linda Cheryl**: born March 29, 1948
794 ii- **BOSSARD Rosalie Jean**: (twin) born January 25, 1949
795 iii- **BOSSARD Carrol Ann**: (twin) born January 25, 1949
796 iv- **BOSSARD Ronald**: born December 28, 1950
Gertrude has four children by her first marriage:
i- **TUCKERMAN Charles**: born November 3, 1938
ii- **TUCKERMAN Dawn**: born May 8, 1946
iii- **TUCKERMAN Patricia**: born October 5, 1950
iv- **TUCKERMAN Arthur**: born October 1, 1959

501 BOSSARD Robert William: (*Arthur, Charles, Anson, George, Melchior, Phillip*) was born August 14, 1920 in Enfield, New York, son of Arthur Alfred Bossard and Mabel Wilson. He married July 11, 1940, Leona Wood. Robert died November 29, 1974 and is buried in Frear cemetery in Ithaca, New York. Leona ia deceased, unknown date.

Children born in Ithaca, New York:
797 i- **BOSSARD Sandy**: (twin) born November 10, 1941 and died April 15, 1976 in Syracuse, New York.
ii- **BOSSARD Sharron**: (twin) born November 10, 1941

502 BOSSARD Betty Jane: (*Arthur, Charles, Anson, George, Melchior, Phillip*) was born April 16, 1926 at Ithaca, New York, daughter of Arthur Alfred Bossard and Mabel Wilson. She married March 2, 1946, Roger Henry Mc Fall born March 30, 1917 in Ithaca, New York, son of Walter Mc Fall and Pearl Palmer. He died November 18, 1979. She married (2) June 30, 1979, Olin Tompkins, son of Olin and Grace Tompkins. They are presently living near Ithaca, New York.

Children:
i- **MC FALL Patricia Ann**: born October 15, 1946
798 ii- **MC FALL Diane Lee**: born September 28, 1949
799 iii- **MC FALL Deborah Elaine**: born March 7, 1955
800 iv- **MC FALL Nancy Jean**: born May 28, 1959
v- **MC FALL Stanley Arthur**: born April 25, 1961

503 KIBBE Vivian Florence: (*Lottie, Charles, Anson, George, Melchior, Phillip*) was born March 30, 1911 in N. Bingham, Pennsylvania, daughter of Bert Kibbe and Lottie Annette Bossard. She married (1) June 17, 1942, Raymond Simmons born February 7, 1916 in Elmer, Pennsylvania. He died June 15, 1975 in N. Bingham and she married (2) May 22, 1976, Martin Regina born October 8, 1914 in Claridge, Pennsylvania. Martin died September 27, 1989 in Mills, Pennsylvania. Vivian is presently living in Mills.

One child:
801 i- **SIMMONS Karen Elaine**: born February 15, 1944

504 **KIBBE Raymon Elbert**: (*Lottie, Charles, Anson, George, Melchior, Phillip*) was born May 6, 1913 in N. Bingham, Pennsylvania, son of Bert Kibbe and Lottie Annette Bossard. He married April 3, 1937 in York, Pennsylvania, Creda Breneman born May 6, 1915 in York. He died July 7, 1963 in Miami, Florida.

Children:
802 i- **KIBBE Justine**: born May 20, 1941
803 ii- **KIBBE Phillip Mark**: born June 23, 1945

505 **MC MILLAN Charles Duncan**: (*Florence, Charles, Anson, George, Melchior, Phillip*) was born May 20, 1923 in Ithaca, New York, son of Roy Duncan Mc Millan and Florence Catherine Bossard. He married January 11, 1946 in New Orleans, Louisianna, Anne Mayfield born March 31, 1926 in Charleston, South Carolina, daughter of Stanwix G. Mayfield and Annie Lartique Sams. Charles served as a Lieutenant in the Navy during World War II and was a Doctor in Temple, Texas.

Children:
804 i- **MC MILLAN Anne Blythe**: born July 23, 1948 in Oakland, California
ii- **MC MILLAN Charles Duncan Jr.**: born September 8, 1950 in Temple, Texas
805 iii- **MC MILLAN Elizabeth** Sams: born April 1, 1951 in Temple, Texas

506 **GENUNG Harold Bowman Jr.**: (*Jessie, Charles, Anson, George, Melchior, Phillip*) was born August 18, 1919 in Ithaca, New York, son of Harold Bowman Genung and Jessie Elizabeth Bossard. He married May 16, 1943, Miriam Briggs, daughter of K. D. and Thelma Briggs.

Children:
i- **GENUNG Karen Olivia**: (twin) born May 27, 1961
ii- **GENUNG Carole Elizabeth**: (twin) born May 27, 1961

507 **GENUNG John Bossard**: (*Jessie, Charles, Anson, George, Melchior, Phillip*) was born January 13, 1922 in Ithaca, New York, son of Harold Bowman Genung and Jessie Elizabeth Bossard. He married (1) Rachel Foulger, born November 2, 1930 in Los Angeles, California. They were divorced and he married (2) June 18, 1961, Barbara Smithwick.

One child:

i- **GENUNG Susan Kay**: born July 20, 1953

508 **BOSSARD Clarence Albert**: (*Claude, William, Anson, George, Melchior, Phillip*) was born August 18, 1913 in Howard, New York, son of Claude Bossard and Cora Voltz. He married January 10, 1936 in Fremont, New York, Edna Mead born October 18, 1917. They are presently living in the Town of Howard.

Children:

i- **BOSSARD Joyce M.**: born April 2, 1943
806 ii- **BOSSARD Jack**: born December 2, 1946

509 **BOSSARD Harold Willis**: (*Claude, William, Anson, George, Melchior, Phillip*) was born February 11, 1916 in Howard, New York, son of Claude Bossard and Cora Voltz. He married October 28, 1940, Beulah Storm born May 28, 1919. Harold died May 27, 1989 in Howard, New York. Beulah is presently living in the town of Howard.

Children born in Hornell, New York.

807 i- **BOSSARD Kermit Lee**: born November 3, 1941
808 ii- **BOSSARD Richard Dale**: born May 4, 1944
809 iii- **BOSSARD Nancy Marie**: born October 16, 1950
810 iv- **BOSSARD David Charles**: born May 19, 1954

510 **BOSSARD Doris Alta**: (*Claude, William, Anson, George, Melchior, Phillip*) was born October 15, 1922 in Hornell, New York, daughter of Claude Bossard and Cora Voltz. She married June 11, 1949 in Hornell, New York, William Lusk born May 5, 1924. They are presently living in Hornell.

Children:

i- **LUSK Steven E.**: born August 29, 1951
811 ii- **LUSK Gail Alice**: born June 8, 1955
812 iii- **LUSK Lucinda Rae**: born August 29, 1957
813 iv- **LUSK Brenda Jo**: born December 30, 1958

511 **HORTON Orlo Lauren**: (*Mary, William, Anson, George, Melchior, Phillip*) was born March 14, 1917 in Hornell, New York, son of Walter Horton and Mary (Matie) Bossard. He married April 29, 1945, Fairiola Taylor. Orlo was in the United States Navy band after graduating from High School in Hornell. He retired from the Navy, and moved to San Diego, California, where they are now living.

Children:

814 i- **HORTON Janice Marie**: born July 27, 1946
815 ii- **HORTON Jerry**: born September 11, 1947

512 **BOSSARD Harriet**: (*Fred, William, Anson, George, Malchior, Phillip*) was born April 11, 1910 in Howard, New York, daughter of Fred Bossard and Anna Coots. She married August 1940, Lee Lemon born November 2, 1914 in Dansville, New York. Harriet died July 9, 1978 in Rochester, New York and Lee died May 1987 in Dansville, New York. They are buried in Dansville.

Children:
816 i- **LEMON Sandra Lee**: born July 23, 1941
ii- **LEMON Gary Lynn**: born March 27, 1943. He is unmarried.

513 **BOSSARD William Anson**: (*Fred, William, Anson, George, Melchior, Phillip*) was born February 16, 1913 in Howard, New York, son of Fred Bossard and Anna Coots. He married June 24, 1934 in Angelica, New York, Alice Harriet Carson born August 27, 1915 in Allen, New York, daughter of Walter Carson and Lelia Luther. They are presently living in South Hornell, New York.

Children born in Hornell, New York.
817 i- **BOSSARD Anna Jean**: born March 26, 1938
818 ii- **BOSSARD Kay Lela**: born October 19, 1941
819 iii- **BOSSARD William W.**: born June 6, 1943
820 iv- **BOSSARD Donald R.**: born November 5, 1946
821 v- **BOSSARD Bruce F.**: born May 20, 1954

514 **BOSSARD Merlin**: (*Fred, William, Anson, George, Melchior, Phillip*) was born November 26, 1915 in Howard, New York, son of Fred Bossard and Anna Coots. He married (1) October 17, 1934, Bernadine Topping born February 12, 1912 in Sayre, Pennsylvania, daughter of Bert Topping and Grace Marley. They were divorced and he married (2) June 24, 1947 in Wellsboro, Pennsylvania, Doris Martin. He married (3) Mrs. Helen Clifford. He died October 1981 in Saratoga, New York.

Children by first marriage:
822 i- **BOSSARD James**: born October 22, 1935
823 ii- **BOSSARD Lois**: born June 3, 1939.
Merlin adopted Sue Martin, daughter of Doris Martin, his second wife.

515 **BOSSARD Marion**: (*Fred, William, Anson, George, Melchior, Phillip*) was born February 11, 1920 in Hornell, New York, daughter of Fred Bossard and Anna Coots. She married January 24, 1942 in Hornell, New York, Boyd Bicknell born January 7, 1918 in Hornell, son of Boyd Bicknell and Catherine O'Neil. They are presently living in Woodbury, New Jersey.

Children born in New Jersey:
824 i- **BICKNELL Boyd Thomas Jr.**: born March 22, 1947
825 ii- **BICKNELL Timothy James**: born March 14, 1953

826 **iii- BICKNELL William John**: born August 31, 1956
iv- BICKNELL James Frederick: born March 23, 1960

516 **BOSSARD Kenneth**: (*Fred, William, Anson, George, Melchior, Phillip*) was born March 10, 1922 in Hornell, New York, son of Fred Bossard and Anna Coots. He married January 15, 1942, Femmie Elizabeth Garrett. Kenneth served in the Marine Corps and retired in Jacksonville, North Carolina. He died May 31, 1985 in Jacksonville, and is buried in the Arlington National cemetery.

Children:
i- BOSSARD Sonja Elizabeth: December 14, 1942. She died June 10, 1953 and is also buried in the Arlington National cemetery.
827 **ii- BOSSARD Kenneth Jr.**: born July 19, 1948
828 **iii- BOSSARD Craig**: born August 5, 1950
829 **iv- BOSSARD Terrel Kay**: born April 1, 1954
830 **v- BOSSARD Lisa Kim**: born May 16, 1961
831 **vi- BOSSARD Kelly**: born August 13, 1963

517 **BOSSARD Aletha Ruth**: (*Roy, William, Anson, George, Melchior, Phillip*) was born May 6, 1916 in Howard, New York, daughter of Roy Bossard and Florence Jaynes. She married November 10, 1934 in Canisteo, New York, Floyd Edward Kame born September 2, 1912 in Hornell, New York, son of Floyd and Edna Kame. He died January 21, 1959 in Hornell, New York and Aletha Ruth died June 2, 1967. They are buried in Arkport, New York.

Children:
832 **i- KAME Irene Joyce**: born October 6, 1935
833 **ii- KAME Lawrence Edward**: born October 2, 1937
834 **iii- KAME Vincent Dale**: born June 8, 1941
835 **iv- KAME Betty Corinne**: born March 30, 1944

518 **BOSSARD Mildred Inez**: (*Roy, William, Anson, George, Melchior, Phillip*) was born April 25, 1922 in Hornell, New York, daughter of Roy Bossard and Florence Jaynes. She married (1) February 7, 1955, Charles Horton. They were divorced and she married (2) December 31, 1960, Harold Flaherty. She died May 22, 1989 in Buffalo, New York.

One child:
i- FLAHERTY Camden David: born July 9, 1962

519 **BOSSARD Merle Roy**: (*Roy, William, Anson, George, Melchior, Phillip*) was born October 8, 1926 in Hornell, New York, son of Roy Bossard and Florence Jaynes. He married August 15, 1948, Emma Jean Doris Campbell born August 25, 1927 in Hornell, New York, daughter of Leonard and Margaret Campbell. They

are presently living in Hornell, New York.

One child:

836 **i- BOSSARD Roy Walter**: born June 22, 1950

520 **BOSSARD Glenn Allen**: (*Roy, William, Anson, George, Melchior, Phillip*) was born June 27, 1931 in Hornell, New York, son of Roy Bossard and Florence Jaynes. He married January 25, 1953, Mary Ellen Dickson born December 17, 1935 in Hornell, New York, daughter of Joseph Dickson and Pauline Renwand. They are presently living in Hornell, New York.

Children:

i- BOSSARD Catherine Ellen: born September 1, 1953 She is unmarried and living in Hornell.

837 **ii- BOSSARD Barbara Jean**: born January 17, 1955

838 **iii- BOSSARD Richard Alan**: born December 14, 1957

839 **iv- BOSSARD Steven Joseph**: born August 10, 1960

v- BOSSARD Bret David: born March 17, 1973. He is unmarried and living in Hornell.

521 **SMITH Ernest Glen**: (*Charlotte, William, Anson, George, Melchior, Phillip*) was born September 13, 1920 in the Town of Hornellsville, New York, son of Frank Hobart Smith and Charlotte (Lottie) Bossard. He married August 23, 1958, Mrs. Fern Buchinger Hankins born August 15, 1924 in Dalton, New York daughter of John Buchinger and Ida Eliza Flint. They are presently living in Hornell, New York.

Children born in Hornell, New York:

840 **i- SMITH Sandra Janine**: born February 9, 1961

841 **ii- SMITH Steven Franklin**: born January 24, 1965

Fern had two children by her first marriage:

i- HANKINS Samuel John: born March 27, 1948

ii- HANKINS Shirley: born November 2, 1951

522 **SMITH Mary Louise**: (*Charlotte, William, Anson, George, Melchior, Phillip*)was born May 30, 1928 in North Hornell, New York, daughter of Frank Hobart Smith and Charlotte (Lottie) Bossard. She married June 2, 1951 in Rochester, New York, Eugene George Jackson born September 6, 1923 in Rochester, New York, son of Wilbert Jackson and Gertrude Elizabeth Tindall. Eugene served in Co. E. 320th Infantry during World War II and was injured during the Battle of the Bulge for which he received the purple heart. He worked for the Defense Department in Rochester until he retired in 1977. He died June 3, 1989 in Canandaigua, New York and he is buried in the Friends cemetery in Farmington, New York. Mary is presently living in Farmington.

Children:
842 i- **JACKSON Edward Frank**: born Januray 25, 1948
843 ii- **JACKSON Allen Eugene**: born May 25, 1953
844 iii- **JACKSON Richard Jay**: born November 21, 1954
845 iv- **JACKSON Cheryl Ann**: (twin) born February 11, 1956
846 v- **JACKSON Gary Lee**: (twin) born February 11, 1956
847 vi- **JACKSON Brian Ernest**: born February 13, 1959
848 vii- **JACKSON Susan Elizabeth**: born March 26, 1960
849 viii- **JACKSON Kevin Scot**: born April 5, 1961

523 BOSSARD Gerald Louis: (*Lawrence, William, Anson, George, Melchior, Phillip*) was born June 19, 1926 in Hornell, New York, son of Lawrence Bossard and Marion Schaumberg. He married October 11, 1945 in Hornell, New York, Doris Elaine Campbell born October 10, 1925 in Elmira, New York. They were divorced and Gerald is presently living in Hornell.

Children:
i- **BOSSARD Robert Joseph**: born August 27, 1946, he was killed in a car accident in October 1964 and is buried in Riverside cemetery.
ii- **BOSSARD William James**: born July 23, 1951

524 BOSSARD Dorothy Jean: (*Lawrence, William, Anson, George, Melchior, Phillip*) was born January 2, 1930 in Hornell, New York, daughter of Lawrence Bossard and Marion Schaumberg. She married September 2, 1948 in Hornell, Max Allen born March 14, 1928, son of Albert Allen and Mabel Jackson. They are presently living in Campbell, New York.

Children:
850 i- **ALLEN Thomas Neil**: born January 20, 1953
ii- **ALLEN Jeffrey Scott**: born December 13, 1954
851 iii- **ALLEN Maxine Susan**: born July 19, 1957
iv- **ALLEN Keith Brian**: born October 4, 1959

525 BOSSARD Jacqueline Lou: (*Lawrence, William, Anson, George, Melchior, Phillip*) was born April 26, 1941 in Hornell, New York, daughter of Lawrence Bossard and Marion Schaumberg. She married May 2, 1960, John Joseph Trewtanelli born February 12, 1934. They are presently living in Florida.

Children born in Lakeland, Florida.
852 i- **TREWTANELLI Elizabeth Ann**: born May 7, 1961
853 ii- **TREWTANELLI Nancy Marie**: born April 22, 1966

526 PALMER Lorena June: (*Inez, William, Anson, George, Melchior, Phillip*) was born July 10, 1928 in North Hornell, New York, daughter of Lloyd C. Palmer and Inez Bossard. She married (1) January 10, 1948, Albert Justin Stillman born January 10, 1929 in Hornell, New York, son of Albert and Roberta Stillman. They were divorced and she married (2) July 17, 1956 in Howard, New York, Joseph Evanosky. They were divorced and she married (3) James Jones. She is presently living in Fairport, New York.

Children born in Hornell, New York.
854 i- **STILLMAN David Lee**: born August 23, 1950
ii- **STILLMAN Marvin Douglas**: born June 19, 1952
Children born in Rochester, New York
iii- **EVANOSKY Greg Steven**: born January 19, 1957
iv- **JONES Jeffrey James**: born September 29, 1970

527 **PALMER Luella Ann**: (*Inez, William, Anson, George, Melchior, Phillip*) was born January 17, 1931 in North Hornell, daughter of Lloyd C. Palmer and Inez Bossard. She married July 7, 1950 in Howard, New York, Harry Lawrence Sharp born August 20, 1928 in Howard, New York, son of Olin Sharp and Nina Brasted. They are presently living in Howard, New York.

Children:
855 i- **SHARP Beverly Ann**: born November 26, 1951
856 ii- **SHARP Patricia Lynn**: born October 19, 1954

528 **PALMER Allen Duane**: (*Inez, William, Anson, George, Melchior, Phillip*) was born May 27, 1932 in North Hornell, New York son of Lloyd C. Palmer and Inez Bossard. He married October 31, 1953 in Wallace, New York, Eleanor Gayle Wise born February 17, 1935 in Avoca, New York, daughter of Lloyd Wise and Nora Fairbrother. They are presently living in Howard, New York.

Children:
857 i- **PALMER Ricky Allen**: born August 22, 1954
858 ii- **PALMER Robert Chester**: born May 8, 1956
859 iii- **PALMER Gary Lee**: born January 20, 1959
860 iv- **PALMER Randy Lynn**: born March 9, 1962

529 **PALMER Betty Joanne**: (*Inez, William, Anson, Geroge, Melchior, Phillip*) was born September 2, 1933 in North Hornell, New York, daughter of Lloyd C. Palmer and Inez Bossard. She married April 24, 1954, Thomas Fairchild Beach born September 19, 1933, son of Thomas Fairchild Beach and Mabel Crandall. They are presently living in South Dansville, New York.

Children born in Hornell, New York.
861 i- **BEACH Michael Thomas**: born January 23, 1956
862 ii- **BEACH Terri Lynn**: born March 13, 1958

530 **PALMER Barbara Jean:** (*Inez, William, Anson, George, Melchior, Phillip*) was born Junuary 14, 1935 in North Hornell, New York, daughter of Lloyd C. Palmer and Inez Bossard. She married May 12, 1956, Phillip Gerald Shafer born July 27, 1928 in Hornell, New York. They are presently living in Poland, Ohio.

Children:
862 i- **SHAFER Susan Kay**: born March 11, 1958
ii- **SHAFER Steven Karl**: born November 5, 1959. He is unmarried and living in Hawaii.
iii- **SHAFER Sarah Kathryn**: born January 6, 1965

531 **BOSSARD Charles Priestly:** (*Anson, Fred, Anson, George, Melchior, Phillip*) was born December 29, 1915 in Hammonton, New Jersey, son of Margaretta Peguese Priestly and her first husband, Herman Priestly. He was adopted by Anson Bossard. He married December 2, 1939, Beverly June Chevalier born January 16, 1918. He died November 30, 1976 and Beverly died November 1978 in Cortland, New York. They are buried in Cortland.

Children born in Cortland, New York:
864 i- **BOSSARD Charles F.**: born May 11, 1943
865 ii- **BOSSARD Richard Aii**: born May 8, 1947
866 iii- **BOSSARD David Warren**: born August 23, 1950
867 iv- **BOSSARD Lorena Sue**: born July 24, 1955

532 **BOSSARD Anson Chester Jr.:** (*Anson, Fred, Anson, George, Melchior, Phillip*) was born August 12, 1927 in Cortland, New York, son of Anson Chester Bossard and Margaretta Peguese Priestly. He married August 12, 1950 in Syracuse, New York, Rita Mae Willoughby born December 24, 1929 in Solvay, New York.

Children born in Syracuse, New York.
868 i- **BOSSARD Beryl Ann**: born June 3, 1954
ii- **BOSSARD Joel Anson**: born May 10, 1956

533 **BOSSARD Margaretta Lorena:** (*Anson, Fred, Anson, George, Melchior, Phillip*) was born August 28, 1936 in Syracuse, New York, daughter of Anson Chester Bossard and Margaretta Peguese Priestly. She married April 26, 1958 in Upper Darby, Pennsylvania, Ira Newton Bush Jr. born September 22, 1931, son of Ira Newton and Dorothy Bush.

Children:
i- **BUSH Phillip Edward**: born May 25, 1960
869 ii- **BUSH Elaine Louise**: born March 25, 1961
iii- **BUSH Jennifer Louise**: born July 27, 1967

534 **BOSSARD Mary Joan Mildred**: (*Anson, Fred, Anson, George, Melchior, Phillip*) was born October 9, 1946 in Philadelphia, Pennsylvania, daughter of Anson Chester Bossard and Mildred Thrasa Myers. She married July 4, 1968 in Verona, New Jersey, Lieutenant Alan M. Mandel born May 18, 1945 in Scranton, Pennsylvania. They are presently living in Parsippany, New Jersey.

Children:
i- **MANDEL Aaron Jacob**: born July 21, 1971 in Denver, Colorado.
ii- **MANDEL Rachel Judith**: born September 19, 1976 in San Francisco, California
Children born in Parsippany, New Jersey:
iii- **MANDEL Seth Joseph**: born May 8, 1981
iv- **MANDEL Beth Janet**: born September 7, 1983

535 **BOSSARD Peter Robert John**: (*Anson, Fred, Anson, George, Melchior, Phillip*) was born June 12, 1949 in Phildelphia, Pennsylvania, son of Anson Chester Bossard and Mildred Thrasa Myers. He married August 16, 1952, Valerie Cicerone, born February 24, 1952, in Phildelphia, Pennsylvania, daughter of Lewis and Theresa Cicerone. They are divorced.

One child born in Phildelphia:
i- **BOSSARD Vanessa Valerie**: born November 5, 1976

536 **BOSSARD Paul Delmer John**: (*Anson, Fred, Anson, George, Melchior, Phillip*) was born May 18, 1950 in Philadelphia, Pennsylvania, son of Anson Chester Bossard and Mildred Thrasa Myers. He married January 19, 1974 in Phildelphia, Elizabeth Tustin, daughter of George and Loretta Tustin. They are divorced and Paul lives in New Jersey.

One child born in Philadelphia:
i- **BOSSARD Amanda Loretta**: born July 11, 1974

537 **BOSSARD Diane Denise Rose**: (*Anson, Fred, Anson, George, Melchior, Phillip*) was born June 5, 1952 in Philadelphia, Pennsylvania, dughter of Anson Chester Bossard and Mildred Thrasa Myers. She married July 13, 1974 in Philadelphia, Joseph Ambruso born January 7, 1952 in Philadelphia, son of Joseph and Margaret Ambruso.

Children Adopted by Joseph and Diane:
i- **AMBRUSO Desiree Denise**: born May 7, 1983
ii- **AMBRUSO Valerie Marie**: born February 19, 1986

538 **BOSSARD Lawrence Alson**: (*Charlie, Fred, Anson, George, Melchior, Phillip*) was born December 5, 1925 in East Lansing, New York, son of Charlie Bossard

and Florence Leola Buck. He married November 29, 1947 in Trumansburg, New York, Ruth H. Mc Fall born June 15, 1926 in Danby, New York. Lawrence died March 12, 1984.

Children:
870 i- **BOSSARD Linda Lou**: born June 17, 1949
871 ii- **BOSSARD Barbara Jean**: born May 16, 1954
iii- **BOSSARD Glenn A.**: born January 6, 1957

539 **BOSSARD Clifton Asil**: (*Charlie, Fred, Anson, George, Melchior, Phillip*) was born June 5, 1926 in West Groton, New York, son of Charlie Bossard and Florence Leola Buck. He married Laura Stevens.

Children:
872 i- **BOSSARD Stephania**: born November 26, 1951
873 ii- **BOSSARD Eric Allen**: born October 25, 1953
iii- **BOSSARD Leigh Ann**: born May 18, 1957

540 **BOSSARD Beverly Ann**: (*Charlie, Fred, Anson, George, Melchior, Phillip*) was born August 11, 1935 in West Groton, New York, daughter of Charlie Bossard and Florence Leola Buck. She married (1) August 17, 1953, Robert Jason Holcomb. They were divorced and she married (2) August 18, 1984, Lloyd Pippin born March 6, 1931.

Children by first marriage:
874 i- **HOLCOMB Florence Ethelyn**: born December 8, 1954
875 ii- **HOLCOMB Rebecca Suzanne**: born March 22, 1957
876 iii- **HOLCOMB Roberta Lynn**: born May 4, 1958
iv- **HOLCOMB Newton William**: born January 19, 1960
877 v- **HOLCOMB Jessica Louise**: born December 15, 1962
vi- **HOLCOMB Charlie Howard**: born August 5, 1964

541 **BOSSARD Charlie Alton**: (*Charlie, Fred, Anson, George Melchior, Phillip*) was born July 3, 1938 in West Groton, New York, son of Charlie Bossard and Florence Leola Buck. He married (1) June 7, 1958, Suzanne Fuller. They were divorced and he married (2) October 5, 1963, Mrs. Judith Leonard Hussey, born June 22, 1942 in Auburn, New York.

Child by first marriage:
878 i- **BOSSARD Russell Leonard**: born February 26, 1959 (Judy's son by first marriage and adopted by Charlie)
879 ii- **BOSSARD Cindy Jane**: born April 17, 1960
Children by second marriage:
iii- **BOSSARD Stephen Alton**: born August 14, 1964
iv- **BOSSARD Randy Lee**: born August 30, 1966

542 **BOSSARD Beth Elaine:** (*Charlie, Fred, Anson, George, Melchior, Phillip*) was born November 9, 1941 in West Groton, New York, daughter of Charlie Bossard and Florence Leola Buck. She married (1) August 4, 1962, Michael Heslin, born February 5, 1936. They were divorced and she married (2) September 12, 1981, Darrell Bacorn born March 23, 1941. They are presently living in Lansing, New York.

Children:
880 i- **HESLIN Ann Theresa:** born August 9, 1963
ii- **HESLIN Joseph Michael:** born April 28, 1965
iii- **HESLIN Garrison Owen:** April 3, 1970

543 **BOGARDUS Neale Fred:** (*Marjorie, Fred, Anson, George, Melchior, Phillip*) was born May 6, 1932 in Corning, New York, son of Charles Wesley Bogardus and Marjorie Eliza Bossard. He married September 22, 1956 in Rochester, New York, Joan Mary Lewis born April 16, 1936. They are presently living in Syracuse, New York.

Children:
i- **BOGARDUS Cythia Ruth:** born July 17, 1957
ii- **BOGARDUS Scott Neale:** born November 18, 1959
iii- **BOGARDUS Peter Gerald:** born November 9, 1963

544 **BOGARDUS Clinton Glen:** (*Irma, Fred, Anson, George, Melchior, Phillip*) was born July 15, 1930 in Buffalo, New York, son of Glen Hoffman Bogardus and Irma Stella Bossard. He married July 7, 1956, Ruth Asmundsen. They are presently living near Buffalo, New York.

Children:
i- **BOGARDUS Jeannette:** born August 2, 1957
ii- **BOGARDUS Lorraine:** born January 4, 1959
iii- **BOGARDUS Debra:** born August 2, 1960

545 **BOSSARD Kermit Jr.:** (*Kermit, Fred, Anson, George, Melchior, Phillip*) was born April 5, 1951 in Troy, New York, son of Kermit Clarence Bossard and Theresa Hebert. He married November 7, 1981, Irene Giaillornardo born November 7, 1955, daughter of William Giallornardo and Mildred Curry. They are presently living in Schenectady, New York.

Children born in Schenectady, New York:
i- **BOSSARD Daniel Kermit:** born July 24, 1983
ii- **BOSSARD Andrew William:** born November 6, 1987

546 **TOWNER Douglas Edward:** (*Winona, Fred, Anson, George, Melchior, Phillip*)

was born February 1, 1941 in Philadelphia, Pennsylvania, son of Edward Towner and Winona Bossard. He married April 3, 1965, Betsey Ketchum. They are presently living near Philadelphia, Pennsylvania.

Children:
i- **TOWNER Lauren Ketchum**: October 15, 1967
ii- **TOWNER Elizabeth Laverne**: born October 12, 1968

547 LONGFELLOW Allen Leroy: (*Louise, William B., Andrew K., Andrew, Melchior, Phillip*) was born October 21, 1913, son of Wilber Leroy Longfellow and Louise Bosard. He married (1) Ethel Williams. They were divorced and he married (2) Virginia Luhr. No further records.

Children:
881 i- **LONGFELLOW Linda**:
882 ii- **LONGFELLOW Susan**:
883 iii- **LONGFELLOW Marnell**:

548 LONGFELLOW Lila Louise: (*Louise, William B., Andrew K., Andrew, Melchior, Phillip*) was born January 6, 1915, daughter of Wilbur Leroy Longfellow and Louise Bosard. She married May 5, 1944, John Walter Houck born January 6, 1915. They are presently living in Seattle, Washington.

One child:
884 i- **HOUCK Catherine Carolyn**: born March 2, 1950

549 PATTISON Helen C.: (*Helen Redfield, Emma, Andrew K. Andrew, Melchior, Phillip*) was born 1912, daughter of John O. Pattison and Helen Redfield. She married (1) Robert B. Carey and (2) Robert S. Cocks.

Child by first marriage:
885 i- **CAREY Helen B.**: born 1940
Child by second Marriage:
ii- **COCKS Mary Irene**: born 1950

550 PATTISON Jane R.: (*Helen Redfield, Emma, Andrew K., Andrew, Melchior, Phillip*) was born 1921, daughter of John O. Pattison and Helen Redfield. She married George E. Tudor.

Children:
i- **TUDOR Susan B.**: born 1957
ii- **TUDOR Jonathan Evans**: born 1959

551 REDFIELD Joseph B. III: (*Mark Redfield, Emma, Andrew K., Andrew, Melchior, Phillip*) was born 1939, son of Mark B. Redfield and Dorothy Bauer. He married Christine Murray. He died in 1971 and is buried in the Keeneyville cemetery in Keeneyville, Pennsylvania.

One child:
i- **REDFIELD Valerie Jean:**

552 REDFIELD Mark B. Jr.: (*Mark Redfield, Emma, Andrew K., Andrew, Melchior, Phillip*) was born in 1942, son of Mark B. Redfield and Dorothy Bauer. He married Anne Cushins.

One child:
i- **REDFIELD William Scott:** born 1965

553 REDFIELD Anthony Lee: (*Mark Redfield, Emma, Andrew K., Andrew, Melchior, Phillip*) was born 1949, son of Mark B. Redfield and Dorothy Bauer. Last known, they were living in Horseheads, New York.

554 BUTLER Franklin Jesse: (*Mabel Treat, Lizzie, Andrew K., Andrew, Melchior, Phillip*) was born September 27, 1917 in Deerfield, Pennsylvania, son of Waldo Butler and Mabel Treat. He married October 26, 1946 in Knoxville, Mary Lucille Hoffa born July 24, 1917.

Children:
i- **BUTLER Charles Waldo:** born February 24, 1949
886 ii- **BUTLER Ronald James:** born April 16, 1950
887 iii- **BUTLER Robert Franklin:** born August 13, 1952
iv- **BUTLER Anne Marie:** born October 1954 and died October 1954
888 v- **BUTLER Richard Seldon:** born February 16, 1961

555 BUTLER Erma Maude: (*Mabel Treat, Elizabeth, Andrew K., Andrew, Melchior, Phillip*) was born April 8, 1920 in Deerfield, Pennsylvania, daughter of Waldo Butler and Mabel Treat. She married January 10, 1953 in Addison, New York, Paul Curtis Plough born September 22, 1924. They are presently living in Round Rock, Texas.

Children:
889 i- **PLOUGH Mark Arthur:** (twin) born April 14, 1955
890 ii- **PLOUGH Martha Ann:** (twin) born April 14, 1955
891 iii- **PLOUGH Scott Curtis:** born March 9, 1958

556 ZUNDEL Ruth Evelyn: (*Ethel Treat, Elizabeth, Andrew K., Andrew, Melchior,*

Phillip) was born May 31, 1918 in Galeton, Pennsylvania, daughter of Louis Jacob Zundel and Ethel Treat. She married June 27, 1946 in W. Branch Township, Potter Co. Pennsylvania, Robert Lincoln Fowler. They are presently living in Potter Co., Pennsylvania.

Children:
892 i- **FOWLER Robert Allen**: born August 21, 1947
893 ii- **FOWLER John Arthur**: born October 27, 1950
iii- **FOWLER Wayne Louis**: born September 24, 1952

557 **ZUNDEL Thelma Louise**: (*Ethel Treat, Elizabeth, Andrew K., Andrew, Melchior, Phillip*) was born May 23, 1925 in Galeton, Pennsylvania, daughter of Louis Jacob Zundel and Ethel Treat. She married December 27, 1947, Gilbert Raymond Schoonover born June 5, 1926.

Children:
894 i- **SCHOONOVER Cheryl Kay**: born September 10, 1949
895 ii- **SCHOONOVER David Raymond**: born March 27, 1951
iii- **SCHOONOVER Ann Marie**: born July 28, 1957 and died the same day
896 iv- **SCHOONOVER Donn Wesley**: born May 5, 1960

558 **ZUNDEL Betty Joette**: (*Ethel Treat, Elizabeth, Andrew K., Andrew, Melchior, Phillip*) was born December 23, 1927 in Potter Co. Pennsylvania, daughter of Louis Jacob Zundel and Ethel Treat. She married August 28, 1948 in Galeton, Pennsylvania, Elmer Dean McAllister.

Children:
897 i- **MCALLISTER Richard Earl**: born July 11, 1949
898 ii- **MCALLISTER Ronald Dean**: born November 18, 1952
899 iii- **MCALLISTER Donna Marie**: born May 12, 1954
900 iv- **MCALLISTER Randall Jon**: born February 10, 1956

559 **TREAT Sondra Ann**: (*Ernest, Elizabeth, Andrew K., Andrew, Melchior, Phillip*) was born June 3, 1938 in Cumberland, Maryland, daughter of Ernest B. Treat and Helen Riser. She married (1) Richard Rouzer. They were divorced and she married (2) William Bowen.

Children:
901 i- **ROUZER Robert Richard**: born November 18, 1958
902 ii- **ROUZER Treta Renee**: born April 13, 1960
903 iii- **ROUZER Ronald Ernest**: born June 28, 1964

560 **WHITNEY Marie**: (*Fay Owlet, Anna, Melchior D., Andrew, Melchior, Phillip*)

daughter of John E. Whitney and Fay Dollie Owlet. She married James Connelly.

561 **OWLET John Bosard Jr.**: (*John Owlet, Anna, Melchior D., Andrew, Melchior, Phillip*) son of John Bosard Owlet and Eva Matteson. He married Coralee Justin.

Children:
- i- **OWLET Kristi**: born 1956
- ii- **OWLET Brent**: born June 22, 1957
- iii- **OWLET Amy**: born 1960

562 **OWLET Florence**: (*John Owlet, Anna, Melchior D., Andrew, Melchior, Phillip*) daughter of John Bosard Owlet and Eva Matteson. She married Richard Schingel.

563 **OWLET Charles B.**: (*Charles Owlet, Anna, Melchior D., Andrew, Melchior, Phillip*) was born July 20, 1924 in Tioga Co., Pennsylvania, son of Charles E. Owlet and Leah Butler. He married May 7, 1954, Lottie (unknown maiden name).

564 **OWLET Gweneth**: (*Charles E. Owlet, Anna, Melchior D., Andrew, Melchior, Phillip*) was born March 26, 1928 in Elkland, Pennsylvania, daughter of Charles E. Owlet and Leah Butler. She married (1) April 5, 1947, Phillip E. Howard. She married (2) John Colletta of Elmira, New York.

Children by first marriage:

904 i- **HOWARD Walter Charles**: born November 7, 1947 in Sabinsville, Pennsylvania.

905 ii- **HOWARD Marlene Ann**: born February 18, 1949 in Elmira, New York.

906 iii- **HOWARD Douglas Earl**: born August 7, 1950, at Blossburg, Pennsylvania

iv- **HOWARD David Phillip**: born August 23, 1954 and died September 9, 1954 in Elmira, New York.

v- **HOWARD Donald Eugene**: born October 4, 1955 in Elmira, New York.

Child by second marriage born in Elmira:

vi- **COLETTA Angelina Marie**: born March 13, 1960

565 **OWLET Andrew V.**: (*Charles E. Owlet, Anna, Melchior D., Andrew, Melchior, Phillip*) was born June 22, 1930 in Davis Station, Pennsylvania, son of Charles E. Owlet and Leah Butler. Andrew was a Senior Chief Aviation Support Equipment for the United States Navy and served aboard the Ticonderga during the Vietnam War. He married February 15, 1953 in Naples, Italy, Maria L. Fusco born in Italy.

Children:

i- **OWLET Charles Eugene**: born December 24, 1953, in Afragola, Italy.
907 ii- **OWLET John Antonio**: born November 21, 1954, in Kittery, Maine.
iii- **OWLET Melinda Ann**: born February 13, 1963, in Willingboro, New Jersey.

566 OWLET Harold: (*Carlton Owlet, Anna, Melchior D., Andrew, Melchior, Phillip*) was born March 8, 1923 in Nelson, Pennsylvania, son of Carlton Andrew Owlet and Fay Leonard. He married September 15, 1951 in Lawrenceville, Pennsylvania, Patricia Cole born January 15, 1930 in Lawrenceville, daughter of Arland L. Cole and Margaret M. Perry.

One child born in Corning, New York.
908 i- **OWLET Julaine**: born August 28, 1956

567 OWLET Wilma: (*Carlton, Anna, Melchior D., Andrew, Melchior, Phillip*) was born February 16, 1918 in Lawrenceville, Pennsylvania, daughter of Carlton Andrew Owlet and Fay Leonard. She married March 25, 1940 in Nelson, Pennsylvania, Phillip Davis, son of Coral Davis.

Children born in Nelson, Pennsylvania.
909 i- **DAVIS Theodore**: born April 10, 1941
910 ii- **DAVIS Charlene**: born December 10, 1942
911 iii- **DAVIS Carlton**: born February 4, 1947

568 OWLET Elva: (*Mark Owlet, Anna, Melchior D., Andrew, Melchior, Phillip*) was born September 9, 1923 in Tioga Co., Pennsylvania, daughter of Mark T. Owlet and Martha O. Buck. She married August 14, 1941, Shirley Baker.

569 OWLET Helen Marie: (*Mark Owlet, Anna, Melchior D., Andrew, Melchior, Phillip*) was born February 28, 1926 in Tioga Co., Pennsylvania, daughter of Mark T. Owlet and Martha O. Buck. She married November 4, 1943, Wilbur Hamlin.

570 OWLET Franklin Deroy: (*Mark Owlet, Anna, Melchior D., Andrew, Melchior, Phillip*) was born November 4, 1928 in Tioga Co., Pennsylvania, son of Mark T. Owlet and Martha O. Buck. He married February 15, 1947, Marjorie Mills.

571 OWLET Marion Louella: (*Mark Owlet, Anna, Melchior D., Andrew, Melchior, Phillip*) was born November 8, 1931 in Tioga Co., Pennsylvania, daughter of Mark T. Owlet and Martha O. Buck. She married February 5, 1951, Edwin Mills.

572 OWLET Kenneth: (*Burton Owlet, Anna, Melchior D., Andrew, Melchior,*

Phillip) was born March 13, 1939 and adopted by Burton Owlet and Alice Bowman. He married Nancy Forbes.

573 ECKERT Leroy: (*Anna Rinker, Sarah Huffsmith, Hanna, Peter, Melchior, Phillip*) was born April 9, 1896 in Stroudsburg, Pennsylvania, son of Franklin Eckert and Anna L. Rinker. He married Julia S. (unknown married name). She died 1976 and Leroy died 1989. They are buried in the Stroudsburg cemetery. Children unknown.

574 RINKER Russell: (*Peter Rinker, Sarah Huffsmith, Hanna, Peter, Melchior, Phillip*) was born January 1893 in Monroe Co., Pennsylvania, son of Peter Rinker and Ella A. Kerrick. He married Florence Dyson, born 1898. He died March 8, 1960 in Stroudsburg, Pennsylvnaia and Florence died November 1973. They are buried in the Stroudsburg cemetery.

Children:
912 i- **RINKER Marguerite**:
913 ii- **RINKER Kathryn**:

575 RHODES Grover C.: (*Mary Rinker, Sarah Huffsmith, Hanna, Peter, Melchior, Phillip*) was born January 17, 1890 in Monroe Co., Pennsylvania, son of Lewis E. Rhodes and Mary F. Rinker. He married Lucy M. (unknown maiden name). He died July 28, 1979 in Stroudsburg, Pennsylvania and Lucy died November 26, 1973. They are buried in the Stroudsburg cemetery.

576 RINKER Horace William: (*Edwin Rinker, Sarah Huffsmith, Hanna, Peter, Melchior, Phillip*) was born January 21, 1899 in Stroudsburg, Pennsylvania, son of Edwin Rinker and Ida Francis Smith. He married Evelyn T. Corn, born 1899. He died October 7, 1963 in Philadelphia and Evelyn died 1987. They are buried in the Stroudsburg cemetery.

Children:
i- **RINKER Franklin H.**:
ii- **RINKER Ray C.**:

577 RINKER Clarence Franklin: (*Edwin Rinker, Sarah Huffsmith, Hanna, Peter, Melchior, Phillip*) was born January 18, 1902 in Stroudsburg, Pennsylvania, son of Edwin Rinker and Ida Francis Smith. He married September 27, 1919 in Stroudsburg, Alice E. Tims born ca 1893, in Reading, England, daughter of Frank and Elizabeth Tims. He died January 2, 1962 in Stroudsburg.

578 HUFFSMITH Clara: (*William Huffsmith, George, Huffsmith, Hanna, Peter,*

Melchior, Phillip) was born August 6, 1907 in Stroudsburg, Pennsylvania, daughter of William Huffsmith and Alta Lee. She married John De Vivo, born June 16, 1909 and they are presently living in Stroudsburg.

Children:
914 i- **DE VIVO Barbara**: born September 7, 1937
ii- **DE VIVO Alta**: born August 24, 1939
915 iii- **DE VIVO John Jr.**: born August 6, 1942
916 iv- **DE VIVO Samuel**: born August 2, 1946

579 **HUFFSMITH Harold**: (*William Huffsmith, George Huffsmith, Hanna, Peter, Melchior, Phillip*) was born January 6, 1915 in Stroudsburg, Pennsylvania, son of William Huffsmith and Alta Lee. He married Mildred (unknown maiden name) and they are presently living in East Stroudsburg.

580 **HUFFSMITH George**: (*William Huffsmith, George Huffsmith, Hanna, Peter, Melchior, Phillip*) was born February 28, 1919 in Stroudsburg, Pennsylvania, son of William Huffsmith and Alta Lee. He married December 8, 1945, Gertrude Partridge. They are presently living in Hornell, New York.

Children:
917 i- **HUFFSMITH Philip Lloyd**: born September 9, 1946
918 ii- **HUFFSMITH Mark Alexander**: born April 1, 1950
919 iii- **HUFFSMITH Susan Claire**: born March 2, 1951
920 iv- **HUFFSMITH George Andrew**: born July 26, 1955
921 v- **HUFFSMITH Sarah Anne**: born June 15, 1956
922 vi- **HUFFSMITH Sandra Lee**: born June 21, 1960
923 vii- **HUFFSMITH Peter James**: born April 17, 1963

581 **RUTH William**: (*Ervin Ruth, Joseph Ruth, Anna C., Peter, Melchior, Phillip*) was born July 1884, son of Ervin Ruth and Mary E. Ward. He married Emma Walters, born in New Jersey. She died in 1914. No further records.

582 **RUTH Virginia**: (*Clarence Ruth, Joseph Ruth, Anna C., Peter, Melchior, Phillip*) was born ca 1901 in Monroe Co., Pennsylvania, daughter of Clarence Ruth and Ida Coffman. She married January 15, 1921, Frank Dewey Fetherman born February 26, 1899 in Stroudsburg, Pennsylvania, son of Frank Fetherman and Eva Fisher.

583 **SULLIVAN Mary**: (*Martha Ruth, Jacob Ruth, Anna C., Peter, Melchior, Phillip*) was born May 2, 1892 in Blairstown, New Jersey, daughter of John Sullivan and Martha Ruth. She married William H. Davey. She died November 17, 1969 in East Stroudsburg, Pennsylvania and is buried in the Stroudsburg cemetery. Her

husband died before 1969. No issue.

584 **SULLIVAN Samuel:** (*Martha Ruth, Jacob Ruth, Anna C., Peter, Melchior, Phillip*) was born June 8, 1894 in Stroudsburg, Pennsylvania, son of John Sullivan and Martha Ruth. He married Adelaide (unknown maiden name). He died December 16, 1974 in Stroudsburg and is buried in the Stroudsburg cemetery.

Children:
924 **i- SULLIVAN Jean:**
925 **ii- SULLIVAN Joan:**

585 **SULLIVAN Anna Marion:** (*Martha Ruth, Jacob Ruth, Anna C., Peter, Melchior, Phillip*) was born January 14, 1898 in Stroudsburg, Pennsylvania, daughter of John Sullivan and Martha Ruth. She married Joseph T. Jagers. Anna died in February 16, 1962 and is buried in the Stroudsburg cemetery.

Children:
926 **i- JAGERS Joan:**
927 **ii- JAGERS Doris:**
928 **iii- JAGERS Phillis:**

586 **RUTH Anna Geneva:** (*Edward Ruth, Jacob Ruth, Anna C., Peter, Melchior, Phillip*) was born August 21, 1897 in Stroudsburg, Pennsylvania, daughter of Edward Ruth and Mary E. Mareau. She married April 13, 1921, Robert Wallace Jr. born ca 1892, son of Robert Wallace and Anna M. O'Donell.

587 **RUTH Theodore Franklin:** (*John Ruth, Jacob Ruth, Anna C., Peter, Melchior, Phillip*) was born February 1, 1908 in Hamilton Township, Pennsylvania, son of John and Sarah Ruth. He married December 15, 1925, Geraldine Kresge.

Child born in Hamilton Township:
i-RUTH Lorraine Evelyn: born April 25, 1930

588 **RUTH Lorraine:** (*John Ruth, Jacob Ruth, Anna C., Peter, Melchior, Phillip*) was born in Hamilton Township, Pennsylvania, daughter of John and Sarah Ruth. She married (1) Albert Idderly and (2) ______ Duffy. They were in New York City in 1925.

589 **HANEY William J.:** (*Clayton Haney, Martha Ruth, Anna C., Peter, Melchior, Phillip*) was born ca 1906 in Hamilton Township, Pennsylvania, son of Clayton E. and Dorothy Haney. He married October 29, 1932 in Hamilton Township, Mildred Heller.

Known Children:
i- HANEY Nancy Elizabeth: born April 15, 1936
ii- HANEY Patricia Ann: born October 24, 1938

590 **BARTHOLOMEW Charles F.**: (*Lillie, Charles, Melchior, Peter, Melchior, Phillip*) was born August 2, 1884 in Hamilton Township, Pennsylvania, son of Edwin A. Bartholomew and Lillie Louise Bossard. He married Emma Wagner. Charles died February 9, 1944 and Emma died December 10, 1957.

591 **BARTHOLOMEW William Edwin**: (*Lillie, Charles, Melchior, Peter, Melchior, Phillip*) was born May 3, 1889 in Hamilton Township, Pennsylvania, son of Edwin Bartholomew and Lillie Louise Bossard. He married Elsie Christina Metzger born May 8, 1892. He died June 28, 1966 and Elsie died February 16, 1984.

One child:
989 **i- BARTHOLOMEW John Elbert**: born December 26, 1915

592 **BARTHOLOMEW Lucy A.**: (*Lillie, Charles, Melchior, Peter, Melchior, Phillip*) was born February 2, 1897 in Hamilton Township, Pennsylvania, daughter of Edwin A. Bartholomew and Lillie Louise Bossard. She married February 21, 1920, Enoch Rinker born May 18, 1894 in Hamilton Township, son of James and Mary Rinker. He died August 13, 1957 and Lucy died May 16, 1981.

Children:
i- RINKER Wilson Herbert: born March 21 1921
930 **ii- RINKER Leroy Frederick**: born April 19, 1923
931 **iii- RINKER Gladys Eleanore**: born May 31, 1925

593 **STREEPY Helen E.**: (*Laura, Charles, Melchior, Peter, Melchior, Phillip*) was born March 26, 1901 in Hamilton Township, Pennsylvania, daughter of William A. Streepy and Laura A. Bossard. She married Wilbur H. Keller. Helen died February 25. 1978. No record found for Wilbur.

594 **MANSFIELD Mary Catherine**: (*Charles Mansfield, Florinda, Melchior, Peter, Melchior, Phillip*) was born July 28, 1905 in Stroudsburg, Pennsylvania, daughter of Charles Mansfield and Gwen Johns. She married Leonard Derrig.

595 **MANSFIELD Ethel Elizabeth**: (*Charles Mansfield, Florinda, Melchior, Peter, Melchior, Phillip*) was born June 16, 1914 in Stroudsburg, Pennsylvania, daughter of Charles Mansfield and Gwen Johns. She married Morris Peckman and they are presently living in Stroudsburg.

596 **MANSFIELD Thomas Cadoo**: (*Paul Mansfield, Florinda, Melchior, Peter, Melchior, Phillip*) was born August 31, 1907 in Stroudsburg, Pennsylvania, son of Paul Mansfield and Eletta Cadoo. He married Lottie Hester, born 1911, daughter of Henry Hester and Laura Carmer. See number 627, Lottie Hester. They were living in El Paso, Texas.

Children:
932 i- **MANSFIELD Kathleen**: born May 31, 1929
ii- **MANSFIELD Richard.**: born August 27, 1930
933 iii- **MANSFIELD Roger**: born April 9, 1932

597 **GIERSCH Donald**: (*Harry Giersch, Mary J., Melchior, Peter, Melchior, Phillip*) was born 1905, son of Harry Giersch and Mary J. Bossard. He married Ethel A. Hartman born December 19, 1907 in Hamilton Township, daughter of Edgar and Elizabeth Hartman. She died March 1982 in Princeton, New Jersey. Donald predeceased his wife.

Children:
i- **GIERSCH Donald W.**:
ii- **GIERSCH Elean**:

598 **HARTMAN Bessie Hilda**: (*Mary Catherine, James, Melchior, Peter, Melchior, Phillip*) was born March 1, 1895 in Hamilton Township, Pennsylvania, daughter of Jacob Hartman and Mary Catherine Bossard. She married Ashton La Due Burrows, born August 1, 1892. She died July 14, 1948 and Ashton died March 5, 1976.

Children:
934 i- **BURROWS Ashton H.**: born March 16, 1915
935 ii- **BURROWS James Ethelbert**: born November 6, 1916
936 iii- **BURROWS Robert Marlin**: born July 24, 1919
937 iv- **BURROWS Jacob Alexander**: born March 24, 1922

599 **HARTMAN Helen Irene**: (*Mary Catherine, James, Melchior, Peter, Melchior, Phillip*) was born September 30 1907 in Hamilton Township, Pennsylvania, daughter of Jacob Hartman and Mary Catherine Bossard. She married (1) John P. Trippett, born September 1, 1908. He died October 10, 1941 and is buried in the Stroudsburg cemetery. She married (2) Raymond B. Farley, born August 12, 1909.

600 **MACKES John Henry**: (*Nettie Haney, Anna C., Melchior, Peter, Melchior, Phillip*) was born January 24, 1895 in Hamilton Township, son of Benjamin Mackes and Nettie Haney. He married Grace Altemose born April 1900 in McIlhaney. Pennsylvania, daughter of Francis Altemose and Sarah Kibler. She died December 3, 1967 and John died March 1, 1977 in Hamilton Township.

One child:

938 **i- MACKES Marguerite Arline:** born November 20, 1919

601 LESH Violet W.: (*Minnie Haney, Anna C., Melchior, Peter, Melchior, Phillip*) was born September 14, 1896 and adopted by Dayton Lesh and Minnie Haney. She married Stewart Hennion. He died April 15, 1936 in Hamilton Township and is buried in the Prospect Hill cemetery in Caldwell, New Jersey. Stewart had three children by a first marriage, Willis, Jetta and Myrtle. Violet died March 18, 1969.

Children:

939 **i- HENNION Lorraine:** born October 14, 1929
940 **ii- HENNION Gernard:** born October 10, 1932
941 **iii- HENNION Dayton:** born May 2, 1935

602 HANEY Ada Blanche: (*Harry Haney, Anna C., Melchior, Peter, Melchior, Phillip*) was born September 16, 1904 in Hamilton Township, Pennsylvania, daughter of Harry Haney and Bertha Snyder. She married (1) June 27, 1924, Evan Green born 1903. He died 1934 and Ada married (2) Martin Henry Hanson, born 1906. Ada died February 22, 1971.

One child:

942 **i- GREEN Dorothy Elizabeth:** born December 7, 1925

603 HANEY Ruth Adaline: (*Harry Haney, Anna C., Melchior, Peter, Melchior, Phillip*) was born June 19, 1909, daughter of Harry Haney and Bertha Snyder. She married (1) _____ Gilland and (2) _____ Stephens. They were living in Bangor, Pennsylvania in 1973. They had one daughter.

604 HANEY Mary Ellen: (*Charles B. Haney, Anna C., Melchior, Peter, Melchior, Phillip*) was born September 9, 1912 in Hamilton Township, Pennsylvania, daughter of Charles B. Haney and Jennie L. Rinker. She married March 11, 1933, William Lotz, born July 25, 1911.

One child:

943 **i- LOTZ William Charles:** born September 29, 1933

605 SNYDER Dora Madlyn: (*Mabel Haney, Anna C., Melchior, Peter, Melchior, Phillip*) was born January 28, 1920 in Hamilton Township, Pennsylvania, daughter of William Ernest Snyder and Mabel Ruth Haney. She married December 20, 1941, Rev. Wilson Herbert Rinker born March 21, 1920, son of Enoch Rinker and Lucy Bartholomew. See children of Enoch and Lucy number 592.

Children:

944 i- **RINKER David Wilson**: born February 10, 1951
ii- **RINKER James William**: born January 30, 1953
945 iii- **RINKER Timothy Paul**: born September 1, 1955

606 **SNYDER Anna Elizabeth**: (*Mabel Haney, Anna C., Melchior, Peter, Melchior, Phillip*) was born February 25, 1922, daughter of William Ernest Snyder and Mabel Ruth Haney. She married John Edwin Sanders, born January 10, 1920.

Children:
946 i- **SANDERS Louise Marie**: born September 29, 1947
947 ii- **SANDERS Stephen Edwin**: born December 8, 1950

607 **BARTHOLOMEW Sarah**: (*Martha, Samuel, Jacob , Peter, Melchior, Phillip*) was born September 23, 1900 in Stroudsburg, Pennsylvania, daughter of George F. Batholomew and Martha Bossard. She married January 26, 1918, John A. Bellis born July 1897, son of Ira L. Bellis and Araminda Oyer. John died September 23, 1980 in Media, Pennsylvania and Sarah died July 1986 in Trumbull, Connecticutt.

One child:
948 i- **BELLIS Susan**: born June 13, 1926

608 **MUSSELMAN Jean**: (*Catherine, Samuel, Jacob, Peter, Melchior, Phillip*) was born in Chester, Pennsylvania, daughter of Allen Musselman and Catherine Bossard. She married Robert Stainton Jr., son of Robert Stainton.

Children:
i- **STAINTON Robert S. III**:
ii- **STAINTON Frederick**:

609 **BOSSARD Katherine**: (*Frederick, Samuel, Jacob, Peter, Melchior, Phillip*) was born February 6, 1913 in Delaware Co., Pennsylvania, twin daughter of Frederick P. Bossard and Elizabeth Morgan. She married March 8, 1941, Owen Morrison. Katherine died November 26, 1958 in Springfield, Pennsylvania. No issue.

610 **BOSSARD Elizabeth**: (*Frederick, Samuel, Jacob, Peter, Melchior, Phillip*) was born February 6, 1913, in Delaware Co., Pennsylvania, twin daughter of Frederick P. Bossard and Elizabeth Morgan. She married Willard G. Reese, born 1907. They were divorced and he died in 1972. Elizabeth is presently living in Wallingford, Pennsylvania.

Children:
949 i- **REESE Richard W.**: born March 18, 1936
950 ii- **REESE Nancy Jean**: born June 6, 1938

611 **BOSSARD Roberta:** (*Robert, Samuel, Jacob, Peter, Melchior, Phillip*) was born December 20, 1907 in Chester, Pennsylvania, daughter of Robert Bossard and Margaret Brennan. She married November 25, 1929 in Bethlehem, Pennsylvania, Allen Corson Du Bois, born May 6, 1903 in Clayton, New Jersey, son of Peter Du Bois and Maria Corson. She died June 21, 1953 and is buried in Hillside cemetery in Plainfield, New Jersey. Allen married (2) Louise Clow, (3) Margaret Raymond and (4) Margaret Mc Cann Quayle. He died December 8, 1987 in Delray, Florida.

Children, first marriage:
951 i- **DU BOIS Peter Bossard:** born December 27, 1939 in Plainfield, New Jersey.
952 ii- **DU BOIS Joan:** born February 19, 1932, Scranton Pennsylvania.
953 iii- **DU BOIS Susan:** born January 25, 1941, Plainfield, New Jersey.

612 **BOSSARD Ina Mae:** (*Curvin, Edwin, Jacob, Peter, Melchior, Phillip*) was born October 10, 1893 in Ida Grove, Iowa, daughter of Curvin Bossard and Minnie Maritz. She married December 23, 1915, William E. Rathbun born April 3, 1893. He died January 29, 1962 and Ina Mae died April 17, 1990. They are buried in Ida Grove. No issue.

613 **BOSSARD Carman Lloyd:** (*Curvin, Edwin, Jacob, Peter, Melchior, Phillip*) was born February 3, 1896 in Ida Grove, Iowa, twin son of Curvin Bossard and Minnie Maritz. He married in Cherokee, Iowa, February 15, 1915, Olga Dibborn born August 24, 1895, in Galva, Iowa, daughter of Peter Jacob Dibborn. She died September 27, 1989 in Loveland, Colorado. Carman is still living in Loveland with his son, Sherlyn Lamont Bossard.

One child born in Moville, Iowa:
954 i- **BOSSARD Sherlyn Lamont:** born July 28, 1915.

614 **BOSSARD Calvin Floyd:** (*Curvin, Edwin, Jacob, Peter, Melchior, Phillip*) was born February 3, 1896 in Ida Grove, Iowa, twin son of Curvin Bossard and Minnie Maritz. He married Amelia Bubash. Calvin died October 10, 1987 in Missoula, Montana and Amelia is living in Butte, Montana.

Children born in Montana:
955 i- **BOSSARD Floyd Carman:** born January 24, 1929
956 ii- **BOSSARD Richard Calvin:** born September 11, 1930
957 iii- **BOSSARD Vera Jean:** born January 1, 1933
958 iv- **BOSSARD Gerald Wayne:** born October 24, 1935
959 v- **BOSSARD Mark Allen:** born October 4, 1951

615 **BOSSARD Gladys Irene:** (*Curvin, Edwin, Jacob, Peter, Melchior, Phillip*) was born August 30, 1898 in Ida Grove, Iowa, daughter of Curvin Bossard and Minnie

Maritz. She married January 20, 1919 in Ida Grove, William Hayden Baxter born April 4, 1898 in Deputy, Indianna. He died February 4, 1981 in Louisville, Kentucky. Gladys is presently living in Austin, Indianna.

Children in Ida Grove, Iowa:
960 i- **BAXTER Hayden Ardell**: born March 13, 1921
961 ii- **BAXTER Marilee**: born April 22, 1928

616 **BOSSARD Vera Emma**: (*Curvin, Edwin, Jacob, Peter, Melchior, Phillip*) was born January 6, 1901 in Ida Grove, Iowa, daughter of Curvin Bossard and Minnie Maritz. She married January 23, 1919 in Ida Grove, Albert Noll born January 20, 1900. He died July 1982 in Ida Grove and Vera is living in a nursing home in Ida Grove.

Children:
962 i- **NOLL Marjean**: born March 25, 1922
963 ii- **NOLL Charles Nowland**: born January 25, 1927

617 **BOSSARD Cecil Alfred**: (*Curvin, Edwin, Jacob, Peter, Melchior, Phillip*) was born August 6, 1904 in Ida Grove, Iowa, son of Curvin Bossard and Minnie Maritz. He married June 26, 1926 in Ida Grove, (1) Sibyl Elizabeth Dillon born April 20, 1907 in Correctionville, Iowa. Cecil died January 6, 1958 in Savannah, Missouri and Sibyl married (2) October 24, 1959, Ralph Gunselman. He died June 2, 1979 in St. Joseph, Missouri and Sibyl died December 6, 1980 in Savannah, Missouri. Cecil and Sibyl are buried in the Savannah cemetery.

Children:
964 i- **BOSSARD Lois Ann**: born July 28, 1928 in Ida Grove
965 ii- **BOSSARD Donna Lee**: born October 15, 1931 in Arthur, Iowa.

618 **BOSSARD Murriel Curvin**: (*Curvin, Edwin, Jacob, Peter, Melchior, Phillip*) was born July 3, 1908 in Ida Grove, Iowa, son of Curvin Bossard and Minnie Maritz. He married Jess Mc Whirter, born August 10, 1918. He died in Great Falls, Montana and Jess is still living there.

Children:
966 i- **BOSSARD Murriel Jr.**: born January 20, 1939
967 ii- **BOSSARD Carl Thomas**: born August 21, 1941

619 **BOSSARD Marcelle Minnie**: (*Curvin, Edwin, Jacob, Peter, Melchior, Phillip*) was born March 20, 1911 in Ida Grove, Iowa, daughter of Curvin Bossard and Minnie Maritz. She married August 22, 1930 in Milwaukee, Wisconsin, Gordon Lee Clark born September 3, 1906 in Cresco, Iowa, son of Kelsie Clark and Ellen Welch. They are presently living in Santa Paula, California.

One child:
968 i- **CLARK Maxine Lavonne**: born November 29, 1931

620 **WILCOX Dewayne**: (*Katie Woodling, Catherine, Jacob, Peter, Melchior, Phillip*) son of George Romain Wilcox and Katie Woodling. He married Hazel Magnuson. No issue.

621 **WILCOX Sylvia**: (*Katie Woodling, Catherine, Jacob, Peter, Melchior, Phillip*) daughter of George Romain Wilcox and Katie Woodling. Unknown married name. She has two children.

622 **BOSSARD Miles Franklin Jr.**: (*Miles, Eugene, Peter K., Peter, Melchior, Phillip*) was born April 22, 1926 in Stroudsburg, Pennsylvania, son of Miles Bossard and Laurette Fabel. He married October 22, 1947 in Stroudsburg, Margaret Ryan, born April 3, 1922. Miles died November 25, 1981 and is buried in the Stroudsburg cemetery. Margaret is presently living in Stroudsburg.

Children born in Stroudsburg:
969 i- **BOSSARD Dianne**: born September 26, 1948
970 ii- **BOSSARD Devon**: born August 2, 1950
971 iii- **BOSSARD Miles Franklin III**: born August 13, 1952
972 iv- **BOSSARD Mary Lynne**: born June 21, 1958

623 **BOSSARD Bettiejane**: (*Miles, Eugene, Peter K., Peter, Melchior, Phillip*) was born March 15, 1928 in Stroudsburg, Pennsylvania, daughter of Miles Franklin Bossard and Laurette Fabel. She married John F. Hogan, born January 14, 1929. He died October 18, 1977 in Stroudsburg and Bettiejane is presently living in Stroudsburg.

One child:
973 i- **HOGAN Janis**: born January 26, 1953

624 **DENNIS Harold Lawrence**: (*Grace Carmer, Alice, Joseph, Peter, Melchior, Phillip*) was born July 4, 1905 in Hamilton Township, son of Amzi Dennis and Grace L. Carmer. He married September 3, 1926 in Hamilton Township, Olive Metzgar born July 27, 1906, daughter of Jesse and Emma Metzger. Olive died April 1980 Harold died April 5, 1962. They are buried in the Stroudsburg cemetery.

Children:
974 i- **DENNIS Clifford Leroy**: born October 19, 1931
975 ii- **DENNIS John H.**: born June 21, 1935

625 DENNIS Nina O.: (*Grace Carmer, Alice, Joseph, Peter, Melchior, Phillip*) was born January 22, 1918 in Hamilton Township, Pennsylvania, daughter of Amzi Dennis and Grace L. Carmer. She married May 14, 1943 in Hamilton Township, Frank T. Talez. No further records.

626 HESTER Leroy: (*Laura M. Carmer, Alice, Joseph, Peter, Melchior, Phillip*) was born June 10, 1904 in Hamilton Township, Pennsylvania, son of Henry Hester and Laura M. Carmer. He married June 27, 1924, Irene Fellencer born June 23, 1904, daughter of Edwin and Ida S. Fellencer. Leroy died June 10, 1979 in Bangor, Pennsylvania and is buried in the Richmond cemetery.

Children born in Hamilton Township:
976 i- **HESTER Louise Shirley**: born January 15, 1926
ii- **HESTER Glenn Franklin**: born May 24, 1925
977 iii- **HESTER Robert**:

627 HESTER Lottie: (*Laura M. Carmer, Alice, Joseph, Peter, Melchior,. Phillip*) was born 1911 daughter of Henry Hester and Laura M. Carmer. She married Thomas Cadoo Mansfield, born August 31, 1907, son of Paul Mansfield and Eletta Cadoo. See number 596 Thomas Mansfield for further records.

628 HESTER Allison A.: (*Laura M. Carmer, Alice, Joseph, Peter, Melchior, Phillip*) was born July 3, 1914 in Hamilton Township, Pennsylvania, son of Henry Hester and Laura M. Carmer. He married October 10, 1937, Helen May Angle born July 12, 1917. They are presently living in Stroudsburg.

Children:
978 i- **HESTER Joan Carol**: born June 8, 1941
ii- **HESTER Keith Allison**: born March 15, 1946

CHAPTER 8

EIGHTH GENERATION

629 **KRETZING Mary**: (*Grace Altemose, Mary Ann Weiss, Daniel, Weiss, Felix Weiss, Eva Catherine, Melchior, Phillip*) was born 1908, daughter of Albert M. Kretzing and Grace Altemose. She married Henry Hoffman. They are presently living in Brodheadsville, Pennsylvania.

630 **KRETZING Kathryn**: (*Grace Altemose, Mary Ann Weiss, Daniel Weiss, Felix Weiss, Eva Catherine, Melchior, Phillip*) was born ca 1912, daughter of Albert M. Kretzing and Grace Altemose. She married March 25, 1934 in Hamilton Township, Pennsylvania, Earl D. Shoemaker born April 25, 1911 in Hamilton Township, son of Harry L. and Ruth Shoemaker. They are presently living in Saylorsburg, Pennsylvania.

631 **KRETZING Martha**: (*Grace Altemose, Mary Ann Weiss, Daniel Weiss, Felix Weiss, Eva Catherine, Melchior, Phillip*) was born in Hamilton Township, daughter of Albert M. Kretzing and Grace Altemose. She married Edward Doney. They are presently living in Kunkletown, Pennsylvania.

632 **EVERITT Abbie M.**: (*Ellen Felker, Julia Altemose, Susannah Weiss, Felix Weiss, Eva Catherine, Melchior, Phillip*) was born 1896 in Jackson Township, Pennsylvania, daughter of J. Ulyssis Everitt and Ellen E. Felker. She married Herman Paul born 1889. He died December 17, 1962 and is buried in the Appenzel cemetery in Jackson Township, Pennsylvania.

Children:

- i- **PAUL Clyde**:
- ii- **PAUL Mary Ardella**:
- iii- **PAUL Avon**:
- iv- **PAUL Leroy Gilmore**: born December 6, 1916
- v- **PAUL Marie Lucille**: born December 26, 1918

633 **FELKER Emma**: (*Stewart Felker, Julia A. Altemose, Susannah Weiss, Felix Weiss, Eva Catherine, Melchior, Phillip*) was born in Jackson Township, Pennsylvania, daughter of S. Ervin and Ida May Felker. She married Thomas Reinhart, born 1910. He died in 1971 and is buried in the Buena Vista cemetery in Chestnuthill Township, Pennsylvania. She is presently living in the town of Saylorsburg, Pennsylvania. No further records.

634 DORSHIMER Arthur: (*Jennie Diana Felker, Julia A. Altemose, Susannah Weiss, Felix Weiss, Eva Catherine, Melchior, Phillip*) was born 1908, probably in Jackson Township, Pennsylvania, son of Benjamin Dorshimer and Jennie Diana Felker. He married Martha (unknown maiden name) born 1906. He was living in Brodheadsville in 1965.

635 BONSER Lloyd Kenneth: (*Florence Miller, Diana Altemose, Susannah Weiss, Felix Weiss, Eva Catherine, Melchior, Phillip*) was born February 10, 1906 in Chestnuthill, Pennsylvania, son of James Bonser and Emma Florence Miller. He married March 26, 1927, Viola A. Weiss born 1909, daughter of Charles and Electa Weiss. See Viola Weiss number 382.

Children:

979 i- **BONSER Elaine Florence**: born August 9, 1927
980 ii- **BONSER Catherine Mae**: born June 8, 1929
981 iii- **BONSER Robert Lester**: born October 7, 1930
iv- **BONSER Geraldine**: born 1933 and died 1940
982 v- **BONSER Leroy Stanley**: born August 1, 1938

636 BONSER Mitchell Fayette: (*Florence Miller, Diana Altemose, Susannah Weiss, Felix Weiss, Eva Catherine, Melchior, Phillip*) was born September 2, 1908 in Chestnuthill, Pennsylvania, son of James Bonser and Emma Florence Miller. He married Jennie Mae Bond born September 22, 1920, daughter of Jesse Wright and Lulu Pearl Bond. He died November 7, 1977 and Jennie died October 20, 1965. They are buried in the Buena Vista cemetery in Chestnuthill.

Children:

983 i- **BONSER Janet**: born April 11, 1935
984 ii- **BONSER Richard**: born September 6, 1936

637 ALTEMOSE Edith Catherine: (*Vernon Altemose, Steward Altemose, Susannah Weiss, Felix Weiss, Eva Catherine, Melchior, Phillip*) was born December 5, 1925, daughter of Vernon Altemose and Anna N. Miller. She married July 10, 1948, Russell Powell born January 9, 1925.

Children:

985 i- **POWELL Deborah F.**: born May 14, 1950
986 ii- **POWELL Melanie H.**: born July 21, 1951
987 iii- **POWELL Michael C.**: born December 28, 1954

638 ALTEMOSE Marion Elizabeth: (*Vernon Altemose, Steward Altemose, Susannah Weiss, Felix Weiss, Eva Catherine, Melchior, Phillip*) was born December 14, 1926. daughter of Vernon Altemose and Anna N. Miller. She married June 4, 1949, Ralph Paul Starner born Jaunary 16, 1924.

One child:

988 i- **STARNER Jed Alan**: born July 23, 1953

639 **ALTEMOSE Elwood Charles**: (*Vernon Altemose, Steward Altemose, Susannah Weiss, Felix Weiss, Eva Catherine, Melchior, Phillip*) was born May 1, 1928, son of Vernon Altemose and Anna N. Miller. He married April 10, 1956, Elizabeth Pruitt born October 26, 1925. She was first married to a Mr. Pruitt and by him, had two children.

Children of Elizabeth Pruitt:

i- **PRUITT Claudia**: born June 8, 1947
ii- **PRUITT Debbie**: born April 27, 1950

640 **ALTEMOSE Frances Louise**: (*Vernon Altemose, Steward Altemose, Susannah Weiss, Felix Weiss, Eva Catherine, Melchior, Phillip*) was born December 24, 1929, daughter of Vernon Altemose and Anna N. Miller. She married June 24, 1950, Donald A. Stoudt born December 18, 1930.

Children:

989 i- **STOUDT Nanette F.**: born February 10, 1952
990 ii- **STOUDT Sheryl L.**: born March 28, 1953
991 iii- **STOUDT Randy Scott**: born August 1, 1955
992 iv- **STOUDT Jeff Donald**: born December 3, 1958

641 **ALTEMOSE Vernon Grover Jr.**: (*Vernon Altemose, Steward Altemose, Susannah Weiss, Felix Weiss, Eva Catherine, Melchior, Phillip*) was born August 23, 1933, son of Vernon Altemose and Anna N. Miller. He married Kathryn Engler born August 15, 1933.

Children:

993 i- **ALTEMOSE Pamela**: born October 17, 1957
ii- **ALTEMOSE Matthew Glen**: born July 2, 1959
iii- **ALTEMOSE Gregory Mark**: born August 12, 1962
iv- **ALTEMOSE David Scott**: born July 9, 1965

642 . **ALTEMOSE Alice May**: (*Vernon Altemose, Steward Altemose, Susannah Weiss, Felix Weiss, Eva Catherine, Melchior, Phillip*) was born April 11, 1939, daughter of Vernon Altemose and Anna N. Miller. She married August 20, 1960, Peter Pristash born October 23, 1929

Children:

i- **PRISTASH Christopher John**: born April 4, 1961
ii- **PRISTASH Tanya Marie**: born August 2, 1962
iii- **PRISTASH Marc David**: March 27, 1966

643 **SEIPLE Marie Bertha**: (*Emma Altemose, Steward Altemose, Susannah Weiss, Felix Weiss, Eva Catherine, Melchior, Phillip*) was born December 23, 1924, daughter of Alfred F. Seiple and Emma Lydia Altemose. She married June 17, 1945, Ronald Triburton Brown Jr. born June 19, 1922. He died June 15, 1966.

Children:

994 i- **BROWN June Marie**: born May 30, 1945
ii- **BROWN Sharon Lynn**: born November 28, 1950
995 iii- **BROWN Gail Naomi**: born June 30, 1953
996 iv- **BROWN Donna Lee**: born July 12, 1956
997 v- **BROWN Ronald Triburton Jr.**: born March 3, 1958
998 vi- **BROWN Keith Alan**: born November 12, 1960

644 **SEIPLE William Henry**: (*Emma Altemose, Steward Altemose, Susannah Weiss, Felix Weiss, Eva Catherine, Melchior, Phillip*) was born October 15, 1927, son of Alfred Franklin Seiple and Emma Lydia Altemose. He married September 19, 1953, Gloria Shulz born December 19, 1927.

Children:

999 i- **SEIPLE Barbara**: born December 19, 1948
1000 ii- **SEIPLE William Henry Jr.**: born July 18, 1954

645 **SEIPLE Alfred Franklin Jr.**: (*Emma Altemose, Steward Altemose, Susannah Weiss, Felix Weiss, Eva Catherine, Melchior, Phillip*) was born July 31, 1930, son of Alfred Franklin Seiple and Emma Lydia Altemose. He married July 12, 1952, Elsa Deuble born November 5, 1931.

Children:

1001 i- **SEIPLE Alfred Franklin III**: born December 16, 1959
ii- **SEIPLE Sandra Lee**: born October 27, 1961

646 **ALTEMOSE Paul Arlington**: (*Ralph Altemose, Steward Altemose, Susannah Weiss, Felix Weiss, Eva Catherine, Melchior, Phillip*) was born September 29, 1926, son of Ralph Altemose and Minnie Schmidt. He married August 5, 1950, Julia Jean Reimert born July 25, 1927.

Children:

1002 i- **ALTEMOSE Bret Harold**: born October 31, 1953
1003 ii- **ALTEMOSE Dee Carol**: born November 23, 1957

647 **ALTEMOSE Geraldine M.**: (*Jacob Altemose, Steward Altemose, Susannah Weiss, Felix Weiss, Eva Catherine, Melchior, Phillip*) was born February 21, 1926, daughter of Jacob Victor Altemose and Irene May Buss. She married August 11, 1948, Howard Eugene Saylor born July 25, 1926.

Children:
i- **SAYLOR Lorrie Lee**: born March 4, 1955
1004 ii- **SAYLOR Wayne Alan**: born July 21, 1956

648 **ALTEMOSE Jean Grace**: (*Jacob Altemose, Steward Altemose, Susannah Weiss, Felix Weiss, Eva Catherine, Melchior, Phillip*) was born June 11, 1927, daughter of Jacob Victor Altemose and Irene May Buss. She married February 27. 1946, Vernon Lewis Messinger born September 22, 1927.

Children:
1005 i- **MESSINGER Melvin Floyd**: born September 14, 1946
1006 ii- **MESSINGER Tim Edward**: born October 4, 1952
1007 iii- **MESSINGER Len Lewis**: born October 10, 1954

649 **ALTEMOSE Richard James**: (*Jacob Altemose, Steward Altemose, Susannah Weiss, Felix Weiss, Eva Catherine, Melchior, Phillip*) was born December 26, 1928, son of Jacob Victor Altemose and Irene May Buss. He married April 19, 1955, Lorain Fritz Deutsch born July 30, 1927.

Child of wife's first marriage:
i- **DEUTSCH Timothy Nicholas**: born December 25, 1947
Children of Richard and Lorain:
1008 ii- **ALTEMOSE Bonnie Sue**: born January 3, 1955
iii- **ALTEMOSE Mark James**: born April 12, 1962

650 **ALTEMOSE Lee Linford**: (*Jacob Altemose, Steward Altemose, Susannah Weiss, Felix Weiss, Eva Catherine, Melchior, Phillip*) was born March 5, 1931, son of Jacob Victor Altemose and Irene May Buss. He married June 30, 1956, Jean A. Kessler born November 5, 1935.

Children:
i- **ALTEMOSE Glenn Taylor**: born September 8, 1957
1009 ii- **ALTEMOSE Marci Lynn**: born April 3, 1959
iii- **ALTEMOSE Ted William**: born March 11, 1964

651 **ALTEMOSE Robert Franklin**: (*Jacob Altemose, Steward Altemose, Susannah Weiss, Felix Weiss, Eva Catherine, Melchior, Phillip*) was born October 21, 1932, son of Jacob Victor Altemose and Irene May Buss. He married April 17, 1954, Ilean Heiserman born June 14, 1936.

Children:
1010 i- **ALTEMOSE Karen Lois**: born December 24, 1954
1011 ii- **ALTEMOSE Keith Robert**: born May 13, 1955

652 ALTEMOSE Wayne Stewart: (*Jacob Altemose, Steward Altemose, Susannah Weiss, Felix Weiss, Eva Catherine, Melchior, Phillip*) was born April 16, 1937, son of Jacob Victor Altemose and Irene May Buss. He married February 14, 1959, Jean Nasatka born February 17, 1940.

Children:
i- **ALTEMOSE Brad Jacob**: born March 29, 1959
ii- **ALTEMOSE Brian Scott**: born July 12, 1960
iii- **ALTEMOSE Cindy Suzanne Laurene**: born November 15, 1965

653 ALTEMOSE Labert Dale: (*Jacob Altemose, Steward Altemose, Susannah Weiss, Felix Weiss, Eva Catherine, Melchior, Phillip*) was born August 5, 1940, son of Jacob Victor Altemose and Irene May Buss. He married August 25, 1962, Carol Sue Johnson born July 8, 1942.

Children:
i- **ALTEMOSE Dean Labert**: born July 1, 1964
ii- **ALTEMOSE Sue Ann**: born September 7, 1967
iii- **ALTEMOSE Jane Kristen**: born December 28, 1971

654 ALTEMOSE Harold Albert: (*Albert Altemose, Steward Altemose, Susannah Weiss, Felix Weiss, Eva Catherine, Melchior, Phillip*) was born February 9, 1936, son of Albert Alvin Altemose and Dorothy Noble. He married May 18, 1957, Barbara Trenberth born July 25, 1937.

One child:
i- **ALTEMOSE Laurie Ann**: born January 31, 1958

655 ALTEMOSE Rollin Amos: (*Albert Altemose, Steward Altemose, Susannah Weiss, Felix Weiss, Eva Catherine, Melchior, Phillip*) was born February 16, 1938, son of Albert Alvin Altemose and Dorothy Noble. He married December 17, 1956, Marlene Uhler born April 9, 1940.

Children:
1012 i- **ALTEMOSE Bruce Alan**: born September 10, 1957
ii- **ALTEMOSE Brian Albert**: born January 31, 1960
iii- **ALTEMOSE Brenda Louise**: born February 16, 1962 and died May 30, 1969.
iv- **ALTEMOSE Brent Andrew**: born November 16, 1970

656 ALTEMOSE Thomas Sherwood: (*Albert Altemose, Steward Altemose, Susannah Weiss, Felix Weiss, Eva Catherine, Melchior, Phillip*) was born June 15, 1943, son of Albert Alvin Altemose and Dorothy Noble. He married July 7, 1962, Barbara Mendham born November 15, 1944.

One child:
i- ALTEMOSE Thomas Sherwood Jr.: born December 31, 1962

657 ALTEMOSE Dorothy Ann: (*Albert Altemose, Steward Altemose, Susannah Weiss, Felix, Weiss, Eva Catherine, Melchior, Phillip*) was born November 18, 1943, daughter of Albert Alvin Altemose and Dorothy Noble. She married July 26, 1968, William W. Sandt born November 1943.

One child:
i- SANDT Kristen Lea: born November 21, 1980

658 ALTEMOSE Carol Ann: (*Woodrow Altemose, Steward Altemose, Susannah Weiss, Felix Weiss, Eva Catherine, Melchior, Phillip*) was born October 3, 1940, daughter of Woodrow Wilson Altemose and Alice Kindt. She married August 18, 1962, Franklin Conrad Jones born March 18, 1940.

Children adopted by Franklin and Carol:
i- JONES David Alan: born August 19, 1969
ii- JONES Louellyn Sue: born November 12, 1970

659 SHRAVER Gary Lynn: (*Alberta Altemose, Steward Altemose, Susannah Weiss, Felix Weiss, Eva Catherine, Melchior, Phillip*) was born June 27, 1941, son of Eugene A. Shraver and Alberta Altemose. He married September 16, 1964, Gloria Jean Kocsis born April 1, 1942.

Children:
i- SHRAVER Gregory Alan: born May 2, 1967
ii- SHRAVER Todd Jared: born February 6, 1971

660 SHRAVER Kirk Lee: (*Alberta Altemose, Steward Altemose, Susannah Weiss, Felix Weiss, Eva Catherine, Melchior, Phillip*) was born November 23, 1946, son of Eugene A, Shraver and Alberta Altemose. He married July 27, 1968, Annette Marie Cook born March 5, 1947.

Children:
i- SHRAVER Brent Darren: born October 29, 1971
ii- SHRAVER Jamie Dawn: born February 26, 1977

661 SHRAVER Bart Altemose: (*Alberta Altemose, Steward Altemose, Susannah Weiss, Felix Weiss, Eva Catherine, Melchior, Phillip*) was born October 8, 1951, son of Eugene A. Shraver and Alberta Altemose. He married Octoboer 30, 1971, Cindy Roe born August 12, 1953.

Children:
- i- **SHRAVER Tracy Kyle**: born April 26, 1972
- ii- **SHRAVER Stacy Lynn**: born January 22, 1976

662 COUNTERMAN Charles: (*Ruth Weiss, Charles Weiss, Felix Weiss Jr., Felix Weiss, Eva Catherine, Melchior, Phillip*) was born 1919 in Bushkill, Pennsylvania, son of George Counterman and Ruth Weiss. He married Pauline Kibler. He died February 6, 1982 in Roseto, Pennsylvania and is buried in the Sand Hill cemetery.

Children:
- i- **COUNTERMAN Debra**:
- ii- **COUNTERMAN Anna**:
- iii- **COUNTERMAN Clair**:
- iv- **COUNTERMAN Claude H.**:
- v- **COUNTERMAN Raymond R.**:
- vi- **COUNTERMAN Lester**:

663 COUNTERMAN Viola: (*Ruth Weiss, Charles Weiss, Felix Weiss Jr., Felix Weiss, Eva Catherine, Melchior, Phillip*) was born in Monroe Co., Pennsylvania, daughter of George Counterman and Ruth Weiss. She married Milton Wolbert and is presently living in Stroudsburg. No further records.

664 COUNTERMAN Idella: (*Ruth Weiss, Charles Weiss, Felix Weiss, Jr., Felix Weiss, Eva Catherine, Melchior, Phillip*) was born in Monroe Co., Pennsylvania, daughter of George Counterman and Ruth Weiss. She married ______ Albert and they were living in Reeders, Pennsylvania in 1982. No further records.

665 COUNTERMAN Dorothy: (*Ruth Weiss, Charles Weiss, Felix Weiss Jr., Felix Weiss, Eva Catherine, Melchior, Phillip*) was born in Monroe Co., Pennsylvania, daughter of George Counterman and Ruth Weiss. She married ______ Consentino and was living in Easton, Pennsylvania in 1982. No further records.

666 TAYLOR Ernest Harrison Jr.: (*Olive Gearhart, Cicero Gearhart, Elizabeth Weiss, Felix Weiss, Eva Catherine, Melchior, Phillip*) was born October 7, 1909 in Stroudsburg, Pennsylvania, son of Ernest Taylor and Olive Gearhart. He married January 14, 1939, Mary Louise Buck born January 1, 1912. Ernest died January 1982 and is buried in Stroudsburg.

Child:
- i- **TAYLOR George Edward**: born October 18, 1943

667 TAYLOR Elizabeth Louise: (*Olive Gearhart, Cicero Gearhart, Elizabeth Weiss,*

Felix Weiss, Eva Catherine, Melchior, Phillip) was born in Stroudsburg, Pennsylvania, daughter of Ernest Taylor and Olive Gearhart. She married January 30, 1940, James T. K. Kitsen, born August 3, 1906.

668 TAYLOR John Fletcher: (*Olive Gearhart, Cicero Gearhart, Elizabeth Weiss, Felix Weiss, Eva Catherine, Melchior, Phillip*) was born May 12, 1916 in Stroudsburg, Pennsylvania, son of Ernest Taylor and Olive Gearhart. He married July 28, 1937, Mary J. Layton born December 5, 1917. They are presently living in Stroudsburg.

669 TAYLOR William Henry: (*Olive Gearhart, Cicero Gearhart, Elizabeth Weiss, Felix Weiss, Eva Catherine, Melchior, Phillip*) was born July 1, 1928 in Stroudsburg, Pennsylvania, son of Ernest Taylor and Olive Gearhart. He married (1) April 13, 1952, Patricia O'Conner born May 28, 1931. He married (2) July 15, 1972, Patricia Connelly born March 3, 1931.

670 GEARHART Joan Agnes: (*A. Greenswald Gearhart, Cicero Gearhart, Elizabeth Weiss, Felix Weiss, Eva Catherine, Melchior, Phillip*) was born September 24, 1927 in Stroudsburg, Pennsylvania, daughter of A. Greenswald Gearhart and Ruth Barthold. She married William Hamilton. They are presently living in Newark, Delaware.

Children:
- **i- HAMILTON Lisa:**
- **ii- HAMILTON Mark:**

671 GEARHART Peter Barthold: (*A. Greenswald Gearhart, Cicero Gearhart, Elizabeth Weiss, Felix Weiss, Eva Catherine, Melchior, Phillip*) was born June 28, 1933 in Stroudsburg, Pennsylvania, son of A. Greenswald Gearhart and Ruth Barthold. He married Antoinette (unknown maiden name). They are presently living in Hershey, Pennsylvania.

One child:
- **i- GEARHART Peter:**

672 JENSON William Keen: (*Helen Gearhart, Cicero Gearhart, Elizabeth Weiss, Felix Weiss, Eva Catherine, Melchior, Phillip*) was born November 6, 1923 in Colby, Kansas, son of Dr. James D. Jenson and Helen L. Gearhart. He married Norma Lutz. Last known, was living in California.

Children:
- **i- JENSON Julie:**
- **ii- JENSON Laurie:**
- **iii- JENSON James:**

673 GEARHART Robert Morris: (*Samuel Gearhart, Cicero Gearhart, Elizabeth Weiss, Felix Weiss, Eva Catherine, Melchior, Phillip*) was born April 23, 1933 in Stroudsburg, Pennsylvania, son of Samuel R. Gearhart and Rebecca Eleanor Mc Call. Robert served as a Corporal in the Korean War. He died 1987 in Stroudsburg. No further records.

674 FELKER Sarah: (*John Felker, Anna Gearhart, Elizabeth Weiss, Felix Weiss, Eva Catherine, Melchior, Phillip*) was born February 19, 1902 in Gilbert, Pennsylvania, daughter of John R. Felker and Flora Shupp. She married (1) Frank Weikel and (2) William Benz. No further records.

675 FELKER Beatrice: (*John Felker, Anna Gearhart, Elizabeth Weiss, Felix Weiss, Eva Catherine, Melchior, Phillip*) was born July 12, 1903 in Gilbert, Pennsylvania, daughter of John R. Felker and Anna E. Gearhart. She married October 22, 1922, Floyd De Haven, born August 6, 1899. No further records.

676 FELKER Elsie: (*John Felker. Anna E. Gearhart, Elizabeth Weiss, Felix Weiss, Eva Catherine, Melchior, Phillip*) was born July 18, 1904 in Gilbert, Pennsylvania, daughter of John R. Felker and Anna E. Gearhart. She married September 20, 1919, Amzi Altemose born August 21, 1899. Amzi died 1978 and is buried in the Buena Vista cemetery in Chestnuthill.

Children:

- i- **ALTEMOSE Beatrice May**: born April 29, 1920
- ii- **ALTEMOSE Arline Winifred**: born April 29, 1922

677 FELKER Paul: (*John Felker, Anna E. Gearhart, Elizabeth Weiss, Felix Weiss, Eva Catherine, Melchior, Phillip*) was born April 20, 1908 in Gilbert, Pennsylvania, son of John R. Felker and Anna E. Gearhart. He married Jessie Smith born March 1, 1909. No further records.

678 FELKER Amelia: (*John Felker, Anna E. Gearhart, Elizabeth Weiss, Felix Weiss, Eva Catherine, Melchior, Phillip*) was born October 8, 1916 in Gilbert, Pennsylvania, daughter of John Felker and Carrie M. Bond. She married Arlington Martin born January 8, 1916. They are presently living in Effort, Pennsylvania.

679 GREGORY Barbara G.: (*Lida Gearhart, Theodore Gearhart, Elizabeth Weiss, Felix Weiss, Eva Catherine, Melchior, Phillip*) was born March 8, 1913 in Stroudsburg, Pennsylvania, daughter of Dr. John C. Gregory and Lida May Gearhart. She married June 18, 1938, Donald A. Gilpin born April 14, 1910. He died 1981 and Barbara is presently living in Stroudsburg.

Children:
1013 i- **GILPIN John Albert**: born April 17, 1941
1014 ii- **GILPIN Mary Jane**: born April 27, 1944
1015 iii- **GILPIN Donald Gregory**: born August 17, 1949

680 GEARHART Gayle: (*Charles Gearhart, Theodore Gearhart, Elizabeth Weiss, Felix Weiss, Eva Catherine, Melchior, Phillip*) was born December 18, 1923, son of Charles Gearhart and Mabel Cooper. He married Lois Todd Dicken born April 9, 1929. They were divorced and he is presently living in Washington D. C.

Children:
i- **GEARHART Neel Reese**: born March 30, 1954
ii- **GEARHART Todd Dixson**: born April 6, 1956
iii- **GEARHART Lyn Parker**: born December 21, 1959
iv- **GEARHART Wayne Cooper**: born February 3, 1959

681 GEARHART Gerald: (*Charles Gearhart, Theodore Gearhart, Elizabeth Weiss, Felix Weiss, Eva Catherine, Melchior, Phillip*) was born Febuary 21, 1926. He married Patricia Leigh and they are presently living in Hingham, Massachusetts

Children:
i- **GEARHART Jan Carol**: born November 12, 1955
ii- **GEARHART Cary Parker**: born April 20, 1957

682 COURTWRIGHT Leslie: (*Edna Gearhart, Theodore Gearhart, Elizabeth Weiss, Felix Weiss, Eva Catherine, Melchior, Phillip*) was born January 29, 1916, son of Albert Courtwight and Edna Gearhart. He married Evelyn Metzger. He died January 10, 1978 in Allentown, Pennsylvania.

683 GEARHART William E.: (*William Gearhart, Theodore Gearhart, Elizabeth Weiss, Felix Weiss, Eva Catherine, Melchior, Phllip*) was born January 25, 1924 in Gilbert, Pennsylvania, son of William J. Gearhart and Mabel Buck. He married Doris M. (unknown maiden name), born November 29, 1924. They are presently living in Silver Springs, Maryland. No issue.

684 GEARHART Leroy M.: (*William Gearhart, Theodore Gearhart, Elizabeth Weiss, Felix Weiss, Eva Catherine, Melchior, Phillip*) was born April 4, 1925 in Gilbert, Pennsylvania, twin son of William J. Gearhart and Mabel Buck. He married Mary P. (unknown maiden name), born January 13, 1925. They are presently living in Denver, Colorado.

One child:
i- **GEARHART May Jane**: born August 27, 1946

685 GEARHART Lemar: (*William Gearhart, Theodore Gearhart, Elizabeth Weiss, Felix Weiss, Eva Catherine, Melchior, Phillip*) was born April 4, 1925, twin son of William J. Gearhart and Mabel Buck. He married Elizabeth L. (unknown maiden name), born June 15, 1929 and they are presently living in Bethlehem, Pennsylvania.

Chldren:
- i- **GEARHART Terry Lee**: born April 21, 1949
- ii- **GEARHART Donna Louise**: born June 15, 1951
- iii- **GEARHART Lemar Lee**: born September 13, 1954

686 GEARHART Barbara J.: (*William Gearhart, Theodore Gearhart, Elizabeth Weiss, Felix Weiss, Eva Catherine, Melchior, Phillip*) was born October 4, 1930 in Gilbert, Pennsylvania, daughter of William J. Gearhart and Mabel Buck. She married Robert J. Kline born November 14, 1929. They are presently living in Adelphi, Maryland.

Children:
- i- **KLINE Janice Joe**: born September 13, 1956
- ii- **KLINE**: a daughter, no name or date.

687 GEARHART James: (*Nevin Gearhart, Theodore Gearhart, Elizabeth Weiss, Felix Weiss, Eva Catherine, Melchior, Phillip*) was born July 25, 1943, in Monroe Co., Pennsylvania, son of Reverend Nevin A. Gearhart and Amelia Mohr. He is presently living in Hamilton Square, New Jersey. No further records.

688 GEARHART Sarah: (*Nevin Gearhart, Theodore Gearhart, Elizabeth Weiss, Felix Weiss, Eva Catherine, Melchior, Phillip*) was born August 8, 1944 in Monroe Co., Pennsylvania, daughter of Reverend Nevin A. Gearhart and Amelia Mohr. She married _____ Meszaros and is presently living in Mt. Kisco, New York.

689 GEARHART Ruth: (*Nevin Gearhart, Theodore Gearhart, Elizabeth Weiss, Felix Weiss, Eva Catherine, Melchior, Phillip*) was born July 14, 1945 in Monroe Co., Pennsylvania, daughter of Reverend Nevin A. Gearhart and Amelia Mohr. She married _____ Cappolino and is presently living in Philadelphia. No further records.

690 GEARHART Charles: (*Nevin Gearhart, Theodore Gearhart, Elizabeth Weiss, Felix Weiss, Eva Catherine, Melchior, Phillip*) was born July 8, 1949 in Monroe Co., Pennsylvania, son of Reverend Nevin A. Gearhart and Amelia Mohr. He is presently living in Warrington, New Jersey. No further records.

691 GEARHART Austin Tuttle: (*Lyster Gearhart, Theodore Gearhart, Elizabeth Weiss, Felix Weiss, Eva Catherine, Melchior, Phillip*) was born April 12, 1933, son of Lyster Gearhart and Frances Tuttle. He married Patricia Smith, born April 19, 1937. No further records.

692 GEARHART David: (*Lyster Gearhart, Theodore Gearhart, Elizabeth Weiss, Felix Weiss, Eva Catherine, Melchior, Phillip*) was born July 29, 1944, probably in Allentown, Pennsylvania, son of Lyster Gearhart and Frances Tuttle. He is presently living in Allentown. He has two children. No further records.

693 GEARHART John: (*Lyster Gearhart, Theodore Gearhart, Elizabeth Weiss, Felix Weiss, Eva Catherine, Melchior, Phillip*) was born August 10, 1946, probably in Allentown Pennsylvania, son of Lyster Gearhart and Frances Tuttle. He is presently living in Allentown. No further records.

694 GEARHART Joanne: (*Martin Gearhart, Theodore Gearhart, Elizabeth Weiss, Felix Weiss, Eva Catherine, Melchior, Phillip*) was born August 11, 1942, daughter of Martin Gearhart and Olga Balson. She was married and divorced. No issue.

695 GEARHART Nadine: (*Martin Gearhart, Theodore Gearhart, Elizabeth Weiss, Felix Weiss, Eva Catherine, Melchior, Phillip*) was born February 12, 1945, daughter of Martin Gearhart and Olga Balson. She is unmarried at this time, and presently living in Nazareth, Pennsylvania.

696 GEARHART John W.: (*Albert Gearhart, John H. Gearhart, Elizabeth Weiss, Felix Weiss, Eva Catherine, Melchior, Phillip*) was born in Stroudsburg, Pennsylvania, son of Albert and Emma Gearhart. He has one daughter born in Stroudsburg. John died 1988 in Stroudsburg. His wife is still living there.

697 GEARHART Claire: (*S. Raymond Gearhart, John H. Gearhart, Elizabeth Weiss, Felix Weiss, Eva Catherine, Melchior, Phillip*) was born in Stroudsburg, Pennsylvania, son of S. Raymond Gearhart and Maizie Arnold. He died in Richmond, Virginia, aged 51.

698 KRESGE Doris: (*Minnie Gearhart, John H. Gearhart, Elizabeth Weiss, Felix Weiss, Eva Catherine, Melchior, Phillip*) was born 1924 in Saylorsburg, Pennsylvania, daughter of Samuel Kresge and Minnie E. Gearhart. She married Wilbur Hoffner, born 1913 in Saylorsburg, Pennsylvania, son of Edwin Hoffner and Sadie Roberts. She died 1961 and is buried in the Buena Vista cemetery in Chestnuthill.

Children:

i- HOFFNER Lee E.:
ii- HOFFNER Ray:
iii- HOFFNER Ann:

699 KRESGE June: (*Minnie Gearhart, Theodore Gearhart, Elizabeth Weiss, Felix Weiss, Eva Catherine, Melchior, Phillip*) was born 1924 in Saylorsburg, Pennsylvania, daughter of Samuel Kresge and Minnie Gearhart. She married Lester W. Hoagland born 1926. No further records.

Children:
i- HOAGLAND Barry:
ii- HOAGLAND Robin:

700 NEWELL Sheldon: (*Carrie Rinker, Susan Shoemaker, Emelie Weiss, George Weiss, Eva Catherine, Melchior, Phillip*) was born in Sroudsburg, Pennsylvania, son of Daniel Newell and Carrie E. Rinker. He is presently living in Stroudsburg.

One child:
i- NEWELL Jack:

701 RINKER Earl R.: (*Sherman Rinker, Susana Shoemaker, Emelie Weiss, George Weiss, Eva Catherine, Melchior, Phillip*) was born ca 1907, son of Sherman and Ada M. Rinker. He married Irene (unknown maiden name). He is presently living in Cherry Valley, Pennsylvania.

Known child born in Hamilton Township:
i- RINKER Hazel Loretta: born January 14, 1919

702 WARRICK Helen: (*Verna Shoemaker, Linford Shoemaker, Amelia Weiss, George Weiss, Eva Catherine, Melchior, Phillip*) was born in Stroudsburg, Pennsylvania, daughter of David H. Warrick and Verna Shoemaker. She married William E. Marshall and they have one daughter. They were living in Bethany Beach, Delaware in 1978. No further records.

703 BUZZARD Beryle Genevieve: (*Roland, Roy, Edwin, Joseph, Phillip, Melchior, Phillip*) was born July 13, 1923 in Bay City, Michigan, daughter of Roland L. Buzzard and Lillie Zelma Burns. She married August 23, 1941, Victor Levi Shatzer. No further records.

704 BUZZARD Lloyd Roland: (*Roland, Roy, Edwin, Joseph, Phillip, Melchior, Phillip*) was born June 27, 1930 in Bay City, Michigan, son of Roland Buzzard and Gertrude Matilda Brown. He married August 1, 1959, Mary Louise Alcorn born

March 24, 1939. They are presently living in Bay City.

Children:
i- BUZZARD Bryan Craig: born August 7, 1960
ii- BUZZARD Darryn Troy: born April 13, 1962. He changed his name to Troy Darryn.
Children adopted by Lloyd and Mary:
iii- BUZZARD Heidi Elizabeth: born May 25, 1969
iv- BUZZARD Heather Christine: born September 26, 1970.

705 BUZZARD Lyle Leroy: (*Roland, Roy, Edwin, Joseph, Phillip, Melchior, Phillip*) was born November 15, 1932 in Bay City, Michigan, son of Roland Buzzard and Gertrude Matilda Brown. He married October 12, 1957, Edna Louise Middleton. They are presently living in Bay City.

706 BUZZARD Gertrude Joy: (*Roland, Roy, Edwin, Joseph, Phillip, Melchior, Phillip*) was born May 10, 1938 in Bay City, Michigan, daughter of Roland Buzzard and Gertrude Matilda Brown. She married November 14, 1959, Earl Duane Engleman.

707 BUZZARD Dale Vernon: (*Roland, Roy, Edwin, Joseph, Phillip, Melchior, Phillip*) was born June 23, 1936 in Bay City, Michigan, son of Roland Buzzard and Gertrude Matilda Brown. He married June 29, 1963, Ruth Eileen Varty. They are presently living in Rees, Michigan.

708 BUZZARD Danelle Kay: (*Roy E., Roy V., Edwin, Joseph, Phillip, Melchior, Phillip*) was born October 24, 1948 in Bay City, Michigan, daughter of Roy Edward Buzzard and Norma Tanner. She is presently living in Bay City.

One child:
i- BUZZARD Christopher Eric: born August 12, 1967

709 BUZZARD Elaine M.: (*Roy E., Roy V., Edwin, Joseph, Phillip, Melchior, Phillip*) was born September 2, 1958 in Bay City, Michigan, daughter of Roy Edward Buzzard and Norma Tanner. She married July 31, 1976, Richard Sisler born May 25, 1956.

Children:
i- SISLER Sean Patrick: born March 5, 1979
ii- SISLER Eric Micah: born June 17, 1980
iii- SISLER Heather Danelle: born January 28, 1983
iv- SISLER Meagan Rose: born August 14, 1984

710 GOULET Eugene Joseph: (*Vera, Roy V., Edwin, Joseph, Phillip, Melchior, Phillip*) was born May 15, 1935 in Bay City, Michigan, son of Emery Joseph Goulet and Vera Marie Buzzard. He married in 1957, Amy Hoppock born February 6, 1948. They were divorced.

Children:
1016 i- **GOULET Andrew Joseph**: born September 13, 1959
1017 ii- **GOULET Ann Elizabeth**: born October 19, 1963

711 GOULET Jerry: (*Vera, Roy V., Edwin, Joseph, Phillip, Melchior, Phillip*) was born April 11, 1937 in Bay City, Michigan, son of Emery Joseph Goulet and Vera Marie Buzzard. He married April 1955, Sharon Lee Cole born September 21, 1937.

Children:
1018 i- **GOULET David Brian**: born January 3, 1956
1019 ii- **GOULET James Allen**: born April 12, 1957
1020 iii- **GOULET Kenneth Matthew**: born June 10, 1959
1021 iv- **GOULET Thomas Michael**: born April 10, 1961
1022 v- **GOULET Wayne Emery**: born May 19, 1964

712 GOULET Donald Emery: (*Vera, Roy V., Edwin, Joseph, Phillip, Melchior, Phillip*) was born February 9, 1949 in Bay City, Michigan, son of Emery Joseph Goulet and Vera Marie Buzzard. He married August 1969, Linda Patricia Perez born March 17, 1948.

Children:
i- **GOULET Derrick Bradley**: born March 20, 1970
ii- **GOULET Dina Michelle**: born March 23, 1973

713 GOULET Michael: (*Vera, Roy V., Edwin, Joseph, Phillip, Melchior, Phillip*) was born August 8, 1951 in Bay City, Michigan, son of Emery Joseph Goulet and Vera Marie Buzzard. He married Debbie Fernier.

Children:
i- **GOULET Sarah Emile**: born February 19,1978
ii- **GOULET Elizabeth Vera**: born October 9, 1979

714 BUZZARD Kenneth Alvin: (*Edwin, William, Edwin, Joseph, Phillip, Melchior, Phillip*) was born in Bay City, Michigan, son of Edwin Howe Buzzard and Alice Lambert. He died in Bay City, unknown date. No further records.

715 BUZZARD Pauline: (*Edwin, William, Edwin, Joseph, Phillip, Melchior, Phillip*) was born July 20, 1936 in Bay City, Michigan, daughter of Edwin Howe Buzzard and Alice Lambert. She married May 28, 1955, James M. Kelly. She died January 7, 1985 in Bay City.

Children:
- **i- KELLY Michael:**
- **ii- KELLY Roger:**
- **iii- KELLY Coleen:**
- **iv- KELLY Kathryn:**

716 BUZZARD Maureen: (*Russell, William, Edwin, Joseph, Phillip, Melchior, Phillip*) was born in Bay City, Michigan, daughter of Russell D. Buzzard and Lillian Griffith. She married October 10, 1951, Norbert Switala, son of Theophile Switala and Mary Wojciechowski.

717 BUZZARD Shirley: (*Russell, William, Edwin, Joseph, Phillip, Melchior, Phillip*) was born in Bay City, Michigan, daughter of Russell D. Buzzard and Lorraine Love. She married June 20, 1953, Bruce Dant, son of Ray Dant and Genevieve Burke.

718 BUZZARD Russell D. Jr.: (*Russell, William, Edwin, Joseph, Phillip, Melchior, Phillip*) was born April 15, 1936 in Bay City, Michigan, son of Russell D. Buzzard and Lorraine Love. He married May 16, 1975, Carolyn May Reynolds, daughter of Verne C. Reynolds and Genevieve Cooper.

719 LEN Linda: (*Noreen, William, Edwin, Joseph, Phillip, Melchior, Phillip*) was born May 27, 1946 in Bay City, Michigan, daughter of Matthew Len and Noreen Buzzard. She married January 19, 1962, Richard Westonburg, son of Edmond Westonburg and Eugenia Grochowski.

720 WESENICK Darlene: (*Noreen, William, Edwin, Joseph, Phillip, Melchior, Phillip*) was born December 3, 1949 in Bay City, Michigan, daughter of Albert Wesenick and Noreen Buzzard. She married July 3, 1976, Keith Perry, son of Roy Perry and Georgina Mc Kenzie.

721 WESENICK Carol: (*Noreen, William, Edwin, Joseph, Phillip, Melchior, Phillip*) was born March 19, 1951 in Bay City, Michigan, daughter of Albert Wesenick and Noreen Buzzard. She married October 7, 1967, Terrance Bouza, son of Edward Bouza and Joan Satkowiak.

722 WESTON Sharon: (*Noreen, William, Edwin, Joseph, Phillip, Melchior, Phillip*) was born August 1, 1959 in Bay City, Michigan, daughter of Ivan Weston and Noreen Buzzard. She married September 19, 1981, John Worthington.

723 **BUZZARD Janice Lea**: (*Robert, William, Edwin, Joseph, Phillip, Melchior, Phillip*) was born March 26, 1948 in Bay City, Michigan, daughter of Robert William Buzzard and Marlan Fayetta Barclay. She married August 3, 1968, James Wojeik, son of Andrew Wojeik and Gladys Novak.

724 **BUZZARD Ellen Marie**: (*Robert, William, Edwin, Joseph, Phillip, Melchior, Phillip*) was born January 6, 1951 in Bay City, Michigan, daughter of Robert William Buzzard and Marlan Fayetta Barclay. She married Kenneth Harring, son of Claude Herring and Marge Chave.

725 **BUZZARD Ruth Evelyn**: (*Robert, William, Edwin, Joseph, Phillip, Melchior, Phillip*) was born July 22, 1953 in Bay City, Michigan, daughter of Robert William Buzzard and Marlan Fayetta Barclay. She married January 8, 1971, David R. Thomas, son of Roy Thomas and Lena Garlets.

726 **VILLAIRE Daniel L.**: (*Doris, William, Edwin, Joseph, Phillip, Melchior, Phillip*) was born July 25, 1950 in Bay City, Michigan, daughter of Laurence Villaire and Doris Buzzard. He married January 22, 1972, Sandra L. Robinson. daughter of Keith Robinson and Maureen Fuhr.

727 **VILLAIRE Barbara E.**: (*Doris, William, Edwin, Joseph, Phillip, Melchior, Phillip*) was born August 3, 1951 in Bay City, Michigan, daughter of Laurence Villaire and Doris Buzzard. She married September 26, 1970, Walter Davis, son of Earl Davis and Caroline Voisine.

728 **WOOD Marcia Jane**: (*Dorothy, William, Edwin, Joseph, Phillip, Melchior, Phillip*) was born September 10, 1954 in Saginaw, Michigan, daughter of Harry E. Wood and Dorothy Buzzard. She married April 7, 1973, Kenneth Spicer.

729 **WOOD Beverly Jean**: (*Dorothy, William, Edwin, Joseph, Phillip, Melchior, Phillip*) was born January 10, 1959 in Saginaw, Michigan, daughter of Harry E. Wood and Dorothy Buzzard. She married June 25, 1977, Joseph Youngs.

730 **WOOD Amy Lee**: (*Dorothy, William, Edwin, Joseph, Phillip, Melchior, Phillip*) was born December 31, 1960 in Saginaw, Michigan, daughter of Harry E. Wood and Dorothy Buzzard. She married October 12, 1985, William Mc Namara.

731 **BOSSARD Sylvia Arline**: (*George, Lewis, George, Peter, Christopher, Melchior, Phillip*) was born June 11, 1933 in Geneva, New York, daughter of George C. Bossard and Emma Graham. She married June 18, 1955, John F. Warren.

Children:
- **i- WARREN John Jr.**:
- **ii- WARREN Susan**:
- **iii- WARREN Michael**:
- **iv- WARREN Jacquelyn**:

732 **BOSSARD Shirley Ann**: (*George, Lewis, George, Peter, Christopher, Melchior, Phillip*) was born November 18, 1935 in Geneva, New York, daughter of George C. Bossard and Emma Graham. She married December 2, 1954, William R. Myers.

Children:
- **i- MYERS Mary Lou**:
- **ii- MYERS William Jr.**:

733 **SNOOK Carolyn Marie**: (*Raymond Snook, Ethelyn, George, Peter, Christopher, Melchior, Phillip*) was born July 20, 1942 in Corning, New York, daughter of Raymond Snook and Corabelle Crumb. She married August 25, 1963, James Newton. They are presently living in Corning, New York.

Children born in Corning, New York:
- **i- NEWTON Christopher Allen**: born March 7, 1968
- **ii- NEWTON Anthony Scot**: born June 1, 1971

Adopted by James and Carolyn:
- **iii- NEWTON Laura**: born March 23, 1974

734 **SNOOK Patricia Ann**: (*Raymond Snook, Ethelyn, George, Peter, Christopher, Melchior, Phillip*) was born February 25, 1945 in Corning, New York, daughter of Raymond Snook and Corabelle Crumb. She married June 6, 1964, Larry Ford. They are presently living in Corning, New York.

Children:
- **i- FORD Kimberly Ann**: born May 23, 1967
- **ii- FORD Stephanie Dawn**: born October 25, 1971

735 **SMITH June**: (*Gladys Stanton, Mabel, George, Peter, Christopher, Melchior, Phillip*) was born March 24, 1922 in Dundee, New York, daughter of Charles F. Smith and Gladys Stanton. She married November 15, 1941, Gordon Miller, born November 21, 1917. They had six prematurely born children, none living. They are presently living in Henrietta, New York.

736 **SMITH William**: (*Gladys Stanton, Mable, George, Peter, Christopher, Melchior, Phillip*) was born April 14, 1923 in Dundee, New York, son of Charles F. Smith and Gladys Stanton. He married Loretta Shaft.

One child:
1023 i- **SMITH David**: born December 15, 1947 and died 1972

737 **SMITH Harry**: (*Gladys Stanton, Mabel, George, Peter, Christopher, Melchior, Phillip*) was born May 5, 1925 in Dundee, New York, son of Charles F. Smith and Gladys Stanton. He married August 11, 1945 in Henrietta, New York, Dorah Williams born May 6, 1925 in Rochester, New York, daughter of Chevalier D. Williams and Elizabeth Perry. They are presently living in Chester, New Hampshire.

Children born in Rochester, New York:
1024 i- **SMITH Cathie**: born October 22, 1946
1025 ii- **SMITH Garrett**: born November 17, 1949
1026 iii- **SMITH Dana**: born September 19, 1953

738 **SMITH Frederick**: (*Gladys Stanton, Mabel, George, Peter, Christopher, Melchior, Phillip*) was born January 2, 1933 in Dundee, New York, son of Charles F. Smith and Gladys Stanton. He married (1) November 28, 1959 Mary Porrica born July 3, 1934. He married (2) January 7, 1978, Dorothy (unknown maiden name), born November 21, 1944.

Children:
i- **SMITH Russell**: born February 15, 1959 and died December 14, 1975. He was adopted by Frederick
ii- **SMITH Robert**: born February 20, 1961 and died September 8, 1979
1027 iii- **SMITH Sueanne**: born October 21, 1962
1028 iv- **SMITH Amy**: born July 23, 1965
v- **SMITH Lenora**: born September 10, 1971. She was adopted by Frederick.

739 **SMITH Charles F. Jr.**: (*Gladys Stanton, Mabel, George, Peter, Christopher, Melchior, Phillip*) was born September 8, 1942 in Dundee, New York, son of Charles F. Smith and Gladys Stanton. He married September 1963, Cherrie Winkler born October 23, 1943.

Children:
i- **SMITH Randall**:
ii- **SMITH Darren**:
1029 iii- **SMITH Brian**:

740 SHARP Mary: (*Zelma Stanton, Mabel, George, Peter, Christopher, Melchior, Phillip*) was born May 10, 1931 in Dundee, New York, daughter of Harry Sharp and Zelma Stanton. She married May 30, 1953, Douglas Pierson born July 16, 1932. They are presently living in Hall, New York.

Children:
1030 i- **PIERSON Martin**: born December 8, 1957
1031 ii- **PIERSON Daniel**: born July 26, 1959

741 STANTON Charlotte: (*William Stanton, Mabel, George, Peter, Christopher, Melchior, Phillip*) was born October 23, 1932, twin daughter of William Stanton and Floreen Morse. She married June 24, 1961, Samuel Di Gennaro born September 30, 1935. They are presently living in Henrietta, New York.

Children:
1032 i- **DI GENNARO Joi Lynn**: born May 23, 1963
ii- **DI GENNARO Michael**: born October 19, 1965

742 STANTON Charleen: (*William Stanton, Mabel, George, Peter, Christopher, Melchior, Phillip*) was born October 23, 1932, twin daughter of William Stanton and Floreen Morse. She married August 7, 1955, Roger Mallard born July 29, 1934.

Children:
1033 i- **MALLARD Scott**: born September 16, 1956
1034 ii- **MALLARD Jeff**: born April 26, 1958

743 STORMS Walter T. Jr.: (*Grace, Truman, Cyrus, Richard, Christopher, Melchior, Phillip*) was born September 1, 1913 in Sugar Grove, Pennsylvania, son of Walter T. Storms and Grace Blanche Bozard. He married Gift Eileen Morris, born April 4, 1918 in Bradford, Pennsylvania, daughter of Claude E. Morris and Elizabeth Skidmore. He died October 10, 1972 in Bradford, Pennsylvania and is buried in the Mc Kean Memorial Park in Lafayette, Pennsylvania. Gift is presently living in Sugar Grove, Pennsylvania.

Children:
1035 i- **STORMS Sylvia Gay**: born June 10, 1940
1036 ii- **STORMS Walter Terrance**: born June 28, 1942
1037 iii- **STORMS Timothy Morris**: October 19, 1944
1038 iv- **STORMS Bruce Allan**: born July 14, 1946

744 STORMS Clifford C.: (*Grace, Truman, Cyrus, Richard, Christopher, Melchior, Phillip*) was born June 15, 1916 in Sugar Grove, Pennsylvania, son of Walter T. Storms and Grace Blanche Bozard. He married August 21, 1938, Eleanor Cadman born March 15, 1920 in Millville, Pennsylvania, daughter of Eugene E. Cadman and

Hilda Pennington. He died March 18, 1983 in Warren, Pennsylvania and is buried in Sugar Grove.

Children:

1039 i- **STORMS Kaye**: born July 15, 1941
1040 ii- **STORMS Charles**: born April 28, 1944
1041 iii- **STORMS Susan**: born November 19, 1956

745 MILLER Charles F. Jr.: (*Ruby, Truman, Cyrus, Richard, Christopher, Melchior, Phillip*) was born December 16, 1919, son of Charles Miller and Ruby Emily Bozard. He was killed in an airplane crash in 1973.

746 MILLER Robert: (*Ruby, Truman, Cyrus, Richard, Christopher, Melchior, Phillip*) was born December 3, 1922, son of Charles F. Miller and Ruby Emily Bozard. He was murdered in San Francisco, California in 1970. He was never married.

747 MILLER Stanley: (*Ruby, Truman, Cyrus, Richard, Christopher, Melchior, Phillip*) was born February 19, 1924, son of Charles F. Miller and Ruby Emily Bozard. He married Mary (unknown maiden name). He died June 25, 1975.

Children:

1042 i- **MILLER Sharron**: born November 25, 1954
1043 ii- **MILLER Jeffrey**: born September 9, 1956
1044 iii- **MILLER Cathy**: born July 13, 1960

748 MILLER Richard: (*Ruby, Truman, Cyrus, Richard, Christopher, Melchior, Phillip*) was born January 20, 1923, son of Charles F. Miller and Ruby Emily Bozard. He married Bunnie, (unknown maiden name), and they were divorced. They had one child.

749 BOZARD Eva: (*Floyd, Truman, Cyrus, Richard, Christopher, Melchior, Phillip*) was born February 7, 1917 in Salamanca, New York, daughter of Floyd C. Bozard and Bessie Harkness. She married November 1, 1941, Dr. Guy Gardner born March 26, 1915, son of Thomas and Mary Gardner. He died May 6, 1980 in Salamanca, New York and Eva is presently living in Salamanca.

Children:

1045 i- **GARDNER Marcia**: born November 5, 1942 in Santa Maria, California.
1046 ii- **GARDNER Susan**: born January 23, 1944 in Harrisburg, Pennsylvania.

Children born in Salamanca:

iii- **GARDNER Ann**: born July 30, 1946
1047 iv- **GARDNER Laura**: born March 18, 1948
1048 v- **GARDNER Thomas**: born September 25, 1953
1049 vi- **GARDNER Jan**: born January 20, 1955

750 **BOZARD Mildred**: (*Floyd, Truman, Cyrus, Richard, Christopher, Melchior, Phillip*) was born January 17, 1919, daughter of Floyd C. Bozard and Bessie Harkness. She married March 25, 1940, Edward Nugent born August 29, 1916. They are presently living in Salamanca, New York.

Children:
i- **NUGENT Michael**: born February 13, 1941
ii- **NUGENT Thomas**: born October 16, 1943
iii- **NUGENT Robert**:

751 **BOZARD Paul Floyd**: (*Floyd, Truman, Cyrus, Richard, Christopher, Melchior, Phillip*) was born December 3, 1920, son of Floyd C. Bozard and Bessie Harkness. He married May 30, 1941, Julia Marie Mohr born July 9, 1921, daughter of Edward Joseph Mohr and Marguerite Weber. They are presently living in Salamanca, New York.

One child born in Salamanca, New York:
1050 i- **BOZARD Paul Edward**: born July 31, 1943

752 **BOZARD Donald**: (*Floyd, Truman, Cyrus, Richard, Christopher, Melchior, Phillip*) was born April 16, 1923, son of Floyd C. Bozard and Bessie Harkness. He married Carol Mc Carthy born April 15, 1924. Donald died April 5, 1982 in Oceanport, New Jersey and Carol is still living there.

Children:
i- **BOZARD Linda**:
ii- **BOZARD David**:
iii- **BOZARD Dennis**:
iv- **BOZARD Jon**:

753 **ZUVER James**: (*Flossie, Truman, Cyrus, Richard, Christopher, Melchior, Phillip*) was born October 22, 1921, son of Arthur Zuver and Flossie Marietta Bozard. He married Marie (unknown maiden name). He died October 20, 1967 in Cuba, New York.

Children:
i- **ZUVER James Jr.**: born May 4, 1944
ii- **ZUVER Sharon**: born April 23, 1952
iii- **ZUVER**: Unknown name or date of birth

754 **ZUVER Eva**: (*Flossie, Truman, Cyrus, Richard, Christopher, Melchior, Phillip*) was born January 8, 1923, twin daughter of Arthur Zuver and Flossie Marietta Bozard. She married Wilford Clark and he is presently living in Olean, New York. Eva died December 31, 1978 In Olean.

Children:
1051 **i- CLARK Linda**: born December 24, 1956
1052 **ii- CLARK Diane**: born November 15, 1957
iii- CLARK Kenneth Ross: born December 4, 1963

755 **ZUVER Kenneth**: (*Flossie, Truman, Cyrus, Richard, Christopher, Melchior, Phillip*) was born December 20, 1931 in Bradford, Pennsylvania, son of Arthur Zuver and Flossie Marietta Bozard. He is presently living in Olean, New York.

One child:
i- ZUVER Debbie:

756 **LANGLEY Beatrice Jean**: (*Bernice, Truman, Cyrus, Richard, Christopher, Melchior, Phillip*) was born June 14, 1922 in Salamanca, New York, daughter of Ralph W. Langley and Bernice Bozard. She married August 3, 1942, Raymond Shearer. They were divorced in 1952 and she is presently living in North Hornell, New York.

Children born in North Hornell:
1053 **i- SHEARER William Raymond**: born December 2, 1943
1054 **ii- SHEARER Richard Langley**: born April 11, 1946
One child born in Greensboro, North Carolina:
iii- SHEARER Genevieve Nancy: born May 15, 1950

757 **LANGLEY Barbara Eva**: (*Bernice, Truman, Cyrus, Richard, Christopher, Melchior, Phillip*) was born August 19, 1925 in North Hornell, New York, daughter of Ralph W. Langley and Bernice Bozard. She married Roland Montgomery. He died March 21, 1986 in Hornell.

Children born in Hornell, New York:
1055 **i- MONTGOMERY Susan Ann**: born February 12, 1947
1056 **ii- MONTGOMERY Marcia Kay**: born February 12, 1948
1057 **iii- MONTGOMERY Ann Langley**: born February 2, 1955
Child born in Berea, Ohio:
iv- MONTGOMERY Robert Roland: born November 23, 1967

758 **HOKANSON Ernest Jr.**: (*Beatrice, Truman, Cyrus, Richard, Christopher, Melchior, Phillip*) was born July 23, 1926 in Bradford, Pennsylvania, son of Ernest Hokanson and Beatrice Bozard. He married (1) in 1945, Zada Ellen Huff. They

were divorced in 1953 and he married (2) Bobbie (unknown maiden name). He married (3) Ruth Sturdevant. They are presently living in Doerun, Georgia.

Children by first marriage:
i- **HOKANSON Paul David**: born May 23, 1946 and died July 17, 1946
1058 ii- **HOKANSON Kathleen Ann**: born December 5, 1947
iii- **HOKANSON Janice Lee**: born June 6, 1949 and died June 7, 1949
Child by second marriage:
iv- **HOKANSON Kenneth Scott**: born July 19, 1961, and he died August 27, 1961
Child by third marriage:
v- **HOKANSON Julia Lynn**: born November 11, 1973

759 HOKANSON Dean Russell: (*Beatrice, Truman, Cyrus, Richard, Christopher, Melchior, Phillip*) was born December 5, 1928, in Bradford, Pennsylvania, son of Ernest Hokanson and Beatrice Bozard. He married Constance Favro born June 6, 1925, daughter of James and Shirley Favro. They are presently living in Atlanta, Georgia.

Children:
1059 i- **HOKANSON Tanyjah Jean**: born April 8, 1949
1060 ii- **HOKANSON April Estelle**: born May 29, 1953
1061 iii- **HOKANSON Roderick Dean**: born September 18, 1954
1062 iv- **HOKANSON James Ernest**: born May 26, 1956
1063 v- **HOKANSON Natasha Lynn**: born October 11, 1961

760 HOKANSON Constance Louise: (*Beatrice, Truman, Cyrus, Richard, Christopher, Melchior, Phillip*) was born August 22, 1932 in Bradford, Pennsylvania, daughter of Ernest Hokanson and Beatrice Bozard. She married April 12, 1958, Charles Arthur Downing. They are presently living in Buffalo, New York.

Children born in Buffalo, New York:
1064 i- **DOWNING Tambri Sue**: born February 2, 1959
1065 ii- **DOWNING Craig Steven**: born July 15, 1960
iii- **DOWNING Julia Lynn**: born March 3, 1964 and died March 4, 1964, buried in Pleasant Valley cemetery Olean, New York.
1066 iv- **DOWNING Christopher John**: born July 30, 1965
1067 v- **DOWNING Tracy Lee**: born September 27, 1966
vi- **DOWNING Charles Ernest**: born September 9, 1969

761 BOZARD Bruce T.: (*Clifford, Truman, Cyrus, Richard, Christopher, Melchior, Phillip*) was born February 3, 1942 in Buffalo, New York, son of Clifford Bozard and Rena Thiel. He married Darlene Spencer born August 5, 1941 in Dalton, Pennsylvania.

Children born in Medina, New York:
i- **BOZARD Laurie**: born June 11, 1966
ii- **BOZARD Lyne**: born January 13, 1970
iii- **BOZARD Kimberly**: born October 16, 1972

762 BOZARD Mary K.: (*Clifford, Truman, Cyrus, Richard, Christopher, Melchior, Phillip*) was born November 26, 1947 in Buffalo, New York, daughter of Clifford Bozard and Rena Thiel. She married Thomas Forese, born February 27, 1945 in Philadelphia, Pennsylvania. They are presently living in Boston.

One child born in Boston, Massachusetts:
i- **FORESE Clifford T.**: born January 2, 1980

763 HALLADAY Harry E.: (*Rena, Edward, Cyrus, Richard, Christopher, Melchior, Phillip*) was born April 6, 1939 in Great Valley, New York, son of Ralph R. Halladay and Rena Bozard. He married April 2, 1964 in Joplin, Missouri, Hazel (unknown maiden name). No further records.

764 HALLADAY Ralph Arthur: (*Rena, Edward, Cyrus, Richard, Christopher, Melchior, Phillip*) was born March 3, 1942, in Great Valley, New York, son of Ralph A. Halladay and Rena Bozard. He married February 17, 1979 in Missouri, Cynthia (unknown maiden name). No further records.

765 SAWDEY Lawrence James: (*Bertha, Edward, Cyrus, Richard, Christopher, Melchior, Phillip*) was born June 11, 1942 in Olean, New York, son of Raymond Sawdey and Bertha Eldene Bozard. He married (1) October 27, 1962, Dorothy Daley. They were divorced and he married (2) July 1971 in Olean, New York, Della Gray.

Children:
i- **SAWDEY Rodney James**: born June 26, 1964
1068 ii- **SAWDEY Patricia Suzanne**: born December 6, 1968
iii- **SAWDEY Lynn Allen**: born July 24, 1965 and died September 7, 1965, buried in Portville, New York.

766 SAWDEY Margaret Mary: (*Bertha, Edward, Cyrus, Richard, Christopher, Melchior, Phillip*) was born September 16, 1943 in Olean, New York, daughter of Raymond Sawdey and Bertha Eldene Bozard. She married December 29. 1962 in Cuba, New York, Lawrence Joseph Fuller. They were divorced in 1989.

Children born in Cuba, New York:
1069 i- **FULLER Daniel Joseph**: born November 3, 1963
1070 ii- **FULLER Mary Jo**: born August 8, 1965

iii- FULLER Marcy Ann: born June 25, 1968
iv- FULLER David Lawrence: born August 22, 1973

767 **SAWDEY Marcia Ann**: (*Bertha, Edward, Cyrus, Richard, Christopher, Melchior, Phillip*) was born February 10, 1945 in Hornell, New York, daughter of Raymond Sawdey and Bertha Eldene Bozard. She married (1) August 19, 1966 in Olean, New York, Douglas Baxter. They were divorced and she married (2) February 3, 1973 in Olean, New York, David Fagnan.

Child of first marriage, name changed to Fagnan:
i- FAGNAN Elizabeth Ann: born August 23, 1969
Child of second marriage:
ii- FAGNAN Sarah Lynn: born June 20, 1975

768 **MOSMAN William Lynford**: (*Lynford Mosman, Blanche, Cyrus, Richard, Christopher, Melchior, Phillip*) was born December 16, 1925 in Olean, New York, son of Lynford Mosman and Harriet Laura Fiester. He married April 15, 1952, Mary Ellen Wilson born June 10, 1928.

Children:
1071 **i- MOSMAN Patricia Marie**: born May 20, 1953
1072 **ii- MOSMAN Mary Lynn**: born September 27, 1955
1073 **iii- MOSMAN Ellen Jean**: born March 17, 1958
1074 **iv- MOSMAN William Lynford Jr.**: born May 28, 1959
1075 **v- MOSMAN Judith Elizabeth**: born August 22, 1960
vi- MOSMAN Timothy Ellis: born March 23, 1962 and died April 25, 1981
vii- MOSMAN Daniel Edward: born March 10, 1963
viii- MOSMAN Nancy Ann: born June 12, 1965

769 **MOSMAN Vivian Harriet**: (*Lynford Mosman, Blanche, Cyrus, Richard, Christopher, Melchior, Phillip*) was born June 3, 1928 in Olean, New York, daughter of Lynford Mosman and Harriet Laura Fiester. She married September 30, 1950, Alan Thomas Kidder born March 19, 1928, son of Chauncy Kidder and Esther May Chant.

Children:
1076 **i- KIDDER Thomas Alan**: born May 8, 1954
1077 **ii- KIDDER Lori May**: born February 5, 1956
1078 **iii- KIDDER David Scott**: born July 28, 1959
1079 **iv- KIDDER Richard Lynn**: born October 29, 1962
1080 **v- KIDDER Jeffery Roy**: born June 22, 1964

770 **MOSMAN Edward George**: (*Lynford Mosman, Blanche, Cyrus, Richard,*

Christopher, Melchior, Phillip) was born September 17, 1931 in Rochester, New York, son of Lynford Mosman and Harriet Laura Fiester. He married September 26, 1953, Winifred Ann Campbell born August 6, 1933, daughter of Kenneth Campbell and Mary L. Pearson.

Children:
1081 i- **MOSMAN Lindy Ann**: born September 6, 1954
1082 ii- **MOSMAN James Edward**: born July 15, 1958
iii- **MOSMAN Michael George**: born April 9, 1971

771 **MOSMAN Phyllis Elaine**: (*Lynford Mosman, Blanche, Cyrus, Richard, Christopher, Melchior, Phillip*) was born December 16, 1938 in Buffalo, New York, daughter of Lynford Mosman and Harriet Laura Fiester. She married July 4, 1958, Frederick Gerhard Koblick born October 8, 1931.

Children:
i- **KOBLICK Christopher Frederick**: born November 10, 1965
ii- **KOBLICK Kenneth Phillip**: born October 6, 1967
iii- **KOBLICK Scott Jeremy**: born October 19, 1974

772 **MOSMAN Judith Marie**: (*Lynford Mosman, Blanche, Cyrus, Richard, Christopher, Melchior, Phillip*) was born August 21, 1944 in Buffalo, New York, daughter of Lynford Mosman and Harriet Laura Fiester. She married July 4, 1966, David Angelo Prieto.

Children:
i- **PRIETO Michelle Marie**: born May 26, 1971
ii- **PRIETO Michael David**: born October 3, 1974
iii- **PRIETO Deborah Katherine**: born March 22, 1978
iv- **PRIETO Matthew Paul**: born September 17, 1986

773 **BOZARD Bernice**: (*Thurman, Glen, Judson, Richard, Christopher, Melchior, Phillip*) daughter of Thurman and Mary Ruth Bozard. She married January 28, 1938, Irvin K. Noll. They are presently living in Cuba, New York. No further records.

774 **GIBSON Eleanor J.**: (*Edward Gibson, Sarah Quin, Amanda Backer, Sarah, George, Melchior, Phillip*) was born in Pulteney, New York, daughter of Edward J. Gibson and Dorothy Cole. She married July 1, 1950, John H. Putnam, son of Harold Putnam and Frances Coryell.

775 **GIBSON Edward J. Jr.**: (*Edward Gibson, Sarah Quin, Amanda Backer, Sarah, George, Melchior, Phillip*) was born in Pulteney, New York, son of Floyd D.

Gibson and Dorothy Cole. He married November 25, 1948, Geraldine E. Preston, daughter of Claire L. Preston and Goldie G. Towner.

776 GIBSON Janice: (*Edward Gibson, Sarah Quin, Amanda Backer, Sarah, George, Melchior, Phillip*) was born in Pulteney, New York, daughter of Floyd D. Gibson and Dorothy Cole. She married November 13, 1959, Frederick V. Mc Callister, born 1927, son of Edward F. Mc Callister and Sylvia Bostick.

777 GIBSON Jerry A.: (*Edward Gibson, Sarah Quin, Amanda Backer, Sarah, George, Melchior, Phillip*) was born in Pulteney, New York son of Floyd D. Gibson and Dorothy Cole. He married March 29, 1969, Elaine L. Niles, daughter of Robert E. Niles and Doris M. Whipple.

778 HEDDEN William Harry: (*William Hedden, Henry Hedden, Jane Backer, Sarah, George, Melchior, Phillip*) was born October 11, 1945 in Hornell, New York, son of William Franklin Hedden and Marjorie Allen. He married February 13, 1971, Sheila Van Arsvale born June 27, 1948.

Children:
- i- **HEDDEN Danielle Marjorie:** (twin) born March 7, 1978
- ii- **HEDDEN Dorothea Beth:** (twin) born March 7, 1978
- iii- **HEDDEN Andrew Jacob:** born January 10. 1983

779 HEDDEN Henry Andrew: (*Raymond Hedden, Henry Hedden, Jane Backer, Sarah, George, Melchior, Phillip*) was born December 21, 1944 in Hornell, New York, son of Raymond Albert Hedden and Dorothy Allen. He married December 27, 1969, Rebecca Briggs born January 30, 1948 in Hornell.

Children:
- i- **HEDDEN Kimberly Sue:** born February 5, 1973
- ii- **HEDDEN Joshua Raymond:** born December 25, 1974

780 HEDDEN Sue Ann: (*Raymond Hedden, Henry Hedden, Jane Backer, Sarah, George, Melchior, Phillip*) was born January 12, 1947, daughter of Raymond Albert Hedden and Dorothy Allen. She married July 8, 1972, Salvatore Buccolo born July 20, 1946 in Hornell, New York.

Children:
- i- **BUCCOLO Adam David:** born September 26, 1974
- ii- **BUCCOLO Larissa Sarah:** born September 12, 1976

781 HEDDEN Marjorie Jean: (*Raymond Hedden, Henry Hedden, Jane Backer,*

Sarah, George, Melchior, Phillip) was born March 5, 1954 in Hornell, New York, daughter of Raymond Albert Hedden and Dorothy Allen. She married November 28, 1973, Gary Eldridge born June 1, 1953 in Hornell, New York.

Children:
i- **ELDRIDGE Cassandra Leigh**: born January 28, 1978
ii- **ELDRIDGE Zachary**: born September 22, 1981

782 HURNE Marcia Joanne: (*Mary Jane Hedden, Henry Hedden, Jane Backer, Sarah, George, Melchior, Phillip*) was born June 15, 1944 in Hornell, New York, daughter of Robert Frederick Hurne and Mary Jane Hedden. She married July 17, 1964 in Hornell, Glen Charles Granger.

Children:
i- **GRANGER Traci Lynn**: born September 11, 1966
ii- **GRANGER Craig Michael**: born July 18, 1968
iii- **GRANGER Sheila Marie**: born October 6, 1969

783 HURNE Marlene Ruth: (*Mary Jane Hedden, Henry Hedden, Jane Backer, Sarah, George, Melchior, Phillip*) was born December 24, 1949 in Hornell, New York, daughter of Robert Frederick Hurne and Mary Jane Hedden. She married February 1970, Gary David Evans.

Children:
i- **EVANS Lori Ann**: born August 20, 1970
ii- **EVANS Robyn Deanne**: born September 21, 1973
iii- **EVANS Mark David**: born September 21, 1975

784 KERR Thomas James: (*Esther Hedden, Henry Hedden, Jane Backer. Sarah, George, Melchior, Phillip*) was born May 4, 1947 in Hornell, New York, twin son of Douglas Leroy Kerr and Esther Hedden. He married October 30, 1971, Linda Kay Kryder, born October 1, 1952.

Children:
i- **KERR Alisha Ann**: born July 23, 1973
ii- **KERR Nicole Jeanne**: born November 23, 1973

785 KERR Douglas Leroy Jr.: (*Esther Hedden, Henry Hedden, Jane Backer, Sarah, George, Melchior, Phillip*) was born May 4, 1947 in Hornell, New York, twin son of Douglas Leroy Kerr and Esther Hedden. He married May 12, 1969, Mary Jane Eubanks born August 23, 1950.

Children:
i- **KERR Shelly Lynn**: born November 14, 1970

ii- KERR Andrew Leroy: born August 21, 1974

786 **KERR Nancy Jane**: (*Esther Hedden, Henry Hedden, Jane Backer, Sarah, George, Melchior, Phillip*) was born May 14, 1949 in Hornell, New York, daughter of Douglas Leroy Kerr and Esther Hedden. She married October 23, 1971, Gary Wayne Hammond born September 27, 1949 in Hornell, New York.

Children:
i- HAMMOND Benjamin Wayne: born August 8, 1978
ii- HAMMOND Christine Joyce: born March 20, 1982

787 **KERR Roger**: (*Esther Hedden, Henry Hedden, Jane Backer, Sarah, George, Melchior, Phillip*) was born February 14, 1957 in Hornell, New York, son of Douglas Leroy Kerr and Esther Hedden. He married June 23, 1978, Kelly Elizabeth Cornish.

Children:
i- KERR Jessica Lois: born February 13, 1984
ii- KERR Katie Lizbeth: born May 3, 1989

788 **BOSSARD Raymond Jr.**: (*Raymond, Clarence, Judd, Simon, George, Melchior, Phillip*) was born October 5, 1953 in West Milford, New Jersey, son of Raymond Bossard and Dolores Furey. He married September 6, 1980.

Children:
i- BOSSARD Raymond III: born June 3, 1982
ii- BOSSARD Michael: born September 24, 1985

789 **KNOWLES Denis**: (*Doris Personius, Adrian Personius, Clara, Anson, George, Melchior, Phillip*) was born February 12, 1952 in Painted Post, New York, son of Daniel Knowles and Doris Personius. He married Kathleen Savage.

Children:
i- KNOWLES Brian: born March 4, 1982
ii- KNOWLES Lauren: born May 4, 1984

790 **KNOWLES Nancy**: (*Doris Personius, Adrian Personius, Clara, Anson, George, Melchior, Phillip*) was born October 31, 1953 in Painted Post, New York, daughter of Daniel Henry Knowles and Doris Personius. She married Claude Perea and they were divorced.

Children:
i- PEREA Marc: born Febuary 14, 1977

ii- PEREA Claudia: born April 24, 1980

791 **HILL Jean Lorraine**: (*Lucelia, Arthur, Charles, Anson, George, Melchior, Phillip*) was born November 8, 1930 in Ithaca, New York, daughter of Harvey Gordon Hill and Lucelia Elizabeth Bossard. She married December 21, 1950, Paul A. Lord born December 7, 1929.

Children:
i- LORD Paul A. Jr.: born March 14, 1952
1083 **ii- LORD Mark Edmond**: born January 31, 1954
1084 **iii- LORD Valorie Ann**: born August 15, 1955

792 **HILL William George**: (*Lucelia, Arthur, Charles, Anson, George, Melchior, Phillip*) was born July 12, 1952 and was adopted by Harvey Gordon Hill and Lucelia Bossard. He married (1) Sharron Graubard and (2) Theresa Bradshaw. They were divorced in 1979 and he married (3) July 6, 1988, Lois Parker.

Child by first marriage:
i- HILL William: born July 13, 1972
Children by second marriage:
ii- HILL David Michael: born October 1977
iii- HILL Richard William: born January 20, 1979

793 **BOSSARD Linda Cheryl**: (*Myron, Arthur, Charles, Anson, George, Melchior, Phillip*) was born March 29, 1948 in Ithaca, New York, daughter of Myron Bossard and Clella Stetson. She married August 7, 1972, Boyd Chamberlain born December 11, 1944.

Children born in Ithaca, New York:
i- CHAMBERLAIN David Boyd: born November 22, 1978
ii- CHAMBERLAIN Christopher Mark: born February 8, 1983

794 **BOSSARD Rosalie Jean**: (*Myron, Arthur, Charles, Anson, George, Melchior, Phillip*) was born January 25, 1949, twin daughter of Myron Bossard and Clella Stetson. She married July 17, 1980, William W. Wood, born November 17, 1940.

Children born in Ithaca, New York:
i- WOOD Valerie Jean: born April 20, 1968
ii- WOOD Nicholas Wayne: born January 7, 1982

795 **BOSSARD Carrol Ann**: (*Myron, Arthur, Charles, Anson, George, Melchior, Phillip*) was born January 25, 1949, twin daughter of Myron Bossard and Clella Stetson. She married March 18, 1967, Amos Little.

Child born in Ithaca, New York:
i- **LITTLE Allen Lee**: born October 29, 1967

796 BOSSARD Ronald: (*Myron, Arthur, Charles, Anson, George, Melchior, Phillip*) was born December 28, 1950, son of Myron Bossard and Clella Stetson. He was married and divorced.

Children:
i- **BOSSARD Jason Christopher**: born 1981
ii- **BOSSARD Theresa Jean**: born 1984

797 BOSSARD Sandy: (*Robert, Arthur, Charles, Anson, George, Melchior, Phillip*) was born November 10, 1941, twin daughter of Robert Bossard and Leona Wood. She married Richard Thorpe and they had three children. She died April 15, 1976 in Syracuse, New York. No further records.

798 MC FALL Diane Lee: (*Betty, Arthur, Charles, Anson, George, Melchior, Phillip*) was born September 28, 1949 in Ithaca, New York, daughter of Roger Henry Mc Fall and Betty Jane Bossard. She married August 16, 1969, Charles Armine.

Children:
i- **ARMINE Jeffrey James**: born December 29, 1971
ii- **ARMINE Jamie**: born August 6, 1975

799 MC FALL Deborah Elaine: (*Betty, Arthur, Charles, Anson, George, Melchior, Phillip*) was born March 7, 1955 in Ithaca, New York, daughter of Roger Henry Mc Fall and Betty Jane Bossard. She married December 29, 1973, Robert Onan.

One child:
i- **ONAN Brandon**: born February 18, 1975

800 MC FALL Nancy Jean: (*Betty, Arthur, Charles, Anson, George, Melchior, Phillip*) was born May 28, 1959 in Ithaca, New York, daughter of Roger Henry Mc Fall and Betty Jane Bossard.

One child:
i- **MC FALL Gavin Henry**: born July 5, 1985

801 SIMMONS Karen Elaine: (*Vivian Kibbe, Nettie, Charles, Anson, George, Melchior, Phillip*) was born February 15, 1944 in Stafford, New York, daughter of Raymond Simmons and Vivian Kibbe. She married February 17, 1967 in Reno,

Nevada, James H. Smith. They are presently living in California.

Children born in San Jose, California:
- i- **SMITH James Raymond**: born November 12, 1967
- ii- **SMITH Elizabeth Ann**: born September 21, 1981

802 KIBBE Justine: (*Raymon Kibbe, Nettie, Charles, Anson, George, Melchior, Phillip*) was born May 20, 1941, daughter of Raymon Elbert Kibbe and Creda Breneman. She married in 1984, Neal Turner. No issue.

803 KIBBE Phillip Mark: (*Ramon Kibbe, Nettie, Charles, Anson, George, Melchior, Phillip*) was born June 23, 1945, son of Raymon Kibbe and Creda Breneman. He married August 14, 1971, Patricia Aldrus.

Children:
- i- **KIBBE Kerri Anne**: born June 14, 1977
- ii- **KIBBE Krista Marie**: born May 13, 1982

804 MC MILLAN Anne Blythe: (*Charles Mc Millan, Florence, Charles, Anson, George, Melchior, Phillip*) was born July 23, 1948 in Oakland, California, daughter of Charles Duncan Mc Millan and Anne Mayfield. She married May 5, 1982, David Moller. No issue.

805 MC MILLAN Elizabeth Sams: (*Charles Mc Millan, Florence, Charles, Anson, George, Melchior, Phillip*) was born April 1, 1953 in Texas, daughter of Charles Duncan Mc Millan and Anne Mayfield. She married December 31, 1973, Lewis Wesley Seay in Paris, Texas.

Children:
- i- **SEAY Amanda Beth**: born November 11, 1976 in Dallas, Texas
- ii- **SEAY Charles Wesley**: born May 25, 1986 in Paris, Texas

806 BOSSARD Jack: (*Clarence, Claude, William, Anson, George, Melchior, Phillip*) was born December 2, 1946 in Hornell, New York, son of Clarence Bossard and Edna Mead. He married July 19, 1969, Susan Knipler born February 6, 1947. They were divorced in 1985 and Jack is presently living in the Town of Howard

Children:
- i- **BOSSARD Kimberly Sue**: born May 1, 1972
- ii- **BOSSARD Katie Elizabeth**: born December 23, 1974
- iii- **BOSSARD Maggie Marie**: born June 28, 1979

807 BOSSARD Kermit Lee: (*Harold, Claude, William, Anson, George, Melchior, Phillip*) was born November 3, 1941 in Hornell, New York, son of Harold Bossard and Beulah Storm. He married September 5, 1964, Carol Wiley born August 15, 1942.

Children:
- i- **BOSSARD Shawn Ethan:** born November 28, 1966
- ii- **BOSSARD Mathew Ryan:** born June 8, 1969

808 BOSSARD Richard Dale: (*Harold, Claude, William, Anson, George, Melchior, Phillip*) was born May 4, 1944 in Hornell, New York, son of Harold Bossard and Beulah Storm. He married July 20, 1968, Eloise Brasted born November 20, 1946.

Children:
- i- **BOSSARD Kari Janelle:** born February 17, 1971
- ii- **BOSSARD Amy Lynn:** born September 12, 1972
- iii- **BOSSARD Jodi Rae:** April 2, 1975

809 BOSSARD Nancy Marie: (*Harold, Claude, William, Anson, George, Melchior, Phillip*) was born October 16, 1950 in Hornell, New York, daughter of Harold Bossard and Beulah Storm. She married August 11, 1973, Douglas Sidney Yaw born September 1, 1949.

One child adopted by Douglas and Nancy:
- i- **YAW Douglas Paul:** born March 27, 1986

810 BOSSARD David Charles: (*Harold, Claude, William, Anson, George, Melchior, Phillip*) was born May 19, 1954 in Hornell, New York, son of Harold Bossard and Beulah Storm. He married October 20, 1979, Kimberly Drepinsted born November 7, 1956. They are presently living in the Town of Howard.

Children:
- i- **BOSSARD Michael Allen:** born July 2, 1980
- ii- **BOSSARD Benjamin Charles:** born March 5, 1986

811 LUSK Gail Alice: (*Doris, Claude, William, Anson, George, Melchior, Phillip*) was born June 8, 1955 in Hornell, New York, daughter of William Lusk and Doris Alta Bossard. She married June 4, 1983, Stephen Fals born October 1, 1954. No issue.

812 LUSK Lucinda Rae: (*Doris, Claude, William, Anson, George, Melchior, Phillip*) was born August 28, 1957 in Hornell, New York, daughter of William Lusk and Doris Alta Bossard. She married June 7, 1980, Richard Giglio born May 30, 1956.

Children:
i- **GIGLIO Nicole Domoneque**: born August 20, 1985
ii- **GIGLIO Colin**: born April 30, 1987

813 LUSK Brenda Jo: (*Doris, Claude, William, Anson, George, Melchior, Phillip*) was born December 30, 1958 in Hornell, New York, daughter of William Lusk and Doris Alta Bossard. She married November 2, 1986, Peter Koener. No issue.

814 HORTON Janice Marie: (*Orlo Horton, Mary, William, Anson, George, Melchior, Phillip*) was born July 27, 1946 in Hawaii, daughter of Orlo Horton and Fairiola Taylor. She married (1) Richard Dunning. They were divorced and she married (2) Robert Scobey. They are presently living in California. No issue.

815 HORTON Jerry: (*Orlo Horton, Mary, William, Anson, George, Melchior, Phillip*) was born September 11, 1947 in Hawaii, son of Orlo Horton and Fairiola Taylor. He married October 1, 1977, Betsy Phanp. They are presently living in Canada. No issue.

816 LEMON Sandra Lee: (*Harriet, Fred, William, Anson, George, Melchior, Phillip*) was born July 23, 1941 daughter of Lee Lemon and Harriet Bossard. She married Phillip Dempelwolf and they are presently living in California.

Children:
i- **DEMPELWOLF Gretchen**: born December 15, 1973, She was adopted by Phillip and Sandra.
ii- **DEMPELWOLF Jeffery**: born December 30, 1977

817 BOSSARD Anna Jean: (*William, Fred, William, Anson, George, Phillip*) was born March 26, 1938 in Hornell, New York, daughter of William Bossard and Alice Carson. She married February 26, 1956, Roland Dale Barnard born June 16, 1936, son of William Barnard and Neola Coots.

Children:
1085 i- **BARNARD Brenda Lou**: born August 16, 1956
ii- **BARNARD Craig Howard**: born September 7, 1957
iii- **BARNARD Lisa Ann**: born May 12, 1959
iv- **BARNARD Lori June**: born June 17, 1967

818 BOSSARD Kay Lela: (*William, Fred, William, Anson, George, Melchior, Phillip*) was born October 19, 1941 in Hornell, New York, daughter of William Bossard and Alice Carson. She married June 17, 1961, De Neil Ives, son of Dewitt and Nella Ives.

Children:
1086 **i- IVES William Neil**: born September 30, 1962
ii- IVES Jodi Lynn: born July 13, 1968

819 **BOSSARD William W.**: (*William, Fred, William, Anson, George, Melchior, Phillip*) was born June 6, 1943 in Hornell, New York, son of William Bossard and Alice Carson. He married on September 11, 1965, Carlise Balschmiter born March 7, 1944, daughter of Carl Balschmiter and Marion Thompson.

Children:
1087 **i- BOSSARD Heather Alma**: born February 24, 1968
ii- BOSSARD Heidi Ann: born May 22, 1971

820 **BOSSARD Donald R.**: (*William, Fred, William, Anson, George, Melchior, Phillip*) was born November 5, 1946, in Hornell, New York, son of William Bossard and Alice Carson. He married July 7, 1968, Kathryn Andrus daughter of Richard Andrus and Bonnie Mc Quire. Kathy died June 28, 1978 in Hornell and is buried in Hillside cemetery. Donald married (2) October 23, 1989, Kathleen Mc Caig.

Children of first marriage:
i- BOSSARD Rebakah Kay: born May 25, 1972
ii- BOSSARD Robin Elizabeth: born February 12, 1974

821 **BOSSARD Bruce F.**: (*William, Fred, William, Anson, George, Melchior, Phillip*) was born May 20, 1954 in Hornell, New York, son of William Bossard and Alice Carson. He married February 24, 1973, Karen S. Alderman born January 28, 1954, daughter of Richard and Geraldine Alderman.

Children:
i- BOSSARD Joshua Richard: born October 15, 1973
ii- BOSSARD Kyle William: born July 22, 1978
iii- BOSSARD Jordan Bruce: born December 16, 1980
iv- BOSSARD Will Tyler: born June 19, 1987

822 **BOSSARD James**: (*Merlin, Fred, William, Anson, George, Melchior, Phillip*) was born October 22, 1935 in Hornell, New York, son of Merlin Bossard and Bernadine Topping. He married (1) Sandra Carr and (2) Bonnie Carlin. They were divorced and he married (3) Mary Quakenbush.

Child by first marriage:
i- BOSSARD James: born October 11, 1957
Child of second wife, Bonnie Carlin, adopted by James
1088 **ii- BOSSARD Steven**: born October 21, 1956
Children by second marriage:

1089 **iii- BOSSARD Alan**: born March 24, 1960
1090 **iv- BOSSARD Terri**: born June 13, 1961
Child by third marriage:
v- BOSSARD Jaime: born June 15, 1975

823 BOSSARD Lois: (*Merlin, Fred, William, Anson, George, Melchior, Phillip*) was born June 3, 1939 in Hornell, New York, daughter of Merlin Bossard and Bernadine Topping. She married September 10, 1960, Robert Taylor born February 21, 1940, son of Robert Taylor and Illean Burdick. They are presently living in Pittsford, New York.

Children:
i- TAYLOR David: born February 11, 1962
1091 **ii- TAYLOR Cindy**: born July 31, 1963
iii- TAYLOR Kim: born November 18, 1968

824 BICKNELL Boyd Thomas Jr.: (*Marion, Fred, William, Anson, George, Melchior, Phillip*) was born March 22, 1947 in Camden, New Jersey, son of Boyd Bicknell and Marion Bossard. He married March 14, 1981, Patricia Kennedy.

Children:
i- BICKNELL Jessica Lynn: born February 17, 1982
ii- BICKNELL Lauren: born November 21, 1984
iii- BICKNELL Boyd Thomas III: born April 11, 1986

825 BICKNELL Timothy James: (*Marion, Fred, William, Anson, George, Melchior, Phillip*) was born March 14, 1953 in Camden, New Jersey, son of Boyd Bicknell and Marion Bossard. He married August 19, 1978, Marilou Corrodetti.

Children:
i- BICKNELL Kelly: born November 3, 1984
ii- BICKNELL Kimberly: born December 7, 1987

826 BICKNELL William John: (*Marion, Fred, William, Anson, George, Melchior, Phillip*) was born August 31, 1956 in Camden, New Jersey, son of Boyd Bicknell and Marion Bossard. He married May 20, 1989, Elizabeth Fox.

827 BOSSARD Kenneth Jr.: (*Kenneth, Fred, William, Anson, George, Melchior, Phillip*) was born July 19, 1948, son of Kenneth Bossard and Elizabeth Femmie Garrett. He married September 8, 1968, Sylvia Jane Yurganious. They are presently living in Jacksonville, North Carolina.

Children:

1092 i- **BOSSARD Tammi Lynn**: born April 21, 1969
ii- **BOSSARD Sonya Elizabeth**: born August 31, 1972

828 **BOSSARD Keith Craig**: (*Kenneth, Fred, William, Anson, George, Melchior, Phillip*) was born August 5, 1950, son of Kenneth Bossard and Elizabeth Femmie Garrett. He married March 31, 1979, Lygia R. Hall.

Children:
i- **BOSSARD Craigery**: born December 18, 1979
ii- **BOSSARD Bryon**: born January 3, 1982

829 **BOSSARD Terrel Kay**: (*Kenneth, Fred, William, Anson, George, Melchior, Phillip*) was born April 1, 1954, daughter of Kenneth Bossard and Elizabeth Femmie Garrett. She married May 12, 1972, Terry Lee Hester.

Children:
i- **HESTER Angela Lynn**: born April 20, 1973
ii- **HESTER Stacie Marie**: born January 22, 1978

830 **BOSSARD Lisa Kim**: (*Kenneth, Fred, William, Anson, George, Melchior, Phillip*) was born May 16, 1961, daughter of Kenneth Bossard and Elizabeth Femmie Garrett. She married June 13, 1980, Jonathan Morton.

One child:
i- **MORTON Amber Beth**: born October 29, 1982

831 **BOSSARD Kelly**: (*Kenneth, Fred, William, Anson, George, Melchior, Phillip*) was born August 13, 1963 in Jacksonville, North Carolina, daughter of Kenneth Bossard and Elizabeth Femmie Bossard. He married July 3, 1988, Marylyn Williams. No issue.

832 **KAME Irene Joyce**: (*Aletha Ruth, Roy, William, Anson, George, Melchior, Phillip*) was born January 5, 1929, daughter of Floyd Kame and Aletha Ruth Bossard. She married May 25, 1952, Nicholas Tychi born January 5, 1929, son of Charles and Mary Tychi. He died April 15, 1979 in Howard, New York. Irene is presently living in Hornell.

Children:
1093 i- **TYCHI Cinthia Gail**: born November 6, 1952
1094 ii- **TYCHI Linda Ann**: born February 24, 1955
1095 iii- **TYCHI Randy Stephen**: born April 5, 1954
iv- **TYCHI Timothy Lee**: born July 8, 1956
1096 v- **TYCHI Patti Kim**: born December 25, 1957

1097 vi- **TYCHI Karen Elaine**: born December 6, 1959
vii- **TYCHI Thomas Michael**: born November 16, 1961
viii- **TYCHI Raymond Neal**: born March 27, 1964
ix- **TYCHI Kristy Lynn**: born September 11, 1969

833 KAME Lawrence Edward: (*Aletha Ruth, Roy, William, Anson, George, Melchior, Phillip*) was born October 2, 1937 in Hornell, New York, son of Floyd Kame and Aletha Ruth Bossard. He married February 27, 1960, Muriel Norton born January 20, 1940 in Arkport, New York. They are presently living in Stephens Mills, New York.

Children:
1098 i- **KAME Tracy Annette**: born July 23, 1961
ii- **KAME Teresa Lynn**: born May 6, 1964
iii- **KAME Laurie Ann**: born September 18, 1969

834 KAME Vincent Dale: (*Aletha Ruth, Roy, William, Anson, George, Melchior, Phillip*) was born June 8, 1941 in Hornell, New York, son of Floyd Kame and Aletha Ruth Bossard. He married June 4, 1960, Patricia Ann Mc Daniel born March 5, 1942. They are presently living in Owego, New York.

Children:
1099 i- **KAME Victoria Lee**: born March 3, 1961
ii- **KAME Cheryl Ann**: born June 21, 1962
1100 iii- **KAME Vincent Dale Jr.**: born April 24, 1963

835 KAME Betty Corinne: (*Aletha Ruth, Roy, William, Anson, George, Melchior, Phillip*) was born March 30, 1944 in Hornell, New York, daughter of Floyd Kame and Aletha Ruth Bossard. She married August 18, 1962, Richard Dresser.

One child:
1101 i- **DRESSER Wendy Sue**: born April 8, 1964

836 BOSSARD Roy Walter: (*Merle, Roy, William, Anson, George, Melchior, Phillip*) was born June 22, 1950 in Hornell, New York, son of Merle Bossard and Doris Campbell. He married August 12, 1972, Sharron Lee Arno born December 15, 1949.

Children:
i- **BOSSARD Kevin Merle**: born August 12, 1972
ii- **BOSSARD Heather Denise**: born April 30, 1978

837 BOSSARD Barbara Jean: (*Glenn, Roy, William, Anson, George, Melchior,*

Phillip) was born January 17, 1955 in Hornell, New York, daughter of Glenn Allen Bossard and Mary Ellen Dickson. She married May 10, 1975, Ronald Hilsdorf born June 9, 1949. They are presently living in Hornell, New York.

Children:
i- **HILSDORF Sarah Jaynes**: born March 27, 1982
ii- **HILSDORF Rian Charles**: born March 24, 1984

838 BOSSARD Richard Alan: (*Glenn, Roy, William, Anson, George, Melchior, Phillip*) was born December 14, 1957 in Hornell, New York, son of Glenn Allen Bossard and Mary Ellen Dickson. He married December 24, 1977, Deborah Carson. They were divorced.

One child:
i- **BOSSARD Rebecca Lynn**: born August 6, 1976

839 BOSSARD Steven: (*Glenn, Roy, William, Anson, George, Melchior, Phillip*) was born August 10, 1960 in Hornell, New York, son of Glenn Allen Bossard and Mary Ellen Dickson. He married October 13, 1989, Julie Eveland.

840 SMITH Sandra Janine: (*Ernest Smith, Charlotte, William, Anson. George, Melchior, Phillip*) was born February 9, 1961 in Hornell, New York, daughter of Ernest Glen Smith and Fern Buchinger Hankins. She is presently living in Wellsville, New York.

Children born in Wellsville, New York:
i- **HURD Scot Lee**: born June 11, 1985
ii- **HURD Shannon Marie**: born January 15, 1988

841 SMITH Steven Franklin: (*Ernest Smith, Charlotte, William, Anson, George, Melchior, Phillip*) was born January 24, 1965 in Hornell, New York, son of Ernest Glen Smith and Fern Buchinger Hankins. He married October 18, 1986, Denise Lanard born July 16, 1969 in Ft. Dix, New Jersey, daughter of Mark Lanard and Donna Burns. They are presently living in Hornell, New York.

Children born in Hornell, New York:
i- **SMITH Amanda Marie**: born January 30, 1987
ii- **SMITH Brandy Nicole**: born July 28, 1988
iii- **SMITH Steven Mark**: born May 25, 1990

842 JACKSON Edward Frank: (*Mary Smith, Charlotte, William, Anson, George, Melchior, Phillip*) was born January 25, 1948 in Rochester, New York, son of Eugene G. Jackson and Mary Louise Smith. He married (1) July 10, 1969,

Kathleen Wilson born December 7, 1951, daughter of Donald and Leola Wilson. They were divorced and he married (2) Fay Aundry Merrill born August 10, 1948, daughter of Albert Merrill and Mildred DuVall. They are presently living in Farmington, New York.

Children of first marriage:

i- **JACKSON Daniel Lee**: born January 13, 1970 in Newark, New York

ii- **JACKSON Michael Scot**: born June 21, 1973 in Cliffton Springs

Child of second marriage, born in Clifton Springs:

iii- **JACKSON Carrie Lynn**: born July 10, 1977

843 JACKSON Allen Eugene: (*Mary Smith, Charlotte, William, Anson, George, Melchior, Phillip*) was born May 25, 1953 in Rochester, New York, son of Eugene G. Jackson and Mary Louise Smith. He married (1) April 29, 1972 in Palmyra, New York, Debria Simmons born March 25, 1954, daughter of William and Delerea Simmons. They were divorced and he married (2) June 23, 1983, Gail Durkee Lent born June 11, 1954, daughter of Ira Durkee and Ardith Cook. They are presently living in Savannah, New York.

Children:

i- **JACKSON Caprice**: born September 29, 1972, in Clifton Springs, New York

ii- **JACKSON Joshua Allen**: born August 5, 1975, in Frankfurt, Germany

iii- **JACKSON Jeromy Eugene**: born March 7, 1980, son of Gail Lent and adopted by Allen.

iv- **JACKSON Kyle Paul**: born August 2, 1982 and died September 5, 1982 in Buffalo, New York. He is buried in Palmyra cemetery.

v- **JACKSON Mary Beth**: born December 10, 1988, in Rochester, New York

844 JACKSON Richard Jay: (*Mary Smith, Charlotte, William, Anson, George, Melchior, Phillip*) was born November 21, 1954 in Rochester, New York, son of Eugene G. Jackson and Mary Louise Smith. He married (1) November 15, 1972 in Rochester, New York, Cathy Scheerens born February 15, 1955, daughter of Wilford and Ruth Scheerens. They were divorced and he married (2) October 22, 1977, Ethel Walton. They were divorced and he married (3) March 15, 1985, Deborah Baker Beug. Richard is presently living in Palmyra, New York.

Children of first marriage:

i- **JACKSON Richard Jay II**: born June 11, 1973, in Rochester, New York

ii- **JACKSON John Paul**: born June 13, 1974 in Germany

Child of second marriage:

iii- **JACKSON Amy Lynn**: born March 31, 1979, in Clifton Springs, New York

845 JACKSON Cheryl Ann: (*Mary Smith, Charlotte, William, Anson, George, Melchior, Phillip*) was born February 11, 1956 in Rochester, New York, twin daughter of Eugene G. Jackson and Mary Louise Smith. She married December 18, 1973, Roderick W. E. Bray born October 26, 1953, son of George Bray and Ethel Weichbrodt. They were divorced and Cheryl is presently living in Farmington, New York.

Children born in Rochester, New York:
i- **BRAY Jeremy Allen:** born December 31, 1974
ii- **BRAY Jason Eugene:** born September 28, 1978

846 JACKSON Gary Lee: (*Mary Smith, Charlotte, William, Anson, George, Melchior, Phillip*) was born February 11, 1956 in Rochester, New York, twin son of Eugene G. Jackson and Mary Louise Smith. He married August 11, 1979 in Newark, New York, Bonnie Lee Nary born July 30, 1956 in Newark, New York, daughter of Eric Nary and Sharron Waldorf. They are presently living in Newark.

One child:
i- **JACKSON Christopher Lee:** born August 7, 1989

847 JACKSON Brian Ernest: (*Mary Smith, Charlotte, William, Anson, George, Melchior, Phillip*) was born February 13, 1959 in Rochester, New York, son of Eugene G. Jackson and Mary Louise Smith. He married (1) July 16, 1980, Jodi Wager. They were divorced and he married (2) August 12, 1988, Elizabeth Noto Huntley born June 7, 1961, daughter of Louis Noto and Jean Keenan. They are presently living in Ontario, New York.

Child of first marriage:
i- **JACKSON Gregory Brian:** born September 16, 1981
Child of second marriage:
ii- **JACKSON Ian Eugene:** born July 29, 1989
Elizabeth has two children by her first marriage:
i- **HUNTLEY Jacob:** born July 2, 1982
ii- **HUNTLEY Jenna:** born January 24, 1986

848 JACKSON Susan Elizabeth: (*Mary Smith, Charlotte, William, Anson, George, Melchior, Phillip*) was born March 26, 1960 in Rochester, New York, daughter of Eugene G. Jackson and Mary Louise Smith. She married June 23, 1979, Lonnie Allison Everett born October 5, 1947 in Canandaigua, New York, son of Floyd Everett and Iona Spears. They are presently living in Farmington, New York.

Children born in Newark, New York:
i- **EVERETT Jeffrey Aaron:** born November 11, 1979
ii- **EVERETT Joseph Clark:** born December 26, 1983
iii- **EVERETT James Lee:** (twin) born November 1, 1986

iv- EVERETT Jennifer Ann: (twin) born November 1,1986

849 **JACKSON Kevin Scot**: (*Mary Smith, Charlotte, William, Anson, George, Melchior, Phillip*) was born April 5, 1961 in Rochester, New York, son of Eugene G. Jackson and Mary Louise Smith. He married September 9, 1989, Kandi Lynn Jackson born August 23, 1964, daughter of David Jackson and Roberta Rush. They are presently living in Perinton, New York.

850 **ALLEN Thomas Neil**: (*Dorothy, Lawrence, William, Anson, George, Melchior, Phillip*) was born January 20, 1953 in Elmira, New York, son of Max Allen and Dorothy Bossard. He married December 21, 1973 in Lakeland, Florida, Susan Cole. They are divorced.

One child:
i- ALLEN Paul: born July 18, 1977

851 **ALLEN Maxine Susan**: (*Dorothy, Lawrence, William, Anson, George, Melchior, Phillip*) was born July 19, 1957 in Elmira, New York, daughter of Max Allen and Dorothy Bossard. She married June 20, 1981, Edward T. Close.

Children:
i- CLOSE Nicole: born October 16, 1985
ii- CLOSE Heather: born December 6, 1987

852 **ALLEN Keith Brian**: (*Dorothy, Lawrence, William, Anson, George, Melchior, Phillip*) was born October 4, 1959 in Elmira, New York, son of Max Allen and Dorothy Bossard. He married January 18, 1986, Lori Jean Phillips.

One child:
i- ALLEN Lauren: born December 20, 1987

853 **TREWTANELLI Elizabeth Ann**: (*Jacqueline, Lawrence, William, Anson, George, Melchior, Phillip*) was born May 7, 1961 in Lakeland, Florida, daughter of John Joseph Trewtanelli and Jacqueline Bossard. She married October 11, 1986 in Tallahassee, Florida, Porter L. Kimball. No issue.

854 **TREWTANELLI Nancy Marie**: (*Jacqueline, Lawrence, William, Anson, George, Melchior, Phillip*) was born April 22, 1966 in Lakeland, Florida, daughter of John Joseph Trewtanelli and Jacqueline Bossard. She married July 16, 1988 in Lakeland, Anthony Todd Blasingame. No issue.

855 STILLMAN David Lee: (*Lorena Palmer, Inez, William, Anson, George, Melchior, Phillip*) was born August 23, 1950 in Hornell, New York, son of Albert Justin Stillman and Lorena June Palmer. He married September 2, 1973 in Penfield, New York, Sandy Topel born April 27, 1952 in Rochester, New York, daughter of Franklin Topel and Betty Crippen. They are presently living in Fairport, New York.

Children born in Rochester, New York:
- i- **STILLMAN Candace Marie**: born June 25, 1974
- ii- **STILLMAN Jason David**: born October 14, 1976
- iii- **STILLMAN Scott Andrew**: born September 15, 1981
- iv- **STILLMAN Sarah Courtney**: born May 13, 1986

856 SHARP Beverly Ann: (*Luella Palmer, Inez, William Anson, George, Melchior, Phillip*) was born November 26, 1951 in Hornell, New York, daughter of Harry Sharp and Luella Palmer. She married (1) Lynn Julian, son of Donald and Delores Julian. They were divorced and she married (2) Karl Anderson. They are presently living in the Town of Howard.

Children of first marriage:
- i- **JULIAN Karl Augustus Karr**: born December 31, 1972
- ii- **JULIAN Aaron David**: born March 28, 1975

857 SHARP Patricia Lynn: (*Luella Palmer, Inez, William, Anson, George, Melchior, Phillip*) was born October 19, 1954 in Hornell, New York, daughter of Harry Sharp and Luella Palmer. She married Vaughn Jackson. They were divorced and she is presently living in Rochester, New York.

858 PALMER Ricky Allen: (*Allen Palmer, Inez, William, Anson, George, Melchior, Phillip*) was born August 22, 1954 in Hornell, New York, son of Allen Duane Palmer and Eleanor Gayle Wise. He married (1) January 10, 1975 Barbara Ridici. They were divorced and he married (2) September 26, 1981, Debra Giglio. They are presently living in the Town of Howard.

Children of second marriage:
- i- **PALMER Brandi**: born September 27, 1982
- ii- **PALMER Michael Joseph**: born May 28, 1985

859 PALMER Robert Chester: (*Allen Palmer, Inez, William, Anson, George, Melchior, Phillip*) was born May 8, 1956 in Bath, New York, son of Allen Palmer and Eleanor Gayle Wise. He married Nadeen May Burns born April 4, 1958, daughter of Kenneth Burns and Margaret Bryan. They are presently living in the Town of Howard.

Children:
i- PALMER Christopher Allen: born May 22, 1979
ii- PALMER Casey Andrew: born July 6, 1982
iii- PALMER Briann Margaret Eleanor: born August 17, 1988

860 PALMER Gary Lee: (*Allen Palmer, Inez, William, Anson, George, Melchior, Phillip*) was born January 20, 1959 in Hornell, New York, son of Allen Duane Palmer and Eleanor Gayle Wise. He married August 6, 1983 in Howard, New York, Karen Sue Slayton born April 4, 1961, daughter of William Slayton and Nancy Hubbard. They are presently living in the Town of Howard.

Children:
i- PALMER Shanna Mae: born November 20, 1984
ii- PALMER Kyle James: born March 19, 1986

861 PALMER Randy Lynn: (*Allen Palmer, Inez, William, Anson, George, Melchior, Phillip*) was born March 9, 1962 in Hornell, New York, son of Allen Duane Palmer and Eleanor Gayle Wise. He married January 16, 1982, Delcie Rae Johner born May 29, 1962, daughter of Harold Johner and Delores Flint.

Children:
i- PALMER Justin Ryan: born December 2, 1984
ii- PALMER Alicia Aaron: born March 15, 1987

862 BEACH Michael Thomas: (*Betty Palmer, Inez, William, Anson, George, Melchior, Phillip*) was born January 23, 1956 in Hornell, New York, son of Thomas Fairchild Beach and Betty Joanne Palmer. He married November 7, 1981, Nancy Caruso, daughter of Anthony and Sally Caruso. They are presently living in Fremont, New York. No issue.

863 BEACH Terri Lynn: (*Betty Palmer, Inez, William, Anson, George, Melchior, Phillip*) was born March 13, 1958 in Hornell, New York, daughter of Thomas Fairchild Beach and Betty Joanne Palmer. She married March 4, 1978, William Clark of Hornell.

Children:
i- CLARK Tanya Arline: born March 21, 1979
ii- CLARK Melissa Lynn: born August 1, 1981

864 SHAFER Susan Kay: (*Barbara Palmer, Inez, William, Anson, George, Melchior, Phillip*) was born March 11, 1958, daughter of Phillip Gerald Shafer and Barbara Jean Palmer. She married October 9, 1983, John Shaub.

Children:
i- **SHAUB Allegra**: born December 20, 1984
ii- **SHAUB Jessica**: born August 22, 1986

865 **BOSSARD Charles F.**: (*Charles, Anson, Fred, Anson, George, Melchior, Phillip*) was born May 11, 1943 in Cortland, New York , son of Charles P. Bossard and Beverly June Shevalier. He married (1) March 7, 1964. Linda Ann Evener, daughter of William and Mildred Evener. They were divorced and he married (2) November 1976, Sandra Riley, daughter of Leo and Louise Riley. They were divorced and he married (3) July 5, 1986, Toni Evangelista, daughter of Phillipe and Grace Evangelista.

Children of first marriage:
1102 i- **BOSSARD Sharri Lynn**: born August 16, 1965, in Cortland, New York
ii- **BOSSARD Jill Ann**: born April 14, 1969 in Ithaca
Child of second marriage:
iii- **BOSSARD Daniel Charles**: born March 17, 1977 in Ithaca, New York

866 **BOSSARD Richard Aii**: (*Charles, Anson, Fred, Anson, Anson, George, Melchior, Phillip*) was born May 8, 1943 in Cortland, New York, son of Charles P. Bossand and Beverly June Shevalier. He married (1) December 3, 1967, Elsa Merihew born May 15, 1944. He married (2) June 13, 1982, Kathy Conger. They were divorced and he married (3) July 25, 1986, Rhonda Shaw born April 2, 1949.

Children:
i- **BOSSARD Melody Ann**: born December 4, 1970
ii- **BOSSARD Richard Aii Jr.**: born June 4, 1972
Children of wife, Rhonda:
i- **BROWN Ray Jr.**: born August 6, 1966
ii- **BROWN Charles**: born January 1, 1969
iii- **BROWN Bobbi Jo**: born January 10, 1973

867 **BOSSARD David Warren**: (*Charles, Anson, Fred, Anson, George, Melchior, Phillip*) was born August 23, 1949, son of Charles P. Bossard and Beverly June Shevalier. He married October 5, 1968, Elaine Regina Mooney born November 31, 1947. She died June 21, 1988.

Children:
i- **BOSSARD Jennifer Elaine**: born December 6, 1969
ii- **BOSSARD Brian David**: born September 21, 1971
iii- **BOSSARD Melissa Maureen**: born January 25, 1979

868 **BOSSARD Lorena Sue**: (*Charles, Anson, Fred, Anson, George, Melchior,*

Phillip) was born July 24, 1955 in Cortland, New York, daughter of Charles P. Bossard and Beverly Shevalier. She married (1) April 27, 1973, Robert Russell, son of Robert Russell and Lucy Little. She married (2) _____ Harrison.

Children born in Ithaca, New York:
- i- **RUSSELL Erik Charles**: born January 12, 1975
- ii- **HARRISON Rebecca June**: born July 29, 1976

869 BOSSARD Beryl Ann: (*Anson Jr., Anson, Fred, Anson, George, Melchior, Phillip*) was born June 3, 1954 in Syracuse, New York, daughter of Anson Bossard Jr. and Rita Mae Willoughby. She married April 12, 1975 in Daytona Beach, Florida, John A. Buice. They have four children.

870 BUSH Elaine Louise: (*Margaretta, Anson, Fred, Anson, George, Melchior, Phillip*) was born March 25, 1961, daughter of Ira Newton Bush Jr. and Margaretta Lorena Bossard. She married October 1986, Paul Kelly. Paul had three children by his first marriage. They are Kimberly, Paul Jr. and Janine.

871 BOSSARD Linda Lou: (*Lawrence, Charlie, Fred, Anson, George, Melchior, Phillip*) was born June 11, 1949, daughter of Lawrence Alson Bossard and Ruth H. Mc Fall. She married November 17, 1979, David Lynn born May 6, 1951. They are presently living in Phoenix, Arizona.

One child born in Phoenix, Arizona:
- i- **LYNN Samantha Kay**: born July 24, 1988

872 BOSSARD Barbara Jean: (*Lawrence, Charlie, Fred, Anson, George, Melchior, Phillip*) was born May 16, 1954, daughter of Lawrence Alson Bossard and Ruth H. Mc Fall. She married April 24, 1982, Danny Carter born February 1, 1950.

873 BOSSARD Stephania: (*Clifton, Charlie, Fred, Anson, George, Melchior, Phillip*) was born November 26, 1951, daughter of Clifton Asil Bossard and Laura Stevens. She married (1) December 1972, James Grant and married (2) Thomas Miller.

874 BOSSARD Eric Allen: (*Clifton, Charlie, Fred, Anson, George, Melchior, Phillip*) was born October 25, 1953, son of Clifton Asil Bossard and Laura Stevens. He married Diane Smith.

875 HOLCOMB Florence Ethelyn: (*Beverly, Charlie, Fred, Anson, George, Melchior, Phillip*) was born December 8, 1954, daughter of Robert Holcomb and

Beverly Ann Bossard. She married September 18, 1982, Steven Carl Brooks born December 8, 1954.

One child:
i- **BROOKS Jessica Lee**: born November 24, 1983

876 **HOLCOMB Rebecca Suzanne**: (*Beverly, Charlie, Fred, Anson, George, Melchior, Phillip*) was born March 22, 1957, daughter of Robert Holcomb and Beverly Ann Bossard. She married 1975, Michael Arnold. They were divorced in 1978.

877 **HOLCOMB Jessica Louise**: (*Beverly, Charlie, Fred, Anson, George, Melchior, Phillip*) was born December 15, 1962, daughter of Robert Holcomb and Beverly Ann Bossard.

One child:
i- **HOLCOMB Natalie Ann**: born December 4, 1988

878 **BOSSARD Russell Leonard**: (*Charlie, Charlie, Fred, Anson, George, Melchior, Phillip*) was born February 26, 1959, son of Judith Leonard and adopted by Charlie Bossard. He married (1) August 10. 1979, Bobbi Dean Hicks born December 11, 1958. They were divorced in 1984 and he married (2) December 16, 1986, Jerri Vaughn born September 29, 1964.

Child of first wife's previous marriage:
i- **WHITE Christopher Glenn**: born December 18, 1976
Children of first marriage:
ii- **BOSSARD Micki Irene**: born April 12, 1979
iii- **BOSSARD Ricki Marie**: born April 18, 1982
iv- **BOSSARD Nicki Louise**: born October 21, 1983
Child by second wife's previous marriage:
v- **ARMENT Joseph**: born October 20, 1984
Child of second marriage:
vi- **BOSSARD Cady Elizabeth**: born March 19, 1988

879 **BOSSARD Cindy Jane**: (*Charlie, Charlie, Fred, Anson, George, Melchior, Phillip*) was born April 17, 1960, daughter of Charlie Alton Bossard and Suzanne Fuller. She married May 19, 1979, Sherwood John Hawley Jr. born July 26, 1954. They are presently living in Moravia, New York.

One child:
i- **HAWLEY Ryan John**: born April 7, 1980

880 HESLIN Ann Theresa: (*Beth, Charlie, Fred, Anson, George, Melchior, Phillip*) was born August 9, 1963, daughter of Michael Heslin and Beth Elaine Bossard. She married June 3, 1989, Garland Massey III.

881 LONGFELLOW Linda: (*Allen Longfellow, Louise, William B., Andrew K., Andrew, Melchior, Phillip*) is the daughter of Allen Leroy Longfellow and Ethel Williams. Have not found her married name, lives in state of Washington. They have four children, Scott, Michael, Lori, and Bret.

882 LONGFELLOW Susan: (*Allen Longfellow, Louise, William B., Andrew K., Andrew, Melchior, Phillip*) the daughter of Allen Leroy Longfellow and Ethel Williams. She married Charles Moody and resides in Washington. No issue.

883 LONGFELLOW Marnell: (*Allen Longfellow, Louise, William B., Andrew K., Andrew, Melchior, Phillip*) is the daughter of Allen Leroy Longfellow and Ethel Williams. She married Kenneth Tolbert. They were divorced and she lives in Washington.

i- **TOLBERT Josh:**
ii- **TOLBERT Katie:**

884 HOUCK Catherine Caroline: (*Lila Longfellow, Louise, William B., Andrew K., Andrew, Melchior, Phillip*) was born March 2, 1950, daughter of John Walter Houck and Lila Louise Longfellow. She married October 1976, Kenneth Clemente. They were divorced in 1980 and she is presently living in Washington.

One child:
i- **CLEMENTE Maria Louise:** born November 13, 1978

885 CAREY Helen B.: (*Helen Pattison, Helen Redfield, Emma, Andrew K. Andrew, Melchior, Phillip*) was born in 1940, daughter of Robert B. Carey and Helen C. Pattison. She married David B. Mc Court. No further records.

886 BUTLER Ronald James: (*Franklin Butler, Mabel Treat, Elizabeth, Andrew K., Andrew, Melchior, Phillip*) was born April 16, 1950 in Corning, New York, son of Franklin Butler and Mary Lucille Hoffa. He married June 1976, Cynthia Margaret Briggs. They were divorced in 1987. No issue.

887 BUTLER Robert Franklin: (*Franklin Butler, Mabel Treat, Elizabeth, Andrew K., Andrew, Melchior, Phillip*) was born August 13, 1952 in Corning, New York, son of Franklin Butler and Mary Lucille Hoffa. He married September 20, 1975 in

Washington D. C., Bari Lynn Nash.

Children:
i- BUTLER Sarah Louise: born April 11, 1984
ii- BUTLER Adam Charles: born September 23, 1988

888 BUTLER Richard Seldon: (*Franklin Butler, Mabel Treat, Elizabeth, Andrew K., Andrew, Melchior, Phillip*) was born February 13, 1961 in Corning, New York, son of Franklin Butler and Mary Lucille Hoffa. He married September 18, 1982, Roxanne Clark.

One child:
i- BUTLER Allison Rae: born January 9, 1987

889 PLOUGH Mark Arthur: (*Erma Treat, Mabel Treat, Elizabeth, Andrew K., Andrew, Melchior, Phillip*) was born April 14, 1955 in Johnson City, New York, son of Paul Curtis Plough and Erma Maude Treat. He married June 21, 1986 in Houston, Texas, Vicki Lee Chrisman born June 24, 1964. They were divorced in 1988. No issue.

890 PLOUGH Martha Ann: (*Erma Treat, Mabel Treat, Elizabeth, Andrew K., Andrew, Melchior, Phillip*) was born April 14, 1955, twin daughter of Paul Curtis Plough and Erma Maude Treat. She married June 27, 1981 in Boca Raton, Florida, Dominick John Pisculli born February 16, 1958.

They adopted one child:
i- PISCULLI Christopher John: born July 8, 1989

891 PLOUGH Scott Curtis: (*Erma Treat, Mabel Treat, Elizabeth, Andrew K., Andrew, Melchior, Phillip*) was born March 9, 1958 in Rochester, Minnesota, son of Paul Curtis Plough and Erma Maude Treat. He married February 14, 1987 in San Marcos, Texas, Maureen Ann Adlof born January 16, 1945.

One child:
i- PLOUGH Jaspa Raine: born February 15, 1988

892 FOWLER Robert Allen: (*Ruth Zundel, Ethel Treat, Elizabeth, Andrew K., Andrew, Melchior, Phillip*) was born August 21, 1947 in Galeton, Pennsylvania, son of Robert Allen Fowler and Ruth Evelyn Zundel. He married August 19, 1967, Mary Lent born June 13, 1947.

Children:
i- FOWLER Michelle Ann: born March 17, 1968

ii- **FOWLER Heather Marie**: born June 20, 1969
iii- **FOWLER Kathleen Mary**: born March 6, 1971
iv- **FOWLER Robert Allen III**: born May 13, 1972

893 FOWLER John Arthur: (*Ruth Zundel, Ethel Treat, Elizabeth, Andrew K, Andrew, Melchior, Phillip*) was born October 27, 1950 in Galeton, Pennsylvania, son of Robert B. Fowler and Ruth Evelyn Zundel. He married September 25, 1971, Carol Hocker born October 27, 1950.

Children:
i- **FOWLER Jeremy John**: born June 21, 1975
ii- **FOWLER Matthew**: born September 27, 1978
iii- **FOWLER Jamie Suzanne**: born December 21, 1979

894 SCHOONOVER Cheryl Kay: (*Thelma Zundel, Ethel Treat, Elizabeth, Andrew K., Andrew, Melchior, Phillip*) was born September 10, 1949, daughter of Gilbert R. Schoonover and Thelma Louise Zundel. She married (1) June 21, 1969 in Maryland, Steve Norwick born May 1, 1946. They were divorced in 1986 and she married (2) July 11, 1987 in Newville, Pennsylvania, Ron Tritt born July 17, 1944.

Children:
i- **NORWICK Mark Christopher**: born June 7, 1975
ii- **NORWICK Kara Louise**: born February 1, 1979
iii- **TRITT Patrick**: born July 4, 1973. He is the son of Ron Tritt, by his first marriage.

895 SCHOONOVER David Raymond: (*Thelma Zundel, Ethel Treat, Elizabeth, Andrew K., Andrew, Melchior, Phillip*) was born March 27, 1951 in Wellsboro, Pennsylvania, son of Gilbert R. Schoonover and Thelma Louise Zundel. He married March 25, 1972, Joann Heckendorn born April 2, 1952.

Children:
i- **SCHOONOVER Karla Dawn**: born June 20, 1978
ii- **SCHOONOVER Krystal Jo**: born November 28, 1983

896 SCHOONOVER Donn Wesley: (*Thelma Zundel, Ethel Treat, Elizabeth, Andrew K., Andrew, Melchior, Phillip*) was born May 5, 1960 in Carlisle, Pennsylvania, son of Gilbert R. Schoonover and Thelma Louise Zundel. He married April 28, 1984 in Greencastle, Pennsylvania, Elizabeth Lillian Streeper born May 16, 1960.

Children:
i- **SCHOONOVER Michael Wesley**: born March 9, 1987
ii- **SCHOONOVER Laura Elizabeth**: born February 28, 1989

897 **MCALLISTER Richard Earl**: (*Betty Zundel, Ethel Treat, Elizabeth, Andrew K., Andrew Melchior, Phillip*) was born July 11, 1949 in Wilmington, Delaware, son of Elmer Dean Mcallister and Betty Joette Zundel. He married August 1974 in Baltimore, Maryland, Jacqueline Popiolek born May 6, 1949. They were divorced in 1984.

Children:
i- **MCALLISTER Sarah Elizabeth**: born August 9, 1976
ii- **MCALLISTER Joshua Allen**: born July 26, 1978

898 **MCALLISTER Ronald Dean**: (*Betty Zundel, Ethel Treat, Elizabeth, Andrew K., Andrew, Melchior, Phillip*) was born November 18, 1952 in Sycamore, Illinois, son of Elmer Dean Mcallister and Betty Joette Zundel. He married August 12, 1971 in Arlington Heights, Illinois, Donna Ann Christopher born November 10, 1952.

Children:
i- **MCALLISTER Michael Christopher**: born December 20, 1978
ii- **MCALLISTER Kristin Lee**: born May 19, 1979
iii- **MCALLISTER Lindsay Beth**: born January 28, 1984
iv- **MCALLISTER Meaghan Ann**: born August 4, 1987

899 **MCALLISTER Donna Marie**: (*Betty Zundel, Ethel Treat, Elizabeth, Andrew K., Andrew, Melchior, Phillip*) was born May 12, 1954 in Sycamore, Illinois, daughter of Elmer Dean Mcallister and Betty Joette Zundel. She married (1) Robert Edwards. They were divorced and she married (2) February 1, 1980 in Savannah, Illinois, Jon Emery Mullen born March 16, 1952.

Children by second marriage:
i- **MULLEN Alicia Marie**: born February 2, 1981
ii- **MULLEN Julie Elizabeth**: born October 22, 1982
iii- **MULLEN Rachel Anne**: born May 27, 1986
iv- **MULLEN Daniel Marshall**: born April 3, 1988

900 **MCALLISTER Randall Jon**: (*Betty Zundel, Ethel Treat, Elizabeth, Andrew K., Andrew, Melchior, Phillip*) was born February 10, 1956 in Sycamore, Illinois, son of Elmer Dean Mcallister and Betty Joette Zundel. He married in Sacramento, California, Karen Beth Larreu born January 5, 1957. He is a Captain in the Air Force.

Children:
i- **MCALLISTER Kandace Renee**: born November 3, 1984
ii- **MCALLISTER Ryan Randall**: born May 20, 1989
iii- **MCALLISTER Timothy Dean**: born January 1990

901 ROUZER Robert Richard: (*Sondra Treat, Ernest Treat, Elizabeth, Andrew K., Andrew, Melchior, Phillip*) was born November 18, 1958 in Cumberland, Maryland, son of Richard Rouzer and Sondra Ann Treat. He married (1) in 1976, Breda Yeager. They were divorced in 1987 and he married (2) June 4, 1988, Marlene Sardelis born July 13, 1963.

Children:
- i- **ROUZER Crystal Marieh**: born February 1977
- ii- **ROUZER Brandy Nicole**: born December 3, 1981
- iii- **ROUZER Katrine Georgette**: born April 21, 1986
- iv- **ROUZER Garet Michael**: born May 20, 1983, son of Marlene and adopted by Robert.

902 ROUZER Treta Renee: (*Sondra Treat, Ernest Treat, Elizabeth, Andrew K., Andrew, Melchior, Phillip*) was born April 13, 1960 in Cumberland, Maryland, daughter of Richard Rouzer and Sondra Ann Treat. She married May 19, 1979, Russell Wheeler. They were divorced in 1985. No issue.

903 ROUZER Ronald Ernest: (*Sondra Treat, Ernest Treat, Elizabeth, Andrew K., Andrew, Melchior, Phillip*) was born June 28, 1964 in Cumberland, Maryland, son of Richard Rouzer and Sondra Ann Treat. He married September 22, 1984, Helen Marie Hogan born October 10, 1966.

One child:
- i- **ROUZER Stephen Luke**: born August 27, 1986

904 HOWARD Walter Charles: (*Gweneth Owlet, Charles Owlet, Anna, Melchior D., Andrew, Melchior, Phillip*) was born November 7, 1947 in Sabinsville, Pennsylvania, son of Phillip E. Howard and Gweneth Owlet. He died March 20, 1966 in Rochester, New York. No further records.

905 HOWARD Marlene Ann: (*Gweneth Owlet, Charles Owlet, Anna, Melchior D., Andrew, Melchior, Phillip*) was born February 18, 1949 in Elmira, New York, daughter of Phillip E. Howard and Gweneth Owlet. She married January 4, 1969, Carl Couglar.

Children born in Elmira, New York:
- i- **COUGLAR Kariane**: born December 24, 1970
- ii- **COUGLAR Karl James**: born June 12, 1974

906 HOWARD Douglas Earl: (*Gweneth Owlet, Charles Owlet, Anna, Melchior D., Andrew, Melchior, Phillip*) was born August 7, 1950 in Elmira, New York, son of Phillip E. Howard and Gweneth Owlet. He married in 1972, Judy Shaut.

One child:

i- HOWARD Jamie John: born January 30, 1974

907 OWLET John Antonio: (*Andrew V. Owlet, Charles Owlet, Anna, Melchior D. Andrew, Melchior, Phillip*) was born November 21, 1954 in Kittery, Maine, son of Andrew V. Owlet and Maria L. Fusco. He married December 6, 1975 in Toms River, New Jersey, Sharron Voorhees.

908 OWLET Julaine: (*Harold Owlet, Carlton Owlet, Anna, Melchior D., Andrew, Melchior, Phillip*) was born August 28, 1956 in Corning, New York, daughter of Harold Owlet and Patricia Cole. She married July 8, 1975, Lawrence E. Miles.

909 DAVIS Theodore: (*Wilma Owlet, Carlton Owlet, Anna, Melchior D., Andrew, Melchior, Phillip*) was born April 10, 1941 in Nelson, Pennsylvania, son of Phillip Davis and Wilma Owlet. He married Linda (unknown maiden name).

910 DAVIS Charlene: (*Wilma Owlet, Carlton Owlet, Anna, Melchior D., Andrew, Melchior, Phillip*) was born December 10, 1942 in Nelson, Pennsylvania, daughter of Phillip Davis and Wilma Owlet. She married Lawrence Davis.

911 DAVIS Carlton: (*Wilma Owlet, Carlton Owlet, Anna, Melchior D., Andrew, Melchior, Phillip*) was born February 4, 1947 in Nelson, Pennsylvania, son of Phillip Davis and Wilma Owlet. He married Jean (unknown maiden name).

912 RINKER Marguerite: (*Russell Rinker, Peter Rinker, Sarah Huffsmith, Hanna, Peter, Melchior, Phillip*) was born in Stroudsburg, Pennsylvania, daughter of Russell Rinker and Florence Dyson. She married _____ Bachman. No further records.

913 RINKER Kathryn: (*Russell Rinker, Peter Rinker, Sarah Huffsmith, Hanna, Peter, Melchior, Phillip*) was born in Stroudsburg, Pennsylvania, daughter of Russell Rinker and Florence Dyson. She married (1) _____ Gould and married (2) Floyd Butz. She is presently living in Stroudsburg.

914 DE VIVO Barbara: (*Clara Huffsmith, William Huffsmith, George Huffsmith, Hanna, Peter, Melchior, Phillip*) was born September 7, 1937 in Stroudsburg, Pennsylvania, daughter of John De Vivo and Clara Huffsmith. She married _____ Stone. They are presently living in Stroudsburg.

Children:

i- STONE Brian: born October 24, ____

ii- STONE Michael: born December 31, ___

915 DE VIVO John Jr.: (*Clara Huffsmith, William Huffsmith, George Huffsmith, Hanna, Peter, Melchior, Phillip*) was born August 6, 1942 in Stroudsburg, Pennsylvania, son of John De Vivo and Clara Huffsmith. He married Jean Danforth, born August 10, 1948.

Children:
i- DE VIVO Crissy: born June 19, 1978
ii- DE VIVO Stacey: born July 1, 1980

916 DE VIVO Samuel: (*Clara Huffsmith, William Huffsmith, George Huffsmith, Hanna, Peter, Melchior, Phillip*) was born August 2, 1946 in Stroudsburg, Pennsylvania, son of John De Vivo and Clara Huffsmith. He married Bonnie Swartz, born May 1, 1946.

Children:
i- DE VIVO Anthony: born April 10, ___
ii- DE VIVO Andrew: born April 10, ___

917 HUFFSMITH Philip Lloyd: (*George Huffsmith, William Huffsmith, George Huffsmith, Hanna, Peter, Melchior, Phillip*) was born September 9, 1946 in Hornell, New York, son of George Huffsmith and Gertrude Partridge. He married July 12, 1969, Linda Cooke born May 24, 1947.

Children:
1103 **i- HUFFSMITH Cindy Marie**: born February 19, 1971
ii- HUFFSMITH Daniel Peter: born March 18, 1974

918 HUFFSMITH Mark Alexander: (*George Huffsmith, William Huffsmith, George Huffsmith, Hanna, Peter, Melchior, Phillip*) was born April 1, 1950 in Hornell, New York, son of George Huffsmith and Gertrude Partridge. He married September 4, 1971, Mary Helen Glynn born February 10, 1950.

Children:
i- HUFFSMITH Erin Elizabeth: born September 19, 1978
ii- HUFFSMITH Kristin Sarah: born December 24, 1980

919 HUFFSMITH Susan Claire: (*George Huffsmith, William Huffsmith, George Huffsmith, Hanna, Peter, Melchior, Phillip*) was born March 2, 1951 in Hornell, New York, daughter of George Huffsmith and Gertrude Partridge. She married July 7, 1973, Matthew Dwyer born October 10, 1951.

Children:
- i- **DWYER Kelly Anne**: born June 6, 1976
- ii- **DWYER John Thomas**: born October 23, 1978
- iii- **DWYER Andrew Thomas**: born August 4, 1983

920 HUFFSMITH George Andrew: (*George Huffsmith, William Huffsmith, George Huffsmith, Hanna, Peter, Melchior, Phillip*) was born July 26, 1955 in Hornell, New York, son of George Huffsmith and Gertrude Partridge. He married May 22, 1976, Joanne O'Brian born February 4, 1956.

Children:
- i- **HUFFSMITH Tasha Elizabeth**: born May 3, 1982
- ii- **HUFFSMITH Chelsea Danielle**: born September 20, 1984
- iii- **HUFFSMITH Janelle Adrienne**: born October 9, 1986

921 HUFFSMITH Sarah Anne: (*George Huffsmith, William Huffsmith, George Huffsmith, Hanna, Peter, Melchior, Phillip*) was born June 15, 1956 in Hornell, New York, daughter of George Huffsmith and Gertrude Partridge. She married July 26, 1980, John Ulrich Knickerbocker born October 3, 1956.

Children:
- i- **KNICKERBOCKER Ann Elizabeth**: born September 1, 1987
- ii- **KNICKERBOCKER Amy Rebecca**: born March 11, 1990

922 HUFFSMITH Sandra Lee: (*George Huffsmith, William Huffsmith, George Huffsmith, Hanna, Peter, Melchior, Phillip*) was born June 21, 1960 in Hornell, New York, daughter of George Huffsmith and Gertrude Partridge. She married July 23, 1983, Theodore John Hillman born September 5, 1960.

Children:
- i- **HILLMAN John Lloyd**: born April 7, 1988
- ii- **HILLMAN Martha Lee**: born July 13, 1989

923 HUFFSMITH Peter James: (*George Huffsmith, William Huffsmith, George Huffsmith, Hanna, Peter, Melchior, Phillip*) was born April 17, 1963 in Hornell, New York, son of George Huffsmith and Gertrude Partridge. He married May 26, 1990, Debra Dick born July 4, 1963.

924 SULLIVAN Jean: (*Samuel Sullivan, Martha Ruth, Jacob Ruth, Anna Catherine, Peter, Melchior, Phillip*) was born in Stroudsburg, Pennsylvania, daughter of Samuel and Adelaide Sullivan. She married _____ Hershberg. No further records.

925 SULLIVAN Joan: (*Samuel Sullivan, Martha Ruth, Jacob Ruth, Anna Catherine, Peter, Melchior, Phillip*) was born in Sroudsburg, Pennsylvania, daughter of Samuel and Adelaide Sullivan. She married _____ Sturdevant. No further records.

926 JAGERS Joan: (*Anna Sullivan, Martha Ruth, Jacob Ruth, Anna Catherine, Peter, Melchior, Phillip*) was born in Stroudsburg, Pennsylvania, daughter of Joseph T. Jagers and Anna Marion Sullivan. She married _____ Rehrig. No further records.

927 JAGERS Doris: (*Anna Sullivan, Martha Ruth, Jacob Ruth, Anna Catherine, Peter, Melchior, Phillip*) was born in Stroudsburg, Pennsylvania, daughter of Joseph T. Jagers and Anna Marion Sullivan. She married James Shiffer born September 10, 1913 in Stroudsburg, Pennsylvania. He died January 28, 1967.

One known child:

i- SHIFFER Donald: born December 12, 1945 and died May 19, 1961. He is buried in the Stroudsburg cemetery.

928 JAGERS Phillis: (*Anna Sullivan, Martha Ruth, Jacob Ruth, Anna Catherine, Peter, Melchior, Phillip*) was born in Stroudsburg, Pennsylvania, daughter of Joseph T. Jagers and Anna Marion Sullivan. She married _____ Hamill. No further records.

929 BARTHOLOMEW John Elbert: (*William Bartholomew, Lillie, Charles, Melchior, Peter, Melchior, Phillip*) was born December 26, 1915, son of William Bartholomew and Elsie Christine Metzgar. He married Emma Mabel Mosteller born March 21, 1922.

Children:

1104 **i- BARTHOLOMEW John Dale:** born March 19, 1941
1105 **ii- BARTHOLOMEW Clark Owen:** born September 3, 1944
iii- BARTHOLOMEW Janice Emma: born February 5, 1959

930 RINKER Leroy Frederick: (*Lucy Bartholomew, Lillie, Charles, Melchior, Peter, Melchior, Phillip*) was born April 19, 1923, son of Enoch Rinker and Lucy Bartholomew. He married Mary Grace Serfass born June 18, 1927.

One child:

i- RINKER Kim Leroy: born December 6, 1954

931 RINKER Gladys Eleanore: (*Lucy Bartholomew, Lillie, Charles, Melchior,*

Peter, Melchior, Phillip) was born May 31, 1925, daughter of Enoch Rinker and Lucy Bartholomew. She married February 21, 1948, James Allen Serfass born January 13, 1921.

932 **MANSFIELD Kathleen:** (*Thomas Mansfield, Paul Mansfield, Florinda, Melchior, Peter, Melchior, Phillip*) was born May 31, 1929 in Stroudsburg, Pennsylvania, daughter of Thomas Cadoo Mansfield and Lottie Hester. She married Robert Smith.

Children:
i- **SMITH Susan:** born February 11, 1957
ii- **SMITH Lonnie:** born January 29, 1958

933 **MANSFIELD Roger:** (*Thomas Mansfield, Paul Mansfield, Florinda, Melchior, Peter, Melchior, Phillip*) was born April 9, 1932 in Stroudsburg, Pennsylvania, son of Thomas Cadoo Mansfield and Lottie Hester. He married Joan (unknown maiden name). No further records.

934 **BURROWS Ashton H.:** (*Bessie Hartman, Mary Catherine, James, Melchior, Peter, Melchior, Phillip*) was born March 15, 1915, son of Ashton La Due Burrows and Bessie Hilda Hartman. He married Esther Barkman. Ashton died October 3, 1956 and Esther died November 6, 1982.

One child:
1106 i- **BURROWS Mary Ann:** born April 6, 1947

935 **BURROWS James Ethelbert:** (*Bessie Hartman, Mary Catherine, James, Melchior, Peter, Melchior, Phillip*) was born November 6, 1916, son of Ashton La Due Burrows and Bessie Hilda Hartman. He married Ruth Elizabeth Taylor born March 31, 1920.

Children:
1107 i- **BURROWS Janice Elaine:** born September 29, 1947
ii- **BURROWS James Ethelbert Jr.:** born June 5, 1949

936 **BURROWS Robert Marlin:** (*Bessie Hartman, Mary Catherine, James, Melchior, Peter, Melchior, Phillip*) was born July 24, 1919, son of Ashton La due Burrows and Bessie Hilda Hartman. He married Ethel Ann Lanternman born July 12, 1920.

Children:
1108 i- **BURROWS Ethel Ann:** born December 26, 1946
1109 ii- **BURROWS Lillian Lorraine:** born January 3, 1951

iii- BURROWS Roberta Marlene: born May 25, 1956

937 BURROWS Jacob Alexander: (*Bessie Hartman, Mary Catherine, James, Melchior, Peter, Melchior, Phillip*) was born March 24, 1922, son of Ashton La Due Burrows and Bessie Hilda Hartman. He married Charlotte Webb born July 1, 1920.

Children:

1110 **i-BURROWS Ronald Ayer**: born December 12, 1951
1111 **ii- BURROWS Wayne Ashton**: born June 14, 1954

938 MACKES Marguerite Arline: (*John H. Mackes, Nettie Haney, Anna, Melchior, Peter, Melchior, Phillip*) was born November 20, 1919, daughter of John H. Mackes and Grace Altemose. She married (1) Burnice Hawk. He died October 26, 1973 and she married (2) William Livingston and (3) Laverne Gildner.

Child by first marriage:

1112 **i- HAWK John William**: born March 18, 1940

939 HENNION Lorraine: (*Violet Lesh, Minnie Haney, Anna, Melchior, Peter, Melchior, Phillip*) was born October 14, 1929, daughter of Stewart Hennion and Violet Lesh. She married William Leap born January 1, 1926 in Hamilton Township, Pennsylvania. They are presently living in Sciota, Pennsylvania.

Children:

1113 **i- LEAP Sandra Lee**: born July 12, 1945
1114 **ii- LEAP William Earl Jr.**: born November 17, 1954
1115 **iii- LEAP Cindy Lou**: born March 12, 1957
1116 **iv- LEAP Scott Matthew**: born April 14, 1965

940 HENNION Gernard: (*Violet Lesh, Minnie Haney, Anna, Melchior, Peter, Melchior, Phillip*) was born October 10, 1942, son of Stewart Hennion and Violet Lesh. He married (1) Joan (unknown maiden name) and (2) Violet Ledora Possinger, born September 11, 1936.

Children:

i- HENNION Stewart Gernard: born July 3, 1963

941 HENNION Dayton: (*Violet Lesh, Minnie Haney, Anna, Melchior, Peter, Melchior, Phillip*) was born May 2, 1935, son of Stewart Hennion and Minnie Haney. He married Gertrude (unknown maiden name).

Children:

1117 i- **HENNION Brenda:**
1118 ii- **HENNION Trudi:**

942 **GREEN Dorothy Elizabeth:** (*Ada Haney, Harry Haney, Anna Catherine, Melchior, Peter, Melchior, Phillip*) was born December 7, 1925, daughter of Evan Green and Ada Blanche Haney. She married (1) September 4, 1947, Mortimer Hall Wells II and (2) James Nicholas. They are presently living in Saylorsburg, Pennsylvania.

Children of first marriage:
i- **WELLS Mortimer Hall III:** born June 18, 1948
ii- **WELLS Joel Mathew:** born June 16, 1955
Child of second marriage:
iii- **NICHOLAS Janie E.:** born March 6, 1962

943 **LOTZ William Charles:** (*Mary Ellen Haney, Charles Haney, Anna Catherine, Melchior, Peter, Melchior, Phillip*) was born September 29, 1933, son of William Lotz and Mary Ellen Haney. He married Martha Jean Kemmerer, born October 8, 1932. They are presently living in Hamilton Square, Pennsylvania.

Children:
i- **LOTZ James William:** born March 6, 1963
ii- **LOTZ Edwin Eugene:** born December 18, 1965

944 **RINKER David Wilson:** (*Dora Snyder, Mabel Haney, Anna Catherine, Melchior, Peter, Melchior, Phillip*) was born February 10, 1951, son of Wilson Herbert Rinker and Dora Madlyn Snyder. He married Janice Lee Hamer, born June 21, 1951.

One child:
i- **RINKER Mathew Davis:** born October 1, 1978

945 **RINKER Timothy Paul:** (*Dora Snyder, Mabel Haney, Anna Catherine, Melchior, Peter, Melchior, Phillip*) was born September 1, 1955, son of Wilson Herbert Rinker and Dora Madlyn Snyder. He married Doreen Ann Broekma born December 30, 1955.

One child:
i- **RINKER Tamatha Lynn:** born February 14, 1978

946 **SANDERS Louise Marie:** (*Anna Snyder, Mabel Haney, Anna Catherine, Melchior, Peter, Melchior, Phillip*) was born September 29, 1947, daughter of John Edwin Sanders and Anna Elizabeth Snyder. She married Newton Joseph

Monschein born June 19, 1947.

947 **SANDERS Steven Edwin**: (*Anna Snyder, Mabel Haney, Anna Catherine, Melchior, Peter, Melchior, Phillip*) was born December 8, 1950, son of John Edwin Sanders and Anna Elizabeth Snyder. He married Deborah Lynn Booth born October 4, 1950.

948 **BELLIS Susan**: (*Sarah Bartholomew, Martha, Samuel, Jacob, Peter, Melchior, Phillip*) was born June 13, 1926 in Stroudsburg, Pennsylvania, daughter of John Bellis and Sarah Bartholomew. She married Frederick Tischler born June 12, 1923. He died August 1, 1978 in Trumbull, Connecticutt. Susan is still living in Trumbull.

Children:
1119 i- **TISCHLER Frederick James III**: born September 18, 1948
1120 ii- **TISCHLER John Jeffrey**: born June 27, 1951
1121 iii- **TISCHLER Sally**: born March 11, 1955

949 **REESE Richard W.**: (*Elizabeth, Frederick, Samuel, Jacob, Peter, Melchior, Phillip*) was born March 18, 1936, son of Willard G. Reese and Elizabeth Bossard. He married October 21, 1959, Sandra L. Melton, born 1939. They are presently living in Delaware Co., Pennsylvania.

Children:
1122 i- **REESE Deborah Jean**: born June 7, 1960
ii- **REESE Alicia Marie**: born June 10, 1961
1123 iii- **REESE Susan Diane**: born September 16, 1963
1124 iv- **REESE Catherine Ann**: born March 19, 1966

950 **REESE Nancy Jean**: (*Elizabeth, Frederick, Samuel, Jacob, Peter, Melchior, Phillip*) was born June 6, 1938 in Delaware Co., Pennsylvania, daughter of Willard G. Reese and Elizabeth Bossard. She married Edward Graham. They are presently living in Wallingford, Pennsylvania.

Children born in Delaware County:
i- **GRAHAM Edward Reese**: born March 8, 1964
ii- **GRAHAM Richard Frederick**: born November 18, 1966
iii- **GRAHAM Suzanne Elizabeth**: born April 7, 1970

951 **DU BOIS Peter Bossard**: (*Roberta, Robert, Samuel, Jacob, Peter, Melchior, Phillip*) was born December 27, 1939 in Plainfield, New Jersey, son of Allen DuBois and Roberta Bossard. He married September 18, 1965 in Virginia Beach, Virginia, Bell Penderel born March 10, 1942 in Norfolk, Virginia, daughter of James and

Virginia Penderel. He died June 1979 in Denver, Colorado and is buried at Eaton's Ranch, Wolf, Wyoming. Bell is presently living in Virginia Beach, Virginia.

Children:

i- **DU BOIS William Mackenzie**: born January 16, 1968
ii- **DU BOIS Charles Corson**: born October 29, 1970

952 **DU BOIS Joan**: (*Roberta, Robert, Samuel, Jacob, Peter, Melchior, Phillip*) was born February 19, 1932 in Scranton, Pennsylvania, daughter of Allen Du Bois and Roberta Bossard. She married June 15, 1955, Robert Hunziker born April 22, 1932. They are presently living in New Canaan, Connecticutt.

Children:

i- **HUNZIKER James Du Bois**: born April 3, 1957, in Ann Arbor, Michigan, now living Portland, Maine.
1125 ii- **HUNZIKER William Mc Kee**: born May 23, 1958, in New York City.
iii- **HUNZIKER Hans Bossard**: born December 26, 1961, now living Richmond, Virginia.
iv- **HUNZIKER Eric Gaston**: born September 30, 1965, now living Newport Beach, California.

953 **DU BOIS Susan**: (*Roberta, Robert, Samuel, Jacob, Peter, Melchior, Phillip*) was born January 25, 1941 in Plainfield, New Jersey, daughter of Allen Du bois and Roberta Bossard. She married (1) May 28, 1959, Brian Mc Kinney. They were divorced in 1965 and she married (2) Michael Shyne born May 18, 1949 in St. Louis, Missouri, son of Joseph Shyne and Millicent Petrov. They are presently living in Alamagordo, New Mexico.

Children by first marriage:

1126 i- **MC KINNEY Colleen Dubois**: born December 17, 1959
ii- **MC KINNEY Carolyn Bossard**: born January 22, 1962. She is presently living in New York City.

954 **BOSSARD Sherlyn Lamont**: (*Carman, Curvin, Edwin, Jacob, Peter, Melchior, Phillip*) was born July 28, 1915 in Ida Grove, Iowa, son of Carman Bossard and Olga Dibborn. He married (1) April 15, 1940, Bonnie Jean Tubbs born July 23, 1917, daughter of Joele Tubbs. She died July 12, 1980 and Sherlyn married (2) Theodora Mary Moorehead born June 19, 1915. She died November 23, 1986 and Sherlyn is presently living in Loveland, Colorado.

Children born in Santa Monica, California:

1127 i- **BOSSARD Barbara Jean**: born February 20, 1945
1128 ii- **BOSSARD Beverly Jo**: born October 30, 1950
1129 iii- **BOSSARD Sherlyn Lamont Jr.**: born December 14, 1952
1130 iv- **BOSSARD Bryan Floyd**: born May 26, 1955

v- **BOSSARD Dorothy Dell**: born August 1, 1956

955 **BOSSARD Floyd Carman**: (*Calvin, Curvin, Edwin, Jacob, Peter, Melchior, Phillip*) was born January 24, 1929 in Missoula, Montana, son of Calvin Floyd Bossard and Amelia Bubash. He married June 23, 1951, Margaret Nevin born January 2, 1930. They are presently living in Butte, Montana.

Children:
1131 i- **BOSSARD Julie**: born April 24, 1952
1132 ii- **BOSSARD Janice**: born August 12, 1953
1133 iii- **BOSSARD Brian**: born July 27, 1958

956 **BOSSARD Richard Calvin**: (*Calvin, Curvin, Edwin, Jacob, Peter, Melchior, Phillip*) was born September 11, 1930 in Missoula, Montana, son of Calvin Floyd Bossard and Amelia Bubash. He married Margaret (unknown maiden name) born April 1933 and they are presently living in Missoula, Montana.

Children:
i- **BOSSARD Michael**: born July 27, 1955
1134 ii- **BOSSARD Patti**: born June 24, 1956
iii- **BOSSARD Kimberly**: born September 13, 1963

957 **BOSSARD Vera Jean**: (*Calvin, Curvin, Edwin, Jacob, Peter, Melchior, Phillip*) was born January 1, 1933 in Missoula, Montana, daughter of Calvin Floyd Bossard and Amelia Bubash. She married Lawrence Le Claire born October 16, 1929. She married (2) Robert Dick born March 22, 1928. They are presently living in Couer D'Alene, Idaho.

Children by first marriage, born in Missoula:
i- **LE CLAIRE Robert**: born May 29, 1953
1135 ii- **LE CLAIRE Gregory**: born December 7, 1956
1136 iii- **LE CLAIRE Diane**: born August 11, 1958
1137 iv- **LE CLAIRE Mark**: born September 29, 1962

958 **BOSSARD Gerald Wayne**: (*Calvin, Curvin, Edwin, Jacob, Peter, Melchior, Phillip*) was born October 24, 1935 in Washta, Iowa, son of Calvin Floyd Bossard and Amelia Bubash. He married December 27, 1952 in Idaho Falls, Idaho, Caroline Cregg born November 28, 1937 in Anaconda, Montana. Caroline is presently living in Tucson, Arizona and Wayne is living in South America.

Children born in Butte, Montana:
1138 i- **BOSSARD Cregg Allyn**: born October 23, 1953
ii- **BOSSARD Krista Lynn**: born September 21, 1955
1139 iii- **BOSSARD Lisa Marie**: born February 15, 1959

Child born in Anaconda, Montana:
1140 iv- **BOSSARD Brenda Louise**: born May 20, 1960

959 **BOSSARD Mark Allen**: (*Calvin, Curvin, Edwin, Jacob., Peter, Melchior, Phillip*) was born October 4, 1951 in Missoula, Montana, son of Calvin Floyd Bossard and Amelia Bubash. He married Nancy Casagrande.

Children:
i- **BOSSARD Lucas**: born July 6, 1977
ii- **BOSSARD Lance**: born December 1978
iii- **BOSSARD Monica**: April 4, 1982

960 **BAXTER Hayden Ardell**: (*Gladys, Curvin, Edwin, Jacob, Peter, Melchior, Phillip*) was born March 13, 1921 in Ida Grove, Iowa, son of William Hayden Baxter and Gladys Irene Bossard. He married November 15, 1945, Jeanne Price born November 26, 1921 in Ada, Kansas. They are presently living in El Cerrito, California.

Children:
1141 i- **BAXTER Terry K.**: born August 27, 1948 in Santa Rosa, California
ii- **BAXTER Kit W.**: born March 16, 1952 in Berkely, California

961 **BAXTER Marilee**: (*Gladys, Curvin, Edwin, Jacob, Peter, Melchior, Phillip*) was born April 22, 1928 in Ida Grove, Iowa, daughter of William Hayden Baxter and Gladys Irene Bossard. She married (1) February 26, 1950, Marvin Homer Gardner. He died July 23, 1968 in Louisville, Kentucky and she married (2) November 3, 1984, Ronald R. Allman born May 8, 1922. They are presently living in Scottsburg, Indiana.

Children:
1142 i- **GARDNER Vicki June**: born October, 10, 1950, in Bluffton, Indiana
1143 ii- **GARDNER Mark Allen**: born April 4, 1975, Seymour, Indiana

962 **NOLL Marjean**: (*Vera, Curvin, Edwin, Jacob, Peter, Melchior, Phillip*) was born March 25, 1922 in Ida Grove, Iowa, daughter of Albert Noll and Vera Emma Bossard. She married Ralph Jack Miller born August 12, 1926. He died July 3, 1970 in Ida Grove and Marjean is presently living in Ida Grove.

Children:
1144 i- **MILLER Connie J.**: born February 13, 1944
1145 ii- **MILLER Candas**: born April 18, 1949

963 **NOLL Charles Nowland**: (*Vera, Curvin, Edwin, Jacob, Peter, Melchior, Phillip*)

was born January 25, 1927 in Ida Grove, Iowa, son of Albert Noll and Vera Emma Bossard. He married Marcella (unknown maiden name) and they are presently living in Kiron, Iowa.

Children:
1146 i- **NOLL Nancy**:
1147 ii- **NOLL Shirley**:
1148 iii- **NOLL Lynette**:

964 BOSSARD Lois Ann: (*Cecil, Curvin, Edwin, Jacob, Peter, Melchior, Phillip*) was born July 28, 1928 in Ida Grove, Iowa, daughter of Cecil Alfred Bossard and Sibyl Elizabeth Dillon. She married June 1, 1947, John O. Trapp Jr. born March 21, 1926 in Savannah, Missouri. They are presently living in Bella Vista, Arkansas.

Children:
1149 i- **TRAPP David Brian**: born January 31, 1951 in Kansas City, Missouri
1150 ii- **TRAPP Sharon Elizabeth**: born November 9, 1955 in Abilene, Kansas.

965 BOSSARD Donna Lee: (*Cecil, Curvin, Edwin, Jacob, Peter, Melchior, Phillip*) was born October, 15, 1931 in Arthur, Iowa, daughter of Cecil Alfred Bossard and Sibyl Elizabeth Dillon. She married November 17, 1951, William C. Wolf. They were divorced February 14, 1983 and they remarried November 17, 1983. They are presently living in Lathrop, Missouri.

Children born in Missouri:
1151 i- **WOLF William Bradley**: born March 9, 1955
1152 ii- **WOLF Jeffrey Dillon**: born July 10, 1958
1153 iii- **WOLF Whitney Kimble**: born November 4, 1962

966 BOSSARD Murriel Jr.: (*Murriel, Curvin, Edwin, Jacob, Peter, Melchior, Phillip*) was born January 20, 1939, son of Murriel Curvin Bossard and Jess Mc Whirter. He married (1) Sandy (unknown maiden name). They were divorced and he married (2) Judy (unknown maiden name). They are presently living in Modesto, California.

Children:
1154 i- **BOSSARD Thomas**:
ii- **BOSSARD Terrence**:
iii- **BOSSARD Robert**:
1155 iv- **BOSSARD Wendy**:
v- **BOSSARD Steven**:
1156 vi- **BOSSARD James**:
1157 vii- **BOSSARD Carrie**:

967 **BOSSARD Carl Thomas:** (*Murriel, Curvin, Edwin, Jacob, Peter, Melchior, Phillip*) was born August 21, 1941 , son of Murriel Curvin Bossard and Jess Mc Whirter. He married Donna Poil born September 20, 1940. They are presently living in Great Falls, Montana.

Children:
i- **BOSSARD Dawn Marie:** born July 9, 1964
1158 ii- **BOSSARD Cindy Rae:** born December 13, 1968

968 **CLARK Maxine Lavonne:** (*Marcell, Curvin, Edwin, Jacob, Peter, Melchior, Phillip*) was born November 29, 1931 in Cresco, Iowa, daughter of Gordon L. Clark and Marcell Minnie Bossard. She married Guy E. Spracklen born April 30, 1928 in Douglas, Wyoming. They are presently living in Santa Paula, California.

Children born in California:
1159 i- **SPRACKLEN Guy Stephen:** born December 19, 1951
1160 ii- **SPRACKLEN Karen:** born March 26, 1957
1161 iii- **SPRACKLEN Kristin Ann:** born October 2, 1959

969 **BOSSARD Dianne:** (*Miles Jr., Miles, Eugene, Peter K., Peter, Melchior, Phillip*) was born September 26, 1948 in Stroudsburg, Pennsylvania, daughter of Miles Bossard Jr. and Margaret Ryan. She married August 7, 1965, William Possinger born September 17, 1945, son of William Possinger and Virginia Gettle. They are presently living in Stroudsburg.

Children:
i- **POSSINGER Bridget:** born January 26, 1966
ii- **POSSINGER Julie:** born October 13, 1969

970 **BOSSARD Devon:** (*Miles Jr., Miles, Eugene, Peter K., Peter, Melchior, Phillip*) was born August 2, 1950 in Stroudsburg, Pennsylvania, daughter of Miles F. Bossard Jr. and Margaret Ryan. She married November 25, 1972, Robert Sherno born March 8, 1950, son of Stanley Sherno and Theresa Chaya. They are presently living in Florida.

Children:
i- **SHERNO Robert Jr.:** born May 16, 1974
ii- **SHERNO Joseph:** born June 13, 1979

971 **BOSSARD Miles Franklin III:** (*Miles Jr., Miles, Eugene, Peter K., Peter, Melchior, Phillip*) was born August 13, 1952 in Stroudsburg, Pennsylvania, son of Miles F. Bossard Jr. and Margaret Ryan. He married Camille Watson born November 17, 1952, daughter of Frank Watson and Paulita Rhoades. He is presently living in Florida.

One child:
i- BOSSARD Christopher: born April 5, 1979

972 BOSSARD Mary Lynne: (*Miles Jr., Miles, Eugene, Peter K., Peter, Melchior, Phillip*) was born June 21, 1958 in Stroudsburg, Pennsylvania, daughter of Miles F. Bossard Jr. and Margaret Ryan. She married Joseph M. C. Mairs Jr. born January 27, 1947, son of Joseph M. C. Mairs and Katherine Graham.

Children:
i- MAIRS Alexandra: born September 15, 1985
ii- MAIRS Sasha: born February 10, 1988

973 HOGAN Janis: (*Bettiejane, Miles, Eugene, Peter K., Peter, Melchior, Phillip*) was born January 26, 1953, daughter of John F. Hogan and Bettiejane Bossard. She married Gary Butz born November 24, 1951, son of Raymond Butz and Janice Singer.

Children:
i- BUTZ Zachary: born April 3, 1974
ii- BUTZ Aaron: born September 3, 1976
iii- BUTZ Katie: born November 24, 1982

974 DENNIS Clifford Leroy: (*Harold Dennis, Grace Carmer, Alice, Joseph, Peter, Melchior, Phillip*) born October 19, 1931 in Hamilton Township, Pennsylvania, son of Harold Dennis and Olive Mezger. He married June 9, 1956, Joan Kresge born July 25, 1935, daughter of Russell Kresge and Gladys Dotter. They are presently living in Saylorsburg.

Children:
1162 i- DENNIS Karen: born May 16, 1958
1163 ii- DENNIS Tracy: born November 9, 1965

975 DENNIS John H.: (*Harold Dennis, Grace Carmer, Alice, Joseph, Peter, Melchior, Phillip*) was born June 21, 1935 in Hamilton Township, son of Harold Dennis and Olive Metzger. He married June 25, 1960, Verna Kay Blakeslee born July 28, 1938, daughter of Jerome Scott and Della Ruth Blakeslee.

Children:
1164 i- DENNIS Diane: born June 11, 1961
1165 ii- DENNIS Jill: born December 5, 1963
iii- DENNIS Jeanne: born January 25, 1969

976 HESTER Louise Shirley: (*Leroy Hester, Laura Carmer, Alice, Joseph, Peter,*

Melchior, Phillip) was born June 15, 1925 in Hamilton Township, Pennsylvania, daughter of Leroy Hester and Irene Fellencer. She married William Rohan born October 31, 1917 in Newburg, New York, son of John Rohan and Mary Fitzgerald. He died January 31, 1989.

Children:
- i- **ROHAN Patrick G.**:
- ii- **ROHAN Robert G.**:
- iii- **ROHAN Michele**: She died 1973

977 **HESTER Robert**: (*Leroy Hester, Laura Carmer, Alice, Joseph, Peter, Melchior, Phillip*) was born in Hamilton Township, Pennsylvania, son of Leroy Hester and Irene Fellencer He married Grace Kirchoffer. Robert is deceased, unknown date.

Children:
- i- **HESTER Richard**:
- ii- **HESTER Sharron**:
- iii- **HESTER Roberta**:
- iv- **HESTER Craig**:
- v- **HESTER Scot**:

978 **HESTER Joan Carol**: (*Allison Hester, Laura Carmer, Alice, Joseph, Peter, Melchior, Phillip*) was born June 8, 1941 in Stroudsburg, Pennsylvania, daughter of Allison A. Hester and Helen May Angle. She married July 11, 1964, Thomas Leonard born December 5, 1941.

Children:

1166 i- **LEONARD Elizabeth**: born April 2, 1965

ii- **LEONARD Thomas**: born August 18, 1966

CHAPTER 9

NINTH GENERATION

979 **BONSER Elaine Florence**: (*Lloyd Bonser, Florence Miller, Diana Altemose, Susannah Weiss, Felix Weiss, Eva Catherine, Melchior, Phillip*) was born August 9, 1927 in Chestnuthill, Pennsylvania, daughter of Lloyd K. Bonser and Viola Weiss. She married September 11, 1943, Albert Lewis Murphy born December 27, 1925, son of Victor Murphy and Beulah Schmear. They are presently living in Saylorsburg, Pennsylvania.

Children:
i- **MURPHY Lambert Lewis**: born March 21, 1946 and died April 6, 1965
1167 ii- **MURPHY Kenneth Albert**: born August 29, 1948
1168 iii- **MURPHY Lisa Ann Florence**: born September 6, 1958

980 **BONSER Catherine Mae**: (*Lloyd Bonser, Florence Miller, Diana Altemose, Susannah Weiss, Felix Weiss, Eva Catherine, Melchior, Phillip*) was born June 8, 1929 in Chestnuthill, Pennsylvania, daughter of Lloyd K. Bonser and Viola Weiss. She married July 6, 1947, Leon Herbert Altemus born February 5, 1929, son of Ambrose W. Altemus and Bessie Pauline Butts. Catherine died March 7, 1989.

Children:
1169 i- **ALTEMUS Linda**: born February 29, 1948
1170 ii- **ALTEMUS Wanda**: born August 14, 1950
1171 iii- **ALTEMUS Kim**: born January 24, 1953
1172 iv- **ALTEMUS Holly**: born December 27, 1963

981 **BONSER Robert Lester**: (*Lloyd Bonser, Florence Miller, Diana Altemose, Susannah Weiss, Felix Weiss, Eva Catherine, Melchior, Phillip*) was born October 7, 1930 in Chestnuthill, Pennsylvania, son of Lloyd K. Bonser and Viola Weiss. He married June 8, 1957, Nancy Jane Brensinger born August 19, 1933, daughter of George Washington Brensinger and Verna Pauline Marshall.

Children adopted by Robert and Nancy:
1173 i- **BONSER James Robert**: born October 21, 1962
1174 ii- **BONSER Jane Ann**: born November 9, 1965

982 **BONSER Leroy Stanley**: (*Lloyd Bonser, Florence Miller, Diana Altemose, Susannah Weiss, Felix Weiss, Eva Catherine, Melchior, Philiip*) was born August 1,

1938 in Chestnuthill, Pennsylvania, son of Lloyd K. Bonser and Viola Weiss. He married November 15, 1958, Mabel Ann Burger born March 12, 1941, daughter of William Burger and Julia Serfass.

Children:

1175 i- **BONSER Leroy Stanley II**: born August 7, 1959
1176 ii- **BONSER Lamont Solomon**: born May 14, 1962

983 BONSER Janet: (*Mitchell Bonser, Florence Miller, Diana Altemose, Susannah Weiss, Felix Weiss, Eva Catherine, Melchior, Phillip*) was born April 11, 1935 in Monroe Co., Pennsylvania, daughter of Mitchell F. Bonser and Jennie May Bond. She married Phillip Niceforo born April 27, 1935. They are presently living in Bangor, Pennsylvania.

Children:

1177 i- **BONSER Barry Russell**: born September 8, 1952
1178 ii- **NICEFORO Philip Nicholas**: born March 12, 1958
1179 iii- **NICEFORO Roxanne Margaret**: born January 4, 1964

984 BONSER Richard: (*Mitchell Bonser, Florence Miller, Diana Altemose, Susannah Weiss, Felix Weiss, Eva Catherine, Melchior, Phillip*) was born September 6, 1936 in Monroe Co., Pennsylvania, son of Mitchell Bonser and Jennie May Bond. He married June 25, 1965, Sue Ann Masters born April 30, 1940.

Children:

i- **BONSER Eric Duane**: born May 27, 1966
1180 ii- **BONSER Laura Michelle**: born April 27, 1968
iii- **BONSER Brenda Cynthia**: born July 25, 1969
iv- **BONSER Rachel Sue**: born December 31, 1970

985 POWELL Deborah F.: (*Edith Altemose, Vernon Altemose, Stewart Altemose, Susannah Weiss, Felix Weiss, Eva Catherine, Melchior, Phillip*) was born May 14, 1950, daughter of Russell Powell and Edith C. Altemose. She married May 24, 1975, Michael F. Montanio born March 14, 1950.

One child:

i- **MONTANIO Jordan**: born February 17, 1978

986 POWELL Melanie H.: (*Edith Altemose, Vernon Altemose, Stewart Altemose, Susannah Weiss, Felix, Weiss, Eva Catherine, Melchior, Phillip*) was born July 21, 1951, daughter of Russell Powell and Edith C. Altemose. She married Mark Anthony Ford.

Children:

i- **FORD Brendan**: born October 14, 1978
ii- **FORD Ryan M.**: born December 26, 1980

987 POWELL Michael C.: (*Edith Altemose, Vernon Altemose, Stewart Altemose, Susannah Weiss, Felix Weiss, Eva Catherine, Melchior, Phillip*) was born December 28, 1954, son of Russell Powell and Edith C. Altemose. He married June 12, 1976, Norma Seifert born March 7, 1956.

Children:
i- **POWELL Ian R.**: born July 12, 1977
ii- **POWELL Andrea L.**: born March 14, 1979

988 STARNER Jed Alan: (*Marion Altemose, Vernon Altemose, Stewart Altemose, Susannah Weiss, Felix Weiss, Eva Catherine, Melchior, Phillip*) was born July 23, 1953, son of Ralph Paul Starner and Marion Elizabeth Altemose. He married April 18, 1980, Jan Wright born September 5, 1950. Jan had three children by a previous marriage to Mr. Blauser.

i- **BLAUSER Lori J.**: born July 19, 1970
ii- **BLAUSER Hilary J.**: born April 12, 1972
iii- **BLAUSER Natalie W.**: born January 7, 1977

989 STOUDT Nanette F.: (*Frances Altemose, Vernon Altemose, Stewart Altemose, Susannah Weiss, Felix Weiss, Eva Catherine, Melchior, Phillip*) was born February 10, 1952, daughter of Donald R. Stoudt and Frances Louisa Altemose. She married December 6, 1975, Edward A. Chladny born July 22, 1951.

Children:
i- **CHLADNY Jessica F.**: born May 28, 1978
ii- **CHLADNY Christy R.**: born May 22, 1980

990 STOUDT Sheryl L.: (*Frances Altemose, Vernon Altemose, Stewart Altemose, Susannah Weiss, Felix Weiss, Eva Catherine, Melchior, Phillip*) was born March 28, 1953, daughter of Donald R. Stoudt and Frances Louisa Altemose. She married September 23, 1978, Thomas Lichner. No issue.

991 STOUDT Randy Scott: (*Frances Altemose, Vernon Altemose, Stewart Altemose, Susannah Weiss, Felix Weiss, Eva Catherine, Melchior, Phillip*) was born August 1, 1955, son of Donald R. Stoudt and Frances Louisa Altemose. He married November 22, 1980, Amy M. Sevi. No issue.

992 STOUDT Jeff Donald: (*Frances Altemose, Vernon Altemose, Stewart Altemose,*

Susannah Weiss, Felix Weiss, Eva Catherine, Melchior, Phillip) was born December 3, 1958, son of Donald R. Stoudt and Frances Louisa Altemose. He married June 16, 1978, Brenda Barlieb born November 16, 1957. No issue.

993 ALTEMOSE Pamela: (*Vernon Altemose Jr., Vernon Altemose, Stewart Altemose, Susannah Weiss, Felix Weiss, Eva Catherine, Melchior, Phillip*) was born October 17, 1957, daughter of Vernon Altemose Jr. and Kathryn Engler. She married May 25, 1980, Paul Forrestal born December 26, 1957.

One child:

- **i- FORRESTAL Paul Jr.**: born August 19, 1980

994 BROWN June Marie: (*Marie Seiple, Emma Altemose, Stewart Altemose, Susannah Weiss, Felix Weiss, Eva Catherine, Melchior, Phillip*) was born May 30, 1945, daughter of Ronald T. Brown and Marie B. Seiple. She married April 15, 1967, Anthony Joseph Rouda born May 12, 1946.

Children:

- **i- ROUDA Anthony Joseph Jr.**: born August 30, 1970
- **ii- ROUDA Denise Ann**: born May 14, 1975

995 BROWN Gail Naomi: (*Marie Seiple, Emma Altemose, Stewart Altemose, Susannah Weiss, Felix Weiss, Eva Catherine, Melchior, Phillip*) was born June 30, 1953, daughter of Ronald T. Brown and Marie B. Seiple. She married March 25, 1972, William Thomas Filer born January 12, 1953.

Children:

- **i- FILER Kimberly Ann**: born August 22, 1972
- **ii- FILER Nicole Marie**: born November 7, 1979

996 BROWN Donna Lee: (*Marie Seiple, Emma Altemose, Stewart Altemose, Susannah Weiss, Felix Weiss, Eva Catherine, Melchior, Phillip*) was born July 12, 1956, daughter of Ronald T. Brown and Marie B. Seiple. She married July 31, 1976, Wayne Victor Joseph Kandravi born September 15, 1953.

Children:

- **i- KANDRAVI Wayne Victor Joseph Jr.**: born May 10, 1977
- **ii- KANDRAVI Kevin Francis**: born July 12, 1978
- **iii- KANDRAVI Christopher Michael**: born January 15, 1980

997 BROWN Ronald Triburton Jr.: (*Marie Seiple, Emma Altemose, Stewart Altemose, Susannah Weiss, Felix Weiss, Eva Catherine, Melchior, Phillip*) was born March 3, 1958, son of Ronald T. Brown Sr. and Marie Seiple. He married

December 23, 1978, Karen Lea Cummins born July 12, 1960.

One child:
i- BROWN Kristen Lee: born November 21, 1980

998 BROWN Keith Alan: (*Marie Seiple. Emma Altemose, Stewart Altemose, Susannah Weiss, Felix Weiss, Eva Catherine, Melchior, Phillip*) was born November 12, 1960, son of Ronald T. Brown and Marie B. Seiple. He married March 8, 1980, Johanna Marie Chiarolanza born January 14, 1964.

Children:
i- BROWN Keith Alan Jr.: born May 10, 1979
ii- BROWN Michael Francis: January 2, 1982

999 SEIPLE Barbara: (*William Seiple, Emma Altemose, Stewart Altemose, Susannah Weiss, Felix Weiss, Eva Catherine, Melchior, Phillip*) was born December 19, 1943, daughter of William H. Seiple and Gloria Shulz. She married April 6, 1968, Richard Mc Clay born November 17, 1946.

One child:
i- MC CLAY Cheryl Lynn: born October 10, 1969

1000 SEIPLE William Henry Jr.: (*William Seiple, Emma Altemose, Stewart Altemose, Susannah Weiss, Felix Weiss, Eva Catherine, Melchior, Phillip*) was born July 18, 1954, son of William Henry Seiple Sr. and Gloria Shulz. He married July 26, 1975, Deborah Warner born October 25, 1953.

Children:
i- SEIPLE Christine: born November 28, 1977
ii- SEIPLE Jennifer: born November 14, 1980

1001 SEIPLE Alfred Franklin III: (*Alfred Seiple, Emma Altemose, Stewart Altemose, Susannah Weiss, Felix Weiss, Eva Catherine, Melchior, Phillip*) was born December 16, 1959, son of Alfred Seiple II and Elsa Deuble. He married July 12, 1980, Gale Holmes born June 20, 1959. No issue.

1002 ALTEMOSE Bret Harold: (*Paul Altemose. Ralph Altemose, Stewart Altemose, Susannah Weiss, Felix Weiss, Eva Catherine, Melchior, Phillip*) was born October 31, 1953, son of Paul Arlington Altemose and Julia Jean Reimert. He married August 23, 1975, Joan Marie Weinheimer. No issue.

1003 ALTEMOSE Dee Carol: (*Paul Altemose, Ralph Altemose, Stewart Altemose,*

Susannah Weiss, Felix Weiss, Eva Catherine, Melchior, Phillip) was born November 23, 1957, daughter of Paul Arlington Altemose and Julia Jean Reimert. She married August 29, 1981, Patrick Arthur Sim born June 6, 1958. No issue.

1004 SAYLOR Wayne Alan: (*Geraldine Altemose, Jacob Altemose, Stewart Altemose, Susannah Weiss, Felix Weiss, Eva Catherine, Melchior, Phillip*) was born July 21, 1956, son of Howard Eugene Saylor and Geraldine M. Altemose. He married August 18, 1979, Rae Lynn Dougherty born May 30, 1956. No issue.

1005 MESSINGER Melvin Floyd: (*Jean Altemose, Jacob Altemose, Stewart Altemose, Susannah Weiss, Felix Weiss, Eva Catherine, Melchior, Phillip*) was born September 14, 1946, son of Vernon L. Messinger and Jean Grace Altemose. He married May 29, 1972, Carol Anstead born September 10, 1950.

Children:
- **i- MESSINGER Tommy James**: born March 29, 1970
- **ii- MESSINGER Jane Marie**: born November 25, 1973
- **iii- MESSINGER Amanda Jean**: born July 15, 1975

1006 MESSINGER Tim Edward: (*Jean Altemose, Jacob Altemose, Stewart Altemose, Susannah Weiss, Felix Weiss, Eva Catherine, Melchior, Phillip*) was born October 4, 1952, son of Vernon L. Messinger and Jean Grace Altemose. He married December 4, 1976, Barbara Shupp born September 25, 1953.

Children:
- **i- MESSINGER Mason Charles**: born November 28, 1979
- **ii- MESSINGER Jeremy Edward**: born July 18, 1981

1007 MESSINGER Len Lewis: (*Jean Altemose, Jacob Altemose, Stewart Altemose, Susannah Weiss, Felix Weiss, Eva Catherine, Melchior, Phillip*) was born October 10, 1954, son of Vernon L. Messinger and Jean Grace Altemose. He married November 11, 1977, Francine Schrenko born November 5, 1955.

One child:
- **i- MESSINGER Lyle Jacob**: born July 22, 1980

1008 ALTEMOSE Bonnie Sue: (*Richard Altemose, Jacob Altemose, Stewart Altemose, Susannah Weiss, Felix Weiss, Eva Catherine, Melchior, Phillip*) was born January 3, 1955, daughter of Richard James Altemose and Lorain Fritz. She married July 9, 1977, Fred Charles Wagoner Jr. born June 19, 1954. No issue.

1009 ALTEMOSE Marci Lynn: (*Lee Altemose, Jacob Altemose, Stewart Altemose,*

Susannah Weiss, Felix Weiss, Eva Catherine, Melchior, Phillip) was born April 3, 1959, daughter of Lee Lynford Altemose and Jean A. Kessler. She married August 19, 1980, Larry D. Hunt born April 27, 1958. No issue.

1010 ALTEMOSE Karen Lois: (*Robert Altemose, Jacob Altemose, Stewart Altemose, Susannah Weiss, Felix Weiss, Eva Catherine, Melchior, Phillip*) was born December 24, 1954, daughter of Robert F. Altemose and Ilean Heiserman. She married February 4, 1978, Robert W. Lugg born July 22, 1954. No issue.

1011 ALTEMOSE Keith Robert: (*Robert Altemose, Jacob Altemose, Stewart Altemose, Susannah Weiss, Felix Weiss, Eva Catherine, Melchior, Phillip*) was born May 13, 1955, son of Robert Altemose and Ilean Heiserman. He married October 3, 1981, Linda Pagotto born December 15, 1954. No issue.

1012 ALTEMOSE Bruce Alan: (*Rollin Altemose, Albert Altemose, Stewart Altemose, Susannah Weiss, Felix Weiss, Eva Catherine, Melchior, Phillip*) was born September 10, 1957, son of Rollin Amos Altemose, and Marlene Uhler. He married June 17, 1978, Calleen Balogh born December 24, 1957. No issue.

1013 GILPIN John Albert: (*Barbara Gregory, Lida Gearhart, Theodore Gearhart, Elizabeth Weiss, Felix Weiss, Eva Catherine, Melchior, Phillip*) was born April 17, 1941 in Stroudsburg, Pennsylvania, son of Donald A. Gilpin and Barbara Gregory. He married August 22, 1967, Sandra Graeter born June 25, 1943.

Children:

- **i- GILPIN Andrea**: born March 18, 1971
- **ii- GILPIN Matthew**: born April 18, 1974

1014 GILPIN Mary Jane: (*Barbara Gregory, Lida Gearhart, Theodore Gearhart, Elizabeth Weiss, Felix Weiss, Eva Catherine, Melchior, Phillip*) was born April 27, 1944 in Stroudsburg, Pennsylvania, daughter of Donald A. Gilpin and Barbara Gregory. She married June 24, 1972, John Seidstricker.

Child:

- **i- SEIDSTRICKER Elizabeth**: born June 24, 1979

1015 GILPIN Donald Gregory: (*Barbara Gregory, Lida Gearhart, Theodore Gearhart, Elizabeth Weiss, Felix Weiss, Ea Catherine. Melchior, Phillip*) was born August 17, 1949 in Stroudsburg, Pennsylvania, son of Donald A. Gilpin and Barbara Gregory. He married August 13, 1971, Carol Ann Frederick.

Children:

i- **GILPIN Barbara**: born October 9, 1976
ii- **GILPIN Donald**: born March 9, 1978
iii- **GILPIN Colleen**: born September 21, 1982

1016 GOULET Andrew Joseph: (*Eugene Goulet, Vera, Roy V., Edwin, Joseph, Phillip, Melchior, Phillip*) was born September 13, 1959 in Bay City, Michigan, son of Eugene Joseph Goulet and Amy Hoppock. He married February 25, 1989, Sue (unknown maiden name).

1017 GOULET Ann Elizabeth: (*Eugene Goulet, Vera, Roy V., Edwin, Joseph, Phillip, Melchior, Phillip*) was born October 19, 1963 in Bay City, Michigan, daughter of Eugene Joseph Goulet and Amy Hoppock. She married July 5, 1986, Craig Parks. No issue.

1018 GOULET David Brian: (*Jerry Goulet, Vera, Roy V., Edwin, Joseph, Phillip, Melchior, Phillip*) was born January 3, 1956 in Bay City, Michigan, son of Jerry Goulet and Sharon Lee Cole. He married Anita Rogers.

Children:
i- **GOULET David Joseph**: born November 5, 1979
ii- **GOULET Yvonne Marie**: born September 21, 1981
iii- **GOULET Ryan Emery**: born November 3, 1982

1019 GOULET James Allen: (*Jerry Goulet, Vera, Roy V., Edwin, Joseph, Phillip, Melchior, Phillip*) was born April 12, 1957 in Bay City, Michigan, son of Jerry Goulet and Sharon Lee Cole. He married Martha June Gillispie.

Children:
i- **GOULET Chad Allen**: born November 20, 1979
ii- **GOULET Katherine Ann**: born July 2, 1988

1020 GOULET Kenneth Matthew: (*Jerry Goulet, Vera, Roy V., Edwin, Joseph, Phillip, Melchior, Phillip*) was born June 10, 1959 in Bay City, Michigan, son of Jerry Goulet and Sharon Lee Cole. He married Lori Ann Smith born June 29, 1959.

Children:

i- **GOULET Tiffany Nicole**: born August 1, 1980
i- **GOULET Melisa Marie**: born February 23, 1983

1021 GOULET Thomas Michael: (*Jerry Goulet, Vera, Roy V., Edwin, Joseph, Phillip, Melchior, Phillip*) was born April 10, 1961 in Bay City, Michigan, son of Jerry

Goulet and Sharon Lee Cole. He married Carla Linnea Hinenbaugh born September 16, 1961. No issue.

1022 GOULET Wayne Emery: (*Jerry Goulet, Vera, Roy V., Edwin, Joseph, Phillip, Melchior, Phillip*) was born May 19, 1964 in Bay City, Michigan, son of Jerry Goulet and Sharon Lee Cole. He married June 2, 1990, Lee Ann Eitel.

1023 SMITH David: (*William Smith, Gladys Stanton, Mabel, George, Peter, Christopher, Melchior, Phillip*) was born December 15, 1947, son of William Smith and Loretta Shaft. He was married, no issue.

1024 SMITH Cathie: (*Harry Smith, Gladys Stanton, Mabel, George, Peter, Christopher, Melchior, Phillip*) was born October 22, 1946, in Rochester, New York, daughter of Harry Smith and Dorah Williams. She married May 8, 1987, Clarke Keenan, son of Richard and Barbara Keenan.

1025 SMITH Garrett: (*Harry Smith, Gladys Stanton, Mabel, George, Peter, Christopher, Melchior, Phillip*) was born November 17, 1949 in Rochester, New York, son of Harry Smith and Dorah Williams. He married August 13, 1972, Janette Robinson, daughter of Roy and Lila Robinson.

1026 SMITH Dana: (*Harry Smith, Gladys Stanton, Mabel, George, Peter, Christopher, Melchior, Phillip*) was born September 19, 1953 in Rochester, New York, son of Harry Smith and Dorah Williams. He married May 27, 1978, Claire Boucher, daughter of Roland and Irma Boucher.

1027 SMITH Sueanne: (*Frederick Smith, Gladys Stanton, Mabel, George, Peter, Christopher, Melchior, Phillip*) was born October 21, 1962, daughter of Frederick Smith and Mary Porrica. She married August 21, 1981, David Wysowski born March 15, 1959.

Child:

i- WYSOWSKI Michael: born March 27, 1985

1028 SMITH Amy: (*Frederick Smith, Gladys Stanton, Mabel, George, Peter, Christopher, Melchior, Phillip*) was born July 23, 1965, daughter of Frederick Smith and Mary Porrica. She married October 3, 1987, Brian Brechue born October 13, 1960. No issue.

1029 SMITH Brian: (*Charles Smith, Gladys Stanton, Mabel, George, Peter,*

Christopher, Melchior, Phillip) was born January 15, ____, son of Charles Smith Jr. and Cherrie Winkler. He married June 9, 1990, Shireen Gazzillo.

1030 PIERSON Martin: (*Mary Sharp, Zelma Stanton, Mabel, George, Peter, Christopher, Melchior, Phillip*) was born December 8, 1957, son of Douglas Pierson and Mary Sharp. He married December 31, 1958, Patricia Kinney.

Children:
- i- **PIERSON Emma**: born September 1986
- ii- **PIERSON Gregory**: born July 3, 1989

1031 PIERSON Daniel: (*Mary Sharp, Zelma Stanton, Mabel, George, Peter, Christopher, Melchior, Phillip*) was born July 26, 1959, son of Douglas Pierson and Mary Sharp. He married June 11, 1983, Elizabeth Meyer born August 1960.

Children:
- i- **PIERSON Nancy**: born February 15, 1986
- ii- **PIERSON Benjamin**: born May 11, 1989

1032 DI GENNARO Joi Lynn: (*Charlotte Stanton, William Stanton, Mabel, George, Peter, Christopher, Melchior, Phillip*) was born May 23, 1963 in Rochester, New York, daughter of Samuel Di Gennaro and Charlotte Stanton. She married June 1, 1985, Gerald Johnson born March 1, 1957.

1033 MALLARD Scott: (*Charleen Stanton, William Stanton, Mabel, George, Peter, Christopher, Melchior, Phillip*) was born September 16, 1958, son of Roger Mallard and Charleen Stanton. He married May 14, 1977, Sue (unknown maiden name) born December 28, 1955.

Children:
- i- **MALLARD Katie**: born December 9, 1977
- ii- **MALLARD Michele**: born July 7, 1980

1034 MALLARD Jeff: (*Charleen Stanton, William Stanton, Mabel, George, Peter, Christopher, Melchior, Phillip*) was born April 26, 1958, son of Roger Mallard and Charleen Stanton. He married November 19, 1977, Kim (unknown maiden name).

Children:
- i- **MALLARD Jeff**: born March 19, 1979
- ii- **MALLARD Kristi**: born January 30, 1981

1035 STORMS Sylvia Gay: (*Walter Storms, Grace, Truman, Cyrus, Richard,*

Christopher, Melchior, Phillip) was born June 10, 1940 in Bradford, Pennsylvania, daughter of Walter T. Storms and Gift Eileen Morris. She married Donald Eckelberger and they are presently living near Binghamton, New York.

Children:
- i- **ECKELBERGER Susan Marie:**
- ii- **ECKELBERGER Bonnie Gay:**
- iii- **ECKELBERGER Dawn Lynn:**

1036 STORMS Walter Terrance: (*Walter Storms, Grace, Truman, Cyrus, Richard, Christopher, Melchior, Phillip*) was born June 28, 1942 in Bradford, Pennsylvania, son of Walter T. Storms and Gift Eileen Morris. He married (1) Rose Marie Walters and (2) Karen (unknown maiden name). Last known, he was living in Seattle, Washington.

Children by first marriage:
- i- **STORMS Kimberly:**
- ii- **STORMS Scott:**
- iii- **STORMS Jennifer:**
- iv- **STORMS Melissa:**
- v- **STORMS Shawn:**

Children by second marriage:
- vi- **STORMS Terry Lee:**
- vii- **STORMS Cassie:**
- viii- **STORMS Jeremy:**

1037 STORMS Timothy Morris: (*Walter Storms, Grace, Truman, Cyrus, Richard, Christopher, Melchior, Phillip*) was born October 19, 1944 in Bradford, Pennsylvania, son of Walter T. Storms and Gift Eileen Morris. He married Eileen Goff.

Children:
- i- **STORMS Mark Timothy:**
- ii- **STORMS Nathan David:**

1038 STORMS Bruce Allan: (*Walter Storms, Grace, Truman, Cyrus, Richard, Christopher, Melchior, Phillip*) was born July 13, 1946 in Bradford, Pennsylvania, son of Walter T. Storms and Gift Eileen Morris. He married Valerie Hamilton.

Children:
- i- **STORMS Faith Elizabeth:**
- ii- **STORMS Joy Ann:**

1039 STORMS Kaye: (*Clifford Storms, Grace, Truman, Cyrus, Richard, Christopher, Melchior, Phillip*) was born July 15, 1941 in Bradford, Pennsylvania, daughter of

Clifford Storms and Eleanor Cadman. She married Sheldon Carlson.

Children:
i- CARLSON Jeffrey:
ii- CARLSON Bradley:

1040 STORMS Charles: (*Clifford Storms, Grace, Truman, Cyrus, Richard, Christopher, Melchior, Phillip*) was born April 28, 1944 in Bradford, Pennsylvania, son of Clifford Storms and Eleanor Cadman. He married (1) Nancy Pestrak and (2) Carol Carpenter. They have three children.

1041 STORMS Susan: (*Clifford Storms, Grace, Truman, Cyrus, Richard, Christopher, Melchior, Phillip*) was born November 19, 1956 in Bradford, Pennsylvania, daughter of Clifford Storms and Eleanor Cadman. She married Stewart Pulliam. They have two children.

1042 MILLER Sharron: (*Stanley Miller, Ruby, Truman, Cyrus, Richard, Christopher, Melchior, Phillip*) was born November 25, 1954, daughter of Stanley and Mary Miller. They are living in Indiana. No further records.

1043 MILLER Jeffrey: (*Stanley Miller, Ruby, Truman, Cyrus, Richard, Christopher, Melchior, Phillip*) was born September 9, 1956, son of Stanley and Mary Miller. They are living in Indiana. No further records.

1044 MILLER Cathy: (*Stanley Miller, Ruby, Truman, Cyrus, Richard, Christopher, Melchior, Phillip*) was born July 13, 1960, daughter of Stanley and Mary Miller. They are living in Indiana. No further records.

1045 GARDNER Marcia: (*Eva, Floyd, Truman, Cyrus, Richard, Christopher, Melchior, Phillip*) was born November 5, 1942 in Santa Maria, California, daughter of Dr. Guy Gardner and Eva Bozard. She married May 1966 in Liverpool, New York, James Kamierski.

1046 GARDNER Susan: (*Eva, Floyd, Truman, Cyrus, Richard, Christopher, Melchior, Phillip*) was born January 23, 1944 in Harrisburg, Pennsylvania, daughter of Dr. Guy Gardner and Eva Bozard. She married Henry Neverett. They were divorced.

1047 GARDNER Laura: (*Eva, Floyd, Truman, Cyrus, Richard, Christopher, Melchior, Phillip*) was born March 18, 1948 in Salamanca, New York, daughter of

Dr. Guy Gardner and Eva Bozard. She married December 3, 1965 in New York City, Roger Domagalski.

1048 **GARDNER Thomas:** (*Eva, Floyd, Truman, Cyrus, Richard, Christopher, Melchior, Phillip*) was born September 25, 1953 in Salamanca, New York, son of Dr. Guy Gardner and Eva Bozard. He married January 1980 in Seattle, Washington, Kim (unknown maiden name). They were divorced in 1989.

1049 **GARDNER Jan:** (*Eva, Floyd, Truman, Cyrus, Richard, Christopher, Melchior, Phillip*) was born January 20, 1955 in Salamanca, New York, daughter of Dr. Guy Gardner and Eva Bozard. She married 1978 in Salamanca, Louis Silvano.

1050 **BOZARD Paul Edward:** (*Paul, Floyd, Truman, Cyrus, Richard, Christopher, Melchior, Phillip*) was born July 31, 1943 in Salamanca, New York, son of Paul Floyd Bozard and Julia Marie Mohr. He married March 20, 1965, Aurelia Marie Puvel born March 3, 1947, daughter of Leo Puvel and Loretta Baker. He is a State Trooper in Cattaraugus Co.

Children born in Olean, New York:

- i- **BOZARD Lisa Anne:** born May 29, 1971
- ii- **BOZARD Clay Edward:** born July 26, 1973

1051 **CLARK Linda:** (*Eva Zuver, Flossie, Truman, Cyrus, Richard, Christopher, Melchior, Phillip*) was born December 24, 1956 in Olean, New York, daughter of Wilford Clark and Eva Zuver. She married Michael Anderson. They are divorced and Linda is presently living in Virginia.

1052 **CLARK Diane:** (*Eva Zuver, Flossie, Truman, Cyrus, Richard, Christopher, Melchior, Phillip*) was born November 15, 1956 in Olean, New York, daughter of Wilford Clark and Eva Zuver. She has one daughter and is presently living in Texas.

1053 **SHEARER William Raymond:** (*Beatrice Langley, Bernice, Truman, Cyrus, Richard, Christopher, Melchior, Phillip*) was born December 2, 1943 in Hornell, New York, son of Raymond Shearer and Beatrice Langley. He married Nancy Ellen Robinson and they are presently living in Webster, New York.

Children:

- i- **SHEARER Mathew William:** born October 6, 1971
- ii- **SHEARER Marcy Ellen:** born November 2, 1975

1054 SHEARER Richard Langley: (*Beatrice Langley, Bernice, Truman, Cyrus, Richard, Christopher, Melchior, Phillip*) was born April 11, 1946 in Hornell, New York, son of Raymond Shearer and Beatrice Langley. He married June 17, 1978, June King.

One child:
i- SHEARER Richard Langley: born December 4, 1979

1055 MONTGOMERY Susan Ann: (*Barbara Langley, Bernice, Truman, Cyrus, Richard, Christopher, Melchior, Phillip*) was born February 12, 1947, daughter of Roland Montgomery and Barbara Eva Langley. She married Steven Steinhilber. No issue.

1056 MONTGOMERY Marcia Kay: (*Barbara Langley, Bernice, Truman, Cyrus, Richard, Christopher, Melchior, Phillip*) was born February 12, 1948 in Hornell, New York, daughter of Roland Montgomery and Barbara Eva Langley. She married Kenneth Schreiber. No issue.

1057 MONTGOMERY Ann Langley: (*Barbara Langley, Bernice, Truman, Cyrus, Richard, Christopher, Melchior, Phillip*) was born February 2, 1955 in Hornell, New York, daughter of Roland Montgomery and Barbara Eva Langley. She married Rex Wilke. They are presently living in Snellsville, Georgia. No issue.

1058 HOKANSON Kathleen Ann: (*Ernest Hokanson, Beatrice, Truman, Cyrus, Richard, Christopher, Melchior, Phillip*) was born December 5, 1947, daughter of Ernest Hokanson Jr. and Zada Ellen Huff. She married ______ Garrett and they are presently living in Atlanta, Georgia.

One child:
i- GARRETT Rhonda: born April 12, 1964

1059 HOKANSON Tanyjah: (*Dean Hokanson, Beatrice, Truman, Cyrus, Richard, Christopher, Melchior, Phillip*) was born April 8, 1949, daughter of Dean Russell Hokanson and Constance Favro. She married (1) in 1966, Kenneth Goodfellow. They were divorced and she married (2) Ashley Deme.

Children by second marriage:
i- DEME Ashley:
ii- DEME Mathew:

1060 HOKANSON April Estelle: (*Dean Hokanson, Beatrice, Truman, Cyrus, Richard, Christopher, Melchior, Phillip*) was born May 29, 1953, daughter of Dean

R. Hokanson and Constance Favro. She married July 2, 1971, Richard Kirkland. They are presently living in Lizella, Georgia.

Children:
- i- **KIRKLAND Michelle:**
- ii- **KIRKLAND Lindsay:**
- iii- **KIRKLAND Rikki:**

1061 HOKANSON Roderick Dean: (*Dean Hokanson, Beatrice, Truman, Cyrus, Richard, Christopher, Melchior, Phillip*) was born September 18, 1954, son of Dean R. Hokanson and Constance Favro. He married Abbie Mansour and they are presently living in Atlanta, Georgia.

Children:
- i- **HOKANSON Dane:**
- ii- **HOKANSON Abbie Lynn:**

1062 HOKANSON James Ernest: (*Dean Hokanson, Beatrice, Truman, Cyrus, Richard, Christopher, Melchior, Phillip*) was born May 26, 1956, son of Dean R. Hokanson and Constance Favro. He married Penny (unknown maiden name). They were divorced and he is presently living in Athens, Georgia.

One child:
- i- **HOKANSON Amber Lynn:**

1063 HOKANSON Natasha Lynn: (*Dean Hokanson, Beatrice, Truman, Cyrus, Richard, Christopher, Melchior, Phillip*) was born October 11, 1961, daughter of Dean R. Hokanson and Constance Favro. She married and they are presently living in Athens, Georgia. No further records.

1064 DOWNING Tambri Sue: (*Constance Hokanson, Beatrice, Truman, Cyrus, Richard, Christopher, Melchior, Phillip*) was born February 2, 1959 in Buffalo, New York, daughter of Charles A. Downing and Constance Louise Hokanson. She married Robert I. Andrews. They are presently living in Blasdell, New York.

Children:
- i- **ANDREWS Shannon Elizabeth:** born August 8, 1978
- ii- **ANDREWS Michael Ian:** born September 7, 1979
- iii- **ANDREWS Sarah Christy:** born October 8, 1983

1065 DOWNING Craig Steven: (*Constance Hokanson, Beatrice, Truman, Cyrus, Richard, Christopher, Melchior, Phillip*) was born July 15, 1960, son of Charles A. Downing and Constance Louise Hokanson. He married Beth Gebhardt and they are presently living in Alden, New York.

One child:

i- DOWNING Steven Michael: born February 13, 1984

1066 DOWNING Christopher John: (*Constance Hokanson, Beatrice, Truman, Cyrus, Richard, Christopher, Melchior, Phillip*) was born July 30, 1965, son of Charles A. Downing and Constance Louise Hokanson. He married Melissa Tomb and they are presently living in Buffalo, New York. No issue.

1067 DOWNING Tracy Lee: (*Constance Hokanson, Beatrice, Truman, Cyrus, Richard Christopher, Melchior, Phillip*) was born September 27, 1966 in Buffalo, New York, daughter of Charles A. Downing and Constance Louise Hokanson. She married David Padilla and they are presently living in Buffalo, New York.

Children:

i- PADILLA Joseph David: born August 16, 1984
ii- PADILLA Elizabeth Ann: born January 20, 1988

1068 SAWDEY Patricia Suzanne: (*Lawrence Sawdey, Bertha, Edward, Cyrus, Richard, Christopher, Melchior, Phillip*) was born December 6. 1968, daughter of Lawrence Sawdey and Dorothy Daley. She married March 4, 1989 in Harrisonville, Missouri, John Mead.

1069 FULLER Daniel Joseph: (*Margaret Sawdey, Bertha, Edward, Cyrus, Richard, Christopher, Melchior, Phillip*) was born November 3, 1963 in Cuba, New York, son of Lawrence Fuller and Margaret Mary Sawdey. He married May 24, 1986 in Cuba, Sue Meade.

1070 FULLER Mary Jo: (*Margaret Sawdey, Bertha, Edward, Cyrus, Richard, Christopher, Melchior, Phillip*) was born August 8, 1965 in Cuba, New York, daughter of Lawrence Fuller and Margaret Mary Sawdey. She married February 3, 1990 in Olean, New York, Richard Wilson.

1071 MOSMAN Patricia Marie: (*William Mosman, Lynford Mosman, Blanche, Cyrus, Richard, Christopher, Melchior, Phillip*) was born May 20, 1953 in Lancaster, New York, daughter of William Lynford Mosman and Mary Ellen Wilson. She married August 29, 1976, Donald E. Smith.

Children:

i- SMITH Zachary William: born November 17, 1981
ii- SMITH Chelsea Elizabeth: born September 11, 1984

1072 MOSMAN Mary Lynn: (*William Mosman, Lynford Mosman, Blanche, Cyrus, Richard, Christopher, Melchior, Phillip*) was born September 27, 1955 in Lancaster, New York, daughter of William Lynford Mosman and Mary Ellen Wilson. She married Wayne Donald Kiefman.

One child:

i- **KIEFMAN Ryan Andrew**: born June 24, 1988

1073 MOSMAN Ellen Jean: (*William Mosman, Lynford Mosman, Blanche, Cyrus, Richard, Christopher, Melchior, Phillip*) was born March 17, 1958 in Lancaster, New York, daughter of William Lynford Mosman and Mary Ellen Wilson. She married Joaquin J. Aymerick.

One child:

i- **AYMERICK Timothy**: born January 6, 1988

1074 MOSMAN William Lynford Jr.: (*William Mosman, Lynford Mosman, Blanche, Cyrus, Richard, Christopher, Melchior, Phillip*) was born May 28, 1959 in Lancaster, New York, son of William Lynford Mosman and Mary Ellen Wilson. He married Paula Ann Wigton.

Children:

i- **MOSMAN Honora Elizabeth**: born August 15, 1979
ii- **MOSMAN Sarah Ann**: born May 3, 1981
iii- **MOSMAN Bridget Ashley**: born May 4, 1989

1075 MOSMAN Judith Elizabeth: (*William Mosman, Lynford Mosman, Blanche, Cyrus, Richard, Christopher, Melchior, Phillip*) was born August 22, 1960 in Lancaster, New York, daughter of William Lynford Mosman and Mary Ellen Wilson. She married Jons Peterson.

One child:

i- **PETERSON Erik**: born November 8, 1985

1076 KIDDER Thomas Alan: (*Vivian Mosman, Lynford Mosman, Blanche, Cyrus, Richard, Christopher, Melchior, Phillip*) was born May 8, 1954, son of Alan Thomas Kidder and Vivian Harriet Mosman. He married August 20, 1977, Constance Marie Schlabach.

Children:

i- **KIDDER Steven Thomas**: born March 16, 1982
ii- **KIDDER Brad Alan**: born March 13, 1984

1077 KIDDER Lori May: (*Vivian Mosman, Lynford Mosman, Blanche, Cyrus, Richard, Christopher, Melchior, Phillip*) was born February 5, 1956, daughter of Alan Thomas Kidder and Vivian Harriet Mosman. She married April 23, 1977, Brian Lee Walker. They seperated in 1987.

One child:
- i- **WALKER Brianne Mae**: born November 4, 1981

1078 KIDDER David Scott: (*Vivian Mosman, Lynford Mosman, Blanche, Cyrus, Richard, Christopher, Melchior, Phillip*) was born July 28, 1959, son of Alan Thomas Kidder and Vivian Harriet Mosman. He married May Gill.

Children:
- i- **KIDDER Christopher James**: born January 19, 1979
- ii- **KIDDER Theresa Gail**: born August 6, 1983

1079 KIDDER Richard Lynn: (*Vivian Mosman, Lynford Mosman, Blanche, Cyrus, Richard, Christopher, Melchior, Phillip*) was born October 29, 1962, son of Alan Thomas Kidder and Vivian Harriet Mosman. He married May 12, 1987, Nancy Herling.

One child:
- i- **KIDDER Richard Lynn Jr.**: born February 1, 1989

1080 KIDDER Jeffery Roy: (*Vivian Mosman, Lynford Mosman, Blanche, Cyrus, Richard, Christopher, Melchior, Phillip*) was born June 22, 1964, son of Alan Thomas Kidder and Vivian Harriet Mosman. He married December 10, 1988, Katherine Theresa Mc Kenny.

1081 MOSMAN Lindy Ann: (*Edward Mosman, Lynford Mosman, Blanche, Cyrus, Richard, Christopher, Melchior, Phillip*) was born September 6, 1954, daughter of Edward George Mosman and Winifred Ann Campbell. She married October 1, 1977, Vincent Anthony Zarcone.

Children:
- i- **ZARCONE Nicholas Anthony**: born May 25, 1981
- ii- **ZARCONE Kimberly Ann**: born December 14, 1983
- iii- **ZARCONE Valerie Marie**: born February 25, 1986

1082 MOSMAN James Edward: (*Edward Mosman, Lynford Mosman, Blanche, Cyrus, Richard, Christopher, Melchior, Phillip*) was born July 15, 1958, son of Edward George Mosman and Winifred Ann Campbell. He married (1) August 15, 1981, Denise Lee Pesch. They were divorced in 1988 and he married (2) June 30, 1990,

Jennifer Stein.

One child:
i- **MOSMAN Jessica Leigh**: born March 10, 1986

1083 LORD Mark Edmond: (*Jean Hill, Lucelia, Arthur, Charles, Anson, George, Melchior, Phillip*) was born January 31, 1954, son of Paul A. Lord and Jean Lorraine Hill. He is married. No issue.

1084 LORD Valerie Anne: (*Jean Hill, Lucelia, Arthur, Charles, Anson, George, Melchior, Phillip*) was born August 15, 1955 daughter of Paul A. Lord and Jean Lorraine Hill. She married December 21, 1950, Gerald J. Jones. No issue.

1085 BARNARD Brenda Lou: (*Anna Jean, William, Fred, William, Anson, George, Melchior, Phillip*) was born August 16, 1956 in Hornell, New York, daughter of Roland Dale Barnard and Anna Jean Bossard. She married Jonathan Ley.

One child:
i- **LEY Allen Edward**: born September 26, 1982

1086 IVES William Neil: (*Kay, William, Fred, William, Anson, George, Melchior, Phillip*) was born September 30, 1962 in Hornell, New York, son of De Neil Ives and Kay Lela Bossard. He married November 9, 1982, Patty Clancy.

Children in Hornell, New York:
i- **IVES Ammi Rachel**: born November 17, 1982
ii- **IVES Danielle Kay**: born October 1, 1987

1087 BOSSARD Heather Alma: (*William Jr., William, Fred, William, Anson, George, Melchior, Phillip*) was born February 24, 1968 in Hornell, New York, daughter of William Bossard Jr. and Carlise Balschmiter. She married July 12, 1986, Steven Kilmer.

One child born in Hornell, New York:
i- **KILMER Kyle William**: born March 18, 1988

1088 BOSSARD Steven: (*James, Merlin, Fred, William, Anson, George, Melchior, Phillip*) was born October 21, 1956, son of Bonnie Carlin and adopted by James Bossard. He married October 25, 1980, Barbara Covert. They were divorced.

One child:
i- **BOSSARD Tammy**: born March 10, 1981

1089 BOSSARD Alan: (*James, Merlin, Fred, William, Anson, George, Melchior, Phillip*) was born March 24, 1960, son of James Bossard and Bonnie Carlin. He married in 1979, Peggy Russell.

Children:
i- BOSSARD Andrew: born January 13, 1980
ii- BOSSARD Tricia Marie: born February 17, 1985

1090 BOSSARD Terri: (*James, Merlin, Fred, William, Anson, George, Melchior, Phillip*) was born June 13, 1961, daughter of James Bossard and Bonnie Carlin. She married October 3, 1981, Steven Jopp. They were divorced.

One child:
i- JOPP Cassandra: born August 24, 1982

1091 TAYLOR Cindy: (*Lois, Merlin, Fred, William, Anson, George, Melchior, Phillip*) was born July 31, 1963, daughter of Robert Taylor and Lois Bossard. She married September 15, 1986, Thomas Simmons. They were divorced. No issue.

1092 BOSSARD Tammi Lynn: (*Kenneth Jr., Kenneth, Fred, William, Anson, George, Melchior, Phillip*) was born April 21, 1969 in Jacksonville, North Carolina, daughter of Kenneth Bossard Jr. and Sylvia Yurganious. She married February 18, 1989, Marvin Wayne Edge.

1093 TYCHI Cinthia Gail: (*Irene, Ruth, Roy, William, Anson, George, Melchior, Phillip*) was born November 6, 1952 in Hornell, New York, daughter of Nicholas Tychi and Irene Joyce Kame. She married July 14, 1973, Michael Hines born May 31, 1945.

One child:
i- HINES Jamie Ann: born June 24, 1981

1094 TYCHI Linda Ann: (*Irene, Ruth, Roy, William, Anson, George, Melchior, Phillip*) was born February 24, 1955 in Hornell, New York, daughter of Nicholas Tychi and Irene Joyce Kame. She married November 16, 1974, Harold Wyant born July 15, 1956. They were divorced.

Children:
i- WYANT Bridget Ruth: born September 24, 1973
ii- WYANT Jennifer: born September 5, 1979

1095 TYCHI Randy Stephen: (*Irene, Ruth, Roy, William, Anson, George, Melchior,*

Phillip) was born April 5, 1954 in Hornell, New York, son of Nicholas Tychi and Irene Joyce Kame. He married October 25, 1975 in Hornell, Judy Wyant born April 29, 1957.

Children born in Hornell, New York:
i- **TYCHI Andy Steven**: born August 13, 1977
ii- **TYCHI Amy**: born January 31, 1980

1096 TYCHI Patti Kim: (*Irene, Ruth, Roy, William, Anson, George, Melchior, Phillip*) was born December 25, 1957 in Hornell, New York, daughter of Nicholas Tychi and Irene Joyce Kame. She married July 19, 1975 in Hornell, James Edward Towner born March 18, 1953. They were divorced.

Children:
i- **TOWNER Kelly Ann**: born January 26, 1978
ii- **TOWNER Lucas**: born June 13, 1983

1097 TYCHI Karen Elaine: (*Irene, Ruth, Roy, William, Anson, George, Melchior, Phillip*) was born December 6, 1959 in Hornell, New York, daughter of Nicholas Tychi and Irene Joyce Kame. She married September 1, 1984, Joseph Carbone born August 5, 1952 in Hornell. No issue.

1098 KAME Tracy Annette: (*Lawrence Kame, Ruth, Roy, William, Anson, George, Melchior, Phillip*) was born July 23, 1961 in Hornell, New York, daughter of Lawrence Edward Kame and Muriel Norton. She married May 5, 1988, Donald Wagoner born May 21, 1962.

One child:
i- **WAGONER Caitlin Aileen**: born August 17, 1987

1099 KAME Victoria Lee: (*Vincent Kame, Ruth, Roy, William, Anson, George, Melchior, Phillip*) was born March 3, 1961 in Hornell, New York, daughter of Vincent Kame and Patricia Ann Mc Daniel. She married April 11, 1987, Joseph Morabita.

Children:
i- **MORABITO Joseph Jr.**: born May 8, 1988
ii- **MORABITO Vincent**: born September 15, 1989

1100 KAME Vincent Dale Jr.: (*Vincent Kame, Ruth, Roy, William, Anson, George, Melchior, Phillip*) was born April 24, 1963 in Hornell, New York, son of Vincent Dale Kame Sr. and Patricia Ann Mc Daniel. He married October 9, 1988 in Hornell, New York, Joan Elizabeth Olshefski.

1101 DRESSER Wendy Sue: (*Betty Kame, Ruth, Roy, William, Anson, George, Melchior, Phillip*) was born April 8, 1964 in Hornell, New York, daughter of Richard Dresser and Betty Corinne Kame. She married April 8, 1989, Mark Rectenwald born April 24, 1965.

One child:
- i- **RECTENWALD Justin Mark**: born April 9, 1990

1102 BOSSARD Sharri Lynn: (*Charles, Charles, Anson, Fred, Anson, George, Melchior, Phillip*) was born August 16, 1965 in Cortland, New York, daughter of Charles F. Bossard and Linda Ann Evener. She married February 24, 1984, Collin Rockwell.

Children:
- i- **ROCKWELL Beth Ann**: born May 19, 1983
- ii- **ROCKWELL Heather**: born June 24, 1985
- iii- **ROCKWELL Lisa**: born May 23, 1988

1103 HUFFSMITH Cindy Marie: (*Philip Huffsmith, George Huffsmith, William Huffsmith, George Huffsmith, Hanna, Peter, Melchior, Phillip*) was born February 19, 1971, daughter of Philip Lloyd Huffsmith and Linda Cooke. She married Matthew Stanley.

1104 BARTHOLOMEW John Dale: (*John Bartholomew, William Bartholomew, Lillie, Charles, Melchior, Peter, Melchior, Phillip*) was born March 19, 1941 in Monroe Co., Pennsylvania, son of John Elbert Bartholomew and Emma Mabel Mosteller. He married Elizabeth Ann Penney born October 13, 1936.

Children:
- i- **BARTHOLOMEW Walter Dale**: (twin) born March 17, 1970
- ii- **BARTHOLOMEW Catherine Ann**: (twin) born March 17, 1970

1105 BARTHOLOMEW Clark Owen: (*John Bartholomew, William Bartholomew, Lillie, Charles, Melchior, Peter, Melchior, Phillip*) was born September 3, 1944, son of John Elbert Bartholomew and Emma Mabel Mosteller. He married (1) Sharron Marie Werkhiser and (2) Dorothy Booth, born March 2, 1947.

Children:
- 1181 i- **BARTHOLOMEW Clark Owen Jr.**: born November 13, 1964
- ii- **BARTHOLOMEW Jeffri Scott**: born November 22, 1967
- iii- **BARTHOLOMEW Staci Nicole**: born March 12, 1972

1106 BURROWS Mary Ann: (*Ashton Burrows. Bessie Hartman, Mary Catherine,*

James, Melchior, Peter, Melchior, Phillip) was born April 6, 1947, daughter of Ashton H. Burrows and Esther Barkman. She married Gregory Warley born January 14, 1947.

Children:
i- WARLEY Sherry Ann: born December 22, 1964
ii- WARLEY Anthony Richard: born February 10, 1966
iii- WARLEY Laura Ann: born Feruary 3, 1967

1107 BURROWS Janice Elaine: (*James Burrows, Bessie Hartman, Mary Catherine, James, Melchior, Peter, Melchior, Phillip*) was born September 29, 1947, daughter of James E. Burrows and Ruth Elizabeth Taylor. She married (1) John Mizalski and (2) Donald E. Ellis born April 6, 1945.

1108 BURROWS Ethel Ann: (*Robert Burrows, Bessie Hartman, Mary Catherine, James, Melchior, Peter, Melchior, Phillip*) was born December 26, 1946, daughter of Robert Marlin Burrows and Ethel Ann Lanternman. She married Curtis V. Groenthal born June 3, 1944.

Child:
i- GROENTHAL Eric Robert: born June 12, 1980

1109 BURROWS Lillian Lorraine: (*Robert Burrows, Bessie Hartman, Mary Catherine, James, Melchior, Peter, Melchior, Phillip*) was born January 3, 1951, daughter of Robert Marlin Burrows and Ethel Ann Lanternman. She married (1) James R. Hahn born October 22, 1946 and (2) Kenneth Carson. She married (3) Steven C. Wicks born July 25, 1950. They are presently living in Candensis, Monroe, Co. Pennsylvania.

Child of first marriage:
i- HAHN James R. Jr.: born February 2, 1968
Children of third marriage:
ii- WICKS Laura Beth: born January 31, 1979
iii- WICKS Aaron Paige: born March 25, 1980

1110 BURROWS Ronald Ayer: (*Jacob Burrows, Bessie Hartman, Mary Catherine, James, Melchior, Peter, Melchior, Phillip*) was born December 12, 1951, son of Jacob Alexander Burrows and Charlotte Webb. He married Victoria Lynn (Kurzinski) Mc Donald born January 1, 1956.

Child:
i- BURROWS Alyse Marie: born August 22, 1981

1111 BURROWS Wayne Ashton: (*Jacob Burrows, Bessie Hartman, Mary Catherine, James, Melchior, Peter, Melchior, Phillip*) was born June 14, 1954, son of Jacob Alexander Burrows and Charlotte Webb. He married Debra Sue Richard born January 3, 1956.

Children:
i- BURROWS Ashton Lee: born April 12, 1981
ii- BURROWS Julie Ann: born February 7, 1983

1112 HAWK John William: (*Marguerite Mackes, John Mackes, Nettie Haney, Anna, Melchior, Peter, Melchior, Phillip*) was born March 18, 1940, son of Burnice Hawk and Marguerite Arline Mackes. He married Marion Schreck born January 9, 1945.

Children:
i- HAWK William John: born October 1, 1965
ii- HAWK Jannifer Lynn: born June 3, 1971

1113 LEAP Sandra Ann: (*Lorraine Hennion, Violet Lesh, Minnie Haney, Anna, Melchior, Peter, Melchior, Phillip*) was born July 12, 1945 in Hamilton Township, Pennsylvania, daughter of William Leap and Lorraine Hennion. She married Ralph Steven Meissee II. They are presently living in Sciota, Pennsylvania.

Children:
i- MEISSEE Ralph Stephen III: born January 16, 1967
ii- MEISSEE Heather Lynn: born February 25, 1970
iii- MEISSEE Danielle Claudette: born May 29, 1971

1114 LEAP William Earl Jr.: (*Lorraine Hennion, Violet Lesh, Minnie Haney, Anna, Melchior, Peter, Melchior, Phillip*) was born November 17, 1954 in Hamilton Township, Pennsylvania, son of William Earl Leap and Lorraine Hennion. He married Amy (unknown maiden name). They are presently living in Sciota, Pennsylvania.

1115 LEAP Cindy Lou: (*Lorraine Hennion, Violet Lesh, Minnie Haney, Anna, Melchior, Peter, Melchior, Phillip*) was born March 12, 1957 in Hamilton Township, Pennsylvania, daughter of William Earl Leap and Lorraine Hennion. She married Donald Paul Bird. They are presently living in Stroudsburg.

1116 LEAP Scott Matthew: (*Lorraine Hennion, Violet Lesh, Minnie Haney, Anna, Melchior, Peter, Melchior, Phillip*) was born April 14, 1965, in Hamilton Township, son of William Earl Leap and Violet Hennion. They are presently living in Sciota, Pennsylvania.

1117 HENNION Brenda: (*Dayton Hennion, Violet Lesh, Minnie Haney, Anna, Melchior, Peter, Melchior, Phillip*) was born in Monroe, Co., Pennsylvania, daughter of Dayton and Gertrude Hennion. She married Scott Bush. They have three children.

1118 HENNION Trudi: (*Dayton Hennion, Violet Lesh, Minnie Haney, Anna, Melchior, Peter, Melchior, Phillip*) was born in Monroe, Co., Pennsylvania, daughter of Dayton and Gertrude Hennion. She was married twice and has three children.

1119 TISCHLER Frederick James III: (*Susan Bellis, Sarah Bartholomew, Martha, Samuel, Jacob, Peter, Melchior, Phillip*) was born September 18, 1948, son of Frederick Tischler and Susan Bellis. He was married and divorced. No issue.

1120 TISCHLER John Jeffrey: (*Susan Bellis, Sarah Bartholomew, Martha, Samuel, Jacob, Peter, Melchior, Phillip*) was born June 27, 1951, son of Frederick Tischler and Susan Bellis. He married Susan Vagvolgi.

Child:
i- **TISCHLER Jessica Sarah Margaret:** born March 5, 1983

1121 TISCHLER Sally: (*Susan Bellis, Sarah Bartholomew, Martha, Samuel, Jacob, Peter, Melchior, Phillip*) was born March 11, 1955. daughter of Frederick Tischler and Susan Bellis. She married Felix Osorio.

Children:
i- **OSORIO Jonathan:** born June 24, 1985
ii- **OSORIO Samantha:** born September 4, 1986

1122 REESE Deborah Jean: (*Richard Reese, Elizabeth, Frederick, Samuel, Jacob, Peter, Melchior, Phillip*) was born June 7, 1960 in Delaware Co., Pennsylvania, daughter of Richard W. Reese and Sandra L. Melton. She married June 23, 1984, Ted Clark. No issue.

1123 REESE Susan Diane: (*Richard Reese, Elizabeth, Frederick, Samuel, Jacob, Peter, Melchior, Phillip*) was born September 16, 1963 in Delaware Co., Pennsylvania, daughter of Richard W. Reese and Sandra L. Melton. She married August 28, 1989, Paul Pittman.

1124 REESE Catherine Ann: (*Richard Reese, Elizabeth, Frederick, Samuel, Jacob, Peter, Melchior, Phillip*) was born March 19, 1966 in Delaware Co., Pennsylvania, daughter of Richard W. Reese and Sandra L. Melton. She married July 3, 1988,

Rex Bornhold.

1125 HUNZIKER William Mc Kee: (*Joan Du Bois, Roberta, Robert, Samuel, Jacob, Peter, Melchior, Phillip*) was born May 23, 1958 in New York City, son of Robert Hunziker and Joan Du Bois. He married October 21, 1989, Theresa Buckley born April 8, 1961. daughter of Edward and Rene Buckley. They are presently living in Westfield, New Jersey.

1126 MC KINNEY Colleen Dubois: (*Susan Du Bois, Roberta, Robert, Samuel, Jacob, Peter, Melchior, Phillip*) was born December 17, 1959 in Washington, D. C., daughter of Brian Mc Kinney and Susan Du Bois. She married August 1, 1987, Stuart Ralston born January 14, 1960, in Portland, Oregon. They are presently living in Phoenix, Arizona.

1127 BOSSARD Barbara Jean: (*Sherlyn, Carman, Curvin, Edwin, Jacob, Peter, Melchior, Phillip*) was born February 20, 1945 in Santa Monica, California, daughter of Sherlyn Lamont Bossard and Bonnie Jean Tubbs. She married August 14, 1966 in Redondo Beach, California, William Simpson. They are presently living in Redondo Beach.

Children:

i- **SIMPSON William Thomas**: born January 17, 1967 in Alexandria, Virginia

ii- **SIMPSON Barbara Jo**: born December 22, 1968

1128 BOSSARD Beverly Jo: (*Sherlyn, Carman, Curvin, Edwin, Jacob, Peter, Melchior, Phillip*) was born October 30, 1950 in Santa Monica, California, daughter of Sherlyn Lamont Bossard and Bonnie Jean Tubbs. She married December 6, 1975 in Redondo Beach, California, John Sweet born August 13, 1953 in Long Beach, California, son of Russell Foster Sweet and Helen Marie Deeble. They are presently living in Los Angeles, California.

Children:

i- **SWEET Sara Elizabeth**: born August 19, 1980

ii- **SWEET Andrew Clark**: born May 14, 1984

1129 BOSSARD Sherlyn Lamont Jr.: (*Sherlyn, Carman, Curvin, Edwin, Jacob, Peter, Melchior, Phillip*) was born December 14, 1952 in Santa Monica, California, son of Sherlyn Lamont Bossard Sr. and Bonnie Jean Tubbs. He married August 2, 1987 in Seattle, Washington, Rebecca Ann Laing born November 23, 1965, daughter of Robert Hubert Laing and Patricia Maher. They are presently living in Seattle.

1130 BOSSARD Bryan Floyd: (*Sherlyn, Carman, Curvin, Edwin, Jacob, Peter, Melchior, Phillip*) was born May 26, 1955 in Santa Monica, California, son of Sherlyn Lamont Bossard and Bonnie Jean Tubbs He married January 7, 1978 in Redondo Beach, California, Janet Anderson.

Child born in Vista, California:
i- BOSSARD Andria Lee: born June 10, 1978

1131 BOSSARD Julie: (*Floyd, Calvin, Curvin, Edwin, Jacob, Peter, Melchior, Phillip*) was born April 24, 1952 in Butte, Montana, daughter of Floyd C. Bossard and Margaret Nevin. She married Jeff Le Fever and they are presently living in Butte.

Children:
i- LE FEVER Jessica: born November 4, 1979
ii- LE FEVER Jocelyn: born August 15, 1982

1132 BOSSARD Janice: (*Floyd, Calvin, Curvin, Edwin, Jacob, Peter, Melchior, Phillip*) was born August 23, 1953 in Butte, Montana, daughter of Floyd C. Bossard and Margaret Nevin. She married Jack Elliot and they are presently living in Las Vegas, Nevada.

Children:
i- ELLIOT Scott: born May 23, 1984
ii- ELLIOT Sean: born August 18, 1986

1133 BOSSARD Brian: (*Floyd, Calvin, Curvin, Edwin, Jacob, Peter, Melchior, Phillip*) was born July 27, 1958 in Butte, Montana, son of Floyd C. Bossard and Margaret Nevin. He married Terri Keller and they are presently living in Butte.

Child:
i- BOSSARD Ryan Andrew: born February 8, 1990

1134 BOSSARD Patti: (*Richard, Calvin, Curvin, Edwin, Jacob, Peter, Melchior, Phillip*) was born June 24, 1956 in Montana. daughter of Richard and Margaret Bossard. She married Douglas Stevens born March 15, 1956.

1135 LE CLAIRE Gregory: (*Vera Jean, Calvin, Curvin, Edwin, Jacob, Peter, Melchior, Phillip*) was born December 7, 1956, son of Lawrence Le Claire and Vera Jean Bossard. He married Susan (unknown maiden name) born June 1, 1959.

Child:
i- LE CLAIRE Elizabeth: born October 31, 1982

1136 LE CLAIRE Diane: (*Vera Jean, Calvin, Curvin, Edwin, Jacob, Peter, Melchior, Phillip*) was born August 11, 1958, daughter of Lawrence Le Claire and Vera Jean Bossard. She married Rod Kelly born February 3, 1955.

1137 LE CLAIRE Mark: (*Vera Jean, Calvin, Curvin, Edwin, Jacob, Peter, Melchior, Phillip*) was born September 29, 1962, son of Lawrence Le Claire and Vera Jean Bossard. He married Debbie Caserma, born November 22, 1965.

Child:

i- **LE CLAIRE Daniel**: born May 1, 1982

1138 BOSSARD Cregg Allyn: (*Gerald, Calvin, Curvin, Edwin, Jacob, Peter, Melchior, Phillip*) was born October 22, 1953, in Butte, Montana, son of Gerald Wayne Bossard and Caroline Cregg. He married August 3, 1974, Charlene Marie Rae born May 26, 1953, daughter of Robert and Alice Rae. They are presently living in Butte, Montana.

Children:

i- **BOSSARD Mathew Cregg**: born September 19, 1978
ii- **BOSSARD Nathan Andrew**: born May 28, 1980
iii- **BOSSARD Gina Marie**: born August 27, 1984

1139 BOSSARD Lisa Marie: (*Gerald, Calvin, Curvin, Edwin, Jacob, Peter, Melchior, Phillip*) was born February 15, 1959 in Butte, Montana, daughter of Gerald Wayne Bossard and Caroline Cregg. She married April 4, 1987 in Tucson, Arizona, Thomas Funk born August 1958. They are presently living in Houston, Texas. No issue.

1140 BOSSARD Brenda Louise: (*Gerald, Calvin, Curvin, Edwin, Jacob, Peter, Melchior, Phillip*) was born May 20, 1960 in Anaconda, Montana, daughter of Gerald Wayne Bossard and Caroline Cregg. She married January 30, 1988 in Tucson, Arizona, Gregory Charles Waddell born October 31, 1959. They are presently living in Tucson.

One child:

i- **WADDELL Brianna Louise**: born August 5, 1988

1141 BAXTER Terry K.: (*Hayden Baxter, Gladys, Curvin, Edwin, Jacob, Peter, Melchior, Phillip*) was born August 27, 1948 in Santa Rosa, California, daughter of Hayden Ardell Baxter and Jean Price. She married in 1969, James Hatcher. They are divorced. No issue.

1142 GARDNER Vicki June: (*Marilee Baxter, Gladys, Curvin, Edwin, Jacob, Peter, Melchior*) was born October 10, 1950 in Bluffton, Indiana, daughter of Marvin Homer Gardner and Marilee Baxter. She married (1) June 1970, John Lewis Wilson born December 10, 1947. She married (2) Robert Bordner born October 2, 1930. They are presently living in Scottsburg, Indianna. No issue.

1143 GARDNER Mark Allen: (*Marilee Baxter, Gladys, Curvin, Edwin, Jacob, Peter, Melchior, Phillip*) was born July 22, 1952 in Seymour, Indiana, son of Marvin Homer Gardner and Marilee Baxter. He married April 4, 1975, Portra Doak born April 28, 1952 in Kokomo, Indiana. They are presently living in Austin, Indiana.

Children:
i- **GARDNER Amy Elizabeth:** born April 28, 1976
ii- **GARDNER Seth Adam:** born November 20, 1980
iii- **GARDNER Alana Eden:** August 8, 1987

1144 MILLER Connie J.: (*Marjean Noll, Vera, Curvin, Edwin, Jacob, Peter, Melchior, Phillip*) was born February 13, 1944 in Ida Grove, Iowa, daughter of Ralph Miller and Marjean Noll. She married (1) James Hausman, born June 21, 1943. She married (2) Wes Wade.

Children of first marriage:
1182 i- **HAUSMAN David:** born January 20, 1963
ii- **HAUSMAN Jodi Lynn:** born March 11, 1966

1145 MILLER Candas: (*Marjean Noll, Vera, Curvin, Edwin, Jacob, Peter, Melchior, Phillip*) was born April 18, 1949 in Ida Grove, Iowa, daughter of Ralph Miller and Marjean Noll. She married (1) Ron Spots and (2) Thomas Marsicek, born February 28, 1938. They are presently living in Omaha, Nebraska.

Child of first marriage:
i- **SPOTS Wendy:** born June 25, 1967
Children of second marriage:
ii- **MARSICEK Kimberly:** born August 4, 1977
iii- **MARSICEK Bradley:** born April 23, 1981

1146 NOLL Nancy: (*Charles Noll, Vera, Curvin, Edwin, Jacob, Peter, Melchior, Phillip*) was born (unknown date), daughter of Charles and Marcella Noll. She married _____ Meyer and they are presently living in Casper, Wyoming.

Children:
i- **MEYER Brenda:**
ii- **MEYER Todd:**

1147 NOLL Shirley: (*Charles Noll, Vera, Curvin, Edwin, Jacob, Peter, Melchior, Phillip*) was born (unknown date), daughter of Charles and Marcella Noll. She married James Motto and they are presently living in Englewood, Colorado.

1148 NOLL Lynette: (*Charles Noll, Vera, Curvin, Edwin, Jacob, Peter, Melchior, Phillip*) was born (unknown date), daughter of Charles and Marcella Noll. She married Kenneth Schwenn and they are presently living in Denison, Iowa.

Children:
- **i- SCHWENN Jessica**:
- **ii- SCHWENN Cassandra**:

1149 TRAPP David Brian: (*Lois, Cecil, Curvin, Edwin, Jacob, Peter, Melchior, Phillip*) was born January 31, 1951 in Kansas City, Missouri, son of John O. Trapp and Lois Ann Bossard. He married August 8, 1983, Virginia Gunion Slusher. They are presently living in Kansas City.

1150 TRAPP Sharon Elizabeth: (*Lois, Cecil, Curvin, Edwin, Jacob, Peter, Melchior, Phillip*) was born November 9, 1955 in Abilene, Kansas, daughter of John O. Trapp and Lois Ann Bossard. She married September 19, 1981, Carl Elmer Jenkins born March 28, 1948 in Wichita, Kansas. They are presently living in Wichita.

1151 WOLF William Bradley: (*Donna, Cecil, Curvin, Edwin, Jacob, Peter, Melchior, Phillip*) was born March 9, 1955 in Kansas City, Missouri, son of William C. Wolf and Donna Lee Bossard. He married June 4, 1977, Jan Krieghauser born April 23, 1954. They are presently living in Strongsville, Ohio.

Children:
- **i- WOLF Andrew Rourke**: born November 23, 1981
- **ii- WOLF Danielle Lee**: born July 6, 1985

1152 WOLF Jeffrey Dillon: (*Donna, Cecil, Curvin, Edwin, Jacob, Peter, Melchior, Phillip*) was born July 10, 1958 in St. Joseph, Missouri, son of William C. Wolf and Donna Lee Bossard. He married August 3, 1980, Patricia Gassman born January 1, 1956, in Kansas City, Missouri. They are presently living in Plattsburg, Missouri.

1153 WOLF Whitney Kimble: (*Donna, Cecil, Curvin, Edwin, Jacob, Peter, Melchior, Phillip*) was born November 4, 1962 in St. Joseph, Missouri, son of William C. Wolf and Donna Lee Bossard. He married February 21, 1986, Sherry Ann Heldstab born March 26, 1963.

1154 BOSSARD Thomas: (*Murriel, Murriel, Curvin, Edwin, Jacob, Peter, Melchior, Phillip*) was born in Modesto, California, son of Murriel and Sandy Bossard. Wife's name unknown.

Children:
i- BOSSARD William: born May 24, 1988
ii- BOSSARD Casey: born February 25, 1989

1155 BOSSARD Wendy: (*Murriel, Murriel, Curvin, Edwin, Jacob, Peter, Melchior, Phillip*) was born in Modesto, California, daughter of Murriel and Sandy Bossard. She married ______ Massengill.

Children:
i- MASSENGILL Laura: born April 15, 1982
ii- MASSENGILL Rhonda: born September 17, 1983
iii- MASSENGILL Tina: born July 10, 1985

1156 BOSSARD James: (*Murriel, Murriel, Curvin, Edwin, Jacob, Peter, Melchior, Phillip*) was born in Modesto, California, son of Murriel and Sandy Bossard. He married Julie, (unknown maiden name). No further records.

1157 BOSSARD Carrie: (*Murriel, Murriel, Curvin, Edwin, Jacob, Peter, Melchior, Phillip*) was born in Modesto, California, daughter of Murriel and Sandy Bossard. She married ______ Emery. No further records.

Children:
i- EMERY Amber: born October 23, 1986

1158 BOSSARD Cindy Rae: (*Carl. Murriel, Curvin, Edwin, Jacob, Peter, Melchior, Phillip*) was born December 13, 1968 in Great Fall, Montana, daughter of Carl Bossard and Donna Poil.

One child:
i- BOSSARD Tyson: born April 30, 1989

1159 SPRACKLEN Stephen Guy: (*Maxine Clark, Marcelle, Curvin, Edwin, Jacob, Peter, Melchior, Phillip*) was born December 19, 1951 in Chico, California, son of Guy E. Spracklen and Maxine Lavonne Clark. He married (1) Camille Fuentes born January 6, 1956. He married (2) October 6, 1984, Mary Scelzi born September 5, 1954. They are presently living in Fresno, California.

Child of first marriage:
i- SPRACKLEN Nathan Ian: born January 12, 1980

Children of second marriage:
ii- SPRACKLEN Andrew Jordan: born June 22, 1987
iii- SPRACKLEN Kaci Danielle: born July 7, 1989

1160 SPRACKLEN Karen: (*Maxine Clark, Marcelle, Curvin, Edwin, Jacob, Peter, Melchior, Phillip*) was born March 26, 1957 in Santa Paula, California, daughter of Guy E. Spracklen and Maxine Lavonne Clark. She married November 19, 1983, Peter Alan Croft born July 5, 1957 in Wellington, New Zealand. They are presently living in Huntington Beach, California.

Children:
i- CROFT Timothy Clark: born May 30, 1986
ii- CROFT Jonathan Alan: born February 21, 1988

1161 SPRACKLEN Kristin Ann: (*Maxine Clark, Marcelle, Curvin, Edwin, Jacob, Peter, Melchior, Phillip*) was born October 2, 1959 in Santa Paula, California, daughter of Guy E. Spracklen and Maxine Lavonne Clark. She married June 27, 1981, Stephen Sistler born December 12, 1960, in Rockford, Illinois. They are presently living in Bakersfield, California.

Children:
i- SISTLER Mathew Stephen: born September 6, 1982
ii- SISTLER Michele Lee: born June 25, 1986

1162 DENNIS Karen: (*Clifford Dennis, Harold Dennis, Grace Carner, Alice, Joseph, Peter, Melchior, Phillip*) was born May 15, 1968 in Hamilton Township, Pennsylvania, daughter of Clifford Dennis and Joan Kresge. She married August 22, 1982, John Saunders born July 14, 1958.

One child:
i- SAUNDERS Daniel: born July 27, 1988

1163 DENNIS Tracy: (*Clifford Dennis, Harold Dennis, Grace Carner, Alice, Joseph, Peter, Melchior, Phillip*) was born November 9, 1965 in Hamilton Township, Pennsylvania, daughter of Clifford Dennis and Joan Kresge. She married December 30, 1989, David Aglio.

1164 DENNIS Diane: (*John Dennis, Harold Dennis, Grace Carner, Alice, Joseph, Peter, Melchior, Phillip*) was born July 11, 1961, daughter of John H. Dennis and Verna Kay Blakeslee. She married Ralph Romepert.

Children:
i- ROMEPERT Bryn: born March 31, 1986

ii- **ROMEPERT Ralph Jr.**: born April 24, 1987

1165 DENNIS Jill: (*John Dennis, Harold Dennis, Grace Carmer, Alice, Joseph, Peter, Melchior, Phillip*) was born December 5, 1963 in Hamilton Township, Pennsylvania, daughter of John H. Dennis and Verna Kay Blakeslee. She married September 1989, James Spinola.

1166 LEONARD Elizabeth: (*Joan Hester, Allison Hester, Laura Carmer, Alice, Joseph, Peter, Melchior, Phillip*) was born April 2, 1965 in Stroudsburg, Pennsylvania, daughter of Thomas Leonard and Joan Carol Hester. She married Steven Hauser. They were divorced. No issue.

CHAPTER 10

TENTH GENERATION

1167 MURPHY Kenneth Albert: (*Elaine Bonser, Lloyd Bonser, Florence Miller, Diana Altemose, Susannah Weiss, Felix Weiss, Eva Catherine, Melchior, Phillip*) was born August 29, 1948 in Monroe Co., Pennsylvania, son of Albert Lewis Murphy and Elaine Florence Bonser. He married Donna Brown born August 4, 1950, daughter of James and Muriel Brown.

Children:
- i- **MURPHY Ericka L.**: born August 25, 1971
- ii- **MURPHY Andrea L.**: born December 4, 1976

1168 MURPHY Lisa Ann Florence: (*Elaine Bonser, Lloyd Bonser, Florence Miller, Diana Altemose, Susannah Weiss, Felix Weiss, Eva Catherine, Melchior, Phillip*) was born September 6, 1958 in Monroe Co., Pennsylvania, daughter of Lewis Albert Murphy and Elaine Florence Bonser. She married September 12, 1981, David Douglas Zinkler born December 19, 1957, son of Leon Zinkler and Barbara Horn.

Children:
- i- **ZINKLER Kyle David**: born March 16, 1987
- ii- **ZINKLER Kristin Lee**: born May 29, 1989

1169 ALTEMUS Linda: (*Catherine Bonser, Lloyd Bonser, Florence Miller, Diana Altemose, Susannah Weiss, Felix Weiss, Eva Catherine, Melchior, Phillip*) was born February 29, 1948 in Monroe Co., Pennsylvania, daughter of Leon Herbert Altemus and Catherine Mae Bonser. She married August 10, 1968, Jeffrey Hinton born November 11, 1945.

Children:
- i- **HINTON Craig**: born September 9, 1972
- ii- **HINTON Janine**: born March 3, 1975
- iii- **HINTON Timothy**: born May 29, 1980

1170 ALTEMUS Wanda: (*Catherine Bonser, Lloyd Bonser, Florence Miller, Diana Altemose, Susannah Weiss, Felix Weiss, Eva Catherine, Melchior, Phillip*) was born August 14, 1950 in Monroe Co., Pennsylvania, daughter of Leon Herbert Altemus and Catherine Mae Bonser. She married May 25, 1974, Terry Hunter born March 20, 1947.

Children:
- i- **HUNTER Matthew**: born August 25, 1978
- ii- **HUNTER Christopher**: born July 24, 1982

1171 ALTEMUS Cindy: (*Catherine Bonser, Lloyd Bonser, Florence Miller, Diana Altemose, Susannah Weiss, Felix Weiss, Eva Catherine, Melchior, Phillip*) was born January 10, 1958 in Monroe Co., Pennsylvania, daughter of Leon Herbert Altemus and Catherine Mae Bonser. She married October 9, 1976, Kim (unknown last name) born January 24, 1953. No issue.

1172 ALTEMUS Holly: (*Catherine Bonser, Lloyd Bonser, Florence Miller, Diana Altemose, Susannah Weiss, Felix Weiss, Eva Catherine, Melchior, Phillip*) was born December 27, 1963 in Monroe Co., Pennsylvania, daughter of Leon Herbert Altemus and Catherine Mae Bonser. She married September 6, 1986, William Schneebeli born September 1, 1962.

Children:
- i- **SCHNEEBELI Joshua**: born February 28, 1982
- ii- **SCHNEEBELI Rachel**: born June 30, 1988

1173 BONSER James Robert: (*Robert Bonser, Lloyd Bonser, Florence Miller, Diana Altemose, Susannah Weiss, Felix Weiss, Eva Catherine, Melchior, Phillip*) was born October 21, 1962 in Monroe Co., Pennsylvania, adopted son of Robert Lester Bonser and Nancy Jane Brensinger. He married October 15, 1983, Christine Evans born April 26, 1962, daughter of Andrew Evans and Anna Gatsche.

Children:
- i- **BONSER James Robert**: born July 26, 1984
- ii- **BONSER Jeremy Lee**: born February 19, 1988

1174 BONSER Jane Ann: (*Robert Bonser, Lloyd Bonser, Florence Miller, Diana Altemose, Susannah Weiss, Felix Weiss, Eva Catherine, Melchior, Phillip*) was born November 9, 1965 in Monroe Co., Pennsylvania, adopted daughter of Robert Lester Bonser and Nancy Jean Brensinger. She married August 16, 1986, Timothy Ott born May 6, 1964, son of Howard and Kathleen Ott. No issue.

1175 BONSER Leroy Stanley II: (*Leroy Bonser, Lloyd Bonser, Florence Miller, Diana Altemose, Susannah Weiss, Felix Weiss, Eva Catherine, Melchior, Phillip*) was born August 7, 1959 in Monroe Co., Pennsylvania, son of Leroy Bonser and Mabel Ann Burger. He married July 14, 1979, Wanda Lynn Snyder born December 27, 1960, daughter of Willard Snyder and Barbara Werkhiser.

Children:

i- **BONSER Leroy Stanley III**: born October 8, 1980
ii- **BONSER Le Ette Nicole**: born May 6, 1984
iii- **BONSER Kyle Matthew**: born July 2, 1988

1176 BONSER Lamont Solomon: (*Leroy Bonser, Lloyd Bonser, Florence Miller, Diana Altemose, Susannah Weiss, Felix Weiss, Eva Catherine, Melchior, Phillip*) was born May 14, 1962 in Monroe Co., Pennsylvania, son of Leroy Bonser and Mabel Ann Burger. He married October 2, 1985, Diane Elizabeth Everett born February 4, 1963, daughter of William and Jean Everett. No issue.

1177 BONSER Barry Russell: (*Janet Bonser, Mitchell Bonser, Florence Miller, Diana Altemose, Susannah Weiss, Felix Weiss, Eva Catherine, Melchior, Phillip*) was born September 18, 1952 in Bangor, Pennsylvania, son of Janet Bonser. He married September 17, 1975, Cathy Gene Walck born May 26, 1950, daughter of George Washington Walck and Thelma Beatrice Drake. No issue.

1178 NICEFORO Philip Nicholas: (*Janet Bonser, Mitchell Bonser, Florence Miller, Diana Altemose, Susannah Weiss, Felix Weiss, Eva Catherine, Melchior, Phillip*) was born March 12, 1958, son of Phillip Niceforo and Janet Bonser. He married April 1, 1987, Edna Mae Sutton born March 16, 1956, daughter of Charles Sutton and Arlene Warmen. They are presently living in Bangor, Pennsylvania.

One child:
i- **NICEFORO Tabitha Lynn**: born August 13, 1987

1179 NICEFORO Roxanne Margaret: (*Janet Bonser, Mitchell Bonser, Flornece Miller, Diana Altemose, Susannah Weiss, Felix Weiss, Eva Catherine, Melchior, Phillip*) was born January 4, 1964, daughter of Phillip Niceforo and Janet Bonser. She married August 25, 1984 Leonard Joseph Riotto III, born February 6, 1961, son of Leonard Joseph Riotto and Joan Reilly.

One child:
i- **RIOTTO Nicole Lynn**: born January 30, 1985

1180 BONSER Laura Michelle: (*Richard Bonser, Mitchell Bonser, Florence Miller, Diana Altemose, Susannah Weiss, Felix Weiss, Eva Catherine, Melchior, Phillip*) was born April 27, 1968, daughter of Richard Bonser and Sue Ann Masters. She married July 1, 1989, Robert Terrence Mueller born September 1, 1966, son of Robert G. Mueller and Minnie Elizabeth Mahan.

1181 BARTHOLOMEW Clark Owen Jr.: (*John E. Bartholomew, William Bartholomew, Lillie, Charles, Melchior, Peter, Melchior, Phillip*) was born November

13, 1964 in Hamilton Township, Pennsylvania, son of John Elbert Bartholomew and Emma Mabel Mosteller. He married Anita Cortwright.

One child:

i- BARTHOLOMEW Amanda Marie: born August 11, 1983

1182 HAUSMAN David: (*Connie Miller, Vera Jean Bossard, Curvin, Edwin, Jacob, Peter, Melchior, Phillip*) was born January 20, 1963 in Ida Grove, Iowa, son of James Hausman and Connie J. Miller. His wife's name unknown.

One child:

i- HAUSMAN Angela:

SPOUSES

Other Heritage Books by Mary Smith Jackson:

Bossards, Bozards, and Buzzards: The Descendants of Phillip Bossard, Who Landed in Philadelphia, September 30, 1740 and Settled in Hamilton Township, Pennsylvania

Marriages and Deaths from Tompkins County, New York Newspapers

Our Smith Family: Descendants of Jasper Smith of Maidenhead, New Jersey, New York and Pennsylvania and Beyond
Mary Smith Jackson and Marsha Smith

Other Heritage Books by Mary Smith Jackson and Edward F. Jackson:

1850 Census for the Town of Howard, Steuben County, New York, and Genealogical Data on the Families Who Lived There

Death Notices from Steuben County, New York Newspapers, 1797–1884

Death Notices from Washington County, New York Newspapers, 1799–1880

Marriage and Death Notices from Schuyler County, New York Newspapers

Marriage and Death Notices from Seneca County New York Newspapers, 1817–1885

Marriage Notices from Steuben County, New York Newspapers, 1797–1884

Marriage Notices from Washington County, New York Newspapers, 1799–1880

www.ingramcontent.com/pod-product-compliance
Lightning Source LLC
Chambersburg PA
CBHW061716270326
41928CB00011B/2002